P9-BZT-236

BRIDE'S BOOK OF
ETIQUETTE

Most Perigee Books are available at special quantity discounts for bulk purchases for sales promotions, premiums, fund-raising, or educational use. Special books, or book excerpts, can also be created to fit specific needs.

For details, write: Special Markets, The Berkley Publishing Group, 375 Hudson Street, New York, New York 10014.

BRIDE'S BOOK OF
ETIQUETTE

(Revised Edition)

BY THE EDITORS OF BRIDE'S MAGAZINE

A PERIGEE BOOK

A Perigee Book
Published by The Berkley Publishing Group
A division of Penguin Putnam Inc.
375 Hudson Street
New York, New York 10014

Copyright © 2003 by The Condé Nast Publications, Inc.
Illustrations by Sharon Watts
Cover design by John Duff
Front cover photo copyright © *BRIDE'S* magazine

Front cover photo by Paul Lange for Langscapes
Model, Melissa Morales
Dress, Alfred Angelo

All rights reserved. This book, or parts thereof,
may not be reproduced in any form without permission.

First five editions by Grosset & Dunlop
First Perigee edition: January 1993
Second Perigee edition: January 1999
Revised edition: January 2003

Visit our website at www.penguinputnam.com

Library of Congress Cataloging-in-Publication Data

Bride's book of etiquette / by the editors of Bride's magazine.—Rev. ed.
    p. cm.
  Includes bibliographical references and index.
  ISBN 0-399-52866-0
  1. Wedding etiquette.

BJ2051.B68 2003
200'.95—dc21

                                                          2002035534

Printed in the United States of America

10   9

CONTENTS

ACKNOWLEDGMENTS

BRIDE'S Magazine would especially like to thank Laurie Sprague for her superb revision of the book, Cynthia Edmunds, Associate Editor, Sally Kilbridge, Managing Editor and Phyllis Richmond Cox, Design Director, for their commitment to this project, and for the many hours spent updating the text for the new century. Thanks, too, to Perigee's Jennifer Repo, editor, and John Duff, publisher, for their continued support of BRIDE'S and this book.

BRIDE'S also acknowledges the contributions of its entire editorial staff, which is constantly reporting on the way couples marry across the country and around the world. Specifically, we thank the following editors for critiquing revisions: Nancy Mattia, Terrie Collymore, Amy Keith, Donna Ferrari, Kate Williams, Rachel Leonard, Denise O'Donoghue, Elizabeth Rundlett, Ellen Heisler, Heather Leo, Yolanda Crous, Chanize Thorpe, and Erin Kettle.

Final acknowledgment is made to the many professionals who devoted their time as expert sources for the material of the book, with particular thanks to Rachel Yohai of Rae Michaels Ltd. in New York City for her expert stationery advice, and wedding consultant JoAnne Gregoli of Elegant Occasions in New York City.

And finally, many words of thanks to our readers, for the inspiration they give us daily through their phone calls, e-mails, faxes, and letters. This book is for them.

FOREWORD

Congratulations on your upcoming marriage! If you're like most brides, your engagement period will be a time of unbelievable activity, anticipation—and anxiety.

Getting engaged, after all, is a life-altering event, and planning a wedding raises questions and issues you may never have dreamed of. Knowing how to do things the "right" way takes on new importance when you're organizing a celebration that's steeped in tradition and protocol. Suddenly, folding and addressing invitations is a more complex task than you ever imagined; you love the idea of wearing red shoes with your wedding dress, but you wonder if the combination will cause ripples of laughter in the reception hall. Friends and family are bound to offer you advice—often unsolicited. When opinions come flying at you, knowing the dos and don'ts will help you keep your cool, and reach the right decisions for your unique set of circumstances.

That's where etiquette comes in.

As you go about planning the wedding of your dreams, you'll have dozens of choices to ponder, decisions to make, and questions—plenty of questions—to ask. How do you choose attendants without hurting feelings? What's the right way to address an invitation to a couple that's unmarried but living together? Where do you seat divorced parents and how can you make sure they'll get along? Is it appropriate to e-mail a thank-you note? Do you really have to keep the—well, interesting—vase Aunt Edna sent as a wedding gift?

Etiquette is not a one-size-fits-all template, but a way to help every bride and groom—regardless of their style and tastes—bring order and ease to this very special occasion. We, the editors of BRIDE'S magazine, have been solving the problems of engaged couples for over half a century, and here, we tackle all the above-mentioned questions and more. Within the pages of this newly revised and updated book you'll find advice and all the how-tos for planning everything from a very formal, traditional wedding to a destination, theme, or long-weekend wedding. Included are tips for personalizing your ceremony, your reception, and even your getaway. You'll learn who traditionally pays for what, how to ask parents for help, and who does what—and when—as well as who wears what—and when. You'll also find helpful charts and timetables to keep you on course.

The perfect wedding isn't the one that goes off without a hitch. It's the one that celebrates your love and commitment in a style that is personally meaningful to you and your fiancé. As such, there is no right or wrong way to host a wedding, as long as you keep your guests' comfort in mind. Go ahead, hire a reggae band. Serve a cherry cheesecake. Your day should be as special and unique as the two of you are.

Also, keep in mind that following some rules—wording and addressing invitations correctly, knowing the procession order, having a receiving line—are some easy ways to be kind to your wedding party and guests. People feel more comfortable and welcome when everyone knows where to go and what to do.

As you read through the pages of this book, we hope you'll discover not what is proper for everyone, but what is right for you, your fiancé, and your families.

All our best wishes for a beautiful wedding and a lifetime of happiness,

Millie Martini Bratten
Editor-in-Chief
BRIDE'S Magazine

YOUR ENGAGEMENT

1

You're engaged! Now what do you do? Whether you've known each other for five years or five months, getting engaged is one of the most exciting—and busiest—times of your life. First, you'll want to share your excitement with family and friends. You might call or visit them spontaneously, invite them over for a small celebration, or break the news on a special occasion. Some couples have even printed the message on a cake or enclosed it in fortune cookies. Once the news is out that you're going to be married, parties and lots of decision-making will follow. Keep in mind that the way that you and your fiancé negotiate with each other and with your families to plan your celebration, honeymoon, and new home now is the best "rehearsal" you could have for marriage.

Sharing the News

Your families should be the first to hear the news of your engagement. What's the best way to let them in on your plans?

If your parents know your fiancé extremely well, choose a time when you're all together. Living far away from your parents, however, means you may not be able to wait to see them in person to share the news. In this case, set up a conference call; make plans to see them as soon as possible.

If your parents aren't acquainted with your fiancé, you should make arrangements to introduce them before springing the news. Ultimately, how you handle this situation will depend a great deal on your relationship with your parents, as well as how feasible it is to get everyone together (i.e., it may not be possible to do this right away if you live in different states or countries). If you aren't able to share the news in person, call your parents and tell them about your engagement. Plan for an in-person introduction as soon as possible.

If your fiancé's schedule doesn't permit a visit to your parents, or you're not sure how they'll react to your decision, then you may want to tell them yourself of your upcoming marriage. No matter what your situation, speaking with your family alone gives them—and you—the opportunity to express yourselves freely.

Your fiancé may want to speak privately with your father. Some guys are sticklers for tradition, and some fathers appreciate the old-fashioned courtesy of the groom-to-be asking for your hand. In this scenario, your fiancé will probably receive congratulations, some loving reminiscences about you, and a warm welcome to the family. If your father is no longer alive, your mother, stepfather, guardian, or whoever raised you may talk with your fiancé. If your parents are divorced, he can visit one parent first, then the other. No matter how you announce your engagement, expect that your parents may have questions about your fiancé's career goals, where you two will live, how you'll deal with education, religion, nationality, or race differences.

If you sense conflict over your choice of a partner, urge your parents to talk to your clergymember or a family member who thinks highly of your fiancé. In any case, it's never a bad idea to seek out a premarital-counseling program (see Chapter 4, "Planning Your Wedding," and Appendix, under Chapter 4).

Your fiancé should tell his own parents the good news. They, too, may appreciate hearing the news privately first, so they can express excitement and any possible reservations. His parents will want to get to know you (if they don't yet) and be reassured that you're both making a carefully considered decision.

If one of you is divorced, the other's parents may be uneasy about what went wrong with the first marriage. Offer them a simple, reassuring statement (*We were much too young when we got married. . . .*). If one of you has children, the other's parents may be apprehensive about their son or daughter becoming an instant parent. Make an extra effort to help them get to know the children before the wedding.

Once your fiancé tells his parents, they traditionally call on your parents so everyone can get acquainted. His mother might drop your mother a note, or phone to invite your parents for drinks, brunch, or dinner. Any way his parents usually entertain their friends is a good way for them to get to know your parents. If your parents are divorced, your fiancé's family might first extend their invitation to the person who raised you. If your families live in different towns, a note from your fiancé's mother to

engagement checklist

- ☐ Shop for a ring.
- ☐ Tell your families.
- ☐ Tell your friends.
- ☐ Tell your boss/co-workers.
- ☐ Buy a wedding-planning book.
- ☐ Surf the Internet for wedding-planning resources.
- ☐ Have an engagement portrait taken.
- ☐ Send newspaper engagement announcement(s).
- ☐ Ask friends/family members to be attendants.
- ☐ Register for china, crystal, silver, other gifts.

your mother saying how pleased she is that you'll be a member of the family is a thoughtful gesture. Even if your parents and his are old friends, this is the perfect excuse for them to have dinner together and toast the occasion (you two—and your brothers and sisters—may or may not be included). Your fiancé's parents haven't contacted your parents? Then your parents might make the first move, inviting them over for a visit. Or, you and your fiancé might get everyone together.

If one or both of you have children, make telling them a top priority; this news is too important to hear from someone else. Tell them far in advance of the wedding, so you'll have time to discuss their concerns. Make the occasion as comfortable as possible and encourage your children to air troubled feelings. Keep in mind that each child, partly depending on his or her age, may react differently. Anticipate worries they may have: Will you still have time for them? Will they still see their own father? Do they have to change their name? Will their stepfather make curfew rules? Will the family have to move? Don't be hurt if your children are less than overjoyed. They may need time to sort things out, regardless of how well they know or "get along with" your fiancé.

There may be other special people you'll want to tell personally, such as friends, bosses, and co-workers. One caveat: Engagements can be distracting, but they're no excuse to act unprofessionally. Use lunch hours and vacation days for wedding-planning chores and appointments.

Tell your ex-spouse, if you are on speaking terms. If not, write a note to say that you're remarrying. It is best if the news comes directly from you. If you two have children together, it is very important that you and your ex-spouse speak to discuss your children's needs and concerns, as well as his or her concerns (Will you be moving to another state? Will your son have to share a room with your new husband's son?). Don't create a situation where your children end up having to answer questions from your ex-spouse about your relationship with your new partner.

Length of Engagement

You can consider yourselves engaged as soon as you officially decide to marry. Today, there is no traditional or expected length of time for an engagement. Many couples wait to announce their engagement until they begin making wedding plans (often twelve months or more before the wedding date in major cities). It is not unusual for couples to be engaged longer than a year, during which time the bride and groom finish school, complete military service, and/or save for the wedding. Some couples, because of new job commitments, a relocation, illness, or pregnancy may speed up their wedding plans so that the engagement lasts just a few months, weeks, or even days.

Sticky Engagement Questions

Engagement often brings a flood of unexpected inquiries, some of which you may find intrusive. Knowing why a friend or family member is asking these questions will help you come up with tactful replies.

"Why do you want to get married?" Don't get defensive. The asker may just be curious about your views. Did you once announce to college friends that you never wanted to marry? They may want to know what changed your mind.

"Why did you choose him?" If this question is coming from family members or close friends, it may signal that they have reservations about your fiancé. Remember that these people care about you and want to make sure you're happy. Invite them to tell you what is bothering them. Be as reassuring as you can. If that doesn't work, don't worry—in most cases their concerns will be calmed near or soon after the wedding day, when they get to know your fiancé better. Finally, while it is always good to try to understand any concerns your family or friends may have, remember it is still *your* choice to marry this person.

"When are you going to have a baby?" This is most likely to come from hopeful future grandparents. If so, you may wish to acknowledge their longing. Then politely—but firmly—tell them that when the time is right for you two to start a family, they'll be among the first to know. Coming from people who aren't so close to you, this question may seem like an invasion of privacy. Humor can often defuse tense moments; you might simply laugh and say, "I think we need to have the wedding first."

"Who's paying for the wedding?" Although this may seem like a rude question, wedding expenses today are shared in many ways. People may be exploring options for future reference. Remember, of course, you don't have to answer. Whenever a question seems impertinent, it's fine to respond, "Why do you ask?" or laugh it off by saying, "We're accepting donations."

"Why are/aren't you changing your name?" People may just be curious. Or, a friend may be looking for confirmation of her own decision. If you choose not to take your husband's name and you sense that his family members are uncomfortable with your choice, reassure them that your decision is not meant as a rejection of his family. Perhaps explain that you have established a professional identity already with your own name. If you've decided to use your surname only professionally, tell his family that you will be "Mrs. Jones" socially. You also might reassure them that any grandchildren will take your husband's surname (as long as you're comfortable with that decision, of course).

"How will the two of you survive financially?" "Were you planning to contribute?" is the perfect answer to anyone asking this question—except a parent with a specific concern (your fiancé is unemployed, for example). By now, you two should have discussed all major issues, including finances.

"Am I invited to the wedding?" Who gets invited depends on the type of celebration you want and what you can afford. If the person asking is someone who probably won't be invited, you can respond, "I'm so flattered that you want to attend." Then, fill in an appropriate excuse ("Unfortunately, we're having a small reception"; "I have a huge family," etc.). If this is someone you wish you could invite, follow up with a post-wedding invitation to dinner, where you can share anecdotes and photographs of your wedding and honeymoon.

Publishing the News

Once you've told close friends and relatives personally about your plans to marry, let the world—or at least your community—know of your good news. Announce your engagement in newspapers in your hometowns and in the cities where you work. Don't forget alumni magazines and organization newsletters.

Announcement styles vary by publication. Call each newspaper's lifestyle department and ask for the correct spelling of the lifestyle editor's name; address all correspondence to her or him. Find out if there is a standardized form that can be mailed or emailed to you. If not, read the paper's announcement section to familiarize yourself with their style. Most engagement and wedding announcements include career information for bride, groom, and all parents; offices held by the couple in professional associations; military service; academic honors; schools attended. Although you might mention the month of the wedding, listing the specific wedding date and your street address, may invite theft. (For submission tips, see the box, "Preparing Your Announcement.")

Ask about the publication's photo policy. Will the editors publish wedding photographs only? Will they accept photos of the bride only, or of the couple, if preferred? Most newspapers require 8 × 10-inch or 5 × 7-inch glossies. Ask if photos should be in black and white or color, if they will be returned and what identifying information should be printed on the back.

Inquire about deadlines. What are the publication deadlines for engagement and wedding announcements? Some newspapers accept information over the phone or via the Internet, while others require that their standardized form be submitted at least ten days prior to publication. Also important to ask: Is there a fee?

Keeping your surname? Include a line such as, *The bride will keep her name* or *The bride will keep her name professionally.*

Divorced or widowed? There is no need to mention it in the announcement. Some newspapers, however, will insist on printing a line such as, *The bride's/groom's previous marriage ended in divorce.* Recently divorced or widowed? Wait and announce your wedding only.

Illness in the family? Most people, ill or not, will want to share in your happiness, so don't delay in making your announcement.

preparing your announcement

If your newspaper doesn't supply announcement forms:

- Type the announcement, double-spaced, on one side of an 8½ × 11-inch sheet of paper.

- In the upper-right corner type your name, address, home and office phone numbers, and e-mail address, or those of someone else who can be contacted to verify the information.

- Include the date on which you would like the announcement to appear. *Note:* Sunday is a popular day for wedding announcements and your news might not get in the paper then; consider typing: *For release Monday, May 26.*

- Protect your 8 × 10-inch or 5 × 7-inch photo with a stiff piece of cardboard. Write your name, wedding date, and phone number on back, lightly in ink (pencil or felt-tip pen might blur). *Note:* Your photo may not be returned.

- Send the announcement to the lifestyle editor, by name.

Announcement Wording

Traditional

Mr. and Mrs. Dennis Brown announce the engagement of their daughter, Ann Marie, to Mr. John Smith, the son of Mr. and Mrs. Thomas Smith of St. Louis. No date has been set for the wedding. [Or, The wedding will take place in December.]

The city is mentioned only when it is not the same as where the paper is published. If your mother uses her maiden name, write *Mr. Dennis Brown and Ms. Ann Hoyt.*

Divorced parent, announcing alone

Mrs. Hoyt Brown announces the engagement of her daughter, Ann Marie, to Mr. John Smith, the son of Mr. and Mrs. Thomas Smith of St. Louis. Miss Brown is also the daughter of Mr. Dennis Brown of Tulsa.

If your parents are divorced, the announcement is made by the parent with whom you've lived, but both parents are mentioned. (A divorced mother's name is traditionally a combination of her maiden and married surnames: *Mrs. Hoyt Brown.* However, she may prefer the contemporary pairing of her given name and married surname: *Mrs. Ann Brown.*)

Divorced parents, announcing jointly

If your parents are divorced but friendly, they might jointly announce the news: *Mr. Dennis Brown of Tulsa and Mrs. Hoyt Brown of Chicago announce the engagement of their daughter, Ann Marie, to Mr. John Smith, the son of Mr. and Mrs. Thomas Smith of St. Louis.*

Remarried mother

Mr. and Mrs. Raymond Jones announce the engagement of Mrs. Jones's daughter, Ann Marie Brown, to Mr. John Smith, the son of Mr. and Mrs. Thomas Smith of St. Louis. Miss Brown is also the daughter of Mr. Dennis Brown of Tulsa.

If your mother has remarried, she uses her current married name: *Mrs. Raymond Jones.*

One parent deceased

The engagement of Miss Ann Marie Brown, daughter of Mrs. Dennis Brown and the late Mr. Brown, to Mr. John Smith, the son of Mr. and Mrs. Thomas Smith of St. Louis, is announced by the bride's mother.

Both parents deceased

If both parents are deceased, the announcement is usually made by an older brother or sister or any close relative—even a close friend:

Mr. Jason Hoyt of Pittsburgh announces the engagement of his niece, Miss Ann Marie Brown, to Mr. John Smith, the son of Mr. and Mrs. Thomas Smith of St. Louis. Miss Brown is the daughter of the late Mr. and Mrs. Dennis Brown.

Should your fiancé be the one whose parents are deceased or divorced, you can adapt the appropriate wording to suit his situation.

Bride and groom sponsoring wedding

If you are sponsoring the wedding, you might still prefer to have your parents announce the engagement, or you can announce it yourselves:

Susan Elizabeth Scott, newscaster for WBIX-TV, is to be married in June to James J. Sampson, vice president, trust accounts, for First National Bank of Denver. Ms. Scott is the daughter of John Z. Scott of Atlanta, Georgia, and Sarah Newberry Scott of New York, New York. Mr. Sampson is the son of Mr. and Mrs. Dudley P. Sampson of Cleveland, Ohio.

Remarriage

Word the announcement in the traditional style, using the bride's legal name: *Mr. and Mrs. Edward G. Dunlap announce the engagement of their daughter, Anne Dunlap Crosby, to Joseph G. Riggs, son of Mr. and Mrs. G. Denton Riggs.*

Engagement Parties

Anyone may give a party in your honor, but your parents should have the opportunity to be the first ones to celebrate your engagement. It may be held shortly before, after, or perhaps on the very day your engagement announcement appears in the paper, if you have chosen to publish the news.

Any style of party is appropriate: a buffet, cocktail party, or barbecue. The invitations may read: *in honor of Howard and Carol.* You and your fiancé—along with your parents and his parents—might greet guests in an informal receiving line.

Gifts are optional at an engagement party and should not be expected. However, since some guests *will* want to mark the occasion with a gift, it's a good idea to list your gift choices and patterns in a Wedding Gift Registry (see Chapter 17, "Wedding Gifts").

At the gathering, your father might propose a toast to you and your fiancé. (Remember: Whenever a toast is proposed to you, remain seated and refrain from raising your glass or drinking.) After your father's toast, it's customary for your fiancé to rise and respond by toasting you and your parents, then his parents. You might also choose to rise and make a toast to your fiancé and both sets of parents.

Surprise guests with your news sometime during the party. Some couples prefer to invite guests to a cocktail party, then announce the news of their engagement during the celebration. It's a perfect occasion to break the news, since so many friends and relatives will be gathered in one place.

Your fiancé's parents may also host a party to introduce you to their family and friends. This might be a luncheon, cocktail party, or dinner, but it shouldn't be a shower. (Since the hosts are members of the groom's immediate family, it should not appear as if they are asking for gifts.)

Thank anyone who entertains you, even if it was a family brunch. Send a note, perhaps accompanied by flowers, to express your gratitude.

Engagement Presents

Your first engagement gift will probably be a ring given to you by your fiancé (although many engaged women prefer not to have a ring). A single diamond (symbolizing love and fidelity) is the classic choice, but other precious and semiprecious gemstones—opals, sapphires, rubies, or emeralds, alone or paired with diamonds—are also appropriate. Some couples choose engagement rings that they will wear as wedding rings. If you plan to wear your engagement ring on the same finger as your wedding ring, or you want your wedding ring to match the groom's, shop for matching sets together. Your fiancé's family may present you with an heirloom ring, instead, or you may have stones belonging to your family placed in a new setting.

In addition to your ring, your fiancé may give you another gift, such as a bracelet, necklace or perhaps a watch—in honor of the engagement, or later as a wedding gift. You may also wish to give him a present—such as a watch (see Appendix, under Chapter 1, "Your Engagement").

An engagement need not be a gift-giving occasion. Those particularly close to you, however, may surprise you with household or trousseau items. Whatever you receive, respond promptly with a written note of thanks, even if you expressed your gratitude in person (see Chapter 17, "Wedding Gifts").

Engagement Customs

Your engagement brings with it a host of customs that have been practiced for centuries by couples throughout the world. Here are some of the most popular traditions.

The engagement ring

The *betrothal ring* dates back to the days of marriage by purchase, when it served as both partial payment for the bride and as a symbol of the groom's honorable intentions. The *gimmal ring* had three parts, and at betrothal the woman, the man, and their witness each donned a portion to wear until wedding day, when the pieces were reunited as a single ring for the bride. In the fourteenth and fifteenth centuries, *posy rings* were popular (a posy, or endearing saying, was inscribed on the outside of the ring). A *regard ring* spelled out a message of love (DEAR) with precious stones such as *d*iamonds, *e*meralds, *a*methysts, and *r*ubies. The diamond, first incorporated into engagement rings in medieval Italy, was chosen to stand for enduring love because of its hardness.

Love tokens

Welsh and Pennsylvania Dutch couples often gave each other handcrafted gifts for their future home. Such things as cake molds, butter prints, and carved spoons were covered with symbols and statements of love. In Wales, a young man carved a wooden spoon for his lady to wear as a "locket" around her neck, signifying engagement (the origin of the term *spooning*). Today's versions are equally romantic.

Wedding gifts

A Finnish bride-to-be was considered snobbish if she did not *go collecting*—door-to-door—to receive her gifts in a pillowcase. An older married man (symbolizing long-lasting marriage) in a top hat, carrying an umbrella (representing shelter), accompanied her and was given a drink at each door. A contemporary bride is more likely to travel to a store's wedding gift registry or Internet site to list preferences and make shopping easier for her guests. She receives gifts at a bridal shower, where an umbrella is often a decoration, still symbolizing protection, shelter, and good luck.

A hope chest

In Europe and later in America, the bride's family began preparing for her marriage when she was born. They collected, embroidered, and crafted items to store in a striking piece of furniture, called a *marriage chest*. Today, the bride's family might purchase a hope chest, which can be used as a place for her to store gifts and purchases before the wedding, and, later, in the couple's home.

Engagement parties

In Guernsey, England, a betrothal party, called a *flouncing*, was held for the engaged couple to meet friends of both families. The flouncing established a formal contract and marked an abrupt change of status. Afterward, the couple could not be seen with or talk to other suitors. Following this formal declaration, if either changed his or her mind

about the marriage, the other could lay claim to half of his or her property.

Formal engagement ceremonies or parties, common in many cultures, bestowed responsibilities (a concept that grew into breach-of-promise lawsuits). For instance, in China, betrothal was a family obligation. If an engaged man died before the wedding, his intended bride was treated like a widow.

Today, your parents will probably want to schedule their own contemporary version of flouncing—a chance to get together to meet both families.

The bridal shower

Legend has it that the first bridal shower took place in Holland when a maiden fell in love with a poor miller. Hoping to discourage the marriage, the maiden's father denied her the customary bridal dowry. To help the young couple set up housekeeping, the miller's friends showered the bride with gifts. Today, there are many kinds of showers (see Chapter 3, "Prewedding Parties").

A matchmaker

In countries where marriages are arranged, *go-betweens* play a respected role. In China, a matchmaker must determine if birth signs are compatible. In Uganda, the bride's elder brother and paternal uncle speak to prospective grooms and barter for the family. You may want to pay tribute to the person who introduced you to your fiancé with a seat of honor at the reception or a toast.

The phrase *tying the knot*

Tying the knot, a phrase associated with getting married, refers to an ancient

Now that you're about to be family, it's time to be more familiar than "Mr. and Mrs. Jones." Have your fiancé ask his parents in private what they prefer to be called.

Your options:

- "Mom" and "Dad"

- "Mother" and "Father" (*not* what you call your parents).

- "Mother J" and "Father J" or "Mrs. J" and "Mr. J"

- their first names

- an endearing name that suits them ("Doc" for a physician).

- whatever your fiancé calls them

what to call stepparents:

- A divorced and remarried in-law? Call the new partner what your fiancé calls him or her (probably by their first name).

- Your fiancé has children? See what they are comfortable with (perhaps you'll be "Mom," or "Sue").

- Give children the option to be more affectionate in the future (say, "You can call me Ann now, but I'll answer to 'Mom' if you ever feel like calling me that.")

Babylonian custom. Threads were taken from the clothes of both the bride and the bridegroom and tied together in a knot to symbolize the union of the couple. In some cultures today, the couple's hands are loosely bound during the ceremony (with plaited grass in Africa, and a rosary in Mexico). (See Chapter 2, "Wedding Customs.")

Broken Engagements

Sadly, not all engagements endure, for a variety of reasons. During this period of planning, the bride or groom may experience cold feet, feel they are not ready to make a lifelong commitment, or realize that there are irreconcilable differences. If you decide to call off your engagement:

Return any engagement, shower or wedding gifts that you were given to celebrate the occasion within two to three weeks after the engagement was broken. Send a note to gift-givers that the wedding has been called off (no need for more elaborate explanation) and that you appreciate the kind gesture. Even if you've already used the gift, or it has your monogram, it should be returned to the sender. Laws differ in each state as to who keeps the engagement ring, but the common etiquette is that whoever initiates the breakup has no claim to the ring. In New York State, regardless of who initiates the breakup, the ring goes back to the giver. If the bride-to-be received a family heirloom, it is honorable to return it to the former fiancé's family. You may keep any birthday or holiday presents received from the fiancé and his family.

If invitations have only been mailed recently, formal cards can be sent reading "The wedding of Miss Anne Marie Brown and Mr. John Smith will not take place."

If it's a last-minute decision, wedding invitations will have to be recalled via notes, telephone calls or e-mails (see Chapter 5, "Invitations & Announcements"). Write a brief personal note to close friends and relatives; there is no need to go into detail.

There's no need to reimburse bridesmaids for their dresses, but it is considerate to see if the bridal salon will offer at least a partial refund. If not, help the attendants find a resale shop.

Send a release to every newspaper that published your announcement, simply stating:
The engagement of Miss Ann Marie Brown and Mr. John Smith has been cancelled/called off by mutual consent.

In the case of a partner's death before the wedding, gifts also must be returned. Someone in the bride's family or a close friend may assume this task, in consideration of the feelings of the survivor and the couple's parents.

You might also send a release to every newspaper that published your announcement, simply stating:
The wedding of Miss Ann Marie Brown and Mr. John Smith will not take place due to the death of Mr. Smith.

WEDDING CUSTOMS

Contemporary Customs

They can clone sheep and send a robot to Mars, but some things—like weddings—are rooted in tradition. Today, couples are choosing to observe centuries-old practices, updating them to reflect their own personalities. And more couples than ever before are including ethnic customs from their heritages in wedding celebrations. Here are the meanings behind many of the traditional marriage customs that are commonly practiced today. (For more on rituals and customs, see Chapter 9, "Religious Rituals & Requirements," and the Appendix, under Chapter 2, "Wedding Customs.")

Why a wedding ring? The circular shape of the wedding ring symbolizes never-ending love. According to folklore, the ring protected the bride against evil spirits; if the bride or groom dropped it during the ceremony, bad luck would follow. Originally, rings were made of rushes, hemp, or braided grass, which had to be replaced every year. Early Romans chose more durable iron to symbolize the permanence of marriage. Gold has always been a popular, but more expensive, choice, symbolizing lasting beauty, purity, and strength. In ancient Egypt, before coins were minted, gold rings were used as currency and as a symbol of the groom's wealth and his intention to wed. To show that he trusted his wife with his money, the Egyptian husband placed a gold ring on the third finger of her left hand.

Only one ring was worn, until the thirteenth century. The declaration of Pope Innocent III that a waiting period was to be observed between betrothal and marriage led to separate engagement and wedding rings. The first recorded account of a diamond engagement ring was in 1477, when Maximilian I, King of Germany, proposed to Mary of Burgundy and offered her a diamond ring to seal his vow.

Why the third finger, left hand? Ancient peoples believed that the vein in the third finger of the left hand ran directly to the heart. Medieval bridegrooms placed the ring sequentially on three of the bride's fingers to symbolize the trinity—first on the bride's thumb ("in the name of the Father"), then on the index finger ("and the Son"), then the middle finger ("and the Holy Ghost")—before sliding it onto the third (ring) finger, saying "Amen." The ring remained on the third finger throughout the marriage. This has since become the customary ring finger for all English-speaking cultures. However, in many European countries, the wedding ring is worn on the right hand. A Greek woman wears her ring on her left hand while she is engaged, but moves it to her right hand once she is married.

Why does the bride wear a veil? Originally, the bride's veil symbolized her youth and virginity. Veils helped brides remain modest and hide themselves from jealous spirits. Even today, in Muslim countries (in the Middle East, Africa, and Eastern Europe), a young man is bound by the constraints of religious modesty to conduct his entire courtship while his bride-to-be remains veiled. He is not permitted to see her face until after the wedding.

In early days, veils were worn to confuse the devil and protect the bride from the "evil eye". Veils were often red (the color of defiance), blue (meaning constancy), or yellow (the classic color of Hymen, god of marriage). Early Greek and Roman brides wore flame-yellow or red veils. The yellow (probably representing fire) was thought to ward off demons. Sometimes, Roman brides swathed their entire body with a long red veil to shield themselves from malicious spirits. Early Christian brides wore white (indicating purity and celebration) or blue veils (a symbol of the Virgin Mary's purity). In America, Martha Custis Washington's daughter, Nellie Custis, is said to have started the custom of wearing a white lace veil. She reportedly decided to cover her head with lacey veiling on her wedding day after her future fiancé, Major Lawrence Lewis, President Washington's aide, caught a glimpse of her through a lace-curtained window.

Why does the bride wear white? White has been a symbol of celebration for some 2,000 years, since the Roman era. In 19th-century Victorian times, white was a sign of affluence—since it was assumed that a woman would only be able to wear a white dress once or twice, before it was soiled. At the beginning of the 20th century, white became synonymous with purity. Today, the color white once again symbolizes joy on the wedding day; women who are remarrying may choose among many shades of white—from bright white to ecru to champagne.

Why does the bride carry flowers? Flowers have long represented a variety of emotions and merits—lilies symbolize virtue; roses, love; and so on. Early Roman brides carried bunches of herbs under their veils to symbolize fidelity and fertility, and to ward off evil. The Greeks used ivy as a sign of indissoluble love. Orange blossoms were originally chosen by the ancient Saracens to represent fulfillment and happiness, as the orange tree blooms and bears fruit at the same time. Today, wedding flowers convey a message of fertility, enduring love, and bounty.

Why do the bridesmaids and the groom have flowers, too? Early bridesmaids' bouquets were made of pungent herbs such as rosemary and garlic—not flowers. The smell was supposed to drive away any evil spirits eyeing the bridal party. Even the groom wore a few sprigs.

Why does the bride carry a handkerchief? Not all brides head down the aisle with one, but if you choose to, it is considered to be a good omen. Early farmers thought a bride's wedding-day tears were lucky and brought rain for their crops. Later, it was believed that a bride who cried at her wedding would never shed another tear about her marriage.

Why is it traditional to have bridesmaids and ushers? Long ago, marriage by capture was the norm. A groom's friends helped him kidnap his mate and defended him against anyone who might try to steal the bride—including her family. The best man and ushers represent the warriors. At the altar, the groom always stood on the bride's right side, leaving *his* right hand—his sword hand—free to defend her.

In later years, it was customary for the bride to travel to her groom's village accompanied by escorts, her "bridesmaids," who were dressed in similar bride-like gowns to confuse rival suitors and robbers. In England, the bride was escorted to the church by boys, or "bride knights," symbolizing her innocent status; on the way home, she was escorted by married men, or "bridegroom men."

Why do wedding attendants all dress alike? Under Roman law, 10 witnesses were required to make a wedding legal. To confuse the netherworld and the evil spirits that lurked at the altar, several witnesses dressed exactly like the bride and groom. Another reason: In Europe, it was common for the bride, groom, and all their friends to walk together to the church. Afraid that someone—perhaps a rejected suitor—would spot the happy couple and put a curse on them, the groom's friends wore clothes almost identical to his, and the women costumed themselves like the bride, in an attempt to trick evil wishers.

Why does a bride shop for a trousseau? Derived from the French word *trousse*, meaning bundle, the trousseau originated as a bundle of clothing and personal possessions the bride carried to her new home. This was later expanded into a more generous dowry that enhanced the value of an unmarried daughter in the eyes of prospective suitors. Today, the trousseau encompasses all the new things—for the household and for the couple themselves—that help make the transition to a new stage of life.

Why is it bad luck for the groom to see his bride before the ceremony? Once, it was considered bad luck for the groom to see his bride *and* for the bride to see *herself* in a mirror in her wedding clothes before the wedding. Because the wedding ceremony marked a break between old and new, never to overlap, people thought that if the groom saw the bride before the ceremony, she would not be pure and new and if the bride saw herself in a mirror before the wedding, she would leave some of herself behind in the reflection.

something old, something new . . .

- Something old: a family heirloom—a Bible, antique veil, jewelry—for continuity.

- Something new: the bride's clothes, lingerie—for optimism.

- Something borrowed: a lace handkerchief, jewelry borrowed from a happily married relative (happiness rubs off!).

- Something blue: blue ribbon threaded through lace, a slip, or the garter, blue toenail polish, blue stones sewn into the train, earrings or necklace, blue flowers—for purity, fidelity, love.

- Penny in your shoe: a sixpence in England, a quarter in Canada, a penny in the U.S.—to ensure a life of fortune.

Why is a white or red aisle runner used? This is not just a decorative detail. In times past, women were carried to a wedding, in part to show respect, but also to protect them from evil spirits that lurked in the ground. The "red-carpet treatment" is a way to honor someone; the white runner, a pure pathway. Rose petals in the bride's pathway lead her to a sweet, plentiful future.

Why does the bride wear something old and something new? This custom stems from an Old English rhyme, "Something olde, something new, something borrowed, something blue, and a sixpence in her shoe. . . ." Brides throughout the decades have taken care to include these touches in their bridal outfit, a nod to tradition and superstition. The symbolism: continuity, optimism for the future, borrowed happiness, fidelity, and good fortune.

Why does the bride wear something blue? Brides in ancient Israel wore a blue ribbon on the border of their fringed robes to denote modesty, fidelity, and love—ideals still associated with that color. Blue is also the color that represents the purity and innocence of the Virgin Mary.

Why is it good luck to put a coin in your shoe? This custom originated in England. Coins were given to young ladies as love tokens. A gentleman burnished the reverse side of a coin, then engraved the initials of his beloved. In Sweden, the bride's father places a piece of silver in her left shoe; her mother, a piece of gold in her right, so that she may never lack in luxuries. Royal brides traditionally have a tiny silver horseshoe sewn in the hem of their gown, for good luck.

Why is the bride given away? She isn't always. Nowadays, although many brides are escorted to the altar by their father, they are no longer "given away." In earlier times, when women were granted fewer personal rights, the bride was literally given to the groom in an arranged marriage. A vestige of that practice can be found in the question in the marriage service, "Who gives this woman to be married to this man?" The bride who keeps the "giving away" ritual in her marriage service often sees it as symbolic of her parents' support for her union and their promise of continued trust and affection. A popular alternative found in ceremonies today is the question, "Who supports this man and this woman in this marriage?" Both parents might respond. "We do." Or, all parents and guests might join together in the response.

Why does the ceremony end with a kiss? From the days of ancient Rome, the kiss was a legal bond that sealed contracts, and thus, the betrothal. Christianity incorporated the betrothal ceremony into the marriage ritual. It was also believed that when a couple kissed, part of each of their souls was left behind in the other when their breath was exchanged. Occurring at the end of the rites, the kiss announces a new status.

Why do couples receive wedding gifts? Once, a bride prepared for marriage by filling a hope chest with hand-sewn linens and other household furnishings. Families endowed offspring with dowries. Today, family members and friends help furnish the couple's new home and lifestyle with shower and wedding gifts (see Chapter 3, "Prewedding Parties"; Chapter 17, "Wedding Gifts").

Why is there a wedding cake? A symbol of good luck and fertility, cake has been a part of wedding celebrations since Roman times, when a small bun was broken above the bride's head at the close of the ceremony. Wheat, the main ingredient, symbolized fertility: crumbs were eagerly sought by guests as good-luck charms. During the Middle Ages, custom required the bride and groom to kiss over a pile of small cakes donated by wedding guests. In Elizabethan times, bridesmaids baked small, sweet buns with currants, which served as the centerpiece for the wedding feast. In the 17th century, it was an innovative visiting French baker who frosted the stack of buns so that they would stand upright—creating the first tiered and frosted wedding cake! The Chinese originated the custom of serving each guest a slice of cake to spread the good luck.

What is the groom's cake? The groom's cake is often a rich, solid fruitcake topped with marzipan and white icing (the traditional wedding cake in England and Ireland) or a cake in the groom's favorite flavor. According to custom, the groom's cake is either served at the reception along with the wedding cake or packed in decorative boxes for guests to take home—a way to share the couple's good fortune and the sweetness of married life. Custom holds that single guests who put a sliver of groom's cake under their pillows that night will dream of their future spouses (see Chapter 13, "Your Reception," "The Groom's Cake" section).

Why are toasts made at the reception? Raising a glass together is a way for everyone to share in wishing health and happiness to the newlyweds. The term *toast* comes from the old French custom of placing a piece of toast at the bottom of the wine cup before filling it. The cup was then passed from hand to hand until it reached the recipient of the good wishes—who drained the goblet and also got the lucky morsel. Toasts may be offered with any beverage, but champagne is a wedding favorite.

Why are there wedding favors? The bride and groom were considered to be lucky—as were any of the things they touched. In times past, guests helped themselves to good-luck souvenirs by tearing off ribbons and bits of lace from the bride's dress, or snatching flowers from her bouquet. Now the bride offers guests boxed pieces of wedding cake, candy, almonds, and often even more elaborate favors, to thank them for sharing their happiness and to impart a little wedding magic.

Why is rice thrown? In the Orient rice at a wedding means, "May you always have a full pantry." In other cultures, grains such as rice and wheat symbolize fertility, prosperity, and bounty. In some countries, the bride wore or carried sheaves of grain. Other societies literally sprinkled the newlyweds with grains or nuts, wishing them abundance and a large family. In Italy, wedding guests flung coins, dried fruit, and candy, called *confetti*. Eventually, shopkeepers sold imitation candies—or colored pieces of cardboard later called confetti—to throw at newlyweds. Today, rice remains a token of a life of plenty, but guests may also throw rose petals, biodegradable streamers, potpourri, wheat, millet seed, safflower seed, birdseed, or corn. Some guests blow bubbles, release birds or butterflies, or ring handheld bells. (See Appendix, under Chapter 2, "Wedding Customs.")

Why is the bouquet tossed? As the bride left the festivities, she tossed her bouquet to a friend—so that the friend would have luck and protection. The custom evolved to imply that whoever caught the bouquet would be lucky and wed next. Flowers were also believed to be pungent enough to ward off evil spirits.

Why is the bride's garter tossed? Since guests in olden times would literally rip off pieces of the bride's gown as good-luck tokens, eventually the bride simply threw her garter to the crowd. Another custom from early England: Friends would follow the newlyweds to their wedding chamber, where the groom's friends would take off their stockings, then hurl them at the groom. The thrower who first hit the groom in the nose would be next to wed.

Why are shoes attached to the getaway car? Shoes represent power. They have been associated with the transfer of authority since early Hebrew times. In ancient cultures, sandals were often exchanged as evidence of good faith in the sale of property. An Anglo-Saxon father transferred his authority over the bride by giving the bridegroom one of her shoes. Tied to the back of the wedding car (as is the custom in England), shoes signify the creation of a new family unit; they also cause a noisy clatter once intended to drive off evil spirits that lurk in the ground.

Why do newlyweds go on a honeymoon? In ancient marriages by capture, the groom kept his bride in hiding for a month to prevent searching relatives from finding her. The term *honeymoon* has its origin in an early Teuton custom: Couples drank a fermented honey drink, known as mead or metheglin, for 30 days after their wedding or until the moon waned. An intoxicant, it might have eased sexual inhibitions. Honey is an ancient symbol of life, health, and fertility; the couple's "month of sweetness" was a time alone—a month of happiness (and, they hoped, fertility) before taking up the everyday responsibilities of marriage.

Why is the bride carried over the threshold? The Roman bride, demonstrating her reluctance to leave her father's home, had to be dragged over the threshold to her new house. It was also believed that evil spirits hovered at the threshold of whatever house the newlyweds would enter. The bride was lifted over the entrance to keep the evil spirits from entering through the soles of her feet.

American Customs

A sampling of our wedding traditions:

Native American

• Hopi Indian weddings still involve the whole tribal village and many feasts. The groom's clan may withhold approval of the marriage until the bride proves herself by grinding corn with the groom's female relatives. As a sign of approval, the whole community spins cotton to weave a fine set of new clothes and a wedding robe, which become the bride's treasured possessions.

• The bride goes to stay at the groom's house before the wedding. There, she makes piki and other traditional breads using blue corn. In an intimate cleansing ritual, both mothers wash the hair of the bride and groom.

• On their wedding day, Hopi couples greet the rising sun, praying for a good life together, children, and faithfulness.

• Navajo Indian brides traditionally marry while facing east, in the direction of the rising sun.

• A Navajo marriage is symbolized by combining corn ground by each family in a porridge referred to as corn mush. The dish is then carried to the ceremony site in a hand-woven wedding basket. The couple share a taste of pudding—symbolizing the first of many meals they'll share in their marriage.

Early American

• In the 1700s and early 1800s up and down the Eastern seaboard, a lower-class bride-to-be brought her blanket to her intended's home, placed it beside his, and spent the night there. After this "bundling" occurred, she woke up as good as "married." Often, a "bundling board" was placed between the couple to ensure that the woman's virtue would be preserved.

• Young Amish boys in the Midwest playfully toss the groom over a low fence to symbolize his passage into a new life.

• Friends serenaded the couple with a shivaree on their wedding night by "playing" pots and pans, and sometimes shooting off their guns.

• In rural Pennsylvania, a centuries-old tradition lives on: Older single siblings of the bride and/or groom do the "Hog's Trough Dance." They dance in an empty wooden hog's trough until it breaks, ensuring future good luck.

• For summer weddings, 19th-century brides often carried fans, usually made of lace, instead of a bouquet. The honor attendant held the bride's fan and scent bottle during the ceremony, in case the bride fainted from the heat. Brides often gave their fans to bridesmaids as favors.

International Customs

Today, couples often honor their heritages by including traditional wedding customs from their countries of origin or adopting others that seem especially meaningful.

Africa/African American

• *Kola Nut* Before a betrothal, the hopeful groom's family visited the bride-to-be's home to arrange the marriage. If her family agreed, a small amount of money and a kola nut were offered to the bride. She accepted the nut, opened it, and shared it with her groom, and family representatives present. A messenger, bearing a small piece of the same kola nut, was then sent to other families to announce the engagement.

• *Crossing Sticks* In the early 1900s, African-American couples demonstrated their commitment to each other by crossing long sticks or stafflike branches against each other. The sticks represented the vitality and strength of trees. The custom blessed their new life together. (In Kenya, a Samburu groom used sticks during the wedding festivities to brand the cattle he would give to his bride when finalizing their vows.)

• *Jumping the Broom* In the times of slavery in this country, African-American couples were not allowed to formally marry and live together. To make a public declaration of their commitment, a man and woman jumped over a broom into matrimony, to the beat of drums. (The broom has long held significant meaning for various African cultures, symbolizing the start of homemaking for a newlywed couple. In Southern Africa, the day after the wedding, a Kgatla bride assisted the other women in the family in sweeping the courtyard, indicating her dutiful willingness to help her in-laws with housework till the newlyweds could move to their new home.) Today, many African-American couples incorporate this symbolic rite in their weddings, directly before the recession.

• *Binding Wrists* Some tribes still perform the ancient rite of binding the bride's and groom's wrists together with plaited grass.

• *Hairstyles* On special occasions, it was traditional for women in most African countries to braid their hair, perhaps covering it with a deep-red ocher dye and animal fat. Today, many African-American brides are choosing to have their hair braided in cornrows or to wear it in plaits for their wedding day.

• *Wedding Dresses* Nigerian brides wear traditional *asooke* cloth (with a textured, pointillistic, geometric pattern); Ghanaian brides and grooms wear the customary *kente* cloth (in colorful, bold, geometric patterns) made into a four-piece *bubah*, a robe worn as a caftan over a *luppa* (skirt). Today, some African-American grooms may wear black trousers under a sport jacket made of *asooke* or *kente* cloth, traditional formalwear with an *asooke* or *kente* vest, cummerbund, bow tie, or pocket handkerchief.

• *Cowrie Shells* Smooth cowrie shells, which encourage fertility, are worn in bridal necklaces or used to embellish gowns, jackets, and headpieces. The shells, found off the coast of West Africa, were once used as money and today represent purification. Cowrie shells are also symbols of beauty and power.

• *Rings* Some African-American couples today are choosing wedding bands that are designed with Khamitic symbols. The Khamites were ancient, pre-Egyptian peoples from the Nile Valley. Cast in silver and gold, the rings have carvings that symbolize truth, love, fertility, or eternal life.

• *Wooden Stools* The Asante tribe in West Africa cherished wooden stools, each carved out of a single piece of wood. The stools and the symbols on them bore the lore and history of each clan and their ancestors. They were considered the receptacle of the owner's soul, and were seats of honor and power for women. Today, at African-American weddings, some couples set Asante stools in the front row—designated as seats of honor for their parents.

• *Corn Kernels* Instead of rice, African couples are showered with kernels of dried corn (symbolizing fertility) as they exit the wedding festivities.

Armenia

• Two white doves may be released to signify love and happiness.

• The bride dresses in red silk and may wear feathers on her head and cardboard wings on her back. Small coins may be thrown at her.

• The bride wears many valuable rings with precious stones on each hand and dons a necklace of fine turquoise.

Austria

• Brides crown their veils with myrtle, which is the flower of life.

Belgium

• The bride embroiders her name on her handkerchief, carries it on the wedding day, then frames it and keeps it until the next family bride marries.

Bermuda

• Islanders top their tiered wedding cakes with a tiny sapling. The newlyweds then plant the tree at their new home—where they can watch it mature as their marriage grows.

Caribbean

• A rich black cake baked with dried fruits and rum is an especially popular wedding dessert on the islands of Barbados, Grenada, Jamaica, and St. Lucia. The recipe is embellished as it is handed down from mother to daughter. It is considered a "pound" cake—with the recipe calling for a pound each of flour, dark brown sugar, butter, glacé cherries, raisins, prunes and currants, plus a dozen eggs, and flavorings. The dried fruits are soaked in rum and kept in a crock anywhere from two weeks to six months.

• Jamaican couples send slices of the fruitcake to all friends and relatives who were unable to attend the festivities.

• In the West Indies, the traditional rum-flavored wedding cake is covered with a fine white tablecloth. Guests pay for a lucky peek, and dine on curried goat and white rice.

China

• Brides receive pocketbooks filled with gold jewelry from female relatives. In doing so, they bestow status on the bride.

• In old China, the color of love and joy was red, the favorite shade for the bride's dress, candles, and gift boxes, as well as the money envelopes that were presented to the bride by guests.

• During the ceremony, the couple drink wine and honey from goblets symbolically tied together with red string.

• The bride is given chestnuts and jujubes in a wish for a son as soon as possible.

Croatia

• Married female relatives remove the bride's veil and replace it with a kerchief and apron, symbols of her new married status. She is then serenaded by all the married women.

• Following the wedding ceremony, those assembled walk three times around a well (symbolizing the Holy Trinity) and throw apples into it (symbolizing fertility).

• The bridal car and guests' cars are all decorated with flowers.

The Czech Republic

• Friends would sneak into the bride's yard to plant a tree, then decorate it with ribbons and painted eggshells. Legend said she would live as long as the tree.

• Brides in the countryside carry on the very old custom of wearing a wreath of rosemary, which symbolizes remembrance. The wreath is woven for each bride on her wedding eve by her friends as a wish for wisdom, love, and loyalty.

• Three symbolic dishes are set before the bride on her wedding day: wheat, symbolizing fertility; ashes mixed with grains of millet—which the bride picks out to demonstrate her patience; and a sparrow under a covered dish, which flies out when she lifts the lid.

• Dried peas—not rice—are tossed at the newlyweds as they exit.

Denmark

• The traditional wedding cake is the cornucopia cake or Danish marzipan ring cake, made of almond paste and pastilage and beautifully decorated with sugarwork. The inside is filled with the good things in life: candies, almonds, perhaps even fresh fruit. The cake may also be decorated with marzipan medallions bearing portraits of the bride and groom.

Egypt

• Families, rather than grooms, propose to brides. In Egypt, many marriages are arranged.

• The *zaffa*, or "wedding march", is a musical procession of drums, bagpipes, horns, belly dancers, and men carrying flaming swords; it announces that the marriage is about to begin.

England

• Traditionally, the village bride and her wedding party walk together to the church. Leading the procession: a small girl strewing blossoms along the road, so the bride's path through life will always be happy and laden with flowers.

• If the bride meets a chimney sweep on her way to the church and he kisses her, it's good luck. (Chimney sweeps kept the home fires burning safely.)

• Brides sew a good-luck charm, such as the silver horseshoe worn by royal British brides, into the hem of their wedding gown.

• The traditional wedding cake of England is a rich fruitcake (sometimes liquor-laced) with golden raisins, ground almonds, cherries, and different spices.

Fiji

• The groom presents the bride's father with a *tabua*—a whale's tooth, which is a symbol of status and wealth.

Finland

• Brides wear golden crowns. After the wedding, unmarried women dance in a circle around the blindfolded bride, waiting for her to place her crown on someone's head. It is thought that whoever she crowns will be the next to wed.

• The bride and groom have seats of honor at the reception. The bride holds a sieve covered with a silk shawl; when guests slip money into the sieve, a groomsman announces their names and the amounts given to those assembled.

• After the wedding, brides have their braids cut off and thereafter wear a white linen cap.

France

• During the reign of Louis XVI, the bride gave her bridesmaids fans, decorated with mythological paintings, as wedding presents.

• Many couples drink the reception toast from an engraved two-handled cup (the *coupe de mariage*), as did newlyweds from days past. This cup is then passed on to future generations.

Germany

• To mark their betrothal, a couple give each other gold bands, which are to be worn on their left hands. Throughout their engagement, the couple are referred to as bride and bridegroom.

• The bride and groom hold candles trimmed with flowers and ribbons for the duration of the service.

• During the ceremony, when the couple kneel, the groom kneels on the bride's hem to show that he'll keep her in line. The bride steps on his foot when she rises, to reassert herself.

• In Hanover and elsewhere, crockery is thrown against the bride's house on her wedding day to bring good luck.

• On her wedding day, the bride carries salt and bread in her pocket; the bridegroom totes some grain, for wealth and good fortune.

Greece

• The *koumbaros*, traditionally the groom's godfather, is an honored guest who participates in the wedding ceremony. Today, the *koumbaros* is very often the best man, who assists in the crowning of the couple (with white or gold crowns, or with crowns made of flowers such as orange blossoms, or of twigs of olive and vine wrapped in silver and gold paper), and in the circling of the altar three times. Other attendants may read Scripture, hold candles, and pack the crowns in a special box after the ceremony.

• To be sure of a "sweet life," a Greek bride may carry a lump of sugar in her glove on the wedding day.

Holland

• Dutch families used to plan a party prior to the wedding where the bride and groom sat on thrones under a canopy of fragrant evergreens. One by one, guests came up to offer their good wishes.

• Dutch weddings traditionally include a big meal, including a sweetmeat called bridal sugar and spiced wine called bride's tears.

Hungary

• The couple exchange betrothal rings. The groom also gives the bride a bag of coins; the bride gives the groom either three or seven handkerchiefs (in Hungary, both are believed to be lucky numbers).

• Guests dance with the bride at the reception, and give her a few pence in exchange for a kiss.

• Guests give pigeons, chickens, and fruit—as well as other edibles—in exchange for a turn on the dance floor with the bride.

Iceland

• The wedding cake indigenous to Iceland is *kransakaka*. It consists of rings of almond pastry of various sizes piled on top of one another to form a pyramid. Swirls of white icing decorate each ring and fine chocolates or decorative candies fill the hollow center.

India

• The families of the bride and groom exchange flower garlands to symbolize their eternal bond.

• The groom's brother sprinkles flower petals on the bridal couple at the end of the ceremony to ward off evil.

• To banish evil spirits, a coconut may be held over the couple's heads and circled around them three times.

• Five days before the wedding, the bride has a ceremonial bath for ritual cleansing, then is painted with henna swirls on her hands and feet, and adorned with makeup and jewels by other women.

• The *thali*, a jewel set in gold and fastened on a yellow string (gold is the color of good fortune and approval) is tied around the bride's neck. Worn throughout the marriage, the *thali*'s three knots remind her of her duty to her parents, her husband, and her sons.

Indonesia

• During an engagement period that may last for years, many ceremonies involving gift exchanges bring the two families together and strengthen their ties.

• During a ceremony on the Indonesian island of Java, the bride and groom sit on the lap of the bride's father, who sits on a ceremonial wedding couch. The bride's mother asks the bride's father who is heavier, the bride or the groom. The father replies that they are the same weight, thereby signifying that from then on, the bride and groom will be loved and treated equally by the parents.

• A Javanese bride is secluded after the marriage blessing and is believed to be visited by an angel, who stays with her throughout the six-day ritual that blends Muslim customs with local folklore.

• The Javanese bride and groom are each served from a bowl of yellow and white rice—then eat from each other's plates—symbolically blending their lives.

• Young people on Bali who have not already done so have their canine teeth filed before marriage to reduce "animal passions" such as anger and jealousy. The ritual is conducted by a member of the Brahmana caste and accompanied by beautiful displays of food.

Iran

• When this country was called Persia, the groom bought the wedding dress— ten yards of sheeting—to wrap around his bride.

• Happily married women hold a sheer cloth over the heads of the wedding pair during the ceremony. Later, the women scrape crumbs from two beautifully decorated sugar cones, known as *kaleh-ghand*, over the couple's heads for luck.

Ireland

• The traditional wedding cake of the Emerald Isle is a rich fruitcake. In true Irish spirit, the recipe is laced with brandy or bourbon.

• A lucky horseshoe is given to the bride and groom to keep in their home.

Italy

• Ribbons signify the tying together of two lives. A ribbon is tied across the front of the church door to symbolize the wedding bond.

• Wedding guests have for centuries tossed *confetti* (sugared almonds, not small pieces of paper) at the newlyweds. Sometimes, these decorate each place at reception tables—in pretty porcelain boxes or tulle bags called *bomboniere*, which are personalized with the couple's names and wedding date—to symbolize the sweet (sugar) and bitter (almonds) in life.

• The newlyweds lead wedding guests in dancing the *tarantella*.

• After a line dance called "The Grand March" (see Chapter 13, "Your Reception," under the "Reception Dancing" section), the reception may end with a second receiving line, where guests are given their *bomboniere*—in exchange for money envelopes. The couple then dance their last dance.

Japan

• Many weddings are held in front of a Shinto shrine, even though a marriage is not considered a religious service. A Shinto priest officiates, but there are no vows. The ceremony brings the bride into the groom's family. Ancestors are honored in the ritual with bows, the ringing of bells, and offerings of food before ancestral shrines. The bride wears a ceremonial kimono. Bridal couples take nine sips of *sake* (rice wine), becoming husband and wife after the first sip. Later, the parents and the couple exchanged sips, both out of respect and to mark the parents' formal acceptance of the marriage.

• On her wedding day, the bride and her parents visit the groom's house. Traditionally, she wears a triangular band on her head, known as a *tsunokakushi*, or horn cover, to hide the horns of jealousy, which supposedly all women possess.

• All of the guests go home with elaborate gifts from the bride's family.

Korea

• Traditionally, the groom traveled to the bride's house on a white pony, bearing fidelity symbols—a gray goose and gander (fowl that mate for life).

• Friends of the groom deliver a *ham* (a box containing gifts for the bride and her new home) several days before the wedding. The *ham* often contains the red and blue fabric needed to make her ceremonial dress.

• Ducks are included in the wedding procession because they mate for life.

• After the ceremony, the couple change into Korean ceremonial clothes for the *p'yeback* ceremony, where families are introduced. There, the groom's mother throws dates, chestnuts, and candies into the bride's lap. The number caught is supposed to foretell the number of children she'll have.

Latin America

• *Padrinos* and *madrinos*, the godparents or wedding sponsors, participate by promising financial and spiritual aid. There may be several sponsors, a pair for each element of the wedding (music, food, and church).

Lithuania

• The wedded couple is served a symbolic meal by their parents—wine for joy, salt for tears, and bread for work.

Malaysia

• The groom's gifts to the bride are delivered to her home by a noisy procession of costumed children, carrying lavish trays of food and currency folded into animal or flower shapes.

• The groom's family pays for the expensive brocade cloth used to make the wedding clothes.

• Although the groom travels with much fanfare to the bride's house for the wedding, he is often denied entry until his best man wages a mock battle against the bride's relatives.

• Each wedding guest is given a beautifully decorated hard-boiled egg, a symbol of fertility.

Mexico

• Guests at many Mexican weddings gather around the couple in a heart-shaped ring at the reception, perhaps before the first dance.

• A "lasso" (a very large rosary) is wound around the couple's shoulders and hands during the ceremony to represent the union and protection of marriage.

• Six sets of godparents, known as *padrinos*, sponsor and participate in aspects of the wedding, such as providing the kneeling pillows to show the comfort of marriage. The groom gives the bride a gift of thirteen *arras*, or gold coins.

Morocco

• As in other Muslim countries, five days before the wedding, the bride has a ceremonial bath, then is painted with henna swirls on her hands and feet and adorned with makeup and jewels by other women.

• Before becoming guardian of her new hearth, the bride circles her marriage home three times.

Norway

• After a reindeer-kabob dinner lit by the midnight sun, nomadic tribes danced, ate, and feasted throughout the night.

• The folk bridal costume is not complete without sterling-silver jewelry and a gold-and-silver crown edged with small silver spoon-shaped bangles, whose tinkling sounds were thought to ward off evil spirits. The bride "dances off" this crown at the wedding feast.

• Bridesmaids wear green, which is considered unlucky in some cultures.

• Traditional wedding gifts are eiderdown beds and pillows.

• Two small fir trees are set on either side of the door to the couple's house until they are blessed with a child.

Pakistan

• A bride and groom traditionally saw each other for the first time in the reflection of a mirror held between the couple during the ceremony. The custom dates to a time when all marriages were arranged.

• The bride's family strings hundreds of

brightly colored lights around the house in anticipation of the wedding.

- The groom wears a long silk coat and is adorned with flowers.
- The bride leaves her family to join her husband's house with the Holy Koran held over her head.

Philippines

- Following the couple's engagement, the groom's parents call on the bride's parents to collaborate on wedding plans.
- A white silk cord is draped around the couple's shoulders to indicate their union.
- The "sponsor" of the wedding is an honored person who stands beside the couple and signs wedding papers as a witness.
- A bell-shaped cage housing white doves (symbolizing peace) is a favored wedding decoration. At a well-timed moment, the bride and groom pull on ribbon streamers to release the birds, a send-off into their new lives.

Poland

- For village weddings, friends weave a wedding crown of rosemary leaves (symbolizing remembrance) for the bride. Long white beaded ribbons— family heirlooms passed from mother to daughter—were tied to the crown.
- Reception guests customarily buy a dance with the bride by pinning money to her veil or tucking bills into a special bridal purse (perhaps of white satin embroidered with the couple's names and the wedding date), to build a honeymoon fund.
- Luck comes to the bride who drinks a glass of wine at the celebration without spilling a drop.

Puerto Rico

- At the reception, a bridal doll, in a dress that replicates the bridal gown, sits on the head table or the cake table.

Romania

- Girls begin making items for their trousseau as young as age six. The trousseau is carried to the annual "maiden market" each June 29, where families camp together on a mountain in hopes of attracting suitors for their daughters.
- Crowns are placed on the newlyweds' heads; sweets and nuts (symbolizing fertility) are thrown at them after the ceremony.

Russia

- The groom comes to claim his bride on their wedding day. She kneels before her parents and asks their forgiveness for all offenses she may have committed toward them. They lift her up and kiss her, then offer her bread and salt—so that she may never want for food as long as they are alive. When the bride leaves, the door is left open—symbolizing that she will never lack shelter if she wishes to return.
- Wedding guests don't only give presents—they get them. The bride gives friends and relatives some sort of sweet as a favor. They give her money after the wedding.
- On a mini-honeymoon, couples often tour the city in commercial wedding taxis, visiting important monuments and having their photos taken. These special nuptial cars are decorated with rings on top, a bridal doll on the front, and streamers. The groom gives out bottles of wine to keep his friends from blocking the way.

• After the couple are crowned in a Russian Orthodox wedding ceremony, they race to stand on a white rug. It is believed that whoever steps on it first will be the master of the household. (The rug can become a wedding keepsake after the ceremony.)

Samoa

• The bride wears a dress of tapa cloth, (made from mulberry bark), fresh flower leis, and a mother-of-pearl crown.

Scotland

• Bridegrooms once traveled to the metalsmiths of Edinburgh to purchase a silver teaspoon, called a wedding *spune*, engraved with the couple's initials and wedding date, to give their brides.

• Another old custom that's still observed: Friends wash the feet of both the bride and groom, preparing them to set off on a new path.

• The sword dance, similar to an Irish jig or a Highland fling, is usually performed at a Scottish wedding gathering.

Spain

• Peasant brides once wore a black silk dress to symbolize devotion until death. They also wore a mantilla, with orange blossoms in their hair. (Orange blossoms symbolize fertility and happiness.)

• Grooms wear a tucked shirt hand-embroidered by the bride in a design of her choosing.

• The groom gives thirteen coins (*monedas* or *arras*) to the bride, symbolizing his ability to support and care for her. During the ceremony, she carries them in a special purse, or a young girl carries them on a pillow or handkerchief.

• Wedding guests dance a *seguidillas manchegas* at the reception, during which each guest presents the bride with a gift.

Sweden

• To frighten away trolls (imaginary beings once thought to bring misfortune), bridesmaids carried bouquets of pungent herbs.

• The groom-to-be gives the bride-to-be a goblet of precious metal, filled with coins wrapped in white tissue paper.

• The bride may place a silver coin from her father in her left shoe; a gold coin from her mother in her right shoe, so she'll never do without. Her shoes are unfastened—symbolizing easy childbirth in the future.

• The bride gives her fiancé a shirt made of fine material to wear on their wedding day; he never wears it again, until he is buried in it.

• Swedish wives wear three wedding rings: for betrothal, marriage, and motherhood.

• Wedding picnics are held outdoors. Carpeting and tableware are laid on the forest floor, and games are played.

• The bride keeps a portion of every type of food from the wedding feast and then distributes it to the poor of the district.

Switzerland

• The junior bridesmaid leads the procession to the reception with handfuls of colored handkerchiefs for the guests. Whoever wants a "lucky" handkerchief contributes a coin toward the newlyweds' nest egg.

• After the vows, the bride's floral wreath, which symbolizes her maidenhood, is removed and set afire by the mistress of ceremonies. It's considered lucky if it burns quickly.

• A pine tree, which symbolizes luck and fertility, is planted at the couple's new home.

Thailand

• An old custom, still practiced in rural areas, is to have an older couple prepare the bridal bed and leave behind lucky talismans—such as bags of rice, sesame seeds, coins, and a tomcat—to wish both fertility and happiness.

• On the morning of their wedding, the couple go to feed the monks (who have taken a vow of poverty), in order to obtain a blessing.

• The timing of the joining ceremony is determined by astrologers.

• Weddings are not religious and do not include vows, but the ceremony of *sai monkon* (white thread) is a sacred ritual. The head of each partner is encircled with the thread, which is then joined together to unite them. A respected elder pours sacred water over their hands to bless them.

Ukraine

• Bridal parties stage a mock capture of the bride at the wedding reception to remind all of the guests of the many times their homeland was invaded.

• Instead of a cake, most couples share *korovai*, a sacred wedding bread decorated with symbolic motifs that represent eternity and the joining together of two families.

Vietnam

• Couples here are lucky enough to be feted twice. They begin their marriage with one wedding celebration, given by the bride's family. The second is given by the groom's family.

• The mother of a Vietnamese groom visits the bride's home on the wedding day to deliver betel (a plant that is used to pay respect) and pink chalk (to represent her wish for a rosy future).

• The groom's procession arrives at the bride's home carrying gifts: clothes, jewelry, and money. Friends and relatives join the parade, but the groom's mother does not, symbolizing her wish that there be no rivalry between her and her daughter-in-law.

Wales

• Here, and throughout the British Isles, the bride gives her attendants cuttings of myrtle (symbolizing love) from her bouquet. According to custom, if the plant roots and blooms, they'll marry soon.

• The churchyard gates are only opened after the village children are bribed with a shower of coins.

• Attendants race home from the ceremony with news of the marriage; the first to arrive wins a pint of ale.

Yemen

• The elaborate costumes worn by the bride and groom may be of gold cloth—indicating their "royal" status. The bride's hair is covered by a jeweled headdress signifying strength and fertility. The groom wears a necklace of gold coins, a talisman for prosperity.

• The whole community is invited to join the celebration. Playing music to "gladden the bride and groom" is a sacred duty, carried out by a variety of people. Professional musicians, performers, and guests take turns with cymbals, drums, and other instruments.

• The bride's female relatives prepare the food, which often includes small sweetened fritters, which promise a sweet life for the newlyweds and all who partake.

American Wedding Trends

North, south, east and west, America has a rich heritage of regional wedding traditions. In many places, the wedding and reception are community events, in keeping with the centuries-old recognition of marriage as a public rite of passage. Here are some of the contemporary customs you may encounter at weddings throughout the United States today. To research more old-country traditions and find out how to incorporate those into your celebration, ask older relatives, or consult cultural associations (see Appendix, under Chapter 2, "Wedding Customs").

Prewedding customs

• At some showers today, friends circulate a beautifully bound blank book so married women can write in their "recipe" for a happy marriage.

• It's a southern custom for guests to drop by anytime during "prewedding teas" (which are often hosted by female friends and relatives of the bride), and leave a gift.

Ceremony Customs

• The custom of "open church" is popular in small communities; it means everyone in the congregation is invited to the ceremony.

• A floral wreath is often hung on the door of the house of worship to let everyone know a wedding is taking place inside.

• Weddings are being held at historic sites—such as mansions, museums, battlefields, or national monuments. Some couples re-create a past era by using replicas of the wedding costumes, accessories, or transportation of that period.

• Ceremony sites are being chosen to reflect the couple's interests: a music hall, winery, art gallery, or beach, for example.

• Brides get to the church on time and in style. Transportation options include horse and carriage or old-fashioned roadsters.

• In the Southwest, western attire is almost always worn in some form—perhaps a traditional string tie or cowboy boots. Fringe-topped surreys and horse-drawn wagons are favorite forms of wedding-day transportation.

• One of the most well-known southern traditions is for the groom to ask his father to be the best man. Today, grooms may choose a best woman; brides sometimes select male attendants, or even a man of honor (see Chapter 6, "The Wedding Party").

• Like the invitation, wedding programs, which list the participants, explain customs, and describe events, become treasured mementos.

• Symbolic bouquets are given to mothers, grandmothers, aunts, godmothers and other female guests of honor.

• Relatives, friends, and members of the wedding party take part in the ceremony by reading Scripture, holding candles, and leading prayers.

• Wine is often sipped from heirloom goblets at the altar; some couples register for or buy and engrave their own.

• Brides and grooms sometimes save a ceremony taper used at the altar and relight it for a romantic first-anniversary dinner.

• During the wedding ceremony, some couples demonstrate family togetherness and the creation of a new family by lighting a Unity Candle. At the altar, three candles are lit in turn: The bride's parents light a candle on one side of the altar; the groom's parents light a candle on the other side; the bride and groom pick up each of their families' candles and jointly set the center taper aflame.

• Some couples arrange for church bells to ring after the vows are said—loud noises were once thought to scare away evil spirits lurking at the altar. Today, however, they herald happiness and new beginnings.

• Instead of rice, guests may throw kernels of wheat to wish the couple good luck and fertility. Many brides make up packets of birdseed, millet seed, or safflower seed to be tossed. Couples can also be sent off in a shower of bubbles. (For more information, see Appendix, under Chapter 2, "Wedding Customs.")

• The bride's father is not always asked, "Who gives this woman in marriage?" Instead, the officiant might ask, "Who supports this man and this woman in this marriage?" Both parents, or all parents (and guests, sometimes) respond, "We do."

• Many couples share their joy with family and friends by partaking in a symbol of peace, a friendly handshake or hug that's passed through the congregation.

Reception Customs

• Weddings are sometimes scheduled during a family reunion or anniversary reaffirmation ceremony when many guests will already be together.

• Long-Weekend Weddings (see Chapter 10, "Special Weddings & New Ways to Wed") allow the celebration to last a few days versus a few hours, and include a variety of different festivities—a welcome cocktail party, a museum tour, a picnic, a bride's-versus-groom's-team softball game, a pool party, or a postwedding brunch.

• Some couples plan a wedding at their honeymoon destination (see Chapter 10, "Special Weddings & New Ways to Wed"), inviting a group of friends and relatives to join them.

• When families and friends are far-flung, some couples plan a Progressive Wedding (see Chapter 10, "Special Weddings and New Ways to Wed")—which means there will be a second, and sometimes third, reception in another town. Invited guests include those friends and relatives who were unable to travel to the first wedding celebration.

• Theme Weddings (see Chapter 10, "Special Weddings and New Ways to Wed") are being woven subtly around a special holiday, such as Christmas, the Fourth of July, or Valentine's Day.

• For African-American couples, the vestibule and stairway of the house of worship may be festooned with African *kente* or *asooke* fabric.

trends for the bride

• Many of today's brides use heirloom lace for their veils. Fingertip-length veils are popular, and are sometimes sprinkled with crystals, or edged with soutache, embroidery or ribbon. Instead of a traditional veil, a bride may choose to wear fresh (or silk) flowers or a headband wrapped in ribbon or made of fresh flowers.

• Instead of a headpiece, African-American brides may braid their hair in Goddess Queen N'zinga braids (piled tall on top of the head).

• Brides often choose to have initials and the wedding date embroidered inside the gown, on the train, or on a handkerchief; the dress is then passed along to the next woman in the family to wed.

• Traditional clothing can be worn by brides to reflect their background and heritage (see "International Customs" section).

• Good-luck symbols—small silver charms, such as horseshoes—are sewn into the hems of brides' gowns. Some brides sew a small pouch filled with a tiny piece of bread, a bit of cloth, a sliver of wood, and a dollar bill—to protect against future shortages of food, clothing, shelter, and money—into the hem of their petticoat.

• Symbolic bridal bouquets, composed of flowers with special meanings are carried. Some brides carry the first type of flower the groom ever gave them.

• At Afro-centric weddings, church pews, pulpits, the ring bearer's pillow, the guest-book table are made of *kente* cloth. The minister might even wear a traditional African robe.

• Rich ethnic foods celebrate the couple's heritages, combining two and sometimes more cultures for a lavish feast.

• The bride and groom may walk to their reception site with young friends (or the couple's children) leading the parade—symbolizing bounty, fruitfulness, and fertility.

• In Louisiana, jazz musicians often lead a procession from the church to the reception site.

• The groom's cake may be served at the reception along with the wedding cake, or it may be cut ahead of time by the caterer and packed in small decorative boxes for wedding guests to take home after the celebration.

• Couples are giving ecologically sound favors to guests—packets of seeds and tree saplings to be replanted (see Appendix, under Chapter 2, "Wedding Customs"), for example. They also sometimes set engraved notes at each guest's place, noting that in lieu of favors, a donation has been made to a favorite charity.

• Reception tables are decorated with state flowers or regional favors (a breakaway arrangement of potted cacti, if the wedding is in a desert setting; splits of wine from a local vineyard) for guests to take home.

• In honor of their wedding, couples appreciate donations to their favorite charity.

• Invitations are printed on recycled paper.

• It's a southern custom, borrowed from the traditional British bridesmaids' tea, to tie tiny charms (an anchor, symbolizing adventure; a ring, symbolizing marriage; a horseshoe, luck) to a ribbon. These ribbons are placed between the layers of the wedding cake. Each bridesmaid pulls out a ribbon with an attached charm before the cake is cut. This custom may be observed at a shower, a bridesmaids' luncheon, or at the wedding reception.

• Today, some wedding cakes are cut with a great-grandmother's sterling-silver cake knife. Or couples start a new tradition by having their initials engraved on a heritage cake knife; when their children wed, they'll add their initials, and so on . . .

• Couples cherish heirlooms. Punch is served with an antique ladle, or the wedding cake is topped with the cake topper from the wedding cake of either the bride's or groom's parents.

• In the Midwest, there's often a Dollar Dance (see "Poland").

• At African-American weddings, African and Caribbean foods are served, tropical flowers decorate the tables, and guests are asked to remove their shoes before entering the reception site (an African custom).

• African-American couples hire traditional African drummers (there are different drumming styles for each region in Africa) for their reception, or for the ceremony when the couple Jump the Broom. Contact a local community center or music school (see Appendix, under Chapter 2, "Wedding Customs") for referrals to African-American entertainment resources.

• Ethnic music and dances are being played at receptions (see Chapter 13,

"Your Reception," under the "Reception Dancing" section).

• Brides plan a special dance with their father at the reception; grooms also have a special dance with their mother.

• Couples honor their parents, by having the band play the first dances their parents chose when they married.

• Couples send joyous wishes skyward—airborne skywritten messages, helium-filled balloons, and fireworks entertaining guests and bringing cheers of congratulations.

• Disposable cameras are set on each reception table so that guests can take candid shots throughout the wedding, then leave the film for the couple to develop later.

• Friends join together and present the couple with a handmade communal gift, such as a wedding quilt. The quilt might consist of commemorative squares, each individually embroidered or appliquéd, to remember a meaningful event or thought. Or, it might re-create traditional quilting patterns such as the Bride's Quilt, the Bridal Wreath, or the Double Wedding Ring.

• Brides save the flowers from their bouquet, pressed and placed into a picture frame.

• Many couples arrange to donate leftover food to needy organizations, and extra floral arrangements to local hospitals.

• Some couples create a time capsule to be saved for a future daughter or granddaughter. In a decorative box, they store wedding mementos, such as wedding checklists; florist, formalwear, gown, and photography orders; the cake topper; an invitation; the bride's garter; and potpourri made from the dried petals of the bride's bouquet.

trends for the groom

• Some grooms wear outfits reflecting their heritage (see "International Customs" section).

• Most men choose to wear a wedding band. The rings are usually of gold or platinum.

• Grooms wear a boutonniere that makes a meaningful statement: a red chrysanthemum ("I love you"), a myrtle sprig (everlasting love), a white rose ("I am worthy of you"), sweet William (gallantry).

• Some grooms choose to have bachelor parties where the focus is on camaraderie. They go camping, enjoy a ski or golf weekend, or take in a game; a few have even hit a local spa.

• It's not uncommon for today's grooms to select their own groom's cake, baked in their favorite flavors (banana, chocolate), or in a clever shape (car, book, canoe).

PREWEDDING PARTIES

Traditionally, the engagement period has been a whirlwind of cocktail parties and dinners hosted by family and friends. Today, however, these celebrations are anything *but* traditional. Whether you're hosting a spa day for your bridesmaids or being toasted at a prewedding breakfast, expect the unexpected! Showers and bachelorette parties are no longer exclusively for women—and gifts are as likely to include cross-country skis and camping gear as lasagne pans and lingerie.

The Shower

A symbol of the dowry that a woman once brought to her marriage, the purpose of a shower is to help a couple outfit their new home or assemble a trousseau. It was traditionally an all-female afternoon tea or luncheon. Not anymore!

Who hosts? Today, friends, bridesmaids, the honor attendant, or the best man might throw a single-sex or coed party, often for the bride *and* the groom.

When is it held? There may be more than one shower during the engagement. All showers should be scheduled a significant amount of time after any engagement parties, but at least two weeks before the wedding. (They should also take place after the couple have registered for gifts.) If the bride lives far away, a shower might be planned for when she's in town for a dress fitting or to get the marriage license, so she won't have to make an extra trip. (See "Long-Distance Shower" question.)

How to celebrate? Showers tend to be informal, whether held at home or in a restaurant, hotel, or at another site. They are most often a lunch, but might be a brunch, barbecue, pool party, or coed

guest-of-honor tips

- Request that your mother, sisters, and/or aunts not cohost your shower; it shouldn't seem like they are asking for gifts.

- Ask your bridesmaids *not* to plan the shower closer than two weeks to the wedding (you'll be busy), unless they or you are arriving from a distance. (See "Long-Distance Shower" question.)

- Urge friends to group together to cohost prewedding parties. Too many activities will wear everyone out.

- Ask friends *not* to invite guests to showers who will not be invited to the wedding. The shower's purpose is to shower the bride with gifts and make guests feel part of the wedding-related festivities.

- Have your groom ask his best man *not* to schedule the bachelor party during the week before the wedding. If the groom is coming from another town or city, ask the ushers to try to schedule something during one of his pre-wedding visits.

- Don't put the same friends on every guest list. Too many parties may make them feel overextended.

- Express your appreciation to hosts afterward with notes of thanks and flowers.

- Reserve some private time the last week or so before the wedding for yourself and your groom.

cocktail party. Most—but not all—showers are a surprise.

What happens at a shower? The host/hostess should ask guests to arrive about thirty minutes before the bride is expected, to help set up a display of presents, perhaps under a shower umbrella (symbolizing good luck and shelter). Eating and opening gifts are the main activities. As the bride or couple unwrap each gift, someone should write down who gave what (to assist the bride with thank-you notes). Another guest might collect all of the ribbons and make a "rehearsal bouquet" (which the bride traditionally carries during the ceremony rehearsal) by taping or stapling them to a paper plate, or tie them together into a long boa. The host and/or hostess might also plan party games.

Who is invited? Usually, shower guests are those who will also be invited to the wedding, unless it is an office shower. The guest list should include your honor attendant and bridesmaids (groomsmen, too, if men will be included), the mothers and sisters of the bride and groom, and other close relatives and friends. The host or hostess usually sends invitations by mail, at least two weeks before the shower.

How is an office/school/club shower planned? This type of shower is often hosted by office coworkers, club members, or school friends who are not necessarily invited to the wedding. It is usually planned for one of the final days or meetings for which the bride will be present before her wedding. Usually as a surprise, the bride's colleagues gather together with refreshments and present her with a group gift.

How can a long-distance shower be planned if the bride and her attendants live in different cities? The attendants might schedule a shower for a long-distance bride once she is in town, days before the wedding. In this instance, a surprise is not a good idea, since the bride's schedule will be tight. Another option: If the couple will be returning to the wedding town after the honeymoon, before traveling home, it is perfectly acceptable to schedule a shower (traditional or coed) then. Again, a surprise may be risky.

Can a remarrying bride have a shower? Today's remarrying brides are often feted with showers and prewedding festivities that aren't all that different from those for first-time brides. Guests may include children, coworkers, parents, relatives, couples, and friends. Since this bride and groom may have already established their homes, they may not need the basic gifts. Instead, friends may chip in for lifestyle gifts (see "Remarrying Shower-Gift Ideas" box 6).

14 New Shower Ideas

Not every bridal shower has to go the traditional route of chicken salad and the ribbon bouquet. Theme showers can put a fun, modern twist on this age-old ritual—and can help family and friends get to know the couple better by highlighting some of their special interests and/or hobbies.

By the Book For the book-loving bride: Send a paperback to each guest with a homemade book jacket listing all party information (title, *A Shower for Katie*; author, name[s] of the hostess[es]; etc.). Re-create a fictional feast, like the tea party in *Alice in Wonderland*. Give the bride a set of bookends, his-and-her reading lights, cookbooks, a bookstore gift certificate, or a guest book and fountain pen.

Into the Garden Clip invitations to assorted seed packets. As for the menu, think summer garden: Serve up a tomato-and-basil salad, ratatouille, and pasta with asparagus. Gifts might include gardening clogs, tools, a watering can, rosebush, sun dial, or lawn furniture.

The Wedding Night Collect do-not-disturb signs from the hotel where you'll be holding the shower (they might charge a small fee) to include in the invitations. What to serve? Room service, of course. Order up champagne, finger sandwiches, and petits fours. The bride might appreciate receiving an overnight bag, perfume, satin sheets, bubble bath, scented candles, and lingerie.

Party Time! For the couple that loves to entertain: Print invitations on recipe cards and attach an extra for guests to share their favorite recipes and/or party-giving advice for a specific type of gathering. Possible themes include Dinner Parties, Desserts, Brunches, Hors d'oeuvres, or Romantic Meals. Serve some of the featured recipes, and give party-appropriate gifts, such as serving plates, knives, trays, cocktail napkins, and decorative placecard holders. Present the bride with a special recipe box to hold all the guests' cards.

Pick a Country To fete a travel-happy couple, border plain notepaper with cutouts from a map. Besides giving party information on the invitation, ask guests to bring a gift associated with a particular country. Plan on serving international fare—individual pizzas, fajitas, sushi. Keeping with the global theme, guests can give the bride a pasta maker, a wok, a gift certificate for a Swedish massage, or some French perfume.

Day at the Spa For the perfect day of female bonding, have the who, what, where, and why printed on a T-shirt that says, "Shelly's Spa." The ultimate in luxury: Hire a masseuse to give everyone a ten-minute neck massage. Put out a healthful spa-inspired spread—e.g., salads, fruit, etc. Gift ideas include massage oil, a terry-cloth robe, monogrammed towels, yoga videos, and a manicure/pedicure set.

creative shower activities

- Play Bridal Jeopardy—The hostess compiles a series of trivia answers relating to the bride and groom, then asks the guests to phrase the questions (ANSWER: "The canoe capsized." QUESTION: "What happened on Bob and Sue's first date?").

- Ask each guest to supply a favorite candid photo of themselves with the bride and/or groom plus a brief caption, and create a scrapbook to present to the bride. Or make the photos into a slide show, or download them onto a CD, with each guest's quips to show at the shower.

- Try Wedding Charades—The hostess passes out squares of paper with wedding-related phrases or superstitions ("In sickness and in health"). Guests are divided into two teams, and take turns acting out the phrases.

- Ask each guest to contribute one line to a free-form "poem" of good wishes that will be read and presented to the bride after all the gifts have been opened.

- "Roast" the happy couple by having guests take turns telling anecdotes and stories about the bride and groom.

- Give the bride some words to live by—invite guests to share their best advice for a happy marriage. Or ask guests to write their thoughts on notecards, then seal them in an envelope for the couple to open together on their first anniversary.

Sunday in the Country Attach invitations to pretty paper fans. Let the menu consist of picnic fare—fried chicken, potato salad, brownies, lemonade, and iced tea. Shower the bride with a picnic basket, car blanket, straw hat, Frisbee, or portable CD player.

That's Entertainment Make up invitations in the form of a ticket ("Admit one to Joanne's Shower"). Tack up posters from classic "wedding movies," such as *Four Weddings and a Funeral, Father of the Bride,* etc. Hot dogs, popcorn, and pizza are the perfect refreshments. Gift options: a VCR, popular videocassettes, a subscription to an entertainment magazine, or sports or theater tickets.

Happy Hour Write the party information on a paper cutout of a wine bottle or champagne glass. Provide a sampling of wines or beers (and a nonalcoholic punch for nondrinkers), as well as traditional happy hour foods like buffalo wings, mini pizzas, and chicken fingers. Gifts might include a wine rack, glasses, coasters, a blender, an ice bucket, a martini set, or a case of wine.

Fitness With a fabric marker, write the invitations on a tennis ball, headband, or small hand towel. The idea: to equip the health-conscious or sports-loving couple with gifts to help them stay in shape. Host the shower at a health club or decorate with a sports theme. Set up a juice bar and a buffet with raw vegetables, salads, and a big fruit platter. Gift suggestions: a nonstick skillet (for low-fat cooking), handheld weights, a new tennis racquet, or gift certificate sessions with a personal trainer.

Tea Time This classic alternative is once again popular, particularly for brides who are being feted at more than one shower. Serve platters of finger sandwiches (crusts cut off, of course!), assorted cookies and small cakes or scones, with jam and lemon curd, and offer two or three varieties of brewed tea. Gift possibilities include a tea pot, tea cups, cookie or cake plates, an assortment of gourmet teas, and decorative napkins.

The Honeymoon Send postcard-style invitations picturing the couple's honeymoon destination. Serve the cuisine of the place they'll be visiting: Caribbean jerk chicken for a visit to the Islands, chowder and sourdough bread for a trip to San Francisco, or gourmet pizzas for a honeymoon to Italy. Guests can give any item that will help the couple enjoy their honeymoon: a travel alarm clock, luggage, a beach blanket for two, or guide books.

Timing Is Everything (a.k.a., "Around the Clock") Invitations might picture a famous clock, like Big Ben. Give each guest an hour of the day and ask them to bring a gift that corresponds to that time. Create an around-the-clock menu: yogurt parfaits, eggs benedict, tea sandwiches, and sliced ham or turkey. Guests might bring a bathrobe for 7 A.M., a teapot for 4:00 P.M., a videocassette for 8:00 P.M., and sexy lingerie for 11:00 P.M.

Holiday Designate a holiday to each guest, asking them to bring a gift that will help the couple celebrate the particular holiday. Serve Thanksgiving turkey, Easter ham, and Christmas cookies. Gift ideas include champagne flutes for New Year's, tree ornaments for Christmas, a seder plate for Passover, or gardening tools for Arbor Day.

Showering with Him:
Tips for a Co-ed Shower

- Choose a theme that men as well as women are bound to enjoy—for example, an entertainment, fitness, or happy-hour shower.
- Forget the finger sandwiches and mini quiches. Serve up fare that will appeal to the guys, too: chili, barbecued ribs, or pizza.

- Get guests mingling with a game of softball or volleyball. Select most-valuable players; have trophies made up. Other games (see "Creative Shower Activities") can also help break the ice.
- Don't feel that you have to schedule every minute. Think more in terms of a fun, leisurely party than a traditional shower. (For example: First hour, eat. Second hour open gifts. Third hour, cut cake and serve dessert.)

remarrying shower-gift ideas

- ☐ a DVD player
- ☐ all the goods for a weekend getaway (e.g., to the beach, or to a specific city)
- ☐ sheets and towels
- ☐ matching pajamas
- ☐ gift certificates for a health spa
- ☐ a donation to a charity
- ☐ an espresso maker and fresh coffee beans
- ☐ a pasta maker and pasta cookbook
- ☐ hobby-related items (e.g., camping gear, gardening tools, sports equipment, specialty cooking utensils)

Bridesmaids' Parties

Bridesmaids' parties are the perfect time to introduce out-of-town attendants, schedule final dress fittings, display wedding gifts, and distribute presents to thank attendants for being in the wedding. (However, the couple may prefer to give all attendants their gifts at the rehearsal dinner.) Bridesmaids might also want to give their gifts to the bride at the bridesmaids' party, particularly if they are going in on one large group gift (see Chapter 17, "Wedding Gifts").

Who hosts? It's customary for the bridesmaids—individually or together—to entertain the bride (if they are not also co-hosting a bridal shower). Otherwise, the bride may want to treat her bridesmaids to a party. Traditionally, this was a lunch or afternoon tea, but today the bride might treat her bridesmaids to margaritas and Mexican food at a favorite local restaurant.

When is it held? More-formal gatherings should be held at least two weeks before the wedding (unless bridesmaids will not arrive until the week of the wedding). Informally, the bride will probably spend time alone with her bridesmaids throughout the days leading up to the wedding. The bride might also treat her attendants to lunch after a dress fitting or invite them to a breakfast on the wedding morning.

Is this when bridesmaids find the "ribbon pulls" in a cake? There is a southern custom that began at a bridesmaids' tea: the baker prepared a traditional pink-iced cake for dessert, with a thimble baked into the layers. Whichever maid found the trinket in her piece would be the next to wed. Today, bridesmaids may gather at a bridesmaids' party or before the cake cutting at the wedding reception to pull ribbons trimmed with tiny charms from between the cake layers: a horseshoe and four-leaf clover mean "good luck"; a fleur-de-lis, "love will flower"; a heart, "love will come"; an anchor, "hope and adventure"; a thimble and button, "old maid"; and a tiny wedding ring, "next to marry."

The Bachelor Party

The bachelor party gives the groom and his attendants a chance to release prewedding tension, celebrate the groom's final days as a single man, and spend time with close friends and relatives.

Who hosts? A friend or relative of the groom (usually the best man) and some or all of the ushers.

When is it held? At least a week (preferably two weeks) before the wedding. Too many ushers and grooms have almost missed the wedding while oversleeping after a late night on the town—so don't plan to celebrate the night before.

What is the purpose? It was once thought that bachelors needed to get philandering out of their system before their wedding day. Poker or gambling was often part of the evening, the winnings going to the groom-to-be. Why? So that he could afford another night out with the boys once his wife took control of his money. Today, the bachelor party is an occasion for the groom's close male friends and relatives to reminisce with him about the past, toast his future, and bid farewell to his single life.

What happens at a bachelor party? While some bachelor parties carry on the tradition of visiting strip clubs or casinos, others gather male guests together for a softball game followed by a keg of beer, a day at the racetrack, or a weekend camping or sailing trip.

Who is invited? The groom's attendants, school and current friends invited to the wedding, brothers, and close cousins.

surviving his bachelor party

- Talk to your fiancé if you feel insecure and hesitant. Don't, however, give him an ultimatum like: "Go to that bachelor party and I'm calling off the wedding." Trust and understanding will serve you well here, as they will throughout your married life.

- Try to understand his point of view. Many men see marriage as an ending of one stage of life, as well as the beginning of another. As such, the bachelor party is often one part mourning, one part celebration.

- If you don't think you can handle the stress of a bachelor party, encourage his groomsmen and friends to plan a co-ed event you'll all enjoy.

The Bachelorette Party

Prewedding revelry is not for men only. The bridesmaids, along with close friends and relatives, may want to take the bride out for one final night alone with them, as a single woman. While some bachelorette parties have the same raucous feel of a stereotypical bachelor party, many are quieter celebrations of female bonding.

Who hosts? A close friend (often the honor attendant), or all of the bridesmaids may plan this celebration, although it may also be hosted by roommates, sisters, or cousins.

When is it held? *Not* the week or night before the wedding. It may be scheduled for the same night as the bachelor party.

Who is invited? Anyone whom the bride would want in attendance. The guest list should include only those individuals who will be invited to the wedding.

How to Celebrate? Some ideas include: hiring a chef from a local restaurant to cook dinner and lead a group cooking lesson; booking a spa weekend, replete with massages, manicures, pedicures, and facials (depending on the number in your party, you may qualify for a group rate); taking off on an adventure for a weekend of white-water rafting, skiing, mountain climbing, or biking; hiring a hairstylist and makeup artist to give you and your party a new look—then renting a limousine and hitting the town.

work-party themes

During the wedding-planning months, gather your attendants together for some fun—and needed assistance. Plan the following theme parties:

- **Inviting Ideas**—Address invitations and announcements; stuff and stamp envelopes.

- **Cake Tasting/Hors d'oeuvre Sampling**—with your attendants, taste the best menus of several bakers and caterers. Most will make mini portions for a fee.

- **Wine/Champagne Tasting**—Ask attendants to help you choose your reception spirits.

- **Battle of the Bands**—Invite bridesmaids and ushers to go with you to clubs and reception sites to "audition" bands live.

- **Treats for Guests**—Make wedding favors for the reception (e.g., rice packets, bags of almonds). Order Chinese takeout and a classic rental movie.

Wedding Work Parties

Getting organized for your wedding day doesn't have to be hard work. One way to lighten the load? Invite your wedding party and closest friends to enjoy a buffet supper (or, order take-out food) while they help get important tasks done.

Who hosts? Usually the bride, at her home.

When is it held? Throughout the engagement, to coincide with each wedding-

planning deadline. (See "Work-Party Themes.")

What is the purpose? To help the bride with wedding–related tasks.

The Rehearsal Dinner

The rehearsal dinner is an occasion for attendants, family, and sometimes out-of-town guests to get acquainted, reminisce, and wish you well. This event will make all arriving guests feel a part of the wedding excitement and give them a chance to get acquainted with other guests. (See Chapter 10, "Special Weddings & New Ways to Wed.")

Who hosts? Though almost anyone can host the rehearsal dinner, the groom's

parents traditionally do the honors. It's perfectly correct, however, for the bride's parents, grandparents, or another relative from either family to host the dinner.

When is it held? The rehearsal and party that follow usually take place the night before the wedding. Participants go directly from the ceremony site to the dinner location. However, if all of the major players will be in town, you may want to schedule the rehearsal and dinner two or three days before the wedding—especially if the ceremony is early in the day—to make sure everyone is well rested.

Who's invited? Invitations are sent after you know who's coming to the wedding. The guest list usually includes attendants, immediate family members, spouses of married attendants, parents of children in the wedding (only if the children themselves are invited to the dinner, which depends on their age), and the officiant and his spouse. You may also decide to invite out-of-town guests. If you prefer to keep the guest list intimate— just the immediate families and the wedding party—be sure to schedule an alternate event for the out-of-town guests at another location. (This can be a relatively casual party and is one wedding-related gathering that you do not have to attend.) An aunt and uncle or family friends might offer to host it in their home or in a restaurant. This will make arriving guests feel welcome, a part of the festivities, and give them a chance to get to know others who will be at the wedding.

How to celebrate? Don't let the name "rehearsal dinner" fool you. This get-together could be anything—a poolside barbecue, a potluck brunch, a cocktail buffet at home, or a traditional seated meal in a restaurant. It can be as informal or formal as you like; just make sure the gathering doesn't upstage the wedding itself.

What happens at a rehearsal dinner? Since the celebration is usually limited to the bridal party, close family members, and sometimes out-of-town guests, the toasts offered to the bride and groom can be longer and more personal than those given on the wedding day. You might also ask each guest to bring a favorite framed picture of you or your fiancé to display near the entrance to the room where the dinner will take place. Your relatives may also compile and show slides or videos of you both as infants and teenagers.

After the hosts say a few words, the best man can offer a toast, followed by good wishes from the groom to you and your parents. Next, you might toast your fiancé and his parents.

The best man or host continues to act as a master of ceremonies, introducing other key guests who may rise to make toasts to you and your fiancé.

The groom should be ready with a closing thought that will bring the evening to an end. Many couples pass out attendants' gifts at the rehearsal dinner. This is also the best time to go over last-minute details, like transportation to the church and reception for the bridal party, seating procedures for ushers, and receiving-line order and instructions.

Any special seating requirements? A rehearsal-dinner seating plan is optional, but if a large group is invited, it's a good idea to use place cards at the table, arranged so that those who don't know one another will become acquainted before the wedding.

Since brides and grooms arrange to sit at a table alone with their parents; it may be the first time that they are all meeting if they live at a distance from each other.

The Wedding Breakfast

The wedding-day breakfast or brunch is a wonderful way to gather guests who are especially close to the bride and groom in an informal setting and give them a chance to wish the couple well—and to distract them from any prewedding stress.

Who hosts? A friend, neighbor, or relative.

Who's invited? Family, friends, out-of-town guests, and anyone to whom you might want to give an extra-warm welcome.

Can there be a postwedding brunch? Just because the wedding's over doesn't mean the celebrating has to stop. Families or friends might host a brunch, lunch, or pool party the next day for guests who have traveled a long distance to attend. Many newlyweds go to this postwedding brunch before leaving on their honeymoon. It's a relaxed way to visit with far-flung family members, old friends, and to talk about wedding highlights.

PLANNING YOUR WEDDING

The beautiful, formal weddings that most couples dream of can take over a year to plan in big cities—less time in rural areas. Even the simplest, most intimate ceremony and reception often require two to three months of planning. Before you get started, though, you'll need to decide when, where, and how you'll marry.

When—Date and Time

The number of other weddings taking place during your chosen month may mean that some dates are eliminated from the start. June is still the most popular wedding month, followed by July, August, September, October, May, and November. Anticipate as many pros and cons as possible when you choose your date and time. But try to secure a date as early as possible. Think about:

Time of day. A busy church or synagogue may schedule multiple weddings on weekends, so reserve a slot as soon as possible. The hour you choose may be influenced by the wedding style and dress that you envision. For example, a *very formal wedding,* in which the groom and ushers wear white tie (full-dress tailcoat, matching trousers, white waistcoat, white bow tie, wing-collared shirt), is held in the evening, with the ceremony beginning after 6 P.M. (see "How—Style and Formality" section and Chapter 7, "Wedding Clothes").

Your wedding time may also be influenced by where you live and your religion. In the South, evening weddings are popular, while afternoon ceremonies are prevalent in the Southwest. For Protestant weddings, afternoon and evening nuptials are common, while Roman Catholic weddings traditionally begin at 11 A.M. or noon. If your heart is set on a Saturday wedding and you are Jewish, it will have to be after sundown, which marks the end of the Sabbath.

If there will be other weddings at your ceremony site that day, be sure there will

key wedding decisions

- religious vs. civil ceremony
- seated meal vs. buffet vs. cocktails and hors d'oeuvres
- large guest list vs. intimate party
- live band vs. DJ
- evening vs. daytime
- weekend vs. weekday
- hometown vs. city of employment or faraway destination

be enough time for your wedding-service professionals to set up flowers, cameras, and food; to assemble your wedding party; and to clear guests out at a leisurely pace when it's over. If another bride will marry shortly before or after you, consider sharing the cost of ceremony flowers, greenery, decorations, or dance floor.

If the church or synagogue is available only in the morning, but you want an evening reception, consider all your options, but do *not* leave your guests with a big block of unscheduled time in between. (If this is unavoidable, arrange for a hospitality suite stocked with drinks and snacks at a local hotel.)

Religious holidays. Consider season, holidays at that time of year, religious observances, and local customs. Some faiths do not allow formal weddings on certain days or during some hours. Ministers and priests may not be willing to perform ceremonies during the solemn days of Lent, for example. Rabbis cannot marry couples during high holy days, such as on Yom Kippur. Remember that some religious holidays fall on different days every year, so take a look at next year's calendar.

Secular holidays. The Fourth of July is a patriotic choice—just remember that the town parade, complete with high school band, may march past the church while you are saying your vows. Spring, summer, and fall festivals, as well as street fairs, races, and walk-a-thons, with accompanying traffic and tourists, can shut down major roads for several hours. Check with the chamber of commerce for upcoming dates. Marrying on a holiday may also require more long-range

planning. Your guests may have booked vacations around long weekends, such as Labor Day, many months in advance. Whether to attend your wedding or go on a longed-for vacation may be a difficult choice.

Season. You may have a season in mind—Christmas, with the church decked out in holly and pine and bridesmaids in deep red velvet; or spring, when tulips bloom and pastel dresses are naturally appealing. Each season has virtues and drawbacks. Snowstorms can cause transportation nightmares not only at the wedding site, but for airline travelers. As you choose a summer date, remember that you'll be responsible for keeping two hundred guests cool in August. Is your house of worship air-conditioned? A faraway wedding on a Caribbean island might be better scheduled before or after hurricane season.

Allergies. Consider your and your family's allergies when selecting a wedding site and season. For example, hay fever strikes in different seasons or year-round, depending on the region. And who wants to say their vows in between sneezes? (See "Allergy-Attack Tips" box.)

Symbolic days. Do you want to marry on the anniversary of the day you met? Perhaps you want to say your vows on your parents' or grandparents' wedding anniversary. Would you like to commemorate your mother's birthday by choosing that date?

Logistics. Maybe you've dreamed of a Valentine's Day wedding, but it's on a Wednesday. If it's a small wedding with few out-of-towners invited, this doesn't

allergy-attack tips

- Visit sites beforehand to be sure they are well ventilated.

- Do you or someone in the wedding party suffer from hay fever? Choose an indoor, air-conditioned site.

- Schedule outdoor photos for late morning or midafternoon when pollen's less prevalent.

- Keep antihistamines and decongestants that don't make you sleepy on-hand.

- Stick to makeup and fragrance you've worn before

- Choose a gown in a natural fiber fabric.

- See an allergist who can determine what you're allergic to, teach you to reduce exposure, and prescribe appropriate medication.

have to be a problem. For a larger wedding, most couples choose the Saturday or Sunday closest to that holiday—to facilitate travel and prevent scheduling conflicts with guests' work commitments.

Cost. Some caterers may offer slightly better deals during less popular wedding months (January or March, for example) in order to stimulate business during slow times. Keep in mind that the earlier you begin to plan, the more time you will have to compare services and choose those best suited to your budget.

Protection. Consider taking out wedding insurance to protect your investment. (See Appendix, under Chapter 4, "Planning Your Wedding.") For a one-time premium, with coverage beginning up to two years prior to the wedding, a policy will usually cover cancellation or postponement and a variety of other optional services, including lost or stolen gifts, damaged rental property, and personal liability.

Where—Choosing the Site

Sit down with your fiancé and make a list of priorities. You may feel a church wedding is essential, or discover that he wants the ceremony and reception to take place under one roof so guests don't have to travel. When weighing locations, first consider the approximate number of guests, activities (dancing, eating—buffet, finger food, or a seated meal?), budget limitations, and proximity to your home or honeymoon site.

Traditionally, the bride and her parents chose the site, since they would be footing the bill. Today, however, many couples either pay for the entire wedding or split the costs into thirds (among themselves and both sets of parents), making both the bride and groom instrumental decision makers. Some couples choose to marry in the city where they are currently working; others travel to the home of the bride's parents for a family wedding, then attend postwedding receptions—otherwise known as a Progressive Wedding—in other towns or cities (see Chapter 10, "Special Weddings & New Ways to Wed"). Below are some site options:

A college. Whether it is your alma mater or a nearby local university, many colleges have exquisite chapels or buildings and halls available for rent.

A vast cathedral with spires and stained glass. This dramatic and inspiring space may be your dream setting.

A stately and dignified judge's chambers. Many interfaith couples choose this type of intimate setting.

A glamorous old hotel ballroom. These large, open spaces offer a multitude of charming possiblities and can accomodate large numbers of people, food preparation and dancing. Plants and decorations can be used to separate the ceremony and reception areas. Or a ceremony setting can simply be removed after the vows.

Your childhood home. This sentimental choice may save on the cost of a hall, but

creative wedding sites

- yacht or yacht club
- art studio or gallery
- mansion or historical landmark building
- private school
- ski lodge
- theater
- fire station
- an ethnic or favorite restaurant
- flower shop
- train station
- lighthouse
- theme museum
- orchard or vineyard
- mountaintop
- ferryboat
- planetarium
- botanical garden
- beachside or lakeside
- sports arena
- aquarium

For more ideas, see Appendix, under Chapter 4, "Planning Your Wedding."

outdoor-site considerations

- accessibility
- parking space
- privacy
- facilities
- presence of traffic
- permits, fees
- inclement weather (rent a tent or have an alternate site)
- noise levels

site decorations

- **Home wedding:** Choose a single color scheme for flowers and linens—to unify a household of objects and elements.

- **Country setting:** Dress up white linens with stripes or gingham checks; go for splashes of color—buckets of vivid wildflowers and fresh fruits, for example; use vines and flowering branches to create an archway or huppah.

- **Outdoor lighting:** paper lanterns, a chandelier hung from a tree branch, or hurricane candelabra with tapers on each table; floating candles in a pond or brook; white lights strung through trees.

- **Outdoor decoration:** oversized slipcovered cushions strewn around the lawn and under trees for guests to lounge on. Tree trunks surrounded at their base with flowering potted plants.

- **Victorian wedding:** Cluster collectibles on tables (porcelain figurines, silver frames, and ribboned nosegays); dress tables with damask cloths, lace runner, doilies, and brocade napkins. Use old valentines for escort cards and/or favors.

- **Formal evening:** Today, this look is tailored, clean, and understated. Use a mono-chromatic color theme, with accents of silver—serene, stately, but simple.

- **Romance:** Grace an altar or podium with 6-foot-tall candelabra; fill windowsills and shelves with votive candles; string strands of white lights around plants and doorways; use pink light bulbs in light fixtures for a natural glow; wrap columns in tulle for a soft, ethereal feel; to toss: rose petals in cones.

- **Seasonal elements:** Place floral arrangements in hollowed-out pumpkins or gourds for fall weddings; in summer, add fresh herbs to bouquets and centerpieces.

(continued)

rental costs of utensils, chairs, etc., add up quickly. (See "Reception Rental Tips" box and Chapter 10, "Special Weddings & New Ways to Wed.")

Your grandmother's/relative's garden. An outdoor ceremony amid blossoming flowers is charming—just make sure that guests have some shelter from the sun (hand out paper parasols), and have an alternate rain plan. Rent a tent, no matter what the weather forecast.

A public park. Many have pretty gazebos on small lakes or ponds, and well-landscaped gardens. Check with authorities in your city or town about permits and regulations.

Rooftops. Are there any local buildings that feature a particularly lovely rooftop garden? The views can be spectacular. Check on the number of people allowed by law, food preparation capabilities, and whether band and lighting equipment can be transported there easily.

How—Style and Formality

Will your wedding be religious or civil? One faith or interfaith? Traditional or offbeat? Formal or informal? A traditional wedding reflects society's accepted patterns. What's traditional can change, depending on your age, region of the country, and what's in fashion. The wedding's formality is dictated by the degree of decorum shown in your invitations, flowers, decorations, attire, mood of entertaining, and number of wedding guests.

When choosing your wedding style, zero in on the type of attire with which you and your families will be most comfortable (see Chapter 7, "Wedding Clothes"). Each of these degrees of formality is altered when the time of day is factored in (very formal evening dress calls for a bride in a traditional gown with a long train; a groom in white tie and tails. Very formal daytime dress calls for a bride in a traditional gown—a shorter train is optional; a groom in a cutaway coat.)

Keeping in mind the four central style considerations (religious vs. civil, one faith vs. interfaith, traditional vs. offbeat, formal vs. informal) you can plan your wedding in either a standard (in a banquet hall or house of worship) or unusual (on a beach or in a sports arena) location.

Visiting Your Clergymember

Before making a final decision about a site, consult your clergymember about religious requirements. The Catholic Church, for example, prefers to celebrate nuptial masses in a church only. Some churches require that you join their congregation. Jewish couples may marry in a synagogue without being members of the congregation,

(continued)

although regular attendees may receive first choice of times and dates. Some houses of worship will rent all or part of their spaces. Check with clergy, however, about their religious requirements for interfaith marriages and remarriages (see Chapter 9, "Religious Rituals & Requirements" and Chapter 11, "Remarriage").

When approaching an unfamiliar house of worship, explain to the clergymember why a religious service is important to you—rather than why you want to borrow the setting for a few hours. Be prepared to field questions about your lack of involvement in the parish (if this applies to you), but remain open to the idea that a wedding can initiate religious affiliation.

If either of you feel uncomfortable for any reason, try another house of worship.

Contact your officiant—minister, priest, rabbi, or judge—so that he or she can check his or her schedule, then make an appointment to discuss your ceremony. Call your local city hall or marriage license bureau for referrals for judges or justices of the peace (see the "Planning a Civil Ceremony" section and Appendix, under Chapter 4, "Planning Your Wedding").

Bring certificates of baptism and confirmation if you are not marrying in the church where you received these sacraments. If either of you is divorced, bring a letter or decree attesting to your marital status. Different faiths? You may need to get special dispensation and/or be required to have religious instruction before your wedding.

Complete or sign documents relating to marriage. Depending on your faith, you may be asked to fill out an "Application to Marry," sign a "Letter of Intention to Marry," or begin a "Preliminary Matrimonial Investigation." Usually, such forms state your willingness to participate in counseling together with your clergymember. These sessions can be opportunities to strengthen your religious understanding of marriage. Most clergymembers require at least one conference with both of you before performing your ceremony. Some religions require several meetings.

Realize that an officiant may bring up topics you'd rather not discuss. A previous marriage, for example, would probably be covered (what went wrong and how you tried to resolve matters in the future). The clergymember is not being intrusive; he or she is required to see that you are marrying in good faith, after taking into account all potential questions and problems.

Consider attending a premarital counseling group. It's worthwhile to pursue any worrisome issues that your clergymember brings up in your initial meeting (see Appendix, under Chapter 4, "Planning Your Wedding," for more information). Counseling groups help couples clarify their feelings about money, sex, children, religion, family relations, goals, how to handle conflicts, and other subjects that often come up after marriage. You may discover some surprises about each other (e.g., he wishes he could work up the nerve to make a job change; you're envious of the time he spends with

- **Unexpected variety:** Vary vases or floral containers to give your site a personal feel—as if you incorporated heirloom treasures. Include framed family photos. Unique furniture can be rented to create atmosphere.

- **Scent:** Fragrant flowers (roses, lilacs, gardenias), scented candles—but not near the food.

- **Garlands:** Adorn with flowers, fruits, vines, and ribbons. Drape across doorways and windows; swag around tables; intertwine among buffet platters; a banister or a staircase.

degrees of wedding formality

- very formal
- formal
- semiformal
- informal

do you need premarital counseling? red flags

- You keep having the same fight, over and over, without ever reaching a solution.

- You have second thoughts about getting married—or he does.

- You're hesitant to discuss certain issues, like how you feel about having children, because you're afraid your partner will call the wedding off and walk away from the relationship.

- You or your fiancé has a problem with drugs, alcohol, or some other substance.

- You constantly feel that your fiancé doesn't understand you.

ceremony and officiant fees

Traditionally, the best man gives the clergymember, organist, and any ceremony assistants an envelope with appropriate payment after the ceremony.

- There is a fee for a civil wedding ceremony performed at city hall. Call for details.

- State law dictates whether judges can accept money. Perhaps give an appropriate gift (e.g., theater tickets, a watch, a key case, a pocket diary).

- Clergymembers usually receive a donation to the house of worship; ask the church secretary or sexton what is the suggested fee, gratuity, or donation made payable to the house of worship. A more generous fee is suitable for a large wedding for which the clergymember attends the rehearsal and reception and performs the ceremony; he or she may have also spent many hours counseling the couple prior to the wedding day.

- Ask if fees for altar servers, sextons, cantors, choir directors, and organists are included in the church or synagogue fee; an additional gift or money amount may be appropriate.

- Consider donating a hymnal, prayer book, memorial window, candelabrum, kneeling cushions, or collection baskets to the house of worship in honor of your marriage.

his friends); these sessions may also help you come to an understanding that will create a stronger, healthier marriage.

Confirm your ceremony date. Have several choices in mind, since many houses of worship and halls may be booked a year or more in advance. (Only when your house of worship, clergymember, and reception site are confirmed for your date is it safe to order invitations.)

Review ceremony details and make a second date to discuss specifics. For starters, ask about the seating capacity of the sanctuary and be sure your wedding party will fit comfortably in front of the altar. Can two or three people walk down the aisle abreast? Are there any church restrictions? Where is the best place for soloists to stand? If it will be an interfaith ceremony, what is the format? (See Chapter 8, "Your Wedding Ceremony" for questions to ask then.)

Are there restrictions on ceremony attire? Ask if men must wear *yarmulkes* in the synagogue sanctuary, if bride's and bridesmaids' shoulders must be covered, or if the bride must wear a veil. Is there a changing room for the bride? How early can you have access on wedding day?

Are there any other restrictions that you should be aware of? If the reception will be in the house of worship, ask whether alcoholic beverages are permitted on the premises. Some congregations will permit a champagne toast but do not allow any other alcoholic drinks.

Will the clergymember perform a ceremony at a nonreligious site? Ask if there are any special requirements that must be met to make this possible. If not, consider which is more important, the location or the person who performs the ceremony.

Will the clergymember marry you in his or her study or chambers? Some couples prefer an intimate ceremony. Is there a small chapel available?

Speak to the sexton, verger, or church secretary. He or she can explain the fire laws governing evening candlelight ceremonies (see Chapter 10, "Special Weddings & New Ways to Wed") and tell you about aisle runners, prayer (kneeling) benches, canopies, candelabra, and any special equipment needed. Ask whether rice, birdseed, or other alternatives (see Chapter 2, "Wedding Customs") can be thrown after the ceremony, and where. Reserve time for your rehearsal, and, if necessary, parking spaces the day of the wedding. Is there adequate air-conditioning in summer and heat in winter? If the reception will be in the house of worship, are there any dietary restrictions? Where can the receiving line be held? Ask about appropriate fees for the house of worship, clergymember, organist, and other staff members (see "Ceremony and Officiant Fees" box).

Meet with the organist, cantor, or choir director. It is wise to discuss your musical program in advance. Get suggestions and make sure that he or she is available for your rehearsal *and* ceremony. If additional musicians or a soloist will perform, schedule extra rehearsals. (For musical selections, see Chapter 14, "Wedding Music.")

Planning an Interfaith Ceremony

You're Catholic, he's Jewish. He's an Episcopalian, you're Muslim. After crossing initial hurdles posed by different cultural backgrounds, there is one more challenge to face: Who will marry you—and how? An interfaith couple might consult an organization that is tolerant of two-religion marriages, such as a campus ministry group, a Unitarian Church, or the Ethical Culture Society for guidance (see Chapter 8, "Your Wedding Ceremony," and Appendix, under Chapter 4, "Planning Your Wedding").

Here are several other options:

Combine both faiths in the service. Start searching for co-officiating clergymembers early. Contact each clergymember to find out if he or she is willing to participate. If they are reluctant, seek out college chaplains, more liberal-minded clergy in your area, as well as referrals from friends or a college dean's office (see Chapter 8, "Your Wedding Ceremony" and Appendix, under Chapter 4, "Planning Your Wedding"). Check out www.weddingofficiants.com or www.interfaith.org/referrals for more sources.

Turn to a third religion that is supportive of interfaith couples. The Unitarian Universalist Society, for example, will perform interfaith marriages for couples who do not belong to its denomination (see Appendix, under Chapter 9, "Religious Rituals & Requirements"). Many Christian/Jewish couples choose this route because Unitarian Universalists encourage couples to participate in structuring a service that reflects both traditions. Societies and fellowships associated with the American Ethical Union and its New York City affiliate, the Ethical Culture Society, perform interfaith marriages. There are twenty-five such societies nationwide in this humanist group, which is dedicated to the ethical guidance of individuals without imposing strict religious dogma (see Appendix, under Chapter 4, "Planning Your Wedding").

Choose one religious ceremony over the other. This may be agreeable if one partner has maintained strong ties with a denomination and the other severed ties with his/her faith long ago. This does not mean that you should exclude the religious heritage of the nonpracticing person. Invite the secondary cleric to offer a special prayer or blessing during the service or at the reception. Prepare family members in advance for the type of ceremony you will have—particularly if you anticipate any strong reactions to your decision.

Plan two ceremonies. When an agreement cannot be reached about combining two faiths, some couples simply marry twice. Only one date of marriage can appear on

choosing an officiant—when you're unaffiliated

- ask friends, neighbors, and wedding professionals living or working in the area where you want to get married for recommendations.

- check the yellow pages and the Internet under "churches" or "synagogues" for houses of worship in your area.

- inquire with the ministry office at a local college; many have chaplains who can perform weddings.

your marriage certificate, but each ceremony can satisfy the requirements of that religion. If you do not want to plan two weddings, some Protestant denominations have a "Blessing of the Marriage" service (the same day or at a later date), which has similar wording to the real wedding ceremony, although no rings are exchanged.

Plan a civil ceremony. Just because you've ruled out a church or synagogue as a ceremony site doesn't mean the only option is a quick ceremony at City Hall. A civil ceremony can be the perfect answer for a couple who prefer to marry without specific religious affiliation.

Planning a Civil Ceremony

A civil ceremony can be short and functional or as formal as you wish, and it can be followed by a reception with a lunch, seated dinner, or simply champagne and cake. It can be held at your home or in a hotel, in a park or garden, or in the county clerk's office at city hall or the local Marriage License Bureau. You might invite just two friends or relatives to be your witnesses, immediate family, or 150 guests or more.

Who can perform the ceremony? Depending on where you live, justices of the peace, superior court clerks, county clerks, judges or magistrates, township committee chairs, mayors, and governors can perform legally binding ceremonies. Since marriage laws vary by state, as well as county, call your local Marriage License Bureau for details; also ask clergymembers, family, and friends for referrals. For a nominal fee, the state of California offers the Deputy Commissioner of Marriage Program that allows a person to perform a civil wedding ceremony. For more information, contact your local county clerk. The Universal Life Church will also ordain a person, but some states do not recognize the ordination. See their website at www.ulc.net for more information. Remember that some public officiants are not willing to work outside their offices or after normal business hours. So if you want to wed in a rooftop garden at sunset, tell prospective officiants up front. If you've planned a large reception and the officiant has traveled to perform the ceremony, it is polite to invite him or her, with their spouse, to your reception. (However, don't worry about including him in a small family party.)

Where can a civil ceremony be performed? Most take place in a courthouse, judge's chambers, or the county clerk's office during regular business hours, or in the home or office of a justice of the peace. A large civil ceremony may be performed at home, in a club or ballroom, or at a public location like a park or beach.

What official documents are needed for a civil ceremony? A marriage license is required for any legally binding ceremony, but keep in mind that obtaining one takes

civil-ceremony officiants

- county clerk
- mayor
- township committee chair
- governor
- clerk of superior court
- judge
- magistrate
- justice of the peace

time. Check specific requirements with your local Marriage License Bureau (see "The Marriage License" section and Appendix, "Marriage Laws" chart). If the ceremony will be in a clerk's office, remember to invite at least two close friends or relatives along, since you may need two official witnesses. Their participation will be more meaningful than having two office employees sign your marriage license.

What should we wear? As the bride, you can wear anything from a traditional bridal gown to a suit or street-length dress. (If you're marrying in an informal dress but are planning a formal reception, change later into a ball gown or evening dress.) The groom can wear a dark suit to city hall, and formalwear for the reception—based on formality and time of day. (See Chapter 7, "Wedding Clothes.")

Can we add personal touches? Of course. The usual civil ceremony is a modernized adaptation from the *Book of Common Prayer*. It doesn't last much more than a few minutes. Ask your officiant if you can add to or customize the ceremony. Many will contribute their own thoughts and good wishes for the future; you should also feel free to read passages from your favorite poems, books or songs. It's also appropriate to include Scripture. Some couples write their own vows; though you should check this out with your officiant beforehand. If it is a second marriage and your children are open to the idea, include them as attendants. You can also ask older children to give a reading. No matter what the scale of the wedding, don't forget to carry a bouquet and pin a boutonniere on your groom. Photographs will be cherished keepsakes regardless of the wedding's size, so hire a photographer, if only for a wedding portrait. Also have champagne or sparkling cider on hand for a toast after the vows. Even if the ceremony is at city hall over your lunch break, plan to take a honeymoon, or at least spend a romantic wedding night in a local hotel.

docu-musts

- birth certificate
- proof of citizenship
- identification
- blood test results if required
- parental consent if underage
- death certificate if widowed
- divorce decree if divorced

The Marriage License

Don't leave this until the last minute. Each state sets its own requirements regarding age of consent, blood tests, documents, and time of validity; you shouldn't apply too early or too late. See "Marriage Laws" chart in the Appendix and follow these steps:

Find out where to apply. Call the city offices in the city in where you intend to marry in order to determine if you apply for a marriage license at city hall, your city or town clerk's office, or the Marriage License Bureau. Don't forget to ask what hours the office is open. (If your wedding will be a civil ceremony in this same office, get precise directions, as well as parking information for yourselves and any guests.)

Find out when to apply. While on the phone, ask when you should apply for a marriage license (usually two to three weeks before the ceremony). The license may be valid for sixty days, and there may be a "cooling-off" or waiting period (i.e., the license will not be valid until several days after you've applied for it).

Find out if you need blood tests. Also ask how long the results will be valid. (Many a couple have scrambled for new blood tests at the last minute.) Each state sets its own requirements for blood tests. If required in your state, go to your doctor or a clinic and ask for the standard prewedding blood test (results for this test for STDs may take several days). Results for an AIDS test may take six to eight weeks.

Bring the right documents. Find out the age of consent to marry. You'll probably need to bring birth certificates for written proof of age; proof of citizenship if you were not born in the United States; identification; parental consent if you are underage; and, in some states, blood test results. If one of you is divorced or widowed, you will also need a divorce decree or death certificate.

Come prepared to pay the fee. Ask about the amount in advance what this will be, so that you'll have a check, credit card, or enough cash on hand.

Plan a lunch date afterward. Since you and your groom will both need to be present to apply, take time out to mark the occasion.

The Marriage Certificate

Before or after your wedding ceremony, in many states two witnesses of your choice (often the best man and maid of honor), the officiant, and the bride and groom must all sign the civil certificate. Some couples include the signing in their ceremony (a Quaker custom; see Chapter 9, "Religious Rituals & Requirements," and Appendix, under Chapter 4, "Planning Your Wedding"). Your church or synagogue may also issue its own certificate—a page written in calligraphy that you can frame later or a decorative booklet (with the words of your ceremony) for participants and even guests to sign. The signing of the marriage certificate makes a memorable photograph, so alert your photographer.

Your clergymember will file your marriage certificate with the proper authorities; you'll receive a copy a few weeks later by mail.

Amish and Mennonite Wedding Certificates. These documents are often illuminated in the *fraktur* folk-art style. Symbolic angels and birds surround the couple's names and wedding date. The crowned angel at the top represents the angel who watches over and blesses mankind; the birds pecking their chests denote sacrificial love.

The *Ketubah*. This traditional Jewish marriage contract is the agreement that specifies the groom's responsibilities toward his bride, including that he "honor and cherish" her. It is required for a valid Jewish marriage and is usually provided by the rabbi. The *ketubah* is mandatory for Orthodox and Conservative Jews; Reform Jews should consult their rabbi for requirements. Originally, the *ketubah* also outlined a financial settlement for the wife in case of divorce or widowhood. Now some rabbis allow a more egalitarian version of the *ketubah,* which pledges equality in marriage. It's signed by two witnesses before the ceremony and is handed to the bride by the groom afterward, for her safekeeping. After the wedding, the *ketubah* (which may be lavishly illustrated) may be framed and hung on a wall.

The Persian Wedding Covenant. This document is traditional, but does not make the marriage legal. It is a modern interpretation of a traditional Iranian wedding certificate. Decorated with birds, flowers, and Islamic symbols, the Persian document is signed by the couple and guests.

The Quaker Marriage Certificate. Often colorfully bordered and written in calligraphy, this certificate records family histories and vows exchanged, and is signed by all the guests. This parchment document, which is often two or three feet long, is customarily framed after the wedding.

Prenuptial Agreements

These documents are no longer requested only by wealthy individuals seeking to protect their estates. Nor are they strictly for second marriages, where one or both spouses hope to protect their children's inheritances. Today, many brides and grooms are entering marriage with earned retirement benefits, 401K plans, IRAs, invested savings, and property; they want to hold on to these hard-earned assets in case the marriage doesn't last a lifetime. Besides protecting your legal rights, a prenuptial agreement is a useful tool for evaluating your financial situations before marriage, and your beliefs about your life together. Such an agreement should be well thought out, reviewed by two lawyers (one representing each of you), signed by you and your groom plus witnesses, and notarized. It's also wise to make it a *pre*nuptial, not a *post*nuptial, agreement.

When should a prenuptial agreement be drawn up? Well in advance of the wedding, to allow time for your careful consideration and for both of your lawyers to review the document. A prenuptial agreement often covers ownership of present property and future ownership of expected inheritances.

When is a prenuptial agreement especially important? If either or both of you have children and personal assets, your agreement should protect the rights of each of the children. If your parents are giving you the family's valuable antiques, your agreement might specify that these heirlooms would remain in your family should you divorce. If you have a family trust fund, or substantial property, you may also want to specify that these things will remain outside marital property. Also, consider a prenuptial agreement if you own property that earns money and will increase in value; if you own part of a family business; or if you expect to receive an inheritance.

before you wed

- Even if you don't plan to draw up a prenuptial agreement, discuss whether you'll pool incomes or keep them separate; also consider what the arrangement would be if one of you stopped working.

- Collect all financial statements from credit cards, banks, pension plans, and student loans. Subtract debts from assets to determine your net worths.

- Draw up a budget together. List all fixed expenses; allow for extras and emergencies.

- If you decide you want a prenuptial agreement, you should each hire your own lawyer. Meet separately to discuss issues of the agreement. Review every word before signing.

prenuptial-agreement tips

- Discuss what you'd each like the agreement to cover *before* you head to your respective lawyers' offices.

- Don't involve family members or friends, unless the agreement directly pertains to them.

- Focus on the big issues—such as inheritances and real estate—and don't sweat the small stuff like the portable CD players.

- Be positive—prenuptial agreements are not precursors to divorce—plenty of couples who have one go on to enjoy long, happy marriages.

- Put the agreement in perspective: having one may be smart, not selfish.

changing places

If one or both of you will be changing your name after marriage, you will need to notify:

- government agencies (e.g., Internal Revenue Service)
- Social Security office
- Department of Motor Vehicles
- telephone company
- bank(s)
- insurance companies
- passport office
- voter-registration office
- your lawyer
- school alumni office
- credit card companies

. . . also change your name on:

- deed(s)
- lease(s)
- will
- stock certificate(s)
- property title(s)

Can lifestyle issues be specified? Yes. A contract may state whether or not you will have children; how you will handle savings and household tasks; whether or not you will keep your maiden name. Some even specify who will do household chores, feed the pet, and care for children.

Will a prenuptial agreement hold up in court? Prenuptial agreements have had mixed success when challenged in court. However, what will matter in determining financial distribution is that each of you had ample time to review the document with your own attorneys prior to signing. Some couples have a videotape made of themselves signing the agreement, which may hold more credence when shown later in court. While lifestyle issues may not be legally enforceable, writing down your expectations about your life together can clarify important issues and help your marriage—whether you sign the agreement or not.

The Name Decision

After marriage, you will have the choice of keeping your maiden name, taking your husband's surname, or choosing an alternative option. Whatever your decision, it will have long-term implications for your career, family relationships, and financial future. Here are the possibilities:

Keeping your own name. Many women who have built a career and an identity around a name are reluctant to give it up. They continue to use their maiden name professionally and socially. If you decide to keep your maiden name, in forty-nine states you simply continue to use it consistently. *Note:* Residents of Hawaii must declare what their married name will be when signing their marriage certificate.

Keeping your own name selectively. It is possible to continue to use your own name professionally and legally, and use your husband's name for social purposes only (correspondence, for invitations, for things relating to your children). Or, you can change your surname to your husband's on all legal (and financial) documents, and use it everywhere *except* at work. Whatever option you decide to go with, it is most important to be consistent in the usage (see "Changing Places" box).

Changing your name. If you decide to change your name, you should assume your new name right after the wedding by notifying various government agencies, so that your name can be changed on official documents and identification cards (see "Changing Places" box). For instance, write and tell the Internal Revenue Service: *Please be advised that social security number____, previously in the name of Jane Smith, should now read Jane Miller.* It's also wise to *keep* one or more credit cards in your own name—to maintain your credit rating should you be divorced or widowed. If you want to take his name but not totally forfeit yours, you have the following options:

Use your maiden name as your middle name. Some women drop their middle name and begin to use their maiden name in its place, before their married name. (*Peggy Lynn Smith* becomes *Peggy Smith Jones*.)

Hyphenate your maiden and married names. For example, *Peggy Smith* could become *Peggy Smith-Jones*. However, if your husband adopts this same hyphenated name as his surname, he must change his name legally, in court.

Create a new hybrid name that both you and your husband adopt. Some couples opt to choose an entirely new name that reflects their newly formed family unit. For example, *Sue Hanson* and *Doug Everly* might become *Sue and Doug Hanly*. Others have simply opened the phone book and chosen a name they particularly like. This name change for bride and groom must be done legally.

Letting everyone know. If you will be changing your name, tell your employer and friends. Send out printed name cards or combine the information with your new address on an at-home card (see Chapter 5, "Invitations & Announcements").

Tell parents and in-laws about your name decision before they hear it from others. If you will keep your own name, be sensitive to your in-laws' concerns. Explain that you've already established a career identity, and reassure them that your children will have your husband's name, if that's the case. Enlist your spouse's support in affirming your decision, especially if you two have *both* opted to change your names. In this situation, you may want to explain that it in no way reflects on your respect for your in-laws' name, but indicates the new commitment you have to each other.

Selecting Your Rings

Some men may prefer to surprise you with a family heirloom ring, or something of their own choosing or design. But shopping together for engagement and wedding rings assures that both of you will be happy with the choices (see Appendix, under Chapter 8, "Your Wedding Ceremony").

Engagement rings vary widely in style and design. Although a diamond solitaire is the classic choice, rings often incorporate gemstones (sapphires, rubies, emeralds). Traditionally, rings are either gold or platinum; finishes can be matte or polished—with surface texture (Florentine) or an etched design (diamond-cut). Diamonds are judged by strict standards (the four C's: color, cut, clarity, and carat; see "A Diamond's 4 C's").

Wedding bands may be chosen to match the engagement ring or to be worn alone. The bride's rings may or may not match the groom's.

Engraving personalizes these keepsakes. Inscribe the couple's initials and their wedding date ("*R. G. S. from J. R. B. 8/22/03*") or a phrase ("*to my love*").

a diamond's 4 C's

- cut—shape, cutting style, proportions, and finish.

- clarity—freedom from flaws (inner cracks, bubbles, and specks); flawless is rated "Fl"; "I3" is imperfect.

- color—rated on a letter scale, from D (absolutely colorless) to Z (yellow). Most contain yellow or brown traces; clear white is most expensive. This rating does not apply to the costly, much-sought-after colored diamonds mentioned in the "Selecting Your Rings" section.

- carat—standard way of measuring the stone's weight; 100 points equals one carat.

stone shapes

- marquise—oblong with pointed ends

- pear shaped—round on one end, pointed on the other

- heart shaped—romantic variation

- round/brilliant—traditional cut (58 facets reflect the most light)

- oval—round adaptation (can appear larger than a round stone with same carat weight)

- emerald cut—rectangular with "steps" on the sides and corners

- princess cut—a brilliant-style shape with sharp, uncut corners; typically square, with 76 facets, giving it more clarity and fire than a round-shaped brilliant diamond

- signature (or branded) cut—specially cut to unleash maximum sparkle and brilliance; stamped with the designer's assurance of quality (often laser-inscribed with trademark and/or serial number)

- cushion cut—an oval cut with squared corners. Its intricate faceting gives the stone a warm brilliance.

Who Pays for What?

SERVICE	BRIDE AND/OR HER FAMILY	GROOM AND/OR HIS FAMILY	ATTENDANTS	OPTIONS TO SHARE
RINGS	The groom's ring	The bride's engagement and wedding rings		The bride's or groom's families may offer heirloom rings
PREWEDDING PARTIES	The bride's family may host the first engagement party to announce the news. The bride hosts the bridesmaids' lunch.	The groom's family may host an engagement party (it should follow any festivities hosted by the bride's family). The groom and/or his family may host a bachelor dinner and rehearsal dinner.	The maid of honor and/or bridesmaids host a bridal shower and may host a "girls' night out." The best man and/or ushers host a bachelor party. Friends may host an engagement party.	The bride's family may host the rehearsal dinner. Out-of-towners' brunch or pool party, barbecue, etc. may be co-hosted.
STATIONERY	Invitations, announcements, enclosures, personal stationery, newsletters, wedding programs, and thank-you notes.	The groom's thank-you notes and personal stationery.	May help with assembling and addressing invitations.	
CLOTHES	The bride's dress, veil, and accessories; her mother's dress and father's formalwear. The bride's trousseau (honeymoon clothes and lingerie).	The groom's formalwear, his mother's dress and father's attire.	The maid of honor and bridesmaids pay for their dresses. Ushers pay for rental or purchase of their outfits.	The bride or her family may pay for bridesmaids' dresses and accessories. The groom or his family may pay for the ushers' rentals and accessories.
FLOWERS	Floral arrangements for the ceremony and reception. Bouquets and corsages for bridesmaids and flower girls.	The bride's bouquet. Boutonnieres for the men in the wedding party. Corsages for the mothers and grandmothers.		The bride's family may purchase bouquets. Bride may give corsages or bouquets to mothers and grandmothers.
CEREMONY	The fee for the church or synagogue, and sexton, organist, and soloist. Rental of aisle carpet, marquee, and *huppah*.	The marriage license and clergymember's or judge's fee.		The couple may cover all ceremony costs.
PHOTOGRAPHY/ VIDEOGRAPHY	The engagements and wedding photos and video.			One family may pay for the photography, the other for videography. The groom's parents or the couple may pay for additional prints not included in the package.
TRANSPORTATION/ LODGING	The transportation of the bridal party to the ceremony and reception sites.		Attendants who live in the wedding area may offer out-of-town attendants a place to stay.	Either family may arrange transportation, pay for fruit baskets, baby-sitters, a welcome buffet for out-of-town guests, or lodging for out-of-town attendants.
RECEPTION	All professional services—food, drinks, decorations, and music/entertainment, etc.			The groom's family may offer to share the reception's cost by covering specific services (hors d'oeuvres, liquor, etc.).
HONEYMOON		Limousine to the airport. The entire honeymoon.		
GIFTS	The bride buys a wedding gift for the groom and each of her attendants.	The groom buys a wedding gift for the bride and each of his attendants.	Attendants may give wedding gifts individually, or pool their resources for a group gift.	The couple may buy thank-you gifts for parents, friends, and relatives who helped with their planning.

Double-ring ceremonies are more popular today, since more men are choosing to wear wedding rings. Your honor attendant should hold the groom's ring and the best man will hold yours, until they are exchanged during the vows. (It's a good idea to have a faux ring attached to a ring bearer's pillow.)

Innovative wedding rings are also an option for some brides, and can include: *colored diamonds* (pink, yellow, blue, cognac); *tension rings* (a center diamond holds the band apart, so almost the entire stone is visible).

Sharing Expenses

Traditionally, the bride's family was responsible for the cost of the wedding. Now, however, sharing expenses is much more the norm, with the bride and groom, as well as the groom's parents, often contributing. Here are the customary guidelines for absolute traditionalists, and a few modern suggestions for those who like to divvy up the expenses (also see "Who Pays for What?" chart):

You and your groom may contribute to your parents' overall budget, or pay for the wedding yourselves. In this case, your parents may still issue the invitations, still be host and hostess, and your fiancé's parents may still be the honored guests. Decisions should be made with the feelings of both sets of parents in mind, no matter who pays the bills.

Your fiancé's family may offer to share the costs. They may suggest splitting the wedding expenses, contributing a set amount, or covering specific things, such as the flowers, music, and/or liquor. All bills should be sent directly to them, to avoid awkward requests for money. (It's best if the groom discusses with them, privately, what they will contribute financially—to avoid tension between families.) There are no firm rules about wedding protocol when families are sharing expenses. Your mother would still head the receiving line and your father make a wedding toast. You would probably, however, want to highlight your groom's parents, too. Both sets of parents' names might appear on the wedding invitations (see Chapter 5, "Invitations & Announcements"); his father might be asked to say a blessing or give a toast, too.

Another alternative: One family might pay for the ceremony; the other, the reception. In this case, the names of the groom's parents would appear on the ceremony invitation or reception card (see Chapter 5, "Invitations & Announcements"). Or the groom's parents may finance the entire wedding. Although they will serve as host and hostess on wedding day, the bride's parents should still be honored in the traditional way.

You may split the wedding expenses (and guest list) in thirds—one third for each set of parents and one third for the couple. It is still the prerogative of the bride's parents to politely decline all offers of financial help, if they wish.

a wedding consultant's duties

The person you hire should:

- listen to your ideas, make suggestions, and research your options

- come up with an overall wedding plan that meets your tastes and budget

- make appointments with wedding-service providers

- help handle the selection of bridesmaids dresses, invitations, flowers, and caterer

- make sure that everything goes smoothly by staying in touch with vendors and service providers

- be on hand on your wedding day to see that all services and details proceed as planned (e.g., the tent is set up correctly, the cake is the one ordered, the flowers arrive, and the service personnel know what is expected)

- deal with any emergencies that occur; an experienced consultant is well versed in wedding etiquette and has directed many weddings

Hiring a Wedding Consultant

If you and/or your mother are busy with work responsibilities, a wedding consultant may be the answer to your wedding-planning needs. This is also a good option if you are planning a wedding in another state (see the "Planning Long-Distance" section) and cannot be on the scene; or for an at-home wedding and reception where there are innumerable details to attend to (you shouldn't be digging out supplies or washing dishes on your wedding day).

How do we find a wedding consultant? Ask friends for recommendations, and contact the Association of Bridal Consultants and June Wedding, Inc. (see Appendix, under Chapter 4, "Planning Your Wedding") for a professional in your area. Bridal salons may also provide leads. Ask florists, caterers, and photographers, and check the Yellow Pages or Internet under "Wedding Supplies and Services," "Wedding Consultants," and "Party Planning Services," as well. Look for someone who has planned at least a dozen weddings.

What kind of service does a wedding consultant provide? Many different kinds. You can hire someone just for a *consultation,* to give you information about sites, photographers, and other recommended wedding vendors, and advice on how to pull off your dream wedding. You can hire a wedding consultant for *day of wedding service,* so that he or she is the on-site director the day of your wedding. You can also hire someone for *full service,* which means they'll help you plan your wedding from start to finish and will be with you on the big day itself.

Besides helping me plan my wedding, what can a consultant do for me? She can act as referee between dueling parents, settle disputes with your vendors, and—even if you're not on a limited budget—show you ways you can save money.

How expensive will it be? Consultants may charge a flat rate, a percentage of the total wedding budget, or by the hour. Be sure to sign, and have countersigned, a contract that specifies responsibilities and fees. (It is to the couple's advantage *not* to have the consultant's fee based on the wedding budget.)

I want this to be *my* wedding, reflecting my taste. Won't I have to agree to what she or he recommends? Absolutely not. A wedding consultant is working for you as your researcher. She or he can scout out the best services and sites, narrowing down each wedding-service category, but you make the final selections. You should meet with the consultant regularly to approve details and assess progress. Hiring a wedding consultant does not mean that you are giving up control of your wedding. Rather, you are simply adding a very competent, knowledgeable facilitator to your wedding staff.

Wedding Countdown

A MONTH–BY–MONTH GUIDE TO PLANNING THE EVENT OF A LIFETIME

12 MONTHS BEFORE

☐ **Visit a bookstore and buy a wedding planner or organizer.** This is where you'll make lists, file pictures of flower ideas, and scribble caterers' numbers. Look for one with space for guest names, extensive to–do charts, plus pockets for contracts, receipts, and photos.

☐ **Talk with your fiancé and all parents about the big picture,** starting with your wedding budget. Also cover the overall style and size of the wedding, possible dates, sites and participants, including the officiant. If you'll be hiring a wedding consultant, do it now—you'll want her on board to help with research.

☐ **Decide on the ceremony and reception sites** and reserve both. Keep in mind that wedding venues in major cities can book up a year or more in advance, especially on summer and fall weekends. Adjust your calendar accordingly.

☐ **Start shopping for your dress.** Even if you haven't nailed down all the wedding details, you'll want to have a good idea of the time and place, in order to search for something appropriate (organza for a noontime garden wedding; silk charmeuse for cocktails in a loft).

☐ **Choose your attendants.** But wait at least a couple of weeks after the proposal—it's easy to get carried away in the excitement of the moment and ask your Pilates instructor to be the maid of honor.

☐ **Mail save–the–date cards,** or notify must–have guests (close family members, your best college buddy) by phone, if you're marrying over a holiday weekend or in a faraway location.

☐ **Send your engagement announcement** to the newspapers where both families live.

10 MONTHS BEFORE

☐ **Start scouting for a caterer, baker, florist, musicians for both ceremony and reception, photographer, and videographer.** Ask recently married friends for recommendations, take notice of the food and music at other functions you attend, and use your network of party–giving pals (or your parents') for referrals.

☐ **Visit your clergymember** with your fiancé if you're marrying in a house of worship, as some religions require that you undergo premarital counseling. This is also a good time to discuss the ceremony wording and whether or not it's possible to personalize the service.

8 MONTHS BEFORE

☐ **Book your caterer, baker, florist, ceremony and reception musicians, photographer, and videographer.** You'll want a signed and countersigned contract for each; if one is not offered by a particular wedding pro, draft it yourself.

☐ **Choose and order your dress.** Many wedding dresses are made to order, then shipped to the salon, where fittings will take place. At some stores you can also decide on a headpiece, lingerie, and shoes.

☐ **Register for your presents.** Choose items in price ranges that can fit every guest's pocketbook, from juice glasses to sterling silver place settings. Check your registry periodically, and, if necessary, add to it as items are purchased. Do a last-minute update. (The bulk of gifts are bought within 48 hours of the wedding.)

☐ **Begin the guest list.** Typically, half the list is allotted to the bride's family and half to the groom's. However, if you know in advance the numbers will be unbalanced (he has 75 relatives within driving distance; most of your family lives in Patagonia) be realistic up front when deciding how many guests each family can invite.

6 MONTHS BEFORE

☐ **Start researching the honeymoon.** Consult books, magazines, and the Internet. Wait to visit a travel agent until you have a general idea of the destination or type of honeymoon you want.

☐ **Plan the details with all the wedding professionals.** Decide on the menu and drinks with your caterer, the bouquets with your florist, the design and flavor of cake with your baker.

☐ **Order all wedding stationery**—invitations, response cards, maps, announcements, programs, and thank-you notes. Proofread them carefully upon delivery for spelling, times, and dates. (Have a second reader check them too.)

☐ **Book a calligrapher,** limos for the wedding party, and a portrait photographer. (Your wedding photographer may not do portraits.)

☐ **Shop for the bridesmaids' dresses.** Ask just one attendant, whose taste you trust, to accompany you. If you're concerned about outfitting a physically diverse group, choose a manufacturer that offers a line of basic dress shapes with variations, then have each bridesmaid select a flattering style.

☐ **Reserve a block of hotel rooms for out-of-town guests.** Offer a luxury and budget option.

☐ **Secure rentals, if you're marrying at home, or in an unfurnished space:** a tent, tables, chairs, glassware, linens, etc.

4 MONTHS BEFORE

☐ **Finalize your honeymoon plans and make bookings**—air, hotel, rental car, cruise ship. Note all reservations numbers. If you don't have passports and are traveling abroad, apply for them.

☐ **Finalize the guest list.** Give complete names, with addresses and zip codes, to the calligrapher so she can start on the envelopes.

☐ **Make an appointment for your first dress fitting.** Bring the lingerie and shoes you'll be wearing on the wedding day.

☐ **Order the wedding rings.**

☐ **Make an appointment with your hairstylist** to do a practice run with your headpiece; book her for the wedding. If you'll be doing your own hair, begin experimenting with styles at home.

☐ **Schedule the rehearsal and rehearsal dinner.** The evening is traditionally hosted by the groom and his family.

☐ **Visit the formalwear shop in the town where you'll be marrying,** if the groom and ushers will be renting their outfits, to select and reserve their morning suits, strollers, or tuxedos.

☐ **Book a hotel room for the wedding night.**

☐ **Choose and order favors.**

2 MONTHS BEFORE

☐ **Visit your officiant (judge, justice of the peace),** if you are having a nonreligious ceremony, to go over vows, readings, music. (Couples marrying in a religious ceremony initially visit their officiant 10 months before.) If you're writing your own vows, start now.

☐ **Buy a guest book** for everyone to sign at the wedding.

☐ **Shop for lingerie and honeymoon clothes.** Make sure your current luggage is up to a trip; if not, buy new or borrow.

☐ **Have your portrait taken.** If you are getting your makeup professionally done for the wedding, this is a good time for a trial run.

☐ **Check to see if the state where you're marrying requires blood tests.** If so, make an appointment with your doctor. The amount of time between when the medical exam is performed and when the marriage license must be issued varies from state to state, but is always fewer than 60 days.

☐ **Mail your invitations.** To ensure that you're using the right postage, take one complete invitation to the post office to be weighed. Buy stamps accordingly. (Mail one to yourself.)

☐ **Choose gifts for all attendants**—bridesmaids, groomsmen, flower girls, and ring bearer.

☐ **Arrange to transport your belongings** if either of you is moving. Send change-of-address information to the post office.

☐ **Get name-change forms** from the department of motor vehicles, Social Security office, credit card issuers, and your place of work, if you'll be taking your fiancé's name.

6 WEEKS BEFORE

☐ **Schedule the final dress fitting.** Bring the shoes and lingerie you'll wear on the wedding day.

☐ **Pick up the rings.** If they've been engraved, check the spelling and date.

☐ **Get programs printed.** Information to include: names of the bride, groom, parents, and bridal party; order of the ceremony; music and readings; explanations of any cultural or ethnic traditions.

☐ **Plan your bridesmaids' party**—anything from a spa day to a barbecue.

☐ **Write thank-you notes as you receive gifts.** Your fiancé should help.

☐ **Send your announcements to the newspapers.**

☐ **Make copies of ceremony readings** for those who'll be doing them. They'll need time to practice.

☐ **Buy each other a wedding gift.**

2 WEEKS BEFORE

☐ **Get the marriage license.**

☐ **Submit lists of must-take shots** to the photographer, and videographer, and your playlist to musicians. (Also, photos and songs you *don't* want.)

☐ **Arrange the seating plan.** Write out table cards to direct guests to their seats, as well as place cards, if you're using them.

☐ **Confirm honeymoon reservations.**

☐ **Break in your shoes.** Scuff the soles to avoid slipping.

☐ **Write toasts for the rehearsal dinner and reception.**

☐ **Pick up your dress a few days before the wedding.** Put a sheet on the floor to protect it from dust, and hang it from a tall hook or a door in a room that's off–limits to kids and pets.

1 WEEK BEFORE

☐ **Pack for the honeymoon;** get your going-away clothes ready.

☐ **Check about using your ATM card** at your honeymoon site. If traveling abroad, purchase a small amount of the local currency.

☐ **Give the final guest count to your caterer.**

☐ **Check final details with all wedding vendors,** from the limousine driver to the florist. Confirm the wedding date, address and their arrival times. Draw up a master list with names and phone numbers of all professionals for you, your maid of honor, or your mom to have on hand on the wedding day.

☐ **Keep up with thank–you notes.**

☐ **Remind all attendants of the rehearsal details.**

☐ **Throw the bridesmaids' party,** at which you can distribute gifts.

1 DAY BEFORE

☐ **Treat yourself and your mom to a manicure and pedicure.**

☐ **Place a "touch base" call to wedding vendors,** especially if there are any last–minute changes or if you want to discuss something that's been nagging at you.

☐ **Hold the rehearsal and the rehearsal dinner.**

DAY OF THE WEDDING

☐ **Eat breakfast—**nerves don't mix with an empty stomach.

☐ **Splurge on a massage.** (Raid your "emergency" fund.)

☐ **Make sure announcements are in the mail.**

☐ **Enjoy.**

Wired Weddings

If you have a computer, you have a high-tech wedding planner. Hundreds of wedding sites are listed on the Web—click on one to get answers to etiquette questions, information on how to register for gifts, and tips on how to entertain out-of-town guests (just input key words such as "wedding" and "planning" and see what shows up). You can even customize your search, so that only the wedding vendors in your state or city pop up, for example. Wedding-planning software (which you download from the Net onto your computer) allows you to keep track of guests, gifts, R.s.v.p.'s, and more. Based on your wedding date, some even give you a personalized checklist of what to do when. Just remember that, in every case, it's important to check the references, reputation, reliability, and taste level of all wedding service providers.

Planning Long-Distance

Few brides today work or live in their hometown, which means that many brides who will return home for their wedding must plan it long-distance. Here are some tips:

Have a planning assistant in that town. Either hire a local wedding consultant (see "Hiring a Wedding Consultant"), consult local websites, or ask a relative or friend who lives there to gather information from various wedding professionals for you. You'll need brochures, photos of reception sites, cakes, and flowers, musicians' audition tapes, etc.

Find out what it will take to plan the reception style you want in this location. An ethnic wedding with dress and foods reflecting your heritage may be difficult to stage unless you find the right resources.

Ask the phone company to send a copy of the Yellow Pages from that town or city. This will put the phone numbers and addresses of a variety of businesses at your fingertips, avoiding the costs of long-distance directory assistance. It will also reveal the services for which you'll have to search further (e.g., in a nearby town). Another option: Consult the Yellow Pages online.

Browse wedding-planning Web sites. Many allow you to customize your search by state or city.

Ask companies you call to send you information. They should be willing to e-mail or send brochures and price lists, as well as a contract.

Keep long-distance calls to a minimum. Do check in regularly, but use postcards, letters, e-mail, and faxes to communicate with service providers. Keep a running list of things to be discussed, then contact once a week—and later, once every two weeks.

Plan at least one visit to the wedding location. Tell your planning assistant or wedding consultant in advance when you will be arriving and have appointments set up with all of the wedding-service professionals you have hired. Make final arrangements and payments in person. Check on hotel reservations for other long-distance travelers. Book a makeup person and hairstylist for the wedding day, if you want one. Thank assistants with a lunch, dinner, and/or gift.

If Someone's Disabled

Whether your college roommate is temporarily on crutches or your grandmother uses a walker, take your guests' physical limitations into account when planning your ceremony and reception. Call your banquet manager and ask what their facility can do to accomodate a handicapped guest at your wedding. See the tips below (and the Appendix, under Chapter 4, "Planning Your Wedding").

Transportation and parking. If your guest doesn't drive and is coming alone, is there an accessible public transportation system or taxi service that he or she can use? If there are not "handicapped parking spaces," allocate a few near the entrance to the site.

Accessibility. If there are no wheelchair ramps, build or rent portable wooden

if one of you is disabled

- If you or your groom uses a wheelchair, arrange for both of you and the rest of the wedding party to be seated during the ceremony.

- Attach your bouquet to your wheelchair—or have an attendant hold it so your hands are free to maneuver.

- Make sure your gown and veil are not so long that they get caught in the wheels.

ones. Rest rooms should have accessible entryways and one stall at least 32 inches across, complete with grab bars for those in wheelchairs. If bathrooms in the house of worship are not accessible, warn guest(s) in advance.

Low elevator controls are needed for guests in wheelchairs, and elevator buttons in Braille that emit a tone at each floor, for the blind. (Describe the physical layouts of both the ceremony and reception sites to a blind guest in advance.) Elevator hallways and doorways should be wide enough for easy wheelchair passage.

Ask a disabled guest if he or she has any other special needs; if so, invite him or her to bring a guest.

Seating. Tell ushers to reserve seats next to aisles for guests in wheelchairs or on crutches, but allow these guests to sit where they are most comfortable. For the reception, tell the banquet manager to set one less chair at a table where a guest in a wheelchair will sit. Try to leave room between tables for a wheelchair to negotiate and fit comfortably for a meal. Seat guests who are hearing impaired near a wooden dance floor, where they'll be able to feel the music's vibrations.

Ceremony. A disabled attendant should dress in the same attire as the rest of the wedding party. If an attendant is on crutches, provide a seat for her or him.

If you or your groom are in any way disabled, be sure to review the ceremony with your clergymember or officiant. Don't assume that he or she won't say the wrong, patronizing thing (*"Who would have thought that this would be possible?"*).

Seat hearing-impaired guests near the front of your church or synagogue, where they can read lips or follow a certified sign-language interpreter. Many houses of worship have amplified earphones in the front pews; ask the sexton to be sure they are turned on. You might also consider a program with a Braille insert that includes the words to prayers and hymns.

Dining and dancing. Serve finger foods or an easy-to-cut entrée if hand and arm motility, or coordination, is a concern for some guests. Have a sign language interpreter for hearing-impaired guests present at the reception to relay toasts and explain traditions and other activities.

Hiring a Caterer

The best way to find a caterer (or a reception site with a banquet manager) with whom you feel comfortable planning your wedding, is through word of mouth, advice from recent brides, your wedding consultant, or other wedding professionals. Book your caterer or banquet location twelve months before your wedding; the best resources will be engaged early. Review the tips below, and be sure to execute a signed and countersigned contract (see "Caterer's Contract Tips" box).

Credentials. Hire only state-licensed caterers, ensuring that they have met the local health-department standards and carry the necessary liability insurance

caterer's contract tips

Put all these points in a signed and countersigned contract:

- date, times, site, and room; adjustment policy if room is switched or party is canceled

- type of food service (buffet, seated meal or cocktails and hors d'oeuvres)

- menu and courses

- attire of the servers (for example, tuxedos)

- type of service (French; see the "Reception Glossary" section); whether the first course will be preset.

- staff-per-guest ratio (including waiters, bartender, valets, and coat-check and rest-room attendants)

- liquor arrangements (Will you supply? How many bottles and brands will there be? Can you return unopened bottles? What will be the hours of the open bar? Will wine or soft drinks be served during the meal? How many bars will there be? What will be the policy for serving after-dinner drinks and liqueurs?)

- payment schedule (never pay everything in advance)

- deposit and refund policies

- sales tax, gratuities, bar fees, and waiter fees

- whether musicians, photographer, and wedding consultant will be fed

- food substitutions and their quality (no prepackaged foods?)

- cancellation and overtime fees

- prices quoted for foods (set ninety days before wedding); services you might add, with a ceiling on menu increases (often 10 percent)

- names of banquet manager and staff members who will be present at your wedding

- insurance (liability) coverage

(see Appendix, under Chapter 4, "Planning Your Wedding," for information about insurance and caterer referrals). If the caterer is not insured, you could be sued if someone gets food poisoning, chokes, chips a tooth, or has a car accident after drinking too much.

Shared halls. If other events will take place during your wedding, be sure there is an empty room or hallway in between parties (and bands). Ask how guests will know which room is for your celebration; whether the entryway and valet-parking staff are large enough to handle crowds from several parties; if there are separate coat checks for each event; whether your attendants have a private suite or if the rest room will be shared. If there is another party that coincides with your starting time, consider making your starting time earlier or later. Ask how much time will be available to set up.

Package deals. Get a detailed list of what is included (cost per person and extras); security deposit, sales tax, gratuities, and bar fees may hike the total over your budget (also see "Wedding Tipping" chart). Ask about overtime fees. Are linen colors and floral arrangements flexible if you pay an additional fee?

Pacing. Review your vision of the reception timetable with the banquet manager. You can request that waiters slow service and let guests dance longer in between courses; you can serve dinner to soft music, then heighten the decibels for dancing after, or you can stick to a tight schedule to avoid overtime fees.

Hidden embarrassments. Check the policy on tipping for valet parking, coat-

check attendant, rest-room attendant, and bartender. You can arrange to cover these fees so baskets soliciting tips will not be left out. (Signs can be displayed that read: *Gratuities have been taken care of by your host*.)

Menu options. Make sure the chef or caterer is flexible and will accommodate your needs. Ask about house specialties and other frequently–requested entrées. (See "Reception Menu" section.) Your caterer should be willing to help you find a menu that pleases you and is within your budget.

Wedding cake. Don't settle for the "house" variety. Ask to speak to the baker about cake flavors and decorations (see Chapter 13, "Your Reception," "The Wedding Cake" section). If you are not pleased, negotiate to hire your own baker. (Ask if you may bring in traditional family cookies, or pastries.)

Reception rooms. Look at the space where your reception will be—when it's empty and when it's set up for a wedding. Evaluate ambience, acoustics. Ask if you can pay more to add decorations, such as a draped ceiling, topiaries, potted plants, if needed (see "Site Decorations" box). Can lighting be adjusted? How will the head table and guest tables be arranged? Where is the dance floor positioned? The band's stage? Is there a sound system, microphone, a generator and back up generator? Is there a piano on the premises?

Thirst quenchers. Tell the caterer whether or not you'll be serving alcoholic beverages. You can opt for an open bar, but a less expensive option is choosing to be charged on a consumption basis. You and the site representative can agree ahead of time that you will purchase specific amounts of wine, liquor, and beer. Should your guests exhaust this supply, you will be informed and can decide whether or not to serve more. (You will be billed for the extra amount later.) If you're serving alcohol, be sure the bar is staffed by a licensed bartender (the catering hall should provide one).

Who's in charge? Insist that someone in authority be present on your wedding day to ensure that all runs smoothly. Meet in advance; find out who will distribute favors, set out alphabetized place or table cards, hang the skirting on tables, etc. Too often, these carefully–planned extras get lost in the shuffle.

Choosing the Right Reception Site

As early as a year before the wedding, you should begin making "walk-arounds" with sales representatives from prospective reception sites. Referrals from friends and wedding professionals help, but don't rely exclusively on someone else's word. Conduct a face-to-face interview with the site representative and examine the room in person.

What to look for. Ask about the room's square footage, the size of the dance floor, and where and when the musicians will be able to set up. Look closely at the space and decide if the decor of the room complements your wedding style. Most halls will be relatively standard, giving you a blank canvas to personalize with your own decorative touches (but make sure to clear your decorating plans with the management).

Little things count. Consider small but important details like the number and location of rest rooms and whether or not a coat room or a coatrack can be set up. Take a good look at where your reception will be held—on the second floor? In an annex? Downstairs? Give guests clear indoor directions so that they'll be able to find your reception once they reach the site. Also find out if you will be sharing the site with another event. You don't want some prom-goers crashing your reception, or worse yet, catching the bouquet.

Leave a paper trail. List all details (e.g., the specific room to be used, when the band and florist can set up, the payment schedule, etc.—see "Reception Rental Tips" for more points to cover) in a contract that's signed by the caterer and countersigned by you. If you feel the contract is too vague, don't be afraid to speak up.

reception rental tips

- Ask for referrals, check Yellow Pages and the Internet under "Party Rentals" (see Appendix under Chapter 4, "Planning Your Wedding").

- Visit the site with the rental agent. Evaluate lighting and sound needs, how the room is laid out, and what you'll need to decorate. Ask about extras (fountains, ice sculptures, etc.).

- Select rentals and finalize three to six months before the wedding.

- Rent ten percent more place settings than guests for a seated meal, one and a half as many for a buffet; ten percent more napkins than guests; one and a half to two times as many glasses as guests, depending on beverages served.

- Outdoors: Rent weatherproof covering (canopies to protect from the sun and rain; tents with sides, and flooring). Control tent temperature with heaters or portable air conditioners.

- Outdoors and at home: Rent portable latrines and coatracks. (The latter for winter only.)

- Sign and countersign an itemized contract. List equipment to be supplied, rental fees, delivery and setup charges, delivery date and location, waivers against damage to equipment, deposit paid (usually 25 percent), if deposit is refundable, and when balance is due.

*creative menu
ideas*

- feature a martini bar (or some other favorite specialty drink, such as margaritas or mojitos)

- serve colorful, tasty hors d'oeuvres and canapés—bruschetta, grilled vegetables, and chicken satay

- include a caviar course--complete with blinis and chilled vodka

- offer a selection of Chinese dim sum

- add a station that makes mini quesadillas with a choice of fillings

- recreate a traditional Japanese sushi bar, or pass a selection of assorted cut maki and mini handrolls

- try a delicious main course alternative: lobster ravioli

- feature an evening of crepes—from chicken to chocolate

- host a New England clambake

- put a fresh spin on the classic wedding supper by offering a main course of grilled duck, fish, or rack of lamb

- serve up a southern barbecue

- include a cheese course, or a "cheese board" station, served with hot, fresh baguettes, and garnished with dried fruit and nuts

- have menu cards printed to show the selections of food and wines paired for each course

Reception Menu

When deciding what to serve your guests, there are certain things to consider.

Time of day. If your reception will be beginning at a time when most people normally eat a meal, it's polite to serve them the amount of food they are expecting. For example, after a noon church ceremony, most guests will be hungry for lunch; if the ceremony ends at 6 P.M. or 7 P.M., they'll most likely be expecting dinner.

Cost. If you're trying to host a large party on a limited budget, simply serve champagne and cake after a 2 P.M. wedding. Or schedule a morning wedding followed by breakfast; a tea or cocktail reception, featuring light nibbles and hors d'oeuvres, following a ceremony between one and four.

Style. For a formal, evening wedding, a seated dinner—with several courses—or a lavish buffet are common options. For large, less formal celebrations, many couples choose a sumptuous cocktail buffet. Food stations—individual buffet tables with a variety of foods (e.g., sushi, pasta, shellfish, stir-fry vegetables, sliced meats)—might also be positioned around the room.

Beverages. A reception should include a bubbly beverage to toast the future. Champagne, or a quality sparkling wine prepared by the *méthode champenoise* technique, is the traditional drink for wedding toasts and can be served at any time of day. Offer nonalcoholic beverages such as ginger ale, club soda, punch, or a non–alcoholic wine for toasting, as well.

Consider your menu and time of day when deciding on beverages. Ice-cold punch (both nonalcoholic and with champagne) might be offered at morning tea receptions: mixed drinks, a selection of wines and micro-brewed beers, and champagne or sparkling wine for lunch and dinner receptions. If you want to serve a sparkling beverage for the entire meal, serve something dry (brut) with the main course and switch to an extra-dry (somewhat sweeter than brut), a sec (sweet) or demi-sec (the sweetest) champagne or sparkling wine with the wedding cake and dessert. (A sweet champagne or sparkling wine will complement the sweetness of cake better than a dry one.)

Special dietary needs. Provide for any special requirements of your guests (e.g., vegetarian, kosher). Offer guests a choice of fish, chicken, or red meat, along with vegetables. (A vegetarian pasta dish should be available if a guest can't eat the other options.)

Ethnic and regional flavor. Offer foods that have special meaning to you and your groom, such as the dim sum you ate on your first date or the Sacher torte that reflects your groom's Austrian heritage. If you're Middle Eastern, borrow from that cuisine; French, design the menu accordingly. Offerings can also reflect a wedding theme, such as barbecue (fried chicken, corn bread, black-eyed peas, biscuits and honey) at a southern-style wedding.

Seasonal foods. Select produce grown in your area and take advantage of in-season prices.

At-home receptions. Give your family heirloom recipes to your caterer to prepare and serve.

reception meal options

- seated breakfast
- seated brunch
- seated lunch
- buffet brunch, lunch, or dinner
- afternoon tea
- punch and cake
- cocktails and passed hors d'oeuvres
- cocktail buffet
- dinner by the bite
- seated dinner

Reception Glossary

Confused by the latest buzzwords? Here is a list of terms to refer to when selecting your reception-food style:

American Plate Service—Food is artfully arranged on plates by the caterer in the kitchen, then presented to seated guests.

Cocktail Buffet—Guests mingle informally while both passed and stationary hors d'oeuvres are served.

Dinner by the Bite/Grazing—Mini portions or salad-sized plates of various foods are served from different food stations positioned throughout the reception room. (This can also include espresso cups of soups, cassoulets, or risottos.) In this way, guests can enjoy a variety of tastes throughout the celebration—starting during the receiving line and continuing throughout the reception.

Edible Flowers—Nasturtiums, roses, pansies, and violets, add visual appeal and delicate flavor to salads and cakes.

English Service—Once a "groaning board" of food set out after a hunt, this is now a buffet from which guests may help themselves.

Ethnic Cuisine—Couples select the foods traditionally linked to their heritages (e.g., sushi and sake—Japanese; a fruitcake—English and Irish; a *croquembouche*, a tall cone of caramel-coated cream puffs—French; fried plantains and baked cheese grits—African-American).

Food Stations—Individual buffet tables that offer everything from crepes and sushi to omelets, enchiladas, shellfish, mashed potatoes, and shish kebabs.

Service *à la Russe*—Waiters serve from platters at the table.

Viennese Table—Sumptuous dessert buffet, including napoleons, mousses, petit fours, crème brulée, tarts, fruits, and ice cream.

thoughtful gestures

- *Recycle flowers.* After the wedding, take or send your floral arrangements to a nearby nursing home or hospital.

- *Share food.* Arrange to have leftover food, hors d'oeuvres, cake, and nonalcoholic drinks delivered to a local soup kitchen or homeless shelter.

- *Make postwedding visits.* Share the wedding excitement with sick or elderly friends and relatives who were unable to attend the wedding. Take along some wedding cake, favors, flowers, photographs, or even your wedding video.

Wedding Tipping

Tipping is a personal expression of gratitude for service delivered graciously and efficiently. The numbers below are only guidelines and apply when gratuities are not included in the bill. If you are unsure whether they're covered, or if you're confused about who and how much to tip, just ask. Tips are generally larger in big cities and upscale establishments. Be sure to work these figures into your overall wedding budget well in advance.

WHOM TO TIP	HOW MUCH TO TIP	WHEN, AND BY WHOM
Caterer, club manager, hotel banquet manager.	15–20% of the food and drink bill. Just 10% of the bill if there is also a maitre d'hotel.	The reception host may be asked to pay the bill in advance. If gratuities are not covered, the host or wedding consultant pays in an envelope during the reception.
Maitre d'hotel.	$1.50–$5.00 per guest.	The reception host or wedding consultant pays the tip in an envelope near the end of the reception.
Waiters, waitresses, table captains.	$10–$20 per person.	Catering manager pays tip at end of reception.
Bartenders.	10-15% of the total liquor bill or $50 per bartender.	The reception host or wedding consultant offers an envelope near the end of the reception.
Powder-room attendants, coat-room attendants.	$1.00 per guest, or arrange a gratuity with the hotel or club management.	The reception host should pay in advance, so that the appropriate sign, "Gratuities Have Been Arranged by the Host," can be displayed.
Parking attendants.	$1.00 per car, or arrange a 15% gratuity with the hotel or club management for valet parking.	The reception host should pay in advance, so guests will not be expected to pay.
Limousine driver(s).	15–20% of the total limousine bill if not already included in final bill.	The host or wedding consultant tips the driver(s) at the reception site.
Delivery truck drivers for florist, baker, etc.	$5.00–$10.00 each.	The host or wedding consultant tips the drivers at the delivery site(s).
Musicians, DJ.	Optional: $20.00–$25.00 each.	The reception host or wedding consultant offers in envelopes at the end of the reception.

INVITATIONS & ANNOUNCEMENTS 5

The style of your wedding should determine the type of invitation you choose. For a very formal wedding, a classic white or ivory invitation engraved with black lettering is the traditional choice, although there are also many decorative designs to choose from. For less formal weddings, there are a large variety of invitations available—including everything from pastel lettering to lace and beads matching the bride's gown. Beyond these considerations, however, there is also a rich tradition of etiquette to be observed in your wedding correspondence. While your wedding and your stationery should still reflect your personal style and tastes, these guidelines are evolving with the times and are the perfect tool to help you navigate the potential pitfalls and sticky situations that will inevitably crop up. The information on the following pages will help you understand all of your options.

Compiling Your Guest List

Decide how many guests you'll be able to invite. Generally, after determining the budget with your families, each family invites half the guests, though sometimes one family will have a longer list (if, for instance, the bride has a small family, or the groom's family must travel a long distance to attend). The guest list may also be split three ways: The bride's parents, the groom's parents, and the couple each invite one third of the guests.

ordering invitations

Before you visit your stationer, you should know:

- how your parents' names will appear on the invitation (and if the groom's parents' names will be included)

- wedding day date and ceremony and reception times

- names and addresses of the ceremony and reception sites

- how many invitations you'll need (count couples, not number of guests)

- whether all guests are invited to both the ceremony and the reception

Make a master wedding-invitation list. The bride usually compiles a list for her side of the family with her parents; the groom, with his parents. Also compile a "wish list"—to invite as guests refuse. (If one of you has divorced parents, rely primarily on the parent who raised you for help in drawing up your list.) Be sure all names (first, middle—if used, and last) are correctly spelled out, (no middle initials), all titles (Dr., Ms., Lt. Col.) are correct, zip codes are included, and addresses are updated. (Use index cards or a computer to easily alphabetize the lists and eliminate duplications.)

Make a master wedding-announcement list. Include all of your acquaintances not invited to the wedding with whom you wish to share the news of your marriage. (Refer to old personal address and telephone books, alumni directories, holiday-card lists, and club rosters to make sure no one is left out.) Announcements should be stamped, addressed, and ready to mail on your wedding day.

Remember, neither an invitation nor an announcement obligates the recipient to send a gift. If you won't be sending announcements, send invitations to all friends and relatives whom you would like to have with you, even if you don't think they'll be able to attend. (Anyone receiving an invitation may, however, decide to come—so allow for this possibility in your budget.)

You are not obligated to invite guests—or escorts—with your single friends. However, if you do decide to, find out beforehand whom they intend to bring and ask for their name and address; you should send a separate invitation to that person. *Don't* write "And Guest" on the inner and outer envelope of your friend's invitation. If the couple live together, you may send one invitation to them both, just as you would to a married couple (list their names alphabetically on the envelope).

Send invitations to the principals in the wedding. This includes your parents, the clergymember and his or her spouse, your fiancé's immediate family, the members of your wedding party (and their parents, if your budget allows), even though they've been invited informally. Mail an invitation to yourself which lets you know which day your guests receive the invitation in the mail.

Printing Techniques

Invitations can be ordered from a printer, jeweler, stationer, or department store (computerized printing and calligraphy services, and computer software packages are also available; see Appendix, under Chapter 5, "Invitations & Announcements"). Some popular printing methods are explained below:

Engraving involves using a steel or copperplate die to "cut" letters into the paper (the die will be given to you as a keepsake). These letters look and feel raised from the surface of the paper, both front and back. The process may take up to eight weeks. Engraving is the most formal—and most expensive—option.

Thermography is a heat process that fuses ink and powder and closely resembles engraving, but is less expensive. The letters are raised on the front, but they cannot be felt on the back. Thermography techniques can reproduce calligraphy and hand-lettered Hebrew or Chinese characters. Ask your stationer to show you samples.

Embossing raises dimensional lettering, borders, and artwork from the surface in relief without printing.

Offset printing uses a rubber cylinder to transfer inked letters onto paper. It is an excellent option for informal invitations and when time and budget are limited.

Letterpress is a process that prints from an inked raised surface.

Working with a Stationer

As when you are working with any wedding-service professional, you should be a wise consumer (see Appendix, under Chapter 5, "Invitations & Announcements").

Get referrals from friends and relatives. Keep a folder of wedding invitations that you've received and like. Once at the stationer's, review sample books. Ask for written price estimates and have a ceiling price in mind.

Order invitations and announcements at least six months before the wedding. This will allow plenty of time for printing (which may take two to eight weeks—engraving takes the longest), proofreading, correction of errors, addressing (allow one to two weeks if using a calligrapher), and mailing (which may take longer near holidays). If possible, have the envelopes sent to you in advance and start addressing them at once; they can be addressed, stamped, and ready to mail when you receive the invitations.

Order extras. It's wise to order 50 extra invitations, perhaps 100 extra envelopes (to allow for addressing mistakes and last-minute additions to your guest list). Your fiancé's mother and your mother should receive three or four unsealed invitations as wedding mementos as soon as they are ready. These may be accompanied by a note from you telling them when the others will be mailed. Also remember to keep a few invitations for yourself.

Print a return address on the back of the envelopes for invitations and announcements to expedite mail handling. This should be the complete address of the host or hostess, including an apartment number, if applicable—but no name. The post office encourages using legible type, rather than the hard-to-read, colorless, embossed return addresses once traditionally put on envelope flaps.

Proofread carefully. Ask the stationer to call you to come in and proofread the master invitation, envelope (if return address is printed), and enclosures before the final

popular lettering styles

Royal Script

Palmer Script

Shaded Antique Roman

London Script

St. James

Flemish Script

Solid Antique Roman

Cathedral Text

Rook Script

Statesman

Prices will vary greatly, based on the order you place. Note the following:

- Colored paper or parchment costs more than white or ivory paper.

- Sheets with printed or embossed designs are more costly than plain.

- Colored inks, a photograph, or illustration increase the bill.

- Enclosure cards will increase the printing-order cost as well as the postage for each invitation.

order is sent to the printer. Proofread slowly and carefully. Double-check the spelling of all names, addresses, and sites; take note of whether the date, time, and punctuation are correct. Check the type. (Are there any broken letters?). If anything needs correcting, this is the time to point it out.

Reread the invitations, envelopes, and enclosures when you pick up your order. If you find any errors, tell the stationer at once so he or she can rush corrections.

Invitation Styles

The invitation will set the tone for your wedding. Its style lets guests know whether the wedding will be formal or informal or whether a theme is indicated (ribbon-tied parchment for a medieval wedding; lacy, floral invitations for a Victorian wedding; graphic black-and-white for an Art Deco wedding).

Formal invitations. For weddings with over 50 guests, it is traditional to have invitations engraved or printed by a stationer. Formal printing is traditionally done with black, brown, or gray ink, although any legible ink is perfectly acceptable. Traditionally the invitation was engraved or printed on the top page of a folded sheet of white, rich ivory, or ecru paper, nowadays flat cards are more common. In either case, it is slipped inside an inner ungummed and unsealed envelope on which the guests' surnames are written *(Mr. and Mrs. Jones),* then placed inside an outer envelope (which is addressed and stamped with full names—*Mr. and Mrs. John Jones).*

Creative, informal invitations. Handwritten or computer-generated invitations may be sent for a small wedding ceremony of fifty or fewer guests. If buying or ordering more personalized invitations, steer clear of those that will embarrass you later. An invitation shaped like a balloon or a baby-picture postcard is not a good choice for a formal wedding. Even for an informal wedding, the invitation style is usually more sophisticated. Less is more. Pick one or two creative elements–ribbon, color, texture. Using too many elements will make your invitation look like a classroom art project. Below are some ways to personalize your invitations:

Color—Order translucent or shiny paper, colored ink, a border or trim.

Decorations—The invitation might be embellished with pearls or feathers, rolled like a scroll, or tied with satin ribbon or cording. (See Appendix, under Chapter 5, "Invitations & Announce-ments," for sources for creative wedding invitations.)

Theme—Coordinate your invitation with the theme of your wedding. For example, simulate the white moiré tablecloths with a white moiré effect on the invitations. Planning a Victorian-style wedding?

Send an invitation with envelopes lined in maroon velvet. If the your scheme includes black, silver, and gold, design the invitation in those three shades.

Tone—Set the mood of your wedding with the invitation. Planning a small, intimate celebration? Personalize the invitations by writing "It is with pleasure that we invite (guest's name) to our wedding . . . "

Artwork—Some couples print a meaningful photograph or a line drawing of their ceremony or reception site on the front of their invitations. Consult with your printer/stationer about what types of artwork will reproduce well, whether a photo can be reduced in size, and what negative quality is best to work with. Allow an extra month for printing if your invitations will include this type of intricate custom work.

Wording Invitations

The typical formal wedding invitation gives the following information—in this order. Keep in mind that these are guidelines and may be adapted to accommodate your family situation.

The hosts of the wedding—usually the bride's parents—issue the invitations and announcements, whether or not the bride still shares their home. (The hosts do not necessarily pay for the wedding, so even if you and your fiancé are paying, the bride's parents can still be listed at the top of the invitation.)

If your parents are divorced, the person who raised you customarily issues the invitations and announcements.

If your parents are deceased, your guardian, closest relatives, or family friends may host the wedding and issue the invitations and announcements.

Spell out words in full. This includes names (don't use nicknames) and numbers *(the twelfth of May)*. Abbreviations are not used, with the exception of *Mr.* and *Mrs., Doctor* and *junior* can be spelled out if space permits, but are also commonly abbreviated. If *junior* is spelled out, it always has a lowercase *j* and a comma before it.

Use the wording . . . *request the honour of your presence* for a religious service in a church or synagogue. It is an honor to witness a religious service. Use . . . *request the pleasure of your company* for a civil ceremony or for the reception. (*Honour* and *favour* ["the favour of a reply is requested"] are spelled with a *u*—the more formal British version.)

Traditionally, the bride's surname is not listed unless it is different from that of her parents. Be consistent with the use of titles (Mr., Miss, Ms., Dr.).—particularly for parents. If you wish to use a title for the groom, then use one for the bride, as well. Or you can simply use first and middle names for both bride and groom.

Military titles are spelled out, with service designations on a separate line. Those with the rank captain and higher in the army, air force, and marines, and commander and higher in the navy, use their titles before their names, with their service designation listed on the next line. (The service designation line is omitted if the invitation is being *issued* by an officer and his wife.) Junior officers list their title on the line beneath their name, before their service designation. Noncommissioned officers list only their service designation, on the line under their name.

The wedding date is written, *Saturday, the sixth of July,* with the year spelled out on the following line. (If the wedding will take place in the same calendar year that the invitations are being sent out, you may omit the year. However, your invitation will be a more meaningful keepsake if the year is included.)

Indicate the correct time of the ceremony. List it as *four o'clock*. If the ceremony will start on the half hour, use the phrase *half after (four o'clock)*. The phrase *in the afternoon* or *in the evening* is optional.

Check the correct name of the ceremony site. If there are churches with similar names in the same city, and most guests will be unfamiliar with the location, indicate the street address beneath the site. Spell out *Saint* in church names, as well as numbers. List the city or town; the state is optional (depending on how familiar guests are with the area).

You may request a reply to the invitation with *R.s.v.p., Please respond, Kindly respond,* or *The favour of a reply is requested*. The most proper version of this ritual requires a handwritten response. However, the more contemporary (and practical) approach is to request that the enclosed reply card be returned by a specific date, usually no less than three weeks prior to the wedding.

Below are examples of the various ways to word invitations:

When the bride's parents host the wedding:	**When the invitation includes the bride's and groom's parents:**
Mr. and Mrs. Charles Andrew Jones	*Mr. and Mrs. Charles Andrew Jones*
request the honour of your presence	*request the honour of your company*
at the marriage of their daughter	*at the marriage of their daughter*
Mary Lynn	*Mary Lynn*
to	*to*
Edward Paul Hill	*Edward Paul Hill*
Saturday, the ninth of May	*son of*
two thousand and three	*Mr. and Mrs. Donald Lawrence Hill*
at four o'clock	*Saturday, the ninth of May*
All Saints Church	*etc.*
Barton, Texas	

Joint sponsorship by the bride's and groom's family: This wording does not clearly spell out the relationship of the hosts to the bride and groom. Some couples may not be comfortable using the word *children*, while others feel it has a warm sound.

Mr. and Mrs. Charles Andrew Jones
and
Mr. and Mrs. Donald Lawrence Hill
request the pleasure of your company at
the wedding reception of their children
Mary Lynn
and
Tyson James
Saturday, the eighth of May
etc.

When a widow who has not remarried hosts the wedding: Although a deceased parent is mentioned in a newspaper engagement or wedding announcement, he or she is not listed on the wedding invitation. This is because an invitation is issued to share an occasion together. Also a wedding is a happy occasion; mentioning the deceased parent's name would strike a note of sadness.

Mrs. Robert Kowolsky
requests the honour of your presence
at the marriage of her daughter
Theresa Louise
etc.

When a widower who has not remarried hosts the wedding:

Mr. Robert Harris Kowolsky
requests the honour of your presence
at the marriage of his daughter
Theresa Louise
etc.

When the bride's mother has remarried after being widowed or divorced:

Mr. and Mrs. Ricardo Rojas
request the honour of your presence
at the marriage of Mrs. Rojas's daughter
[or, if the bride is close to her
stepfather, *their daughter*]
Angela Madelena Mendoza
etc.

When the bride's father has remarried after being widowed or divorced:

Mr. and Mrs. Victor Mendoza
request the honour of your presence
at the marriage of Mr. Mendoza's
daughter/
[or, if the bride is close to her
stepmother, *their daughter*]
Angela Madelena Mendoza
etc.

When the bride's parents are divorced, the invitation is generally issued by the parent who raised her.

When a divorced mother has not remarried: If issuing the invitations, she may use the traditional divorcée's combination of her maiden and married surnames (*Mrs. Sarah Collins Anderson*), or she may drop *Mrs.* and use just her first name (*Sarah Collins Anderson*). It is also acceptable for her to use her first name, middle name, and married surname (*Mrs. Sarah Beth Anderson*). The rest of the invitation is worded as for a widowed parent.

Sarah Collins Anderson
requests the honour of your presence
at the marriage of her daughter
Abigail Blake
etc.

When a divorced father has not remarried: If he issues the invitation, it carries his full name and the phrase *his daughter*. The wording is the same for a widower who has not remarried (above).

When divorced parents send a joint invitation: This may be sent if parents are still on good terms. Avoid using *Mr.* and *Mrs.*, since that is no longer the case, and list their names on separate lines—remarried or not.

Sarah Collins Anderson
[or *Mrs. Peter Smith*, if remarried]
Steven Randolph Anderson
[or *Mr. Steven Randolph Anderson*]
request the honour of your presence
at the marriage of their daughter
Abigail Blake
to
Christopher Howard Geist
etc.

When divorced parents send two separate invitations: If divorced parents don't want their names to appear together, but the bride wants to acknowledge them equally, a solution is to have one parent issue the invitation to the ceremony and the other to the reception. These are assembled and mailed together like any other wedding invitation.

The ceremony invitation:
Sarah Collins Anderson
[or *Mrs. Peter Smith*, if remarried]
requests the honour of your presence
at the marriage of her daughter
Abigail Blake
to
Christopher Howard Geist
etc.

The reception invitation:
Steven Randolph Anderson
requests the pleasure of your company
Saturday, the ninth of May
at five o'clock
Glen Oaks Country Club
R.s.v.p.
Sixty-two Laurel Lane
Barton, Texas 12345

When the groom's parents are divorced and included on the invitation, adapt the previous examples or follow this:
Mr. and Mrs. Charles Andrew Jones
request the honour of your presence
at the marriage of their daughter
Mary Lynn Jones
to
Edward Paul Hill
son of
Mrs. Sheila Jane Smith
Mr. Donald Lawrence Hill
etc.

When a married mother of the bride or groom goes by her maiden name, the parents' names are listed on separate lines. This is similar to an invitation for divorced parents sending a joint invitation (see previous example).

When a single parent hosts the wedding with a live-in partner, grandmother, aunt, etc.: This form lists the sponsors separately and indicates which is the parent.

Mrs. Mayuri Bhatt
Mr. Stephen J. Barkley
request the honour of your presence
at the marriage of Mrs. Bhatt's daughter
Ellen Victoria
etc.

When relatives other than parents of the bride, host the wedding: The host's relationship to the bride is spelled out with such words as *his sister, her sister,* or *their niece* substituted for *their daughter.*

If friends host the wedding: The invitation lists the bride's full name with *Miss* (or *Ms.*) before it:

Mr. and Mrs. George Anthony Donato
request the honour of your presence
at the marriage of
Miss (Ms.) Cheryl Diane Callas
to
Mr. Arnold Lee Gregory
etc.

The bride's surname appears on the invitations in these special circumstances:

The bride's mother has remarried and is hosting the wedding with her new husband (see previous example).

The bride has been previously married and has retained her ex-spouse's name:

Mr. and Mrs. George W. Harvey
request the honour of your presence at
the marriage of their daughter
Ms. Stephanie Harvey Milsap
to
Mr. G. Allen Montclair
etc.

When the couple host the wedding: If the bride and her fiancé wish to host their own wedding, they may issue the invitations themselves.

The honour of your presence
is requested at the marriage of
Miss Margaret Jean Murphy
to

Mr. Leo Stanley Stark
Saturday, the seventh of November
at eleven o'clock
Saint Cecilia's Church
South Bay, California

Personalized printed invitations: Some couples and their parents word their own invitations as a personal expression or to share religious feelings with their guests. Adapt the traditional invitation any way you wish (don't feel you must spell out numbers—7 P.M., for instance), but be sure the necessary information (the hosts' names; the ceremony site, date, and time; the reception site, date, and time; and the address, if any, for replies) is included and easy to follow. The invitation should be warm and concise and should fit the formality of the celebration:

Warner and Paula Sampson
and
William and Mary Marcus
invite you to share in the joy
of the marriage uniting our children
Nicole and Jerry
Saturday, August 29, 2003
at 4 p.m.
at the First Baptist Church
607 Lincoln Avenue
New Petersburg
Worship with us, witness their vows,
and join us afterward at
the Church Fellowship Hall.

If you are unable to attend, we ask your
presence in thought and prayer.

R.s.v.p.
Warner and Paula Sampson
(301) 223-1234

Double wedding: The brides are usually sisters, and a single invitation is issued.

Mr. and Mrs. Nicholas Pappas
request the honour of your presence
at the marriage of their daughters
Katherine Denise
to
Milton Zara
and
Christina Eugenia
to
Enrique Gonzalez
Saturday, the first of August
at half after seven o'clock
Saint Barbara's Greek Orthodox Church
Inport, Connecticut

When the brides are not sisters, separate invitations may be sent by each family, or they may issue a joint invitation:

Mr. and Mrs. Samuel Catt Saulsberry
and
Mr. and Mrs. Gaylord Rogers
request the honour of your presence
at the marriage of their daughters
Susan Ann Saulsberry
to
Bruce Raymond Harnett
and
Brenda Lou Rogers
to
Jisoo Kwan
etc.

Professional Titles

Traditionally, only the groom's full name was used on a wedding invitation, preceded by a title *(Mr.* or *Doctor/Dr.)*. The bride's professional title and last name, as well as the title of her mother, were omitted in favor of social titles—*Miss* and *Mrs.* Today, couples often want their names to be printed in the same form: Both either use or omit their titles, and both use their first and middle names. They're also choosing to include their mother's professional titles (if she is a doctor, clergymember, or member of the armed services on active duty). Titles of senators and judges and other high officials may be used, but those of lesser officials are usually omitted.

When the bride has a professional title:

Mr. and Mrs. George W. Harvey
request the honour of your presence
at the marriage of
their daughter
Dr. Stephanie R. Harvey
to
Mr. G. Allen Montclair
etc.

When the bride's father is a doctor: The name of a medical doctor is preceded by *Doctor/Dr.* instead of *Mr.*

Dr. and Mrs. Charles Andrew Jones
request the honour of your presence
at the marriage of their daughter
Mary Lynn
to
Edward Paul Hill
etc.

When the bride's mother is a doctor: The names of the two parents appear on separate lines, in the format of divorced parents.

Mr. Charles Andrew Jones
and
Dr. Susan Jones
request the honour of your presence
at the marriage of their daughter
etc.

When the bride's mother is a judge:
Mr. John Smith
and
The Honorable Jane Smith
request the honour of your presence
at the marriage of their daughter
Jessica Ann
etc.

When the bride's father is a clergymember: A clergymember's title *(The Reverend, The Reverend Doctor, Rabbi)* is spelled out in full before his or her name.

The Reverend and Mrs. Charles Andrew
Jones
request the honour of your presence
at the marriage of their daughter
Mary Lynn
etc.

When the bride's mother is a clergymember: The parents' names would appear on separate lines, in the format of divorced parents.

Mr. Charles Andrew Jones
and
The Reverend Susan Jones
request the honour of your presence
at the marriage of their daughter
Mary Lynn
etc.

Military Titles

When used with social invitations, military titles are subject to changing regulations and should always be verified with the protocol office of the specific branch of service. The titles *Mr., Mrs., Miss,* or *Ms.* should never precede a name that mentions a rank and branch of service. A bride or mother in the military may choose not to use her title in favor of the familiar first-name form; if she uses her title on the invitation, she would also use her last name, as she would with any title. Reserve officers do not use military titles unless they are on active duty at the time of the marriage.

When the bride's father is a military officer hosting the wedding with the bride's mother, his title is spelled out and precedes his name; the branch of service is not mentioned.

Captain and Mrs. Gregory Connor
request the honour of your presence
at the marriage of their daughter
Margaret Kelly
etc.

The groom's or bride's military title appears before his or her name only if he

or she holds a rank equivalent to or higher than captain in the army or commander in the navy.

Mr. and Mrs. Michael Simmons
request the honour of your presence
at the marriage of their daughter
Commander Karen Ann Simmons
United States Navy
to
Major Mark William Burns
United States Marine Corps
etc.

- Fold the traditional engraved double sheet like a book, with the type on top, the fold to the left.

- Enclosures can be inserted inside the invitation (or announcement).

- Enclosures may also be placed directly on top of the invitation, before all are slipped inside the inner envelope.

- Tissue paper—inserted by the printer to keep ink from smudging—is usually tossed away but may be left in place.

- The proper order in which to insert enclosures into the inner envelope is, bottom to top, most important to least important: Invitation, then reception card, and finally the R.s.v.p. card. For each piece, the print should be facing up, toward the back side of the envelope.

- The unsealed inner envelope is inserted into the outer envelope, so that handwritten guests' names are visible when the outer envelope is opened.

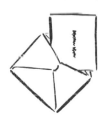

If the bride or groom occupies a lesser rank, it may be listed on the invitation with the branch of service.

> *Mr. and Mrs. William MacGregor*
> *request the honour of your presence*
> *at the marriage of their daughter*
> *Lisa Susanne*
> *to*
> *Malik Jeffrey Johnson*
> *Lieutenant, United States Army*
> etc.

If the bride or groom is enlisted, the branch of service may be listed without the rank.

> *Mr. and Mrs. William MacGregor*
> *request the honour of your presence*
> *at the marriage of their daughter*
> *Lisa Susanne*
> *to*
> *Jeffrey Ronald Sherman*
> *United States Marine Corps*
> etc.

When the bride's father is a military officer hosting the wedding alone, the line after his name indicates his branch of service (include the word *Retired* if applicable).

> *Captain Gregory Connor*
> *United States Navy, Retired*
> *requests the honour of your presence*
> *at the marriage of his daughter*
> *Margaret Kelly*
> etc.

When the bride's parents are divorced and one is in the military, the civilian is listed first, the military person on a separate line, with branch of service on the next line:

> *Mrs. Jane Hanson*
> *and*
> *Admiral John Hanson*
> *United States Navy*
> *request the honour of your presence*
> *at the marriage of their daughter*
> *Joan Mary*
> etc.

When the bride's mother is a military officer, she has the option of following the same wording for a military officer issuing an invitation alone (see previous example). However, if issuing the invitation with her husband, the civilian is listed first, the military person second on a separate line, with the branch of service on the next line (similar to when parents are divorced, and one is in the military; see previous example):

> *Mr. Gregory Connor*
> *and*
> *Captain Barbara Connor*
> *United States Navy*
> *request the honour of your presence*
> *at the marriage of their daughter*
> *Margaret Kelly*
> etc.

another formal invitation option

Some formal invitations are folded twice—reminiscent of the time when envelopes were smaller than the invitations.

- Fold these formal invitations first in half, from left to right (forming a "book"), then again, from top to bottom. Printing may run across both sides of the second fold.

- Enclosures are inserted inside the second fold of the invitation.

- Insert the invitation in the inner envelope fold-side down.

- The unsealed inner envelope is inserted into the outer envelope (address side facing the back flap), so that handwritten guests' names are visible when the outer envelope is opened (see illustration, previous page, bottom).

Addressing Envelopes

Address all invitations by hand. Never use a typewriter, though you may consider some computers that are able to print envelopes in script type. Do not, however, use computer–generated mailing labels. Many couples address invitations together, often with their families, and wedding-party members' help (see Chapter 3, "Prewedding Parties").

Consider hiring a calligrapher or secretarial service to address invitations. Calligraphy is elegant handwriting done with pen and ink. If you don't know anyone who can execute this classic style, ask friends and family, your stationer, or wedding consultant for referrals. Your stationer will also be able to tell you about computerized calligraphy services (see Appendix, under Chapter 5, "Invitations & Announcements").

Don't abbreviate streets, cities, or states, and be sure to use zip codes. The only abbreviations used are *Mr., Mrs., Ms., Jr., Dr.,* and *Esq.,* which is abbreviated in social correspondence for an attorney. (Never use *Esquire* or its abbreviation on an invitation addressed to both husband and wife.)

Note that the guests' full names and addresses (*Mr. and Mrs. James Wallace McDermott*) are written only on the outer envelope, which is stamped and sealed. First names and addresses are *not* written on the inner envelope (just titles and last names—*Mr. and Mrs. McDermott*—are written), which is ungummed and remains unsealed when it is slipped inside the outer envelope.

The proper way to address mail to your guests:

A divorcée is addressed by either the very traditional *Mrs. Joan Ross* or by her maiden name (*Ms. Joan Phillips*).

A separated woman is addressed on an envelope as *Mrs. Joan Ross.*

A widow is addressed on an envelope as *Mrs. Earl Jones.*

A single woman, even a child, is addressed as *Miss (Ms.) Sandra Lightner.*

A boy under age 13 is addressed as *Master Jordan Sullivan.*

Follow these guidelines when sending invitations:

Children under 18 are not listed in the address on the outer envelope. Their names *should* be listed under their parents' names on the inner envelope.
  Mr. and Mrs. McDermott
  Kevin, Christopher, and Mary
Avoid using the phrase "*And Family*" so that everyone who is invited feels the invitation is especially for him or her, and to ensure an accurate head count.

A person over 18 years old should receive a separate wedding invitation, whether or not he or she is currently living with his or her parents.

If two siblings live together at another address, one invitation may be sent, with the siblings' names listed alphabetically on the envelope:
  Mr. Arthur Reed
  Ms. Kellie Reed

mailing invitations

- Weigh a sample assembled invitation to gauge correct postage, since enclosures may require extra postage. (The last problem you want to deal with: All invitations are missing, or returned, because of insufficient postage.)

- Mail invitations six weeks before the wedding (eight weeks before if the wedding falls on a holiday or long weekend, or if you're inviting many out-of-town guests).

- Expect regrets. Look at your list realistically (i.e., are the majority local, or do most people live out–of–state), but on average, roughly 10 to 15 percent of those you invite will not be able to attend. These refusals will give you the opportunity to invite people who had to be eliminated from your original guest list— now on a "wish list."

- It's acceptable for guests to receive invitations up to four weeks before the wedding. After that, any invitations should be extended personally, via a phone call.

A married woman who uses a military title, and her husband:
Outer Envelope:
Captain Sheila Vincente
Mr. David Vincente
1010 Maplewood Road
Metropolis, Ohio 12345
Inner Envelope (on one line):
Captain Vincente and Mr. Vincente

Married woman who uses a professional title, and her husband:
Outer Envelope:
Dr. Carol Kim
Mr. Keith Kim
Inner Envelope (on one line):
Dr. Kim and Mr. Kim

A married couple who are both doctors are addressed as follows:
Outer Envelope:
The Doctors Klein

Inner Envelope:
The Doctors Klein

A married couple with different last names or an unmarried couple living together receive one invitation with their names listed alphabetically. An "and" should be inserted between the names of a married couple on the outer envelope, but not between the names of an unmarried couple.
Outer Envelope:
Mr. Joshua Adams
         (and)
Ms. Isabella Dolesji
393 Atlantic Boulevard
Metropolis, Ohio 12345
Inner Envelope:
Mr. Adams and Ms. Moore

Two unrelated friends who are roommates should be sent two invitations.

Quick Invitations

If you're getting married quickly—between one and six weeks from now—there may not be time to get invitations formally printed and mailed. You might be able to rush-order thermography invitations in as little as five working days; if time is really short, there are formal preprinted invitations available with space to fill in names, date, and place, as well as computerized calligraphy services, available at many stationery stores.

If possible, guests should receive an invitation at least two weeks before the wedding. If time is very tight, your parents may send handwritten notes or invite guests personally by telephone or e-mail. However you spread the word, be sure that all information that would be included on a printed invitation—who's getting married, where, when, style of the service, location of the reception, R.s.v.p. address, and a return address (so that guests know where they may send gifts)—is passed along to guests. If you are telephoning, and want to indicate that your parents are the sponsors, say *"Mom and Dad wanted you to be with us . . ."*

Forms of Address

PERSONAGE	INVITATION: OUTER ENVELOPE	INVITATION: INNER ENVELOPE/ NAME CARD
Clergymember* Protestant (no degree)	The Reverend Paul Jones	The Reverend Jones
Clergymember Protestant (with degree)	The Reverend Doctor Paul Jones or The Reverend Paul Jones, Ph.D.	The Reverend Doctor Jones
Clergymember Roman Catholic	The Reverend Paul Jones	Father Jones
Eastern Orthodox Priest	The Reverend Father George Kontos	Father Kontos
Roman Catholic Bishop	The Most Reverend Daniel Bell, Bishop of Texas	Bishop Bell
Vicar	The Reverend Robert MacDonald	Monsignor MacDonald
Dean	The Reverend Samuel Brandon	The Reverend Brandon
Rabbi (no degree)	Rabbi Nathan Ziff	Rabbi Ziff
Rabbi (with degree)	Rabbi Nathan Ziff, D.D.	Dr. Ziff
Cantor	Cantor David Levy	Cantor Levy
Professor (no degree)	Professor Katherine Lyle	Professor Lyle
Professor (with degree)	Martin Steven Severino, Ph.D., or Professor Martin Severino	Dr. Severino or Professor Severino
Judge	The Honorable Walter Reynolds	Judge Reynolds
Lawyer	Mr. Alfred Standish or Alfred Standish, Esq.	Mr. Standish
Mayor	The Honorable Patricia Kelly, Mayor of Middletown	Mayor Kelly or Ms. Kelly
Army Officer	Captain Lee Wainwright, United States Army	Captain Wainwright
Navy Officer	Commander William Gordon Smith, United States Navy	Commander Smith
Physician	Marcella Duarte Hopkins, M.D.	Dr. Hopkins

*Check with your clergymember's office to confirm his/her title, as there are many variations.

Handwritten quick invitation:

Dear Rose,

Judith and Michael are to be married at half past three on Sunday, the sixth of September, in the chapel of Temple Emanuel in Green Heights. It will be a small wedding with a reception afterward at our house. You know how much we all want you to be with us on that day.

Affectionately,

Ruth

Please respond to:

Mr. and Mrs. Andrew Hirsch

Fifteen Stone Drive

Birmingham, Alabama 12345

Enclosures

These small printed cards are enclosed with the invitation and match the invitation in style and paper quality.

The simplified reception card:

Reception

immediately following the ceremony

Glen Oaks Country Club

Kindly respond

Sixty-two Laurel Lane

Barton, Texas 12345

A combined ceremony-and-reception invitation without enclosure cards: This popular contemporary invitation solution is often used when all guests are invited to both ceremony and reception. (If you are having both the ceremony and the reception at home, there is no need to mention the reception, since it will be assumed that one will follow and all guests will be included.)

Mr. and Mrs. Charles Andrew Jones

request the honour of your presence

at the marriage of their daughter

Mary Lynn

to

Edward Paul Hill

Saturday, the ninth of May

at four o'clock

All Saints Church

Barton, Texas

and afterward at

Glen Oaks Country Club

Please respond

Sixty-two Laurel Lane

Barton, Texas 12345

When parents are divorced and one hosts the reception:

Mr. James Gilrod

requests the pleasure of your company

at the wedding reception of his daughter

Sarah Jessica

Saturday, the twentieth of June

at six o'clock

Maple Hill Inn

Little Rock, Arkansas

etc.

When the couple host the reception, they may enclose this reception card (or a *simplified reception card*—see earlier example):

The pleasure of your company is
requested
Saturday, the seventh of November
at half after eleven o'clock
The Waterside
South Bay, California

R.s.v.p.
1600 Ocean Parkway, Apartment 12L
South Bay, California 12345

Ceremony Cards: If you will invite people to the reception who will not be included at the ceremony, send invitations to the reception and enclose ceremony cards (or informal notes) for a select few.

Reception Invitation:

Mr. and Mrs. Charles Andrew Jones
request the pleasure of your company
at the wedding reception of their
daughter
Mary Lynn
and
Edward Paul Hill
Saturday, the ninth of May
at five o'clock
Glen Oaks Country Club
Barton, Texas

R.s.v.p.
Sixty-two Laurel Lane
Barton, Texas 12345

The separate ceremony card:

Mr. and Mrs. Charles Andrew Jones
request the honour of your presence
Saturday, the ninth of May
at four o'clock
All Saints Church
Barton, Texas

A simplified ceremony card: If very few people are invited to the ceremony, the ceremony invitations may be printed or handwritten on informal note cards.

Ceremony
at four o'clock
All Saints Church

Ceremony-admittance cards: These small cards are printed when there is a chance that an uninvited person may try to attend the ceremony or when the wedding is held in a public place (a museum, art gallery). Ceremony cards are enclosed with the invitation; upon arrival, guests present the cards to ushers for admittance.

Please present this card
The First Congregational Church
Saturday, the twelfth of March

At-home cards: These small cards may be enclosed with formal invitations, but are more often included with announcements (see "Announcements" section). They announce your new address and the date that it is effective. You may either print your names on the cards or not, and mail them with your invitations and announcements.

Traditional at-home card:

Mr. and Mrs. John Simon Eagle
after the tenth of April
1035 Fifth Avenue, Apartment 9B
New York, New York 12345

If the bride is keeping her name, or decides to hyphenate it with her husband's surname, she may announce it on the at-home card:

Dr. Mary Ann Janacek
(or *Dr. Mary Ann Janacek-Eagle*)

Mr. John Simon Eagle
after the tenth of April
123 Robin Lane
Phoenix, Arizona 24689

Name cards: If you wish, you may send separate name cards in invitations or announcements, or alone, after the honeymoon. These cards will inform professional colleagues of your decision to change or hyphenate your name.

Kirsten Andrews
will be changing her name to
Kirsten Andrews Sullivan
following her marriage
June 6, 2003

When a couple adopt a new surname together:
Kirsten Andrews and Roger Sullivan
will be adopting the surname
Andrews-Sullivan
following their marriage
June 6, 2003

Pew cards: These small cards are used to assign special seating to very close friends and relatives at the ceremony. They may be sent with the invitation—or better still, after the acceptance has been received. Pew cards may be handwritten notes from the bride's parents or printed cards.

Please present this card
The First Congregational Church
Saturday, the fourteenth of March

Pew number 9

Within-the-ribbon cards: For large formal weddings, small printed cards may be sent with the phrase *within the ribbon* in the lower left corner, where the pew number is usually listed. This phrase will indicate to ushers that guests should be seated in a special reserved section; the *last* row is decorated with festive bows or ribbons.

Please present this card
The First Congregational Church
Saturday, the twelfth of March

Within the ribbon

Reception response cards: Traditionally, response cards were avoided for formal weddings, as they implied that the person invited would not know that proper etiquette required them to respond with a handwritten note. (See Chapter 18, "Wedding Guests," for how to word handwritten responses.) Today, however, for convenience and immediacy, they are almost always sent with wedding invitations. (Guests can also enclose a personal note with the response card, expressing their best wishes.)

Check post-office regulations regarding size of cards and envelopes and placement of the return address. Return envelopes should be stamped and have printed addresses.

Some response cards are blank, with an *R.s.v.p.* date (usually three weeks before the wedding) printed in the bottom left corner. They allow guests to write a personal note on the card; these cards become keepsakes for the bride.

Blank response cards:
The favour of a reply is requested
by the fifteenth of September
or
Kindly respond
by September 15

Fill-in response cards: To accommodate today's busy lives, one alternative to the completely blank response card is one that allows guests to simply fill in their name and circle or check appropriate wording; adding the word *not* next to *attend* if they will not accept the invitation.

The favour of a reply is requested
by the fifteenth of September
M_____
will _____ attend

Rain cards: If an outdoor wedding is planned, enclose rain cards with an alternate location, just in case.
In case of rain
the wedding and reception
will be held in
Myers Park Methodist Church
424 River Road
one o'clock in the afternoon

Travel cards: Enclose travel cards to let guests know that you've chartered a bus or ferry to get them to a distant or out-of-the-way site.

Special-transportation cards:
A private bus will leave
Saint Mary's Parish Hall
at three o'clock in the afternoon
and arrive back in Washington
at ten o'clock in the evening.

Travel cards are also used to inform guests that you've arranged for them to park at a nearby garage. The card can serve as an admission pass if you've arranged to pick up the cost and gratuity.

Parking-arrangements card:
Parking provided

McKenzie Parking Garage
2018 Main Street
Gratuities included. Please present this
card to the parking attendant.

Direction Cards/Maps: Directions to the ceremony and reception sites should be enclosed with the invitation and printed in a manner as beautiful and professional as the invitation itself. Check that they are accurate, and arrange to have extras available at the ceremony site. After the ceremony, the ushers should see that guests have directions and transportation to the reception.

Accommodation cards: These cards are sent to out-of-town guests who will need hotel reservations. The cards, which may be printed by the hotel or reprinted by you in a style that matches your invitation, let guests know that a block of rooms has been reserved, and include the hotel's phone number. Guests can then call and make their own reservations.

Long weekend wedding response cards: A weekend wedding filled with festivities calls for several invitations (see "Long-Weekend Wedding Invitations" section). Along with the wedding invitation, enclose an itinerary of weekend events, and one longer R.s.v.p. card with boxes to check off for each event. Or, enclose small printed R.s.v.p. cards for each additional party. Print addresses on each stamped response envelope, since each might have a different host. (Hosts of each weekend party may instead opt to send separate invitations and response cards.)

long-weekend wedding response cards

Have response cards printed for these or other similar festivities, and enclose them with the invitation (or have the host of each party/event send them separately):

- welcome cocktail party
- rehearsal dinner
- museum tour
- bride's team vs. groom's team softball game
- golf or tennis outing
- pool party and picnic
- wedding-day breakfast
- postwedding brunch

invitation-response tips

Suggestions for keeping track of R.s.v.p.'s:

- *Index cards* Create an alphabetical file with each couple's/family's information on 3×5-inch cards. Later, you can reorganize and group cards by tables.

- *Notebooks* Reserve a page for each couple's/family's information.

- *Ledgers/Planners* Many wedding planners have pages set aside for guest responses.

- *Computer* Programs are available to keep track of all planning information—from florists and bakers to guests and gifts.

Moveable–Wedding Invitations

When a number of relatives of either the bride or the groom live in another city than that where the wedding is held, someone (a parent, grandparent, or even the couple) may host one or more postwedding parties. Then friends and relatives in those towns and cities can meet and celebrate with the newlyweds (see Chapter 10, "Special Weddings & New Ways to Wed"). These second or third receptions don't have to be gift-giving occasions but are often formal events with receiving lines, and require invitations that are equally formal.

Moveable-wedding invitation:

Mr. and Mrs. Albert Hughs Hudson
request the pleasure of your company
at a reception in honour of
Mr. and Mrs. Theodore Russell Hudson
Sunday, the eighteenth of January
at four o'clock
Castle Mountain Inn
Woodtown, Vermont

R.s.v.p.
263 Spruce Road
Woodtown, Vermont 12345

Formal moveable-wedding invitations or handwritten notes are appropriate. If you are sending announcements the day of the wedding, you can tuck in the appropriate second or third reception card (use the wording for reception cards in previous examples) to invite those who weren't at the wedding to the follow-up celebration(s). It is not unusual to have different guest lists for each moveable-wedding reception—depending on the city where each celebration takes place.

Long-Weekend Wedding Invitations

The weekend-long wedding celebration is a very popular option today, giving the couple and their families more time to interact with guests—often at a resort or some other special destination. Regardless of the circumstances, if you are undertaking the time, effort and cost of planning a long-weekend wedding, plan to send simple, elegant Save the Date cards at least six months prior to ensure that the maximum number of people will be able to join you—particularly if the celebration will take place over a holiday weekend. Long-distance guests may be more likely to make the trip if they know there will be many opportunities for them to visit with other friends and relatives. If several celebrations are planned during your wedding weekend, send wedding guests a letter or a computer-generated calendar of events detailing all of the festivities. Perhaps include a sketch of the wedding site. When mailing the official wedding invitation, additional inserts might include a map outlining the wedding route, invitations to the rehearsal dinner, brunch, and other events. Also enclose a chronological list of events, with suggested clothing (*bathing suits and shorts for the Saturday afternoon barbecue*). However, do your best to keep it simple and elegant—the last thing you want to do is to confuse or overwhelm your guests.

Keeping Track of Responses

Once invitations arrive, you will receive formal written acceptances or regrets, informal notes, response cards, even phone calls. Set up a system to record who's coming and who's not (see "Invitation-Response Tips"). Also track the gifts you receive (include each guest's complete name, address, gift, and when the thank-you note was sent). Finally, note their table number once the seating plan is complete.

No response. If your R.s.v.p. date arrives and you still haven't heard from some guests, call them and ask if they received the invitation. Your caterer or banquet manager will need a final head count, and you will have to finish your seating plan.

Recalling Invitations

If a formal wedding must be canceled or postponed after the invitations have gone out, guests should be notified as soon as possible. It is best to do this with printed cards rush-ordered from a stationer.

If there has been a death in the family:

Mrs. Gerald Timothy Allen
regrets that the death of
Mr. Allen
obliges her to recall the invitations
to the wedding of her daughter
Sarah Louise
Saturday, the seventh of February

The above wording indicates that the wedding will not take place *as planned.* A death or serious illness in the family means that a large wedding would be inappropriate, but the marriage may still take place as a small family ceremony. The couple may dress in their formal wedding attire, but the only attendants to participate are the honor attendants.

If the wedding is postponed and a new date has been set:

Mr. and Mrs. Stuart Dean Jefferson
announce that the marriage of their
daughter

Virginia Ann
to
Frank Martin Gallagher
has been postponed from
Saturday, the sixth of June
until
Saturday, the seventeenth of October
at four o'clock
Grace Episcopal Church
Wilfordshire, Connecticut

or

...has been postponed
and will now take place
Saturday, the seventeenth of October
etc.

If the wedding is canceled, invitations are recalled with engraved or printed cards if there is time. If time is short, however, invitations may be recalled with personal notes, or by phone, fax, or e-mail. Calls are made in the name of the bride's parents. Reasons other than a

*who gets
announcements?*

- business associates
- guests invited by phone
- friends and relatives not receiving invitations

death or illness in the family need not be mentioned.

If the wedding is canceled:

Mr. and Mrs. Warren Troy Peterson
announce that the marriage of

their daughter
Ellen Marie
to
Henry Carl Smith
will not take place

Announcements

Wedding announcements may be sent directly after a small, family ceremony or an elopement. They should not be mailed to anyone who received an invitation and do not obligate the receiver to send a gift; they simply spread the happy news.

Include the date, year, and city in which the marriage took place. It is optional to mention the actual ceremony site.

Printing, paper, style, and addressing should match invitations. Order announcements when you order invitations and enclosures. Ask bridesmaids to help address announcements and invitations at a wedding work party (see Chapter 3, "Prewedding Parties"). Use computer–generated calligraphy, or, bring the announcement and invitation envelopes to the same calligrapher. In any case, make sure your announcements are handled in the same manner as the invitations. No matter how tempting, never use computer–generated mailing labels.

Enclose at-home cards and name cards, if you decide to send them, with your announcements (as well as with your wedding invitations).

Mail announcements immediately after the ceremony. Ask a bridesmaid or usher to drop them in the mail within twenty–four hours of the wedding.

Traditional announcement wording:

Mr. and Mrs. Peter Young Chow
have the honour of announcing
the marriage of their daughter
Annette Elizabeth
to
Leonard Park Ling
on Friday, the tenth of July
Two thousand and three
Our Redeemer Lutheran Church
Seattle, Washington

Other announcement wording:

Mr. and Mrs. Peter Young Chow
announce the marriage of their daughter
etc.

Announcements are also an ideal option for the groom's family to send and can be adapted accordingly:

Mr. and Mrs. Richard Park Ling
announce the marriage of their son
etc.

When the bride or her parents are divorced or widowed: wording is varied as in printed invitations. For example:

Sarah Collins Anderson
Steven Randolph Anderson
have the honour of announcing
the marriage of their daughter
etc.

When the bride and groom issue the announcement: This is an option if you have no parents or close relatives to send announcements, have been previously married, or have been on your own and want to announce your own wedding. It is also a good way to include business associates.

Deborah Suzanne Schwartz,
[Dr. Deborah Schwartz, etc.]
and
[Mr.] Eric Davis Fisher
announce their marriage
Friday, the twenty-seventh of November
Two thousand and three
Chicago, Illinois

Other Printing Needs

It will save time if you order all of your stationery when you order your invitations. That way, all printed material will be compatible and will be on hand as you need it throughout your engagement.

Thank-you notes: It is best for the bride and groom to each choose formal notes, since each will be writing thank-you notes before the wedding. The couple's name *(Mr. and Mrs. Jon Word)* or a joint monogram can be printed on the stationery they will use after their wedding. You should never use stationery printed with your married name or initials until after the wedding. (See Chapter 17, "Wedding Gifts.") Be sure to check post-office regulations regarding size of cards and envelopes and placement of the return address before you order.

Gift-received cards: If you're planning a long honeymoon or a large wedding and know that you won't be able to send thank-you notes as promptly as you should (see Chapter 17, "Wedding Gifts"), order printed gift-received cards. These acknowledge your receipt of the gift and promise that a personal thank-you will follow.

Ann Marie Brown
[or Steven Ray Jones, if two sets are ordered]
acknowledges with thanks
the receipt of your wedding gift
and will take pleasure in writing a
personal note at an early date.

Notepaper can be engraved with your new address only, so you can both use it after the wedding (or before, if you live together). City and street names are printed in full, not abbreviated. Numerals may be spelled out if you prefer.

A wedding program is extremely helpful in guiding your guests through the ceremony and can be a special keepsake. It includes the date, time, and place of the ceremony, as well as a listing of the participants (the couple, parents, wedding party, officiant, organist, soloist, and choir members). A program is useful for translating prayers and explaining customs at an interfaith or intercultural wedding that may be unfamiliar to some guests. It can also include your vows, a special greeting you have written, or a tribute to a deceased relative or friend. Your program can be elaborate or simple. Some couples prepare a booklet that matches their wedding colors; others use a preprinted wedding bulletin (from religious supply houses) with their wedding service photocopied inside; still others choose a calligraphy-inscribed scroll, while some have formal programs printed to match their stationery (see Appendix, under Chapter 4. "Planning Your Wedding" for samples, as well as information on wedding program styles and options).

Reaffirmation of Vows

Whether they have eloped, gotten married in city hall, or reached a special wedding anniversary, many couples decide to have a reaffirmation ceremony, during which they repeat their marriage vows to each other. The officiant often designs the service, which may take place at a house of worship or at home (see Chapter 20, "Reaffirmation").

Reaffirmation-invitation wording:
The honour of your presence is requested
when Mr. and Mrs. Walter May reaffirm
their wedding vows
Saturday, the sixth of June
at three o'clock
Christian Reformed Church
Amsterdam, Michigan
and afterward at a reception in
the church parlour

Wedding-Anniversary Invitations

You may issue a formal invitation to a formal celebration with fifty or more guests. Often, the couple's children and their spouses are the hosts for this event.

Wedding-anniversary invitation wording:

Mr. and Mrs. Joshua Spiegel
request the pleasure of your company
at a reception to honour the fortieth
wedding anniversary of her parents
Mr. and Mrs. Morris Weidman
Wednesday, the fifth of August
at half after eight o'clock
1614 Greatfalls Avenue
Minneapolis, MN 12345
Kindly reply to
Mr. and Mrs. Spiegel
6643 Bergen Place
Minneapolis, Minnesota 12347

or

In honour of Mr. and Mrs. Morris Weidman
on the occasion of their
Fortieth Wedding Anniversary
Mr. and Mrs. Joshua Spiegel
request the pleasure of your company
etc.

THE WEDDING PARTY

A wedding celebrates family and friends as well as the bride and groom. Although the marriage can be legally performed with as few as three people present—the couple and an officiant (witnesses are not required by every state)—most couples want those who are important in their lives to be part of the wedding party. The traditional roles of best man, maid of honor, bridesmaids, ushers, flower girl, and ring bearer have changed dramatically over the years. Couples are marrying at a later age, and the nuclear family has often been replaced by the blended family, which includes stepparents and stepsiblings. The groom's honor attendant may be a woman; the bride's matron of honor may be her mother. The logistics of organizing the wedding party may also be more complex, since friends often live long distances apart. (The earlier they are asked to be in the wedding party, the sooner they can make travel and vacation plans.) Below are the members of the wedding party and their responsibilities.

The Bride's Role

Traditionally, the coordinators of the wedding have been the bride and her mother. Today, however, the bride and groom may plan—and pay for—all or part of the wedding. Sometimes they enlist the help of a wedding consultant—a wedding-planning professional who will do the legwork for the couple, interview wedding-service professionals, present all the options, and coordinate the details of the prewedding parties and the wedding itself

THE BRIDE:

Discusses the budget with the groom, her family, and the groom's family (if appropriate). This is the first step in planning.

Chooses the wedding date, style, and site. In most major cities, a formal wedding should be planned one year—sometimes two years—in advance, in order to book the sites and wedding-service professionals of preference.

Visits the ceremony officiant with her fiancé to discuss procedures and any special requests. Signs up for premarital counseling, if required or desired (see Chapter 4, "Planning Your Wedding").

Chooses the honor attendant and bridesmaids. Once the bride and her fiancé have settled on the size of the wedding party, the bride asks her close friends or family members to be a part of that group. (While it's not customary to pay for bridesmaids' dresses, hotel accommodations, or travel, the bride may make that her thank-you gift to her attendants. If so, she should tell them this when she invites them to be in the wedding party. If not, she should be forthright about expenses.)

Compiles her family's guest list, with help from her parents. Then informs the groom how many people may be included on his and his family's guest list.

Seeks recommendations for photographers, florists, stationers, and other wedding-service professionals from family and friends. (See Chapter 4, "Planning Your Wedding.")

Shops for bridesmaids' dresses. Considers attendants' budgets, prospects for wearing the dress again, body shapes, and tastes. Lets bridesmaids make the final selection from the three styles she likes the most (see Chapter 7, "Wedding Clothes").

Delegates duties among attendants. Tries not to overload her bridesmaids with requests to shop for dresses and audition bands, or for help in addressing invitations, making favors, or sampling menus. Doesn't expect any one person to share every planning trauma or delight.

Gives each attendant a small thank-you gift (a pendant or silver picture frame, perhaps engraved with the attendant's initials and wedding date). This may be presented at the rehearsal dinner, or at the bridesmaids' lunch or tea, if she is hosting one (see Chapter 17, "Wedding Gifts").

Plans a bridesmaids' lunch. Getting the bridesmaids together is a fun way for them to get acquainted, if they don't already know each other. (See Chapter 3, "Prewedding Parties.")

Arranges lodging for any long-distance bridesmaids, if needed. (The bride may choose to pay for this cost as her thank-you gift to them.)

Shops with the groom for wedding rings and has them engraved. More grooms than ever before are choosing to wear wedding rings, and most ceremonies are double-ring ceremonies. Traditionally, the bride pays for the groom's wedding ring; the groom, for the bride's. The groom may have strong opinions about the style and should be consulted. Many couples choose matching bands.

Shops for a wedding gift for the groom. This is an optional but meaningful gesture. Gifts may range from the traditional, such as gold cuff links to wear down the aisle, to the more creative—a scrapbook filled with courtship mementos (see Chapter 17, "Wedding Gifts").

Stands in the receiving line with the groom. If you have fewer than 50 guests, the receiving line is optional, but regardless of the number of guests, most couples realize that family and friends want to share their congratulations with them immediately after the ceremony ends. A receiving line offers them that opportunity. Mothers and attendants also stand in the line, but today, attendants, as well as fathers, may circulate among guests.

May be introduced by the bandleader— with groom (after the wedding party)— to all reception guests.

Dances a first dance to a preselected song with the groom. She can also dance during the same song with both fathers and the best man (see Chapter 13, "Your Reception"). Later, she might dance again with her father to a special song she's selected for the father-daughter dance (see Chapter 14, "Wedding Music"). She may also dance with her brothers, the ushers, and special guests at the reception.

Takes time before leaving the reception to spend a few moments alone with her parents.

Sends thank-you notes. With help from the groom, the bride acknowledges every gift in a personal note to the sender (see Chapter 17, "Wedding Gifts").

The Groom's Role

Grooms today play an active role in wedding planning—sharing the finances and decisions. Often, the partnership skills developed during the engagement months set a precedent for the way the couple will work as a team throughout their marriage. Together, the bride and groom should decide early on what responsibilities and areas of wedding planning he is interested in—and best able to handle.

THE GROOM:

Discusses the wedding's budget with the bride, his family, and the bride's family (if appropriate).

Makes sure that his family's guest list is compiled early. Ensures that titles (Miss/Ms., Sgt.), first and last names,

and middle names (for formal invitations), are filled in, and that the list includes all cities and states, street numbers, zip codes, and phone numbers.

Helps fiancée research and compare the services of wedding professionals. Helps compile a list of the caterers, photographers, videographers, florists, musicians, and other individuals they want the wedding consultant to interview. Or, if the couple will not be hiring a wedding consultant, the groom divides up the list so that he and his fiancée each visit a few. Reviews the information gathered with fiancée before making decisions.

Visits the ceremony officiant with fiancée to discuss procedures, music, and special requests.

Chooses the best man and ushers. Asks them to stand up for him shortly after he tells them the news of his engagement. Tells them about the wedding attire that will be required, and the expected rental fee and travel fees (unless he will cover this, as his gift to them).

Reminds his parents of their role in planning the rehearsal dinner. Traditionally, this prewedding party is hosted by the groom's parents (see Chapter 3, "Prewedding Parties"). However, the groom may take responsibility for it, especially if he is financing it. That evening, he presents his ushers with thank-you gifts, such as cuff links or silver razors (see Chapter 17, "Wedding Gifts").

Pays for the flowers for the bride (her bouquet and going-away nosegay), mothers, and any women of honor (grandmothers, aunts, friends). Although the bride will most likely choose the floral arrangements, some traditional grooms make the romantic gesture of picking up the tab.

Shops with the bride for the wedding rings and has them engraved.

Shops for a gift for the bride (optional). He might give her a strand of pearls to wear with her gown (the traditional gift) or new golf clubs (see Chapter 17, "Wedding Gifts").

Sets up the day and time for getting the marriage license and any other necessary documents (see Chapter 4, "Planning Your Wedding"). Afterward, he might take his fiancée to lunch or cocktails to celebrate the occasion.

Makes all reservations and arrangements for the honeymoon. Usually, the bride and groom will decide together where they want to go, but traditionally, the groom surprises the bride with some of the details and pays the tab.

Reserves a block of rooms in a local hotel for out-of-town wedding guests. The groom is also responsible for arranging lodging for any long-distance ushers, if needed. (He may choose to pay for this cost, as his gift to them.)

Helps the bride research, hire, and oversee contract details for one or more specific areas of the wedding—unless involved in everything. Many couples target key areas—for example, music, liquor, and photography—as the groom's responsibility.

Stands in the receiving line (if there is one) with the bride.

May be announced by bandleader with the bride (after the wedding party)—to all reception guests.

Dances a first dance to a preselected song with the bride. Can also dance during the same song with both mothers and the honor attendant (see Chapter 13, "Your Reception"). Later in the reception, he might dance again with his mother to a preselected song (see Chapter 14, "Wedding Music").

Responds to the best man's toast at the reception. The groom should rise to thank the best man for his good wishes, then toast his bride and thank her parents for hosting the celebration.

Takes time before leaving the reception to spend a few moments alone with his parents.

Sends thank-you notes, together with his bride, to acknowledge each gift (see Chapter 17, "Wedding Gifts").

The Honor Attendant's Role

The role can be filled by anyone who is very close to the bride—single or married, young or old, usually female. The matron of honor is a married woman, the maid of honor is a single woman, and the maiden of honor is a young girl or child. A male might be called an honor attendant (see "New Attendants' Roles" section). You may choose your sister, a longtime friend, favorite cousin, or roommate. Some brides have asked their mother or grandmother, or a favorite aunt, to fill this role. *Note:* You needn't ask your fiancé's sister to be your honor attendant unless she also happens to be a friend. If you have two sisters, or two best friends, ask both to be honor attendants and divide the duties between them.

THE HONOR ATTENDANT:

Assists the bride with prewedding tasks whenever possible. There are no responsibilities that necessarily set an honor attendant apart from the bridesmaids during the engagement months. She might help address invitations and take charge of recording shower gifts.

Arranges a date to have all bridesmaids' gowns fitted. A lot of logistics are involved in coordinating the schedules of several bridesmaids for fittings and prewedding festivities. It helps if the honor attendant oversees all the details, making sure all the bridesmaids know where they have to be and when. She might even send out a "wedding newsletter" to all attendants—to communicate information about clothing, travel plans, and prewedding parties (see Appendix, under Chapter 4, "Planning Your Wedding"). On the wedding day, the honor attendant acts as team leader to the bridesmaids, making sure that accessories are in place, and that the bride's party is on time for the ceremony.

Pays for her entire wedding outfit, except the flowers. The bride may offer to help out with, or completely cover these expenses, as her thank-you gift.

a pregnant attendant

Today, pregnancy does not rule out an attendant's participation in the wedding ceremony, as long as both the bride and the mother-to-be feel comfortable with the role. Below are some questions to discuss and consider.

- How pregnant will the attendant be by the wedding date? Is she due near the wedding date?

- Will the attendant be uncomfortable standing at the altar for a long period of time? If so, arrange to have chairs set up for the entire wedding party.

- What style of dress could she wear to match what the other bridesmaids will wear? What will her dress size be at the time of the wedding? Can you order extra material to enlarge her dress, just in case it doesn't fit?

- What other positions of honor might she fill if she chooses not to walk down the aisle? Perhaps she might read a poem or Scripture, sit near the guest-book table, carry a bouquet, and be escorted to the first or second pew before the first attendant walks down the aisle.

Attends all prewedding parties and may host one with the other attendants. Along with the other bridesmaids, she may co-host a shower, lunch or tea for the bride, or a wedding breakfast the morning of the wedding for the bride and her close female relatives and friends.

Greets the ceremony officiant and shows him or her where the ceremony will be performed, if it's a home wedding. The bride and her immediate family will be too busy to deal with these details.

Precedes the bride and her father down the aisle. Two honor attendants might walk side-by-side in the procession and recession.

Arranges the bride's train and veil, holds the bride's bouquet as she stands next to her during the ceremony. Two honor attendants divide the responsibilities for veil, train, bouquet, and ring.

Holds the groom's ring during the ceremony, until it is needed. The honor attendant might slip it onto her finger or thumb or carry it in a hidden pocket for safekeeping.

May sign the marriage certificate if witnesses are required by law. The witness, who must be at least 18 in order to sign a legal document, and the maid or matron of honor, do not have to be the same person. For example, if the bride's best friend breaks her leg and can't walk down the aisle, she could still be designated as the witness and sign the certificate. A second-time bride might choose to have her young daughter as the honor attendant, then designate someone of legal age to be the legal witness.

Stands next to the groom in the receiving line and sits on his left at the head table if it's a seated reception. Once the receiving line disperses, she's free to enjoy the reception as an honored guest.

May be announced—with the best man—to all reception guests immediately before the newlyweds.

Can dance with the best man, then the groom, during the newlyweds' first dance.

Takes time out to help the bride bustle her train, remove her headpiece, and change for the honeymoon. She should be alert to the bride's needs throughout the wedding and be available to run short errands, such as retrieving accessories from the changing room. She may also take charge of bringing the bride's gown home or to a dry cleaner, and with the best man, may deposit any gifts of checks or money in the bank while the couple are on their honeymoon (first listing the guests' names and the amount of each gift). She may also be asked to move gifts from the wedding site to the newlyweds' home.

The Best Man's Role

This indispensable role is usually filled by the groom's most trustworthy friend or relative. His brother, cousin, best friend, father, or even a close female friend—called an honor attendant (see the "New Attendants' Roles" section)—are all appropriate choices. The best man's duties are many and varied. He usually organizes the bachelor party, is chief of staff at the wedding, toastmaster at the reception, and personal aide and adviser to the groom. Although any of his tasks may be assigned to one of the ushers, the best man is expected to hold the bride's ring during the ceremony, offer the first toast, and just generally lighten the groom's load.

THE BEST MAN:

Checks on such wedding details as accommodations for out-of-town ushers.

Sees that the groom is properly outfitted and at the ceremony site on time for the ceremony. The best man is the groom's personal bodyguard/valet for the hours leading up to the wedding.

Hands the ceremony officiant a sealed envelope with his fee (from the groom) immediately after the ceremony. He will also make sure any altar servers are remembered with a gift, cash, or whatever is recommended.

May sign the marriage license as a witness. The officiant will file the license at the municipal hall after the wedding, and may give the couple a copy on their wedding day. It is the best man's job to make sure the groom knows where this copy is at the end of the wedding.

Carries the bride's wedding ring down the aisle. (He may keep it in a pocket; check first for holes.) At the appropriate moment in the ceremony, he hands it to the officiant.

Oversees the ushers, making sure that all are uniformly dressed (e.g., cummerbunds are pleat-side up), thoroughly briefed, and at the ceremony site at the appointed hour. Someone will have to remind ushers how to properly seat guests (see "The Bridesmaids' and Ushers' Roles" section).

May stand in the receiving line or circulate among guests. Attendants' participation in this tradition is optional.

May be announced—with the honor attendant—to all reception guests, immediately before the newlyweds.

Can dance with the honor attendant, then the bride, during the newlyweds' first dance. Later, at the reception, he should dance with any single attendants or guests. The best man should also encourage the ushers to do the same.

Sits to the right of the bride, if it's a seated reception, and proposes the first toast to the new couple. The best man should rise, raise his glass, mention the couple by name and his relationship to them. It is also traditional to offer a wish for health, happiness, and prosperity (see Chapter 13, "Your Reception").

why you should have a wedding party

- You'll have people to share in the excitement and planning.
- You'll have help with such duties as shopping, addressing invitations, etc.
- You'll have help on the wedding day with errands, changing, bustling your gown, and dealing with the caterer.
- Close friends and relatives might be hurt if they're left out.

Collects any congratulatory notes or faxes and reads them aloud if the couple wish, after the toasts. He makes sure these documents get back to the couple's home after the wedding.

He may also introduce other guests. This will help make guests feel comfortable and get them mingling.

Ensures that the reception goes as planned, and that no unpleasant practical jokes are played on the bride and groom. In particular, he is the guardian of the couple's luggage until they leave the reception and makes sure it does not disappear and is not tampered with (it should be locked in the car's trunk).

He makes sure that the windshield of the honeymoon car isn't overdecorated. For safety, the driver's view should be unobstructed. Also, he should make sure that only removable materials are used to decorate the car (no paint).

Escorts the bride and groom to the limousine or car, or may drive the couple to the airport or hotel. As they leave, he hands over any keys, tickets, and baggage checks given to him for safekeeping.

Sees to it that all the men's rental clothes are returned to the formalwear store the first business day after the wedding.

With the honor attendant, he may make sure that any gifts of money received at the wedding are deposited in the bank (after making a list of guests and amount of each gift). The honor attendant may take the checks, the best man the cash, or vice versa.

New Attendants' Roles

Some brides choose a *man of honor* (as their honor attendant) or a male attendant (instead of bridesmaid) when they want to include a close male friend or family member in the bridal party. The groom may choose a woman to fill many of the traditional roles of the best man (she's referred to as an honor attendant) or a *female usher*. These new roles can be incorporated into the most traditional wedding if done tastefully. Inform wedding professionals, such as photographers, in advance that you have nontraditional attendants, to ensure that they are not left out of photos or inserted by the photographer into traditional portrait positions (the male attendant with the ushers, the best woman with the bridesmaids).

THE MAN OF HONOR/MALE ATTENDANT/BEST WOMAN/FEMALE USHER:

Helps run errands and address invitation envelopes. Assists in many of the ways that other attendants might be helpful.

Should not have to perform awkward duties usually reserved for an individual the same sex as the bride or groom. A bride should not ask a man to attend all-female showers (it would be awkward) or ask him to help bustle her gown at the reception (her bridesmaids, who will be allowed into rest rooms and fitting rooms, can assist). Similarly, a groom should not expect his female attendant to try on tuxedos with him or attend the bachelor party (unless it is co-ed).

Usually wears the same attire as the other attendants of his/her sex in the wedding party. A male attendant to the bride can be given some distinction with a unique boutonniere, vest, or bow tie.

A male attendant walks down the aisle with the bridesmaids and stands with them during the ceremony. If the bridesmaids are being escorted by ushers during the recessional, the bride's male attendant can escort an unaccompanied female family member, such as the bride's grandmother. Another option: Each attendant can walk back up the aisle alone.

A female honor attendant to the groom stands beside the groom at the altar if she's filling the role of best man.

May be announced—with the best man or honor attendant—before the wedding party and before the newlyweds, to all reception guests.

Can dance with other attendants during the newlyweds' first dance.

The Bridesmaids' and Ushers' Roles

The number of bridesmaids and ushers in your ceremony will depend on its size and style. At a small, informal wedding, you may have just one maid or matron of honor and a best man. At a large, formal wedding, you may have twelve or more. (You will need at least one usher to seat every 50 guests, to avoid seating delays.) Don't worry about having an equal number of male and female attendants: the clergymember will arrange the aesthetics of the procession and altar lineup. And remember, attendants do not have to walk up and down the aisle in pairs (some of the ushers can escort a bridesmaid on each arm, for example).

It is the bride's and groom's prerogative to choose attendants from among their close friends and relatives. Although it's not necessary, it is thoughtful to invite at least one of the groom's sisters to be a bridesmaid and one of the bride's brothers to be an usher. If one of your attendants is married, it is *not* necessary to invite his or her spouse to be in the wedding party. If you and your fiancé *do* ask a couple to be in the wedding, they need not be paired in the recession (an usher can escort a bridesmaid, even if his wife is the matron of honor). And if an attendant's spouse, girlfriend, or boyfriend is not in the wedding party, you don't have to seat them together at the reception (see Chapter 13, "Your Reception").

If a bridesmaid or usher drops out at the last minute for whatever reason, remember that you do not need balanced pairs for the procession and recession. (Besides, it is impolite to ask someone else to stand in at such a late date.) Send flowers and wedding keepsakes (a table favor, for example) to the attendant who wanted to be there but couldn't.

solving bridesmaids' dilemmas— without hurting feelings

- **A friend has hinted around at being your maid of honor—yet you have no intention of asking her. How do you break the news without ruining the friendship?** Share your feelings in a way that doesn't spark a major fight (i.e., *don't* say something insensitive like, "I just don't feel close to you anymore.") Tell her it's a difficult decision and that you value her friendship. Thoughtfully explain why so-and-so is a more logical candidate. Maybe she introduced you to your fiancé or helped you through a particularly tough time.

- **You have two sisters or two best friends (or any combination thereof) that you adore. Which one do you ask to be maid of honor?** Don't play King Solomon. If you have two sisters or two best friends, ask them each to be in your wedding. Split duties among them—one can help you shop for shoes, the other can arrange a schedule for bridesmaids to have their dresses fitted. Have them both stand with you during the ceremony.

- **You were a bridesmaid in a friend's wedding four years ago, and since then you've lost touch. Should you invite her to be in your wedding party to reciprocate?** You're under no obligation to include someone as a bridesmaid just because you were in her wedding party years ago. If you don't feel close to her, she probably feels the same about you. *She might feel as uncomfortable as you if you asked her to be in the wedding party.*

(continued)

(continued)

- **Your sister is 15 years older than you, and your mom is pressuring you to ask her to be your maid of honor. You'd rather ask your best friend. What should you do?** If your sister is married but your best friend isn't, let your sister be a matron of honor and your friend be a maid of honor. Or, ask your sister to take part in the wedding in some other honored way—say by reading a piece of Scripture during the ceremony.

Custom dictates that bridesmaids and ushers are close to the bride's age. If you have sisters or cousins between the ages of nine and fourteen, however, you may ask them to participate as junior bridesmaids (see "The Child Attendants' Roles" section, and Chapter 7, "Wedding Clothes").

THE BRIDESMAIDS:

Offer to run errands, address invitation envelopes, and help the bride in any way they can. They may scout out bridesmaids' dresses, research hotels, write place cards, or assemble favors.

Are invited to all prewedding parties and may co-host a bridesmaids' lunch or bachelorette party. Consideration should be given to out-of-town attendants when planning events for which they may have to travel. If most bridesmaids are long-distance, showers can be planned for the week of the wedding, when everyone will be in one location (see Chapter 3, "Prewedding Parties").

Usually pay for their own wedding outfit, chosen by the bride. As a gift to her attendants, the bride may assume the entire clothing expense for her bridesmaids, or present them with an accessory to be worn on the wedding day. (Junior bridesmaids' dresses are usually paid for by their parents.)

Pick up their bouquets at the bride's home an hour or so before the ceremony, unless all the flowers are being delivered directly to the ceremony site. It is customary for the bridesmaids to also participate in the prewedding photograph session at the bride's house or in the dressing room at the ceremony site.

Walk first in the procession. Junior bridesmaids precede the maid of honor in the procession. Bridesmaids usually stand at the bride's side during the ceremony. Younger attendants stand next to the bridesmaids.

Walk back up the aisle alone or escorted by groomsmen. Junior bridesmaids need no partners in the recession.

May greet guests in the receiving line. Some brides and grooms, however, prefer to have their attendants circulate among guests.

May be announced—with the wedding party—to all reception guests, before the newlyweds.

Can dance with the ushers during the newlyweds' first dance.

Sit alternately with the ushers at the head table, if there is one.

Along with single attendants and guests, are often called onto the dance floor or into a hallway to catch the bride's bouquet.

If there is no honor attendant, one bridesmaid, designated by the bride, may take responsibility for the wedding gown if the bride changes at the reception. After the couple depart for their honeymoon, this bridesmaid carefully hangs or packs the gown to take to the bride's home or to a dry cleaner to be professionally cleaned and preserved.

THE USHERS:

Attend all prewedding parties the groom goes to and may host a bachelor party.

Provide their own wedding clothes, renting the appropriate formal attire if they don't own it. The groom supplies the boutonnieres, neckwear, and gloves when these are not included in the rental package. He may also offer, as a gift, a shirt, cuff links, or other accessories.

May pick up ceremony flowers and the aisle runner from the florist. This is usually done the day of the wedding.

Seat the guests at the wedding ceremony. Ushers should arrive at the ceremony site forty-five minutes to an hour before the ceremony begins. They assemble near the entrance and review any special seating requests by families.

Step forward and offer their right arm to each woman, as guests arrive. When a couple enters, traditionally the woman takes the usher's arm, and the man follows them down the aisle. Ushers make quiet conversation as they walk unhurriedly down the aisle with guests. A new trend at informal ceremonies: Ushers just lead people to their seats. As they greet each guest, they can simply say, "Please follow me."

Seat the oldest woman first if several guests arrive together. Unless a man is elderly and needs assistance, he may simply be accompanied to his seat.

Ask if the guest is a friend of the bride or the groom if he or she does not have a pew card and is unknown to the usher. In a Christian ceremony, the bride's guests are seated on the left (facing the altar); the groom's guest on the right. The opposite is true for Jewish ceremonies.

If one side has many more guests than the other, explain that everyone will be sitting together. This will give all guests the best view.

Unroll the aisle runner and tie pew ribbons (if used). Usually, the groom appoints two ushers to handle the aisle runner and pew ribbons.

Participate in both the procession and the recession. Ushers escort mothers, as well as elderly or disabled guests, from the church or synagogue first.

Loosen pew ribbons after the recession. Two ushers loosen the ribbons at the end of each pew, then pause at the side of each, signaling guests to file out row by row, from front to back.

Are prepared to direct guests to parking and restroom facilities, and to the reception site. They also make sure all guests have rides.

Escort guests from their cars—and back to them after the ceremony—with umbrellas if it rains.

Make certain the ceremony site is cleared of the wedding party's belongings before leaving. This avoids unnecessary trips back later in the day.

the head usher

- The groom designates one groomsman as head usher to supervise special seating arrangements.
- If the bride or groom has divorced parents (see Chapter 8, "Your Wedding Ceremony"), one parent may be seated in the first row, one in the third row.
- If there are elderly guests, they'll be seated up front.
- If there are guests in wheelchairs or on crutches, they'll be seated at the front or end of pews, near family and friends.
- If the bride and groom do not each have brothers in the wedding party to seat their respective mothers, the head usher will seat them.

Sit at the head table, if there is one, but do not stand in the receiving line, if there is one. Ushers circulate among guests at the reception and help make sure that everyone has a good time. They also dance with the bridesmaids and single female guests.

Can be announced—with the wedding party—to all reception guests, before the newlyweds.

Can dance with the bridesmaids during the newlyweds' first dance. Should also invite single attendants and guests to dance throughout the reception.

Are alert to potential problems. Ushers (as well as bridesmaids) should keep their ears and eyes tuned to any difficulties that might interrupt the smooth flow of the reception. They may help to resolve problems or questions that the caterer, photographer, or other wedding-service professionals have.

Propose toasts to the bride and groom. After the best man makes the first toast, and the groom thanks him (perhaps followed by the bride), the ushers may keep the festive comments going.

Decorate the couple's going-away car. The ushers may drape the car with flower garlands, streamers, balloons, and signs that won't be hazardous on the road. The windshield is left clear.

The Child Attendants' Roles

Having young children in the wedding party is a popular European custom that can delight guests and add charm to the ceremony—especially if they're supervised and well behaved. When the children are from a previous marriage, including them in the festivities will go a long way toward making them feel included in their parents' lives (see Chapter 11, "Remarriage"). A young son may even escort his mother, the bride, down the aisle. If no children are to be part of the ceremony, you may want to have them pass out programs in the sanctuary, or oversee the signing of the guest book.

Very young children who are not often dressed up or are never in a crowd may behave unpredictably. Consider having only one or two child attendants, between the ages of four and eight, as *pages, ring bearer(s),* or *flower girl(s)*—the most often included child attendant. *Junior bridesmaids, junior ushers,* and *candlelighters* (for safety's sake) are between the ages of nine and fourteen. Although traditionally a boy, today the *ring bearer* may be a girl. *Candlelighters,* common in some regions, are often two boys from either (or both) family(ies) who light the ceremony candles.

THE FLOWER GIRL:
May walk alone, with the ring bearer, or with another flower girl about the same height. The flower girl immediately precedes the bride down the aisle in the procession.

Dresses in a younger version of the bridesmaids' outfits. Usually, this is a tiny, floral print or all-white dress accented with a silk sash (no low back or neck). Another option: a white pinafore over a velvet dress, with black or white patent-leather shoes.

Traditionally carries a basket of rose petals to scatter in the bride's path. Due to the very real possibility of someone slipping on dropped petals, flower girls now often carry a tiny nosegay. The flower girl's flower arrangement should be the same front and back—so blossoms will look pretty no matter how they are held.

THE RING BEARER:

Immediately precedes the flower girl (if there is one) or the bride down the aisle. The ring bearer may also be paired with the flower girl or another ring bearer.

Balances a white lace or satin pillow with a faux bride's ring tied to the center with ribbons, or stitched down lightly with satin thread. (A second ring bearer might carry a pillow with a groom's ring attached.) The real rings are safe with the honor attendants. After the ceremony, turn the cushion upside down to hide the dummy ring.

If a boy, the ring bearer wears a satin or velvet suit (perhaps a dark-blue Eton suit, or white shorts, a navy blazer, and white or blue knee socks). If a girl, a pretty dress, similar to what a flower girl wears, is appropriate.

THE PAGES/TRAIN BEARERS:

Follow the bride down the aisle and carry her train. Pages are very common in English weddings. If pages are four to six years old, Eton suits may be worn. If older, they dress to match the ushers. If the page is a girl, she dresses similarly to a flower girl, or if older, to a junior bridesmaid.

Always walk down and up the aisle in pairs and are about the same height. Generally, they are little boys, but girls may also carry the bride's train. (Pages are needed only when the wedding gown has a very long train.)

THE CANDLELIGHTERS:

Wear dress clothes similar to junior ushers and junior bridesmaids. Dress styles should be complementary, but not identical to bridesmaids' gowns.

Step forward to light the candles just before the mother of the bride is seated. Ceremony musicians may begin a new prelude selection as the candlelighters step forward.

Snuff the candles after the recession, as guests are filing out of the sanctuary. The ceremony musicians may continue to play selections in a postlude.

child attendants' dos & don'ts

DO include child attendants in the rehearsal so they can practice their parts and become familiar with the site.

DON'T invite children to attend an evening rehearsal dinner or other prewedding parties.

DO invite child attendants to the reception, along with their parents.

DO seat the parents of child attendants on the aisle, in one of the front pews. Parents are familiar faces, and can offer encouragement to their children as they walk past. Children may also sit with them after going down the aisle. This eliminates the risk of young attendants fidgeting while standing at the altar and distracting everyone's attention from the ceremony.

DO assign a relative (or hire a baby-sitter) to supervise young attendants at the reception. A teenage guest might set up a play area with activities and snacks. Or include a children's table in your seating plan. (Arrange for an adult or teen to supervise; provide coloring books and crayons.)

DO choose outfits in which young attendants will be comfortable, and which are appropriate for their age (nothing too low cut for young girls).

DON'T insist on a cummerbund, bow tie, or other accessory if a child resists wearing it.

DO thank the children for their participation with a gift (a teddy bear or charm bracelet). Thank their parents, as well, perhaps with a framed photograph of their child walking down the aisle.

Follow these etiquette tips if your parents are divorced.

- Your father may still escort you down the aisle and give you his blessing at the altar.

- The parent who raised you sits in the front row. (See Chapter 8, "Your Wedding Ceremony.")

- If you like, split father of the bride duties between your father and stepfather. *Both* may escort you down the aisle, if they are comfortable with the idea. (For example, one can escort you down the first half of the aisle, the other the rest of the way.) Or have one do the honor during the ceremony and the other dance with you at the reception (see Chapter 13, "Your Reception").

- Be certain each parent has a partner if invited onto the dance floor during the first dance.

- Do not position your parents together in the receiving line. Even if they're on friendly terms, guests may misunderstand their relationship.

- Seat divorced parents at different reception tables (see Chapter 13, "Your Reception").

The Mother of the Bride's Role

Your mother is the official hostess of your wedding, unless you are serving in that capacity yourself, or some other close relative or friend is filling this role. Her duties will vary, depending on whether you're planning an out-of-town wedding *and* on the amount of free time you and she have.

THE MOTHER OF THE BRIDE:

Helps the bride compile the guest list. She, or the bride, should tell the groom how many people can be included on his and his parents' guest list.

Helps arrange the details of the ceremony and reception. She may be the main contact between the bride and all wedding-service professionals (unless a wedding consultant is hired)—particularly if the bride lives in another city.

May assist with selecting the bride's wedding outfit and trousseau. It is the bride's choice whether her mother comes with her to shop for the wedding dress.

Is invited to most prewedding parties. The mother of the bride attends (but never hosts) all showers. She also attends the prewedding breakfast (if there is one). She is generally not invited to the bridesmaids' lunch or bachelorette party (see Chapter 3, "Prewedding Parties").

Helps keep track of wedding gifts. She can see that they are displayed attractively in a safe place. She may also be invited to advise the couple regarding their wedding gift registry.

May scout out reception sites, photographers, florists, caterers, and other wedding-service professionals—especially if the bride lives out of town. She can purchase two identical wedding planners (one for herself and one for the bride) and schedule regular long-distance calls—if the bride lives far away—to communicate information.

Chooses her dress first, then informs the groom's mother of her selection. The wedding attire of the two mothers should be the same in length, similar in style (formality), and complementary in color.

Keeps the bride's father and the parents of the groom posted on the progress of the wedding plans. The groom's parents will want to feel included in the planning process.

Runs errands as the need arises. These might include mailing and following up on invitations or addressing and mailing announcements and change-of-address cards the day of the wedding (see Chapter 5, "Invitations & Announcements").

May also give the bride family heirlooms to wear on the wedding day (the pearls *she* wore when she got married, a grandmother's lace handkerchief, a blue garter, or a family sixpence to tuck in her shoe).

May accompany the bride down the aisle. This traditional Jewish wedding-ceremony custom, in which the mother *and* father of the bride flank the bride and link arms (or hold hands), as they all walk down the aisle, is being adopted by many couples in all religions.

Is seated in the first pew on the bride's side of the aisle. If walking the bride down the aisle with the bride's father, she will slip into the front row with him after leaving the bride at the altar (if not standing under the *huppah* at a Jewish ceremony). If not walking the bride down the aisle, the mother of the bride is the last to be seated before the procession begins. If her son is an usher, he escorts his mother to her seat. Otherwise, the head usher does the honor.

Is the first guest to be ushered out, with her husband or escort, after the recession is over. Two ushers unhook pew rib-bons (if used) and stand at each row, motioning guests to file out in order.

Serves as official hostess. The mother of the bride greets guests at the head of the receiving line, sits in a place of honor at the parents' table, makes sure everyone has a good time, and stays until the reception's end to say good-bye to guests.

Joins the newlyweds on the dance floor with the father of the bride during the first dance. If divorced or widowed, she dances with her escort or the best man. She may also dance with her new son-in-law at some time during this dance.

Is on hand to keep the bride calm, smooth out last-minute crises, and offer moral support throughout the wedding.

The Father of the Bride's Role

As the official host of the reception, the father of the bride often plays a prominent role in prewedding decisions and organization on the day of the wedding. Although today expenses are most often split among the couple and both families (see Chapter 4, "Planning Your Wedding"), the father of the bride still plays a major role in wedding finances.

THE FATHER OF THE BRIDE:

May share in scouting out wedding sites and assorted wedding services. How much the father of the bride involves himself in wedding plans varies with family situation and interest.

May set up travel arrangements for out-of-town guests. Many fathers pick up arriving relatives and friends at the station or airport, and arrange for rides to and from prewedding parties and the wedding.

Might draw maps of the various wedding sites with directions. These may be printed and sent to guests as invitation enclosures (see Chapter 5, "Invitations & Announcements").

Gets fitted for formalwear that blends with that of the groom and other men in

special members of the wedding

- Ask young girls or boys to distribute Mass books, yarmulkes, or wedding programs, or to serve as acolytes during the ceremony.

- Ask an uncle to read a Scripture or poem at the ceremony.

- Ask family members to join in "sentence prayers"—each adding a line to continue the prayer.

- Include grandparents in the procession (traditionally a Jewish custom).

- Give your grandmother a corsage or nosegay; your grandfather, a boutonniere.

- Ask children to take charge of the guest book, pass out groom's cake or packets of birdseed, or help with refreshments.

- Designate friends and relatives as "persons of honor." Ask them to greet guests at the door, direct them to rest rooms, help seat guests, carry the guest book at the cocktail hour, or hand out programs. They need not walk down the aisle or wear a tuxedo or a bridesmaid's gown. Still, you might order a small bouquet, corsage, or a boutonniere to honor them; ask them to wear the same color dress or suit as your attendants.

- Some couples include well-behaved dogs in the procession. They may be decked out in a flower collar and walked down the aisle by a friend or family member.

the wedding party. He should inform the father of the groom if he must be fitted for matching formalwear. (Traditionally, all men walking down the aisle wear matching formalwear.)

Rides to the ceremony with the bride in the limousine and escorts her into the ceremony site. Prior to the procession, he waits in the vestibule with her.

Walks the bride down the aisle (perhaps with her mother on the bride's other arm). If the bride's father is deceased, her brother, uncle, or other male relative; a close family friend; or an usher may escort her down the aisle, then serve as her mother's escort for the reception or the bride's mother may walk her down the aisle if the bride feels closer to her than to any male relative or friend. The bride may also choose to walk alone.

At the altar, offers his support or blessing (what has traditionally been called "giving away the bride"). Many clergymembers will offer the traditional or updated wording for this part of the wedding ceremony.

Joins the bride's mother in the first pew. If divorced, he may sit in the third pew (see Chapter 8, "Your Wedding Ceremony").

May mingle with guests, instead of standing in the receiving line. If the bride prefers, her father may stand in the receiving line, to the left of her mother (unless they're divorced) (see Chapter 13, "Your Reception").

Keeps an eye on the bar and champagne supply and alerts banquet manager if more is needed. Also is attentive to any other problems that may arise and may speak with the banquet manager, wedding consultant, or bandleader to resolve them.

Joins the newlyweds on the dance floor—with the mother of the bride (unless they've divorced, in which case the custom may be omitted)—during the first dance. Later in the reception, he dances with the bride to a preselected song appropriate for a dance with his daughter.

May make a short toast or welcoming speech. At Jewish weddings, the father of the bride traditionally offers blessings over the wine and bread before the reception meal begins. At all weddings, he may make a toast after the best man gives the first toast, and the groom (and perhaps the bride) have responded.

Leaves the reception last, after bidding all guests good-bye. He may also settle outstanding bills at this time with caterer, bandleader, coat-check, rest-room, and parking attendants.

The Parents of the Groom's Roles

Although their roles are smaller than those of the bride's parents, they are considered co-hosts of the wedding, regardless of whether or not they've contributed financially. It is a gracious gesture to include their names on the wedding invitation (see Chapter 5, "Invitations & Announcements").

THE PARENTS OF THE GROOM:

Contact the bride's parents by phone or letter. They should let them know they're pleased about the upcoming marriage. They should also arrange a prewedding get-together with the bride's parents—at their home or in a restaurant (see Chapter 1, "Your Engagement").

May host an engagement party (after the bride's family first hosts one), or lunch to introduce the bride to their friends (see Chapter 3, "Prewedding Parties").

Provide a list of an agreed-upon number of guests. Included are full names, titles, addresses, zip codes and telephone numbers.

Let bride know about family traditions (ethnic dances or festive dishes) to consider including in the celebration. A wedding is a merging of both families.

Consult with the bride's parents on the proper wedding attire. The dress of the groom's mother should be the same in length as that of the mother of the bride, and in a shade that complements the wedding color scheme. The father of the groom should wear an appropriate suit or jacket—if a tuxedo is not required. (See Chapter 7, "Wedding Clothes.")

Traditionally, they do pay for some wedding expenses. These may include the engagement and wedding rings, marriage license, clergy fees, corsages, boutonnieres, bride's bouquet, ushers' gifts, liquor, music, and honeymoon.

May give the couple a special gift. Possibilities include a family heirloom, china, silver, or crystal, shares of stock, or perhaps a monetary gift to be put toward a car, a home, or the honeymoon.

Are invited to all prewedding parties. The mother of the groom attends (but never hosts) all showers. She also attends the prewedding breakfast, if there is one (see Chapter 3, "Prewedding Parties").

Attend the rehearsal and practice any special duties (lighting the Unity Candle or reading Scripture).

Traditionally host the rehearsal dinner. If the parents of the groom are from out of town, the bride's mother may suggest a site or caterer. (The groom's parents are invited to the rehearsal dinner if they are not hosting it.)

Arrive fifteen minutes before the ceremony's scheduled starting time. The mother of the groom is escorted to her seat by the head usher (unless she has another son in the wedding party), followed by the father of the groom. As honored guests, the groom's parents are seated in the first row on the groom's side of the aisle (unless they will stand under the *huppah* at a Jewish ceremony). If his parents are divorced and remarried, or not on amicable terms, the parent who raised him is seated in the first pew, his other parent in the third (behind grandparents and siblings).

Escort the groom (one on each side) down the aisle, if the couple chooses to include this traditional Jewish wedding-ceremony custom.

The groom's mother stands second in the receiving line, after the bride's mother and before the bride. The groom's father usually mingles with guests; otherwise, he stands to the left of his wife in line, before the bride.

Sit at the parents' table with the bride's parents. The wedding day is the perfect time to establish warm relations for future holidays to come. If the reception is a large one, each family can host their own table. The same is true when parents are divorced.

Dance with the newlyweds. During the first dance, they may be invited onto the dance floor together, or to dance with the newlyweds. If they've divorced, this custom may be omitted. Later in the reception, after the bride's special dance with her father, the groom should ask the band to play a meaningful song to which he'll dance with his mother. The father of the groom may also ask the bride to dance sometime during the reception.

May be served the fifth and sixth pieces of wedding cake (after the newlyweds each cut pieces to feed each other, and after the bride's parents are served). This is a lovely gesture of respect.

Play a more visible role if they are solely sponsoring the wedding. The father of the groom then oversees the wedding-reception personnel. The mother of the groom presides as hostess and first greeter in the receiving line. Both parents stand near the door for good-byes.

WEDDING CLOTHES

Ever since Britain's Queen Victoria caused a stir by choosing to wear a majestic white dress created especially for her wedding to Prince Albert—at a time when most women simply donned their best dress for the occasion—women have devoted weeks, months, even entire childhoods to the contemplation of this utterly romantic garment. Your wedding gown is the dress of a lifetime—and will set the style and tone for the entire wedding. Before you shop, have fun and explore your fantasies. Look through magazines with friends, and don't forget to surf the Internet; mark the pages of anything that catches your eye, whether it's a particular fabric, cut, trim, or the entire dress. You may fall in love with a specific dress, then plan your wedding around it. However, it's usually best to determine the day, time, and formality of your reception first, then shop for the most beautiful and appropriate look (see the "Guide to Wedding Clothes" chart for the appropriate style of dress for each type of wedding, daytime and evening).

Once you've found your dream dress, select bridesmaids' and ushers' attire that is complementary in formality and style. Mothers' dresses should also complement the wedding color scheme.

Shopping for Your Gown

Choosing a wedding gown is a unique experience, one you might want to share with a close friend or your mother. They can provide valuable input, insight, and honesty (just don't shop with an entourage—all the varying opinions will make your head spin). Before you begin shopping, think about how you picture yourself walking down the aisle. Will you have a formal church wedding, an intimate garden ceremony, or an informal ceremony on the beach? You should choose a dress that fits the formality of your celebration. As you familiarize yourself with what styles are available, you'll begin to narrow down your preferences (see Appendix, under Chapter 7, "Wedding Clothes").

Finding a gown that suits your personality, flatters your figure, *and* meets your budget may seem like a daunting task, but you can shop smart without compromising on style. To get the best service and quality for your money, don't leave home without first reading these savvy shopping tips:

Start shopping at least nine months before the wedding. You'll be able to shop for good prices rather than settle on a dress because time is running out. Order your gown at least six months before the wedding. This allows three to four months for the dress to be made and delivered to the store, another two months for fittings and portraits.

Make an appointment. Bridal shops are busy places, and the most popular wedding months are May through October. Remember that other brides will be shopping nine months before their wedding date and having final gown fittings the month before their wedding date. For the most relaxed, attentive service, avoid Saturdays and evenings.

Take advantage of the bridal-shop consultant's expertise. He or she can recommend cleaning or heirloom services (see Appendix, under Chapter 7, "Wedding Clothes"), wedding pros like photographers and caterers, as well as advice on what formalwear looks are appropriate for the time and style of your wedding.

If you are plus-sized or concerned about specific figure flaws, stick with long, A-line, or simple styles. In general, stay away from lightweight, clingy fabrics, and pay close attention to the cut of the dress. The most flattering gown is the one that helps balance your proportions.

If you are petite, avoid exaggerated details. The point is to elongate the body, so proportion is very important here, as well—embellishments should flatter, not overwhelm you.

Tell the salespeople your price ceiling. This will save time—yours and theirs—because you'll only see gowns that are within your price range.

If you fall in love with a gown that's out of your budget, explore possibilities. Ask if the salon owner or bridal consultant can find you a similar dress that is priced more moderately, perhaps in poly-satin instead of silk satin, or with laces and beading that are applied by machine rather than by hand.

gown-shopping list

Here is a list of what to wear and bring when shopping for your gown:

- a strapless bra—to give you the versatility to try on all gown styles (you may buy a specific nude or white bra or bustier and a slip after selecting your gown)

- sheer control-top panty hose or regular sheer panty hose

- shoes the same heel height you'll wear on your wedding day (a one-and-a-half to two-inch heel is comfortable for dancing); buy wedding shoes to match the style of the dress before the first fitting

- The hairstyle you plan on wearing on your wedding day (certain hairpieces are better for hair worn up or down)

- photos or tearsheets of dress styles you like

- photos and/or description of ceremony and reception site

Ask about quality. Are the beads, crystals pearls or sequins sewed or glued on? Were appliqués applied by hand or machine? Can the gown be dry-cleaned? Ask, in advance, about on-the-spot cleaning advice for spills on the particular fabric of your gown.

Take advantage of discontinued samples or stock dresses. These gowns are usually reduced and often will look like new once they are dry-cleaned. Also consider out-of-season gowns, bridesmaids' dresses in white or ivory (for an informal wedding).

Inquire about special payment and layaway plans. Some shops offer minimal interest that isn't charged until the dress arrives. Make all payments by credit card or check. Never pay cash.

Get a price quote for alterations before buying your dress. Avoid major changes to the dress structure, such as reworking the neckline or repositioning the waist, which are costly.

Consult bridal stores about updating or restoring an heirloom veil. If you have your heart set on a veil and headpiece worn by your mother and grandmother, but worry that it looks faded or dated, find out how you can make it look more contemporary (see "Wearing an Heirloom Gown" section).

Ask for a description of the dress in writing (including fabric and lace types, neckline, and sleeves). This description will come in handy when talking with the florist, and coordinating the attire for the rest of the bridal party.

Put all points of the sale in a signed and countersigned contract or bill of sale. The best protection for you—and for the bridal salon—is to clearly list the specifications of the gown you have ordered and the terms of the sale. (See "Wedding-Dress Contract Tips" box.)

10 questions to ask before buying your gown

1. Does the store have a good reputation with recent brides and wedding consultants I've talked to? Have any complaints been lodged against the store with the Better Business Bureau?

2. Do the salespeople put me at ease?

3. Does the salesperson pay attention to my comments? Is she showing me the kinds of dresses I want to try on?

4. Does the salesperson seem genuine when she tells me how I look in a dress—or is she telling me only what I want to hear?

5. If I want a different neckline or sleeve on a gown, can it be ordered that way?

6. What are the store's alteration fees? Can I get those fees in writing?

7. How long will it take for the dress to come in after I place my order?

8. Can I place a rush order if necessary? Will there be an extra charge?

9. How much money do I need to put down for a deposit? When is the balance due?

10. Can I borrow the dress for my bridal portrait and then bring it back to the store for safe-keeping until my wedding day?

Your Fashion Dilemmas

Many questions will come to mind while you are finalizing your wedding-fashion decisions. Here are answers to a few of the more common ones:

Which fabrics would be most comfortable on a warm spring or summer day?
Organza—a light, stiff, sheer fabric; *chiffon*—a fluid, slightly sheer fabric woven of silk or rayon; *linen*—a stiffer, lightweight fabric that is best for structured couture dresses in simple designs (note: It wrinkles easily); *voile*—a sheer, fine fabric of cotton,

wedding-dress contract tips

Specify these points in a signed and countersigned contract or bill of sale.

- the dress's manufacturer, style number, size, and color (white, eggshell, ecru)

- embellishments (hand-embroidered Alençon lace, sequins, pearls, etc.)

- special order requests and costs

- the delivery date

- the price and payment schedule, deposit paid, and fitting and pressing costs

- the store's policy on refunds (there should be a 100 percent refund if the garment is never delivered) and cancellations

- the store's policy for gown storage and pickup (can the gown be borrowed for prewedding photo sessions and returned for safekeeping?)

silk, or rayon, that drapes easily; *Alençon* lace—a delicate, handmade pattern often used as an overlay on sheer fabrics.

Which gown fabrics are best for a fall or winter wedding? Choose year-round fabrics with a light, lush feel—*shantung, brocade, tulle, taffeta, satin.* Perhaps wear a gown with a full taffeta skirt and long sleeves of medium-weight lace. If you prefer a low-cut or strapless gown, cover up for the ceremony in a matching or lace jacket, hooded velvet cape, kimono-inspired coat, or silk shawl. For chilly evenings, snuggle in a fur or faux-fur wrap.

When should I choose my headpiece—when I select the gown or during my first fitting? If you have the stamina (and are sure about your wedding-day hairstyle) choose it when you choose your gown. Otherwise you can wait until the first fitting.

What is the best headpiece and veil-length for my gown? Your choice of headpiece and veil should be based on your height, proportions, face, hairstyle, and dress style. Proportions must be balanced: A ballgown calls for a headpiece with a longer veil. Choose a shoulder-length veil, flowers or jewelled hair clips to go with a short dress. Ask your bridal salon representative to help you experiment so that you can find the right headpiece and veil for your personality and dress.

What shoe styles are best for a wedding gown? For bridal footwear, select evening shoes in white or cream. Consider innovative styles: modern or medieval pumps, ballet slippers, or slingbacks, satin lace-up boots for Victorian wedding gowns. Select luxurious fabrics: brocade, linen, silk, and peau de soie. The mood of the shoe should match the mood of the gown. Wearing a Renaissance gown? Select a baroque, court-heeled shoe. Also echo your dress's trim or appliqués in your shoe details: rosettes, pearls, bows, or rhinestones.

Do I have to wear hosiery? It won't really show, anyway. Your ankles and legs may indeed show as you waltz around the dance floor, are swept up on a chair during the traditional *horah,* or when your groom removes your garter to toss it at the reception. However, you should do what is most comfortable and appropriate, given the tone of the wedding, the season, and your style of dress and footwear. If you do choose to wear hosiery, it should complement, not overpower, your gown. Consider ultra-sheer, shimmery hose in white, pearl, or pale pink.

Is there a way to bustle my gown for reception dancing? Most trains today are designed to "bustle" for the reception and dancing. Many manufacturers and bridal shops automatically sew in special fasteners to draw the fabric up to floor-length in back (ask if this is the case). If yours isn't, have your salon arrange for the alteration department to sew in snaps, hooks, or other methods of securing the train into a bustle. Bring your honor attendant along for the final dress fitting so she can learn how to bustle the train for you.

Today, many long and short dresses are made with detachable trains (which are fastened with Velcro™, hooks, buttons, or snaps). Sweep trains are short enough to maneuver without bustling. Or, have a loop attached to the train, to slip around your wrist for dancing.

We're getting married during the holidays. What fashion accents can I add to a Christmas wedding? Choose colors and details that evoke the spirit of the season. Consider velvet or doupioni silk gowns with fur collars, cuffs, or metallic embroidery, dresses in gold lace; metallic trimming. Choose gloves with a tartan trim or satin purse and shoes. Select jewel-tone bridesmaids' gowns—in ruby red, amethyst, or emerald green. (See Chapter 10, "Special Weddings & New Ways to Wed.")

Are there any special rules for choosing my wedding colors? The colors that you select will help set the tone that you want to convey, so be sure to give this some thought. Consider the setting and style of your wedding, and stick to just two or three complementary colors. In general, it's best to stay away from dark colors or jewel tones for summer weddings, and to avoid pastels or other pale shades in the winter months. White and taupe work all year round.

My fiancé and I, and our attendants, are all in the military. What should we wear? Men and women in a military wedding may wear the full ceremonial dress uniform of the appropriate service and rank—precedent is usually set by the groom. (Ushers not in the military may wear formalwear appropriate to the time and style of the wedding.) Brides almost always choose to wear a wedding gown (bridesmaids may also wear bridesmaids' dresses). A bride in uniform can carry a bouquet; grooms and ushers in uniform may wear appropriate military decorations —but never boutonnieres. The type of dress uniform that is worn is determined by season and regional regulations. States with warm weather may require summer dress longer than states with a cool season. (See Chapter 10, "Special Weddings & New Ways to Wed," and Appendix, under Chapter 10.) Also, be sure to check with the officer in charge of protocol for your branch of the military.

Sizing Your Gown

Your salesperson should measure your bust, waist, hips, and length—from shoulder or nape of neck to the floor. (Dress sizes usually differ by one inch.)

When deciding on the size of your gown, choose the size that matches the largest part of the gown. (For example, if your bust is 36 inches and your waist is 23 inches, order the size gown that fits a 36-inch bust; take in the waist.)

Order the size you are _that_ day. If your weight tends to fluctuate or you plan to lose some pounds before the wedding, schedule fittings six weeks to a month before the

flattering dress features for every body type

- Hourglass figure—a rounded V-neck or off-the-shoulder portrait neckline flatters a large chest; a dropped waist highlights a narrow waist; a V-shaped basque waist and full skirt slim waist and hips.

- Short waist—a princess shape creates a long, slim silhouette; a high-low waist lengthens the torso.

- Thick waist—an Empire line with skirt flowing from just below the bust creates a long, lean silhouette.

- Boyish figure—ornamentation at the neckline enhances the bust; a wide band of pleating at the waist or around the bodice adds dimension to a lanky upper body.

- Full figure—long, sheer sleeves slenderize arms, a V-neck and dropped V-waist deemphasize bust and hips.

- Small bust—flowers or other ornamentation around a strapless bodice balance a pear-shaped figure; bows or lace appliqués on a neckline add shape to a slim torso.

- Petite—a simple gown flatters a tiny figure; the long, fluid shape of a sheath or princess-line gown elongates; subtle shoulder detail, like delicate cap sleeves—or opting for strapless—keeps the focus up and adds height.

- Great legs—an above-the-knee sheath with detachable overskirt or a simple minidress lets you play up terrific legs.

wedding day, with the final fitting within ten days of the wedding (timing will depend on the workload of the seamstress). If you do lose weight, the gown can always be taken in. A too-small gown, however, cannot be made more than one size larger.

Fitting Your Gown

Since most gowns are made to order, you're not likely to find a shop that has samples of every dress in every size. However, if you are either petite or plus–sized, do call ahead and ask the salon if they carry samples in smaller or larger sizes, as this can make the entire experience more helpful and enjoyable for you. To get a sense of how a gown will look, a consultant will pin the gown to fit or have you try on a similar dress that fits. The gown you choose will be ordered in your size—most dresses can be made to fit any size—then altered to fit perfectly. Don't be surprised if the size that is ordered is larger than you generally wear. Wedding dresses are sized differently than ordinary clothes. For the best results:

Inquire in advance about the fee for alterations. Costs for alterations are not usually included in the price of the gown. Some shops charge a flat fee, others bill according to the work required, which can range from taking in the waist, shortening sleeves and hems, to adding appliqués or beadwork. If there is hem detail (such as lace), order the gown in the length you need, so the hem will not have to be altered.

Expect to return to the shop for at least two fittings. Three or four visits are sometimes necessary. Make and write the appointments in your calendar shortly after ordering your gown, so that the time is reserved on your schedule. And don't forget to bring along the appropriate bra, slip and hosiery to make sure you get an accurate fit.

Be sure that your gown is short enough. *The bottom line:* The hem of the gown should gently skim the front of the shoe's toe area. If the gown is too long, the front of the skirt will skim the floor, causing the gown to wrinkle and you to step on it. This is why it is important to bring your wedding shoes with you to all fittings.

Wedding-Dress Glossary

SILHOUETTES

Ball gown—fitted waist and bodice, full skirt.
Basque—natural waist with V-front.
Empire—small, scooped bodice, gathers at a high waist; a slender, yet elegant and graceful skirt.

Princess/A-line—slim-fitting; vertical seams flow from shoulders to hem. There is no seam on the waist.

Sheath—narrow, body-conscious style indented at the waist or sculpted, following the bust, waist, and hips.

Mermaid—narrow to knee, then flairs out.

LENGTHS AND TRAINS

Short—above-the-knee length.

Knee-length—hem just covers the knees.

High-low—hem falls from slightly below the knee to ankle length in front; ankle to train-length in back.

Mid-calf/Ballet-length—hem reaches to center of the calf or to ankle length.

Floor-length—hem fully skims the floor.

Sweep train—shortest train; extends back eight to twelve inches after touching floor.

Fishtail—a narrow train; same length as a sweep train.

Chapel train—trails three-and-one-half to four-and-one-half feet from the waist.

Semicathedral train—extends four-and-one-half to five-and-one-half feet from waist.

Cathedral—flows six-and-one-half to seven and-one-half feet from waist.

Extended-cathedral/Monarch train—cascades twelve feet from waist.

Watteau train—extends from upper back to floor.

FABRICS

Brocade—a Jacquard-woven fabric with raised designs.

Charmeuse—a lightweight, smooth, semi-lustrous satiny fabric.

Chiffon—delicately sheer, a thin, transparent fabric of silk or rayon with a soft finish.

Crepe—a silk or rayon fabric made with crepe yarn, with a slight pebbly texture.

Eyelet—an open-weave embroidery; may be allover or decorative.

Linen—a cloth made of flax, noted for its strength, coolness, and luster.

Moiré—a silk taffeta; wave-patterned to glisten like water when illuminated; dramatic.

Organdy—a sheer, transparent, crisp silk or rayon fabric; is sometimes printed or embroidered.

Organza—a sheer, crisp fabric like chiffon, but with a stiff finish.

Silk Gazar—a four-ply silk organza with a box weave.

Silk-faced satin—a smooth, lustrous silk fabric woven with a glossy face and dull back.

Silk Mikado—a crisp, woven fabric with a twill–like texture.

Shantung—a plain-weave silk or man-made fiber fabric; it has a rough texture, like slubs.

Taffeta—a crisp, smooth fabric with a small, crosswise rib.

Tulle—a fine, sheer, open-weave net in silk, nylon, or rayon; for skirts and veils.

LACES

There are many kinds of laces; below are today's most popular:

Alençon—a needlepoint lace with designs in deep relief on sheer net; originated in Alençon, France; can be reembroidered.

---

how to walk in a gown

Here are tips for walking—without tripping—in a floor-length gown, with or without a train:

- Scuff new bridal shoes in advance, so that the soles are not slippery.

- Practice walking at home in your gown and shoes.

- Keep your head erect and shoulders back, so the gown hangs properly on your body.

- Hold the gown from the sides and pull it smoothly upward a few inches when ascending and descending stairs.

- If your dress has a train, always walk forward don't back up.

Guide to Wedding Clothes

	VERY FORMAL EVENING 200 GUESTS OR MORE; CEREMONY AFTER 5:00	VERY FORMAL DAYTIME 200 GUESTS OR MORE; CEREMONY BEFORE 5:00	FORMAL EVENING 100 GUESTS OR MORE; CEREMONY AFTER 5:00
BRIDE	A beaded, embroidered, or ornamented dress with a long, cathedral or monarch train. (Veil often the same length as the train to complement the dress.) Long sleeves, sleeveless, or strapless with or without gloves. Full bouquet or flower-trimmed prayer book.	Similar to very formal evening, but with more subdued accents, such as embroidery and/or pearls; a shorter, chapel or sweep train is also appropriate.	A long dress with a chapel, sweep, or detachable train; any length veil. Accessories the same as for a very formal wedding.
GROOM AND USHERS	Full-dress tailcoats with matching trousers; white waistcoats and bow ties; wing-collared shirts. (Optional: Black top hats and white gloves.)	Cutaway coats, gray striped trousers, waistcoats, wing-collared shirts and ascots or striped ties. (Optional: Top hats, and gloves.)	Tuxedos with matching trousers, dress shirts, bow ties or four-in-hand ties, and vests or cummerbunds. (Summer option: White or ivory dinner jackets.)
BRIDESMAIDS	Between 4 and 12 attendants, including the honor attendant. Long dresses in evening wear styles; any style bouquet.	Between 4 and 12 attendants, including the honor attendant. Same overall style as very formal evening, but dresses may be less elaborate.	Between 2 and 6 attendants, including the honor attendant. Similar to very formal, but the dresses may be short.
MOTHERS OR HOSTESSES	Long, glamorous evening dresses in colors that complement the bridesmaids' dresses and each other.	Long or short dresses, not as formal as those for evening, in fabrics such as chiffon, lace, taffeta, crepe or silk satin.	Long or short dresses, or evening suits.
GUESTS	Women: Long or short evening or cocktail dresses. Men: Black-tie (tuxedos) or white-tie (tails).	Women: Elegant short dresses or suits. Men: Suits.	Women: Elegant long or short evening dresses or suits. Men: Dark suits or Black-tie (tuxedos).

FORMAL DAYTIME	INFORMAL EVENING	INFORMAL DAYTIME
100 GUESTS OR MORE; CEREMONY BEFORE 5:00	100 GUESTS OR LESS; HOME, CHAPEL	100 GUESTS OR LESS; OFTEN HOME
Same as formal evening, or a shorter dress that can have a detachable train, in a daytime-appropriate fabric, such as organza or tulle. Headpiece and veil.	A long or a short dress in white or pastel. No train. Any length veil. Same accessories as for a formal wedding, but with a simpler bouquet.	Simple dress in white or pastel; short veil; no train. A small bouquet or flower-trimmed prayer book.
Strollers, waistcoats, striped trousers, shirts, and striped ties. (Optional gloves.) Or, the groom may choose a dark suit, dress shirt, and tie.	Dark suits, dress shirts, and four-in-hand (straight) ties.	Suits or blazers (navy and gray are good choices), dress shirts and four-in-hand (straight) ties.
Between 2 and 6 attendants, including honor attendant. Dresses either long or short, but not too elaborate.	Seldom more than one bridesmaid, plus an honor attendant. Cocktail-length dresses or suits and small bouquets.	Seldom more than an honor attendant. A suit or dress, less elaborate than semiformal wedding. Small bouquet.
Elegant dresses or suits.	Stylish short evening dresses or dinner suits.	Daytime suits or dresses, somewhat less elaborate than formal evening.
Women: Elegant daytime dresses or silk pant suits. Men: Suits.	Women: Short dresses or dinner suits. Men: Suits.	Women: Stylish dresses or suits. Men: Suits or blazer and trousers. (No business attire.)

Belgian—pillow laces (or bobbin laces) made with machine-made grounds from Belgium.

Chantilly—delicate scrolls and floral designs on fine mesh, often with scalloped edges; from Chantilly, France.

French—machine-made lace fabrics made in imitation of handmade French lace (Chantilly and Alençon, for example).

Guipure—a heavy lace with large patterns in needlepoint or bobbin over a coarse mesh background fabric.

Schiffli—a machine-made lace with delicate floral embroidery.

Venise—a heavy needlepoint lace with floral sprays, foliage, or geometric designs; first made in Venice, Italy.

NECKLINES

Halter—rises high and fastens at the neck; arms and back are generally bare.

High—a high band collar; fits close to the neck.

Jewel—a round neckline at the base of the throat.

Off-the-Shoulder—fits below the shoulders, with short or long sleeves.

Portrait—off-the-shoulder; extra fabric framing neckline.

Queen Anne—rises high at the back of the neck; sculpts low to outline a bare yoke.

Sabrina—gently follows curve of the collarbone, almost to the tip of the shoulders—same across the back.

Scoop—square with rounded edges.

Sweetheart—shaped like the upside-down top half of a heart.

V–neck—a v–shaped neckline, falling from shoulders or collarbone.

SLEEVES

Bell—a sleeve that's narrow at the top and set into a regular armhole; it has a bell flare at lower edge.

Cap—a short, fitted sleeve.

Fitted—a narrow sleeve set into a small armhole; it is fitted all the way to wrist.

Poet—an extravagant sleeve rounded from shoulder to wrist or beyond.

Puff—a short sleeve gathered into a gentle, rounded shape.

Three-quarter—a sleeve ending between the elbow and wrist.

HEADPIECES

Bow—positioned at the back of the head; usually made of lace or satin and often flower–trimmed.

Floral wreath—a circle of flowers that can nestle on top of the head or at the mid-forehead.

Hair clips—with jewels, crystals, or pearls; often scattered around the head.

Headband—a raised hairband, decorated and ornamented.

Mantilla—a fine-lace veil, usually secured to an elegant comb; it gently frames the face.

Tiara—crown or half-crown resting atop the head; often encrusted with crystals, rhinestones, other semiprecious stones, or pearls.

VEILS

Ballet-length—falls just above the ankles.

Blusher—a loose veil worn forward over the face, and at the end of the ceremony, turned back, over the headpiece; it's often attached to a longer, two- or three-tiered veil.

Cathedral-length—cascades at least three and one-half yards from the headpiece, and is usually worn with a cathedral train.

Chapel-length—falls two and one-third yards from the headpiece.

Elbow—falls to the elbow.

Fingertip—multiple layers of veiling that touch the fingertips.

Fly-away—a veil comprised of multiple layers that brush the shoulders; usually worn with an informal, ankle-length dress or a style with details in back.

Wearing an Heirloom Gown

Do you dream of walking down the aisle in the gown your mother—or her mother—wore? Here are suggestions on how to update and restore a family treasure.

Contact an experienced dressmaker or wedding-gown designer who specializes in antique gowns and lace. He or she can assess what alterations and adjustments are possible and recommend a good dry-cleaner (see Appendix, under Chapter 7).

If parts of the dress are stained or torn, you can mix new lace with old. Consider replacing the sleeves or bodice fabric. You might also update the look with new accessories, such as a headpiece and veil.

If the gown is deteriorating or is too small for you, you might remove the lace and have it added to the bodice or skirt of a new gown. Heirloom lace can also be used to create your headpiece or mantilla. Also consider transferring buttons, beads, and other detailing from a family gown to personalize a new dress.

Preserving Your Gown

If you want your dress to last until *your* daughter grows up or to remain in perfect condition for sentimental reasons, take these protective measures:

Have your dress and veil cared for by a professional dry cleaner immediately after the wedding. Point out where any sugar-based beverages (champagne, etc.) spilled on the dress—they may be invisible at first, but can stain later.

9 ways to personalize your wedding look

1. Weave fresh miniature orchids or roses into your veil or hair (choose sturdy blossoms that will last throughout the day).

2. Going sleeveless? Wear a pair of opera-length vintage gloves.

3. Choose a dramatic wrap—perhaps a faux fur capelet or a gothic velvet cape for a winter wedding; a silk cape for springtime nuptials, a bolero, shrug or cashmere shawl.

4. Wear a delicately jewelled tiara or some other unique piece of hair jewelry (sticks, combs, etc.), or a vintage veil.

5. Celebrate your heritage—a Chinese-American bride might wear a crimson cape or carry a bouquet of red roses (red is the customary shade for a Chinese bride's wedding dress); a Japanese-American bride might dress in a white kimono before changing into a traditional white wedding gown.

6. Follow a theme—for a Victorian wedding, wear a vintage lace dress or romantic corset–style bodice.

7. Consider having some small but meaningful symbol (e.g., your wedding date, or a lucky horseshoe) embroidered into the hem of your dress or veil.

8. Select interesting shoes, such as court slippers in bright pink, gold or silver sandals; or try a pair of turn-of-the-century–style boots.

9. Opt for dramatic–yet–romantic jewelry, such as "chandelier earrings" with dangling crystals; or a large South Sea pearl pendant necklace, hung on a wire circle.

Ask the dry cleaner to test the beads and trim with solvent before cleaning. Some dresses can't be dry-cleaned if beads are glued (not sewed) on; the glue may dissolve during the cleaning process, and you could lose all of the decoration.

Remove protective shields and bra inserts. They may cause staining over time.

Have the dress hand-pressed and wrapped in acid- and linen-free tissue paper. Store it in a box that's free of acid. Use the acid- and linen-free tissue paper to protect against creases and to puff up sleeves and bodice. Avoid "vacuum-packed" boxes (there is no such thing) and cellophane windows that keep air from circulating and can discolor fabric. Also, don't wrap it in plastic.

Alternative idea: Wrap the gown in a white muslin sheet. Fold it over two well-padded hangers in a closet on an inner wall.

Store the gown at room temperature. Never leave it in an attic (too hot) or basement (too damp). Make sure the room is dark—sunlight causes fibers to decompose.

Never store a wedding gown in mothballs. Fumes can damage some textiles.

Don't smoke, drink, or eat in the storage area. Cigarette butts, crumbs, and sweet residues may attract silverfish and mice—all a threat to your fabric.

Check the gown yearly. If slow-to-emerge stains have appeared, bring the dress back to your dry cleaner. Rewrap it in the same method as before.

Accessories

Whether you want to create a romantic Victorian mood or evoke the refined, elegant modern look, accessories can help express the theme of your wedding. The perfect finishing touches:

Jewelry. Brides often wear a sentimental present—a family heirloom or a present from their groom. Wedding-day jewelry should work in proportion with the elaborateness of your dress; the more heavily beaded or ornate the gown, the simpler the jewelry.

If you choose, move your engagement ring to your right hand until after the ceremony, when you'll return it to your left hand.

Underpinnings. Fine lingerie will enhance the overall line of your wedding dress, hide bulges and give you a smooth shape. When you are buying your wedding dress, the bridal-shop consultant will tell you what type of slip and bra your dress requires.

A petticoat made of firm fabric (nylon taffeta, for instance) adds body to a full skirt; soft body-shaping lingerie smooths the lines of a sheath silhouette. Below are some shopping tips:

Buy all foundations before the first fitting. Undergarments should be chosen with a critical eye—a sheer bodice may call for a lacy camisole; a clingy fabric may require control-top panty hose and a fitted slip or body suit for the best look.

Choose the right petticoat: white to wear under any shade of white gown. Some brides, however, choose to make a theatrical statement by wearing a brilliantly colored petticoat that flashes with every turn. Today, most slips are built-in, however you may need a small additional one to improve the shape of the dress. Be sure to choose the proper fullness so that the dress falls as it was meant to.

Make sure your slip is short enough. It's wise to wear a petticoat two to three inches shorter than your dress—so it doesn't show while you dance (unless you want it to show, in which case, ask the bridal consultant for advice).

Have your bra fitted professionally. Bras should be well made, comfortable, and fit correctly. Check that the cup is the right size and that the bra isn't too tight. In general, it's best to opt for smooth styles, since lace embellishments may show through your dress unintentionally. Secure bra straps at the shoulders with lingerie straps. For halter, backless or strapless styles try a three-way convert-ible bra. Or wear a strapless corset or push-up bra and check that the shape conforms to your dress. Wedding dresses are heavy—don't let yours flatten you out. You need something to help lift and support you, and to give the dress the proper shape, whether it's padded, push-up or made of foam. Cups, or a complete bra, can be sewn into a low-cut dress so that nothing shows. Full-busted and full-figured women should shop for a strapless bra with underwire—to offer the best support and enhance their figure. Or, they might opt for a long-line bra with vertical boning (to prevent rolling)—for waist control and to smooth back bulges.

Hosiery. Stockings can be plain, patterned, or embroidered. Choose a color that is harmonious with the shade of your gown; ultra-sheer or shimmery in white, ivory, or blush. Follow these shopping tips:

Shop at legwear stores and bridal shops. You'll find an assortment of stockings and bride's garters in various colors and styles. The garter, an optional accessory, is worn just above the left knee. Some garter options: Wear your mother's; make one yourself with lace, satin, or a sentimental ribbon (perhaps a piece of blue ribbon that your groom's mother saved from his baby sweater). (See Chapter 2, "Wedding Customs," for more on the bride's garter.)

Buy an extra set of hosiery for yourself and for each bridesmaid. Stockings do run—even on your wedding day.

---

wedding-day jewelry ideas

- a new take on the classic strand of pearls: combine them with gem stones or colored crystals, such as seed pearls paired with aquamarine, topaz, or rose quartz

- a simple strand of freshwater pearls

- a 3-to-5 strand pearl choker

- a diamond-solitaire necklace

- symbolic jewelry (such as a cross or Star of David)

- a multi-strand elastic pearl bracelet

- romantic earrings in floral, bow, or chandelier motifs

- drop earrings with diamonds or pearls

- diamond stud earrings

Wedding Shoes. White is the most popular shade for the bride's shoes, but be sure they are same shade of white as your wedding gown. Materials range from lace-covered fabric to ornamented satin to peau de soie. Follow these guidelines:

Shoes may be dyed to match the bridesmaids' gowns. Or they can opt for silver, gold or metallic shades that complement the dress, or black.

Choose a medium heel for maximum comfort. You'll want shoes that will walk you steadily down the aisle, let you stand through a long receiving line, and dance for hours. Options include shoes with ornamentation such as lace, pearls, or embroidery; ankle straps with jeweled or pearl buckles; slingbacks and open-toed shoes.

Shop for shoes late in the day. This is when feet are most tired and swollen. If the shoes are comfortable then, they'll carry you throughout your wedding day.

Scuff the soles of new shoes to avoid slipping on polished floors and carpets.

additional bridal accessories

• bridal handbag
• prayer book
• heirloom handkerchief (your "something old")
• wrap, stole, or shawl
• heirloom jewelry—a cameo, earrings

Gloves. Gloves should reflect the formality of your wedding, the season, and the style of your gown. Follow these guidelines:

Choose the right fabric for the season. For a summer wedding, options include cotton, or stretch-lace gloves. For a winter wedding, select cotton or white kid gloves.

Choose the right color and accents. White or ivory is the best choice. Search for custom touches—lace, beading, or other designs, such as rosettes, that echo the accents on your gown. Reminder: The minute there's a spot on your gloves, remove them.

Select the right length for your gown. If you'll wear a sleeveless gown, wear opera-length gloves that extend past the elbow. Wrist-length gloves are appropriate for short or cap sleeves or even sleeveless dresses.

Plan in advance what you will do with your left glove during the ring exchange. If you wear short gloves, simply remove the left glove and hand it to your honor attendant once you reach the altar. Or, beforehand, unstitch, or slit the underseam of the left glove's ring finger lengthwise, so that you can slip your finger out. (Gloves can be restitched later.)

Remove your gloves during the receiving line. These days, women remove their gloves to shake hands with their wedding guests as a friendly gesture. Also remove your gloves during the meal and any other time you're eating or drinking that day.

Groom, Attendants, Fathers

Clothes for the groom and other men in the wedding party are governed by tradition, style, and time of day of the wedding—with the exception of outfits that reflect heritage (a Scottish kilt) or military service (see "Your Formalwear Dilemmas" section). The groom and his attendants wear the same formalwear; accessories distinguish the groom and best man—they wear matching ties and or cummerbunds, and vests that differ from those worn by the other ushers.

Fathers may walk the bride down the aisle, stand in the receiving line (if they choose), and pose in wedding portraits; their attire should coordinate with that of the other members of the wedding party.

Although you can buy a tuxedo, most grooms and ushers decide to rent. The groom should try on the suit style and color that match the formality, colors, and theme of the wedding (see "Groom's Formalwear Glossary" section). Formalwear should be ordered at least three months before the wedding, and tried on by each attendant as soon as it is picked up to be sure the outfit (with accessories) fits correctly and is complete.

Today there are a range of formalwear accessories with a contemporary twist. New hues, fabrics, and accessories are creative, witty, and appropriate, as long as they complement your gown and the time and style of the wedding. (See "Guide to Wedding Clothes" chart for the correct formalwear for each style of wedding, daytime and evening.) Black tuxedos always look elegant and are appropriate after 6 P.M.

Your Formalwear Dilemmas

Your groom and his ushers will have many questions when they are ordering and being measured for their formalwear.

Can the men in our wedding wear dress oxfords with their tuxedos? A heavy everyday business shoe clashes with the elegant style of a tuxedo. Formal shoes are sleeker, lighter; the most traditional formal shoe (perfect with a full-dress tuxedo or white tie) is a black tuxedo pump—a plain slip-on shoe in silk, velvet, dress or patent leather, often with a grosgrain bow; or a suede or quilted slipper. Other formal options: black slip-ons, lace-ups made of fine leather with a soft matte finish (for a morning suit—or cutaway, stroller, or tuxedo). Or add pizzazz with a black silk handwoven slip-on (available for rent at most men's formalwear stores).

If the ceremony begins in late afternoon with the reception taking place after six o'clock, what is the appropriate formalwear? If the ceremony is scheduled for five o'clock in the afternoon, and a very formal reception will follow at six or seven o'clock, men wear black tie or white tie.

My ushers live in different cities. How can I be sure their formalwear matches? The only guarantee is to order everyone's complete ensemble in one store, or try ordering via the Internet. The groom can choose a formalwear store convenient to the wedding site. After he chooses his formalwear style, the store gives the groom measurement

formalwear contract tips

Specify these points in a signed and countersigned contract or bill of sale:

- size, style, and color of each outfit; number of suits ordered

- specific accessories covered in suit-rental fees (shirt stud sets, striped ascots, etc.)

- additional accessories (black matte-leather lace-up shoes)

- date outfits will be ready for pickup

- total rental cost, deposit paid, and payment schedule

- additional charges (fitting, cleaning, late-return fees)

- what the store will do if the formalwear is fit incorrectly, or is soiled, or ripped when tried on after pickup

- refund and cancellation policies

forms to mail, fax or email to his ushers. They then visit a formalwear store in their own area to try on a jacket and be measured (most stores will do this as a courtesy and a precaution against ending up with incorrectly fitted formalwear). It's not enough to measure chests; some men have muscular biceps, triceps, and thighs.

The groom may be able to secure the entire order with his credit card; later, as each usher comes in for a final fitting, he can pay for his own outfit. Even if an usher will wear his own tuxedo, the shirts and accessories should all be rented, since colors, styles, ties, shirt studs, and cuff links may vary.

Can my groom's outfit distinguish him from his ushers? Everyone, including your fathers, wears the same type of formalwear. (The only possible exception: the ring bearer, who may fit into a different style suit or tuxedo that is appropriate to his age.) What can vary, however, are the accessories. Creative ways to set the groom apart:

Texture. If the ushers are wearing black vests and four–in–hand ties, have your groom's (and perhaps best man's) accessories be of woven or jacquard fabric.

Colors. Ushers might wear black and white houndstooth vests and black bow ties. Order solid accessories for your groom (and best man), or vice versa. Or, if the male attendants are all wearing color accents, the groom can wear black accessories. (Or the groom can wear a white tie, while the groomsmen wear gray.)

Patterns. If wearing ascots, the groom's and best man's might be in a different pattern than the ushers'.

Boutonnieres. The best man and ushers wear identical flowers in their left lapels. The flowers worn in the groom's left lapel may be a different variety and color to indicate his position of honor.

Accessories. The groom may also stand out by being the only one to wear a top hat (with tails), a cummerbund (instead of a vest), or gemstone studs (a gift from his bride).

What accents can we add to the formalwear for a Christmas wedding? Choose bow ties and vests or cummerbunds in holiday colors or tartan plaids to coordinate with bridesmaids gowns. Rent or buy vests with flecks of gold, or other metallic accents.

Can my groom wear an outfit that reflects his heritage? Yes, in the most formal version. For instance, a groom of Scottish descent may wear his own clan tartan kilt with either a daytime or evening jacket. As with a military wedding (see "Your Fashion Dilemmas" section), only those men eligible to wear a specialized formal outfit do so; other attendants wear traditional formalwear appropriate to the time of day and style of the wedding.

Anatomy of a Tuxedo

Today, there are many creative options in formalwear that can reflect the personalities of those wearing it. Before your groom and his attendants begin to shop for their wedding-day outfits, they should consider these basic points. (For more information on formalwear, see the "Guide to Wedding Clothes" chart and the Appendix, under Chapter 7, "Wedding Clothes.")

The jacket. Tuxedo jackets may have notched or peak lapels, or shawl collars. Single-breasted or double-breasted styles are equally appropriate. Jackets come in 2– and 4–button styles; the 4–button jacket is longer in length.

The trousers. Trousers should break once, about five inches above the ankle. Bottoms are hemmed, never cuffed.

The shirt. Traditionally, a pleated shirt is worn with a tuxedo. The proper closures: studs in black, white, or gold, or with precious stones. No black shirts, and always wear a tie.

The shirt sleeve. Allow one-half inch of shirt sleeve to show beneath the sleeve of the jacket.

The cuff links. These may match the shirt studs or you may opt for whimsical shapes (such as champagne bottles), classic finishes (enamel, mother of pearl), or geometric shapes in gold or silver.

The collar and tie. Choose from among the wing collar, the lay down collar, and the stand-up collar. All are paired with a bow tie for formal evening dress, or the popular four–in–hand tie. Bow ties rest in front of the wings. Mandarin-collar shirts have a jeweled-button closure.

The cummerbund. Always wear a cummerbund with pleats facing upward. Cummerbunds were once referred to as *crumb catchers* because they caught the crumbs when a gentleman ate. The pleats held theater tickets, keys, or money, so that bulging pockets wouldn't ruin a tuxedo's slim line. (Many cummerbunds from England still have hidden cummerbund pockets.)

The vest. Instead of a cummerbund, a popular option is a colorful—though never loud—solid or patterned vest, which can add personality to the most conservative tuxedo. (Buy them as ushers' gifts; they can be worn again after the wedding.) Neutrals, like black, white, silver or gold are always popular, as well.

The boutonniere. The boutonniere is always worn on the left lapel, but never with a pocket square (see below), or with a high–button jacket. A vibrantly colored flower is a dramatic accent for black-and-white formalwear. However, the overall effect should be simple and masculine.

Pocket squares. Instead of a boutonniere, some men prefer to tuck a pocket square in the jacket's left breast pocket.

tying a bow tie

It's as simple as tying a shoelace:

- Place tie around your neck, with ends hanging down.
- Tie a bow.
- Don't look in mirror or look down; it will confuse you.
- Once tied, use a mirror to straighten bow.
- Practice making a bow around your knee, before tying around your neck.

Your formalwear specialist can show you examples of each of the four proper handkerchief folds: The multipronged, the pouf, the square-ended and the triangle.

The shoes and hose. Black patent oxfords or pumps are the best shoe choices; patent for tuxedos and matte leather for morning coats. Men should wear socks that match the color of their trousers.

Formalwear Sizing

Here are some helpful tips for ordering the formalwear for the groom, ushers and fathers.

Ask if the store has a tailor on the premises. If trouser legs are too long or too short (the most common fitting error), they can be hemmed in a few minutes.

If not, ask if the store has an affiliation with a tailor. Can he or she do small alterations such as turning up sleeves and sewing on buttons?

Have each attendant come into the store to check the fit of his formalwear and all accessories.

Shirts should hug the neck; if a shirt is too tight, ask for a collar extender (an elastic hoop or button).

Trousers should touch the top of shoes.

Waistbands are often adjustable—check for side buckles.

Jackets should fit snugly, yet comfortably, around shoulders—no arm bulges—with some room at the waist.

The *collar* should hug the neck; the lapels shouldn't buckle.

"Vents," or panels, found on the side or in the back of the coat, should lay smoothly, following body lines.

Jacket sleeves should end at the wrist bone, each with the same number of sleeve buttons.

Also: Ask ushers to check their formalwear for any stains, fabric snags, or cigarette burns before leaving the store. They should also be sure they have all accessories that go with their outfit.

Appoint an attendant to return all formalwear to the store on time. Late fees may be five to ten dollars per day, per outfit. Food and beverage stains can usually be dry-cleaned out. If there are more serious stains (grease, blood), or damage, expect to be asked to pay the cost of replacing the clothing.

Groom's Formalwear Glossary

THE COAT

Shoulders—can be natural or padded.

Lapels—the pieces of fabric that extend from the collar and lay folded back on the chest.

Peaked—a cut in the lapel points upward, adds to a broad, V-line look.

Notched—a triangular piece in the lapel is cut at the collar line and points outward.

Shawl—there is no cut in the lapel, creating a rounded effect.

Pockets—may be flapped or may have a decorative border at the top.

Besom—inset pockets with a narrow trim (often satin) across the top.

Single-Breasted a coat with one vertical row of buttons to close the front.

Double-Breasted—a coat with two rows of vertical buttons; one to close the coat front, the other for decoration.

CLASSIC FORMALWEAR

Tails—a formal coat that is short in front and extends to two "tails" in back; a stiff-front white piqué vest, a white shirt, and black patent-leather shoes complement tails.

Black full dress—the tailcoat and trousers are black; accessories are black.

White tie—the tailcoat, trousers, and shoes are black; accessories are white.

White or dark gray full dress—the tailcoat, trousers, and accessories are all white or gray.

The Tuxedo—the most popular evening formalwear; it can be single-or double-breasted (see above definitions).

Black tie—the tuxedo, trousers, bow tie, or four-in-hand tie, and vest or cummerbund are black or charcoal gray.

Cutaway Coat/Morning Coat—a long coat that tapers from the waistline button to one broad tail in the back, with a vent; usually gray or dark gray.

Stroller Coat—a semiformal suit jacket cut like a tuxedo; worn in the afternoon; usually dark gray or black.

Dinner Jacket—tuxedo-cut jacket in white, or ivory; worn with black, satin-striped trousers. This is a great option for an after-6 p.m. destination wedding, as well as hot summer nights.

THE SHIRT

Traditional Formal Shirt—white; some have buttons, others need pearl, onyx, gold, or diamond studs as closures.

Shirt with French Cuffs—calls for elegant cuff links.

Pleated Shirt—the front panels on either side of the buttons are pleated.

Wing collar—the collar has downward points; it looks great with an ascot or bow tie.

Spread or Lay–down collar—similar to a business-shirt collar; looks good with a four-in-hand tie or bow tie.

THE TROUSERS

Most are adjustable at the waist. Variations include:

Striped—all-over gray striped trousers worn with cutaway or stroller.

Double-pleated a double pleat in the front of trousers.

Black with side stripe—a satin or silk stripe down the outside of each leg.

shopping for bridesmaids' gowns

- Keeping the style and formality of your wedding gown in mind, look for ideas in bridal magazines, in stores and bridal salons, and on the Internet.

- Shop with honor attendant; choose her dress first.

- Narrow the choices for the bridesmaids' dresses to three styles. Or select a special fabric and color by a particular manufacturer and let bridesmaids pick their own styles. Another option: Choose a design that includes many coordinated pieces that can be mixed and matched to flatter attendants of various shapes and sizes.

- Let bridesmaids make the final decision since they are, most likely, buying their own dresses.

ACCESSORIES

Neckwear—is selected to match the coat, vest, or cummerbund; various options include the following:

Bow tie—a short tie resembling a small bow; can be worn with any collar.

Four-in-hand tie—a knotted tie that hangs vertically, like a business-suit tie; can be fastened with a tie tack and is worn with a spread collar.

Ascot—a broad neck scarf looped under the chin; fastened with a tie tack or stick pin, worn with a wing collar.

Cummerbund—pleated sash made of brocade, silk, or satin; worn instead of a vest to cover the trouser waistline. The pleat width, either horizontal or slanted to the right, varies; pleats are worn facing up.

Vest/Waistcoat—worn instead of a cummerbund under the coat; adjustable behind the neck and waist.

Other options—tie tacks, stick pins, cuff links, studs, pocket squares, suspenders (braces), top hats, shoes, and scarves; all can be rented from formalwear shops. Personalize formalwear with creative but tasteful accessories.

Bridesmaids and Honor Attendants

Proper dress varies with the hour and season, but your wedding party will look most striking if they have a uniform appearance. This used to mean that the bride chose one dress for all of her attendants to wear, regardless of body types or tastes. Today it is increasingly popular to let bridesmaids take a more active role in choosing their dresses, with certain parameters set by the bride (e.g., choosing a specific fabric or designer, then letting them choose the style of dress). Not only does this allow for some individuality, but it can also improve the chances that your bridesmaids will like and wear their dresses again.

Whether or not they are all wearing the same thing, bridesmaids and honor attendants should wear dresses that complement the style and formality of your gown. Attendants may wear short dresses, even if the bride wears a floor-length gown, but *never* a long dress if the bride is in a short gown. As far as hair is concerned, here too it is generally best to let each maid maintain her individual style. If you feel strongly about requesting a uniform hair look, consider some of the beautiful hair accessories (jewelled sticks, clips, combs, etc.) that are now available.

If you don't want all bridesmaids to dress alike, ask each to select her own style of dress in the same color family. To accommodate their various heights and weights, consider choosing dresses that are similar but not identical in style (a sleeveless dress for the friends with toned arms; one with sleeves for those who prefer to be covered up). The dresses should be in the same fabric and color, and from the same manufacturer. Something to watch for: Many manufacturers are now making separates that can be mixed and matched.

You may wish to distinguish your honor attendant. Order her a dress in a shade that's slightly different from the other bridesmaids' dresses—in a contrasting color (deep rose instead of pink, for example), or with contrasting trim or accessories.

If there is just one attendant, she should dress in a style similar to that of the bride, but simpler. For instance, if the bride's gown is strapless, the honor attendant might opt for a similarly-cut gown, or at least one with the same neckline.

Order similar bouquets for attendants. Select flowers and colors that match or harmonize with the dresses. Bouquets should resemble the style of the bride's bouquet and have similar colors (unless it is all white).

Shoes should be similar. They should match the mood and color of bridesmaids' dresses and be the same heel height. Strappy sandals, slingbacks and pumps are all popular options. They may be dyed to match gowns; they may also be metallic—silver, gold, copper, or pewter.

Jewelry should be an elegant complement. Bridesmaids can wear something as simple as a pendant or a single strand of pearls (perhaps a thank-you gift from you). Or something more dramatic like a multi-strand crystal necklace.

Mothers of the Bride and Groom

The dresses of the mothers of the bride and groom should be elegant, stylish and flattering, without upstaging the bride. The two mothers should choose dresses that complement each other, as well as those worn by the bridesmaids.

Traditionally, the mother of the bride selects her outfit first. She then describes it to the mother of the groom, allowing her enough time to shop. The mothers will most likely talk about the wedding's style and agree on complementary colors before either shops, however. Style and length should be appropriate to the style and time of the wedding (see "Guide to Wedding Clothes" chart). The color should blend with (rather than match) the color worn by the wedding party. Mothers should avoid all black or all white—black is too somber and white is reserved for the bride. Both mothers may wear the same color, but not the *same* dress, although they should be the same degree of formality, and, preferably, the same length.

Order flowers for both mothers. Some choices include a nosegay, a handtied bouquet, one striking bloom, a wrist corsage or floral bracelet, or a pocket posy (for a suit). If walking down the aisle, mothers should leave handbags and wraps with seated family members and carry only flowers.

Child Attendants

Children will perform better if they're happy and comfortable with the way they look (see Chapter 6, "The Wedding Party").

Dresses for junior bridesmaids (girls over the age of eight) should be styled for their age (no low-cut necklines). They might wear the same color and fabric as the bridesmaids, with a wreath or hair flower; bouquets should also match the bridesmaids' (see Chapter 15, "Wedding Flowers").

Flower girls' dresses may echo the bride's gown. For example, shop for a dress with the same cap sleeves, but in a floral print, with a silk sash to match the bouquets. Other style options: white organza pinafores over deep-green velvet dresses; miniature flowers and pastel hair ribbons; ballet slippers or flat-soled black (or white) patent leather pumps trimmed with bows, flowers, or buckles.

Ring bearers or pages (if males) might wear traditional satin-and-velvet suits. Other style options: dark blue, gray or black Eton suits, with white shorts, and white or blue knee socks. For a summer wedding: white linen suits with white knee socks and white shoes. For a semiformal or an informal wedding: matching suits or matching long pants and jackets or, a replica of the ushers' attire for boys over the age of five; boutonnieres to match those of the ushers. Ring pillows should only be carried by boys younger than ten; otherwise, they can carry the ring in their jacket pocket.

Children in a semiformal or informal remarriage ceremony wear "special occasion" outfits. Boys might wear matching neckties; girls, lacy tights and identical bouquets (see Chapter 15, "Wedding Flowers").

Familiarize your child attendants with the outfits they'll wear. Together, look at pictures, wedding photos, and page through bridal magazines. Rent videos or films that have child attendants in them. Point out the flower girl's and ring bearer's clothing. Draw pictures of wedding clothes with the children (you might display their efforts at the rehearsal or rehearsal dinner).

Shop together for the flower girl and ring bearer outfits. Let your child attendants feel part of the wedding excitement. Spend time with them (and their mothers) shopping for and trying on the clothes.

Try to have your child attendants' outfits fitted at the same time that the ushers' and bridesmaids' outfits are fitted. This will make your child attendants feel special, part of the wedding party, and very grown up.

Encourage your child attendants to try on their outfits briefly at home. This will get them accustomed to wearing and walking in the clothes in advance.

Encourage the mothers of your child attendants not to dress them hours in advance of the ceremony on wedding day. They may get fidgety and wrinkle, soil or tear their outfits before it's time for them to walk down the aisle.

YOUR WEDDING CEREMONY

All wedding planning culminates in the moment you two turn to each other and begin to say your vows. Your wedding ceremony will seal your status as a married couple. More than any other part of the day, it will convey the importance of getting married, as well as express your own personalities through unique touches.

Questions for Clergy

By this time, you should have already settled general logistics with your clergymember such as the date, time, size, religious requirements, and general style of the wedding. (If you haven't, turn back to Chapter 4, "Planning Your Wedding," and contact your officiant as soon as possible.) Perhaps you have scheduled counseling sessions, if they're required by your religion. To make sure you have all the wedding-ceremony details covered, take along this checklist and ask your officiant about the points that apply to your situation.

☐ When do we give our marriage license to you? How many witnesses do we need? When is the document signed?

☐ May our photographer use a flash during the ceremony? How close to the altar may he or she stand?

☐ Are wedding guests allowed to throw rice or flower petals within the building or on the steps? What about birdseed, or the releasing of doves?

☐ When can we gain entry into the church or synagogue on our wedding day?

☐ What area is recommended for setting up the receiving line?

☐ Do you have samples of wedding programs? When are they passed out?

☐ Which accessories are provided (the *huppah*, candelabra, aisle runner)?

☐ Can we include a wine ceremony, communion, or ethnic traditions?

☐ How long will the ceremony last? Will you be delivering a homily or speech? Can we preview it so we're not surprised by your comments on our wedding day?

getting guests involved

- If marrying in a house of worship, reverse positions with the officiant so you and your groom face guests.

- Move the *huppah* or portable altar closer to pews to increase the feeling of community.

- At a small wedding, have guests stand around the altar in a semicircle.

- Stand outside the house of worship to greet arriving guests—an Asian custom.

- Welcome guests with bagpipers, saxophonists, or classical guitarists outside the ceremony site; a flutist or harpist can play indoors.

- Choose a prayer for attendants or guests to say in unison.

- After sealing your vows with a kiss, ask the clergymember to pass the Kiss of Peace— once a kiss, but now most often a handshake passed from clergymember to you, to attendants, to all guests.

- Ask ushers to distribute candles to each guests as he or she is seated. After lighting the Unity Candle, the bride and groom walk to the first pew on their sides of the church. With their own candles they each light the candle of the guest in the first seat of the first pew, who lights the candle of the person next to him or her, till all of these Candles of Peace are lit, throughout the room.

☐ Can we write our own vows, personalize our ceremony? Can we read the wording of the service and make phrases more contemporary?

☐ Must all readings be religious? When will they be performed?

☐ Will you explain the symbolism of the ceremony to guests who may not be familiar with the rituals?

☐ Is a kiss permitted at the end of the marriage ceremony?

☐ Is it possible to reserve seats for family members?

☐ Can you suggest roles for children from previous marriages? May children of another religion serve as altar servers or candlelighters?

☐ When is the rehearsal held? Will you coordinate the procession and recession?

☐ Will you (and your spouse, if applicable) be attending the rehearsal dinner, and reception? Will you bless the meal?

☐ Can you arbitrate between divorced parents or feuding in-laws?

Planning the Ceremony

Ask your priest, minister, or rabbi to review the ceremony with you step by step. You may have some options: the number of readings, if communion is celebrated, if you can include poetry, prose, favorite song lyrics, or write your own vows. A common misconception is that a wedding without witnesses or the exchange of vows is illegal. Matrimonial laws vary by state; some require witnesses, others specify just that the couple and the officiant be present. A ceremony may not be required to legally join a couple in wedlock. However, most states require that the bride and groom assure the officiant they are entering into marriage of their own free will. Most religious ceremonies include the following elements, which may be personalized.

The Greeting/Call to Worship. These first words will welcome the guests and set the tone. For example, the traditional, well-recognized greeting from *The Book of Common Prayer* of the Episcopal Church is:

"Dearly beloved: We have come together in the presence of God to witness and bless the joining together of this man and this woman in Holy Matrimony . . ."

At this part of the ceremony, you might include a favorite poem or quotation, a wish for your family, or a reading from a friend about love and friendship.

Your clergymember might also express your personal philosophy about marriage.

"Jane and Kevin feel that their lifelong companion should be . . ."

The Charge to the Couple. This is the part of the ceremony that determines that the bride and groom have come together to marry of their own free will. For example, the well-recognized questions from the Protestant ceremony:

"Will you have this man/woman to be your wedded (husband/wife) to live together in holy matrimony . . . ?"

The Presentation/Giving Away. Traditionally, at a point in the ceremony, the clergymember asks:

"Who gives this woman to be married to this man?" (Episcopal)

The bride's father, who has escorted her down the aisle, replies, *"I do."*

The "giving away" dates back to the time when patriarchal ownership of a daughter was transferred to a husband in marriage. Today, many couples choose to vary these traditional words. For example, the minister might ask, *"Who blesses/supports this marriage?"* Both your parents and your groom's parents (and sometimes the entire wedding party and congregation) may respond, *"We do."*

At this point, the couple and their attendants move toward the altar from the head of the aisle to say their vows.

The Vows. These public promises join you together emotionally and proclaim your intentions to love, trust, and honor each other. In traditional Christian wed-dings, the couple promise *"to have and to hold . . . for better or for worse."* Most couples today choose to substitute the word *"cherish"* in the woman's tradi-tional pledge for the words *"to obey."*

The Exchange of Rings. Traditionally, the bride and groom place a wedding ring on each other's left ring finger, stating, *"With this ring, I thee wed."* You may, however, want to also state what the rings mean to you as a couple.

The Pronouncement. At the end of the ceremony, the officiant will declare to those assembled that you are legally wed. The words traditionally heard:

"I now pronounce you man and wife. Those whom God has joined together, let no man put asunder."

Today, most clergymembers have changed the pronouncement to the more egalitarian words, *"I now pronounce you husband and wife."* He or she might also personalize the pronouncement.

Ceremony Readings

Whether you and your groom compose your own poem or prayer to accompany your vows or choose a verse from another source, a brief reading is a lovely way to express any special thoughts you may have. You might also include close friends or siblings by asking them to recite the reading for you. The best time for readings to be offered is before the vows and after the exchange of rings (although some officiants will have other recommendations). Guests may enjoy following along with their own copy of the reading, perhaps included in a wedding program. Be sure to consult with your cler-gymember for approval, as well as other suggestions.

Sacred Scripture

To find meaningful readings, ask your clergymember for suggestions or check your local library or bookstore for compilations of wedding readings, and be sure to look

creative ceremony touches

- Have children pass out candles, flowers, or yarmulkes (skullcaps) for a Jewish ceremony.

- Print greetings, poetry, and tributes in your wedding program (see "The Wedding Program" section).

- Hang a floral wreath on the door of the house of worship, announcing "a wedding is in progress."

- Line the windowsills with votive candles; wrap greenery or tulle around columns.

- Walk down the aisle on a hand-painted runner decorated with flowers.

- The bride and groom walk down the aisle escorted by both parents—a Jewish tradition.

- As the bride is escorted to the altar, she might pause at the first pew to give her mother a flower and a kiss; as she leaves the altar with the groom, she'd do the same for her mother-in-law.

- Sip from two goblets of wine—a Jewish tradition—to symbolize the joy and sorrow of life.

- Seal your vows with nine sips of sake (three sips from three cups)—as the Japanese do.

- Have attendants ring bells, release doves, or blow bubbles as you emerge from the house of worship.

- Travel to the reception in creative transportation—a horse and buggy or an unique car (see Chapter 19, "Going Away").

on the Internet. Read many translations before you choose your Scripture selections. Wording may vary and one might seem more meaningful, but remember that not all versions are acceptable in every church. Keep the passage short—generally a few sentences are enough to convey your message. Don't only look at verses pertaining to love and marriage; perhaps one that refers to happiness sums up your thoughts perfectly. If the verse contains some language that bothers you, see if your officiant will let you delete part of it. Give whomever will read the passage a copy of it, so he or she can practice it. Below are sections from both the Old Testament (the Jewish Scripture), appropriate for a Jewish or Christian wedding, and the New Testament, appropriate for a Christian wedding. Check Today's English Version of the Bible (see Appendix, under Chapter 8, "Your Wedding Ceremony," for source).

to find Scripture

If you remember several words or phrases from a particular passage, but don't know how to find it:

- Type the words "Bible" or "Scripture" into a search engine; then search for marriage- and love-related phrases.

- Look in a religious *concordance*, a reference book in libraries and bookstores, that lists key words ("love," "marriage") alphabetically; under each word is listed every verse and phrase where that word appears, and the citation where it can be found in the Bible.

- Compare translations in the King James version and today's English version of the Bible, to select the version you prefer.

- Check a Bible dictionary, which is filled with entries about phrases and words from the Bible. If you turn to "children," "family," "marriage," or "love," you may pick up other references to Scripture.

On husbands and wives:
- Proverbs 17; 20; 25–29, 31:10–13
- Hosea 2:21–22
- Ephesians 5:28–33
- Ruth 1:16
- Genesis 2:18–24
- Song of Solomon 4:1–3; 5:10–14; 7; 16
- Isaiah 61:10–62:5

On marriage:
- Hebrews 13:4
- Ecclesiastes 4:9–12
- Matthew 19:4–6
- Mark 10:6–9
- John 2:1–11

On home and family:
- Matthew 7:21, 24–27
- Ephesians 3:14–19
- Proverbs 24:3–6

Secular readings

The use of poetry and prose is allowed in most civil, Jewish, and some Christian ceremonies (check with your officiant). Visit your local library or bookstore or use the Internet to research inspirational prose and poetry that express your convictions (see Appendix, under Chapter 8, "Your Wedding Ceremony," for some

On praise and joy:
- Psalms 23; 33; 34; 63; 90; 100; 103; 139; 145; 150
- Isaiah 61:10–11
- Jeremiah 33:10–11
- Ecclesiastes 9:7–9
- John 15:9–17

On love:
- 1 John 3:16; 3:18–24; 4:7–19
- John 15:9–17
- 1 Corinthians 13:1–13
- Song of Solomon 7:11–12; 8:6b–7
- Ephesians 4:1–4; 5:1–2
- Isaiah 43:1–5; 54:10; 60:19–22
- Matthew 22:35–40
- Romans 12:1–2, 9–18
- Colossians 3:12–13
- Proverbs 3:3–6
- 1 Peter 3:7

sources). Here are some reliable sources of readings:

Poetry from the works of e. e. cummings, Robert Frost, Rainer Maria Rilke, Sara Teasdale, Percy Shelley, Elizabeth Barrett Browning, John Keats, and Shakespeare. Also consider the work of Pablo Neruda and Kahlil Gibran *(The Prophet).*

Novels and plays from such writers as John Updike, Thornton Wilder, D. H. Lawrence, Emily and Charlotte Brontë Anne Morrow Lindbergh (*Gift from the Sea*) and Gabríel García Marquez.

Song lyrics from classic or current love songs (see Chapter 14, "Wedding Music," for suggestions).

Unity Symbols

Many couples choose to incorporate symbols of unity into their wedding ceremony to demonstrate that two families are becoming one through marriage.

The Unity Candle. Both the bride's and the groom's parents light a candle on their respective sides of the altar, which remain burning throughout the ceremony. A taller candle remains unlit in the center till the officiant pronounces the couple husband and wife. The bride and groom then carry their respective candles to the center, to jointly light the Unity Candle, then return their candles to the sides of the altar. The lighting of the Unity Candle symbolizes the joining of their families and the merging of two individuals into one married couple.

The Unity Cup. Each family fills goblets from separate decanters. The bride and groom each pour half of the wine into a separate cup, from which each sips. The half-filled goblets are a reminder of your individuality; the single cup marks your new life together.

Writing Your Own Vows

Writing vows that express your own beliefs and feelings is the most significant way to personalize your ceremony (see Appendix, under Chapter 8, "Your Wedding Ceremony"). Working on the ceremony together will also bring you closer—you'll explore all the reasons the two of you chose to get married in the first place. Here are tips for pledging your love:

Share your plans with your officiant. If you are having a religious wedding, he or she must make sure that your wording does not conflict with the beliefs of your house of worship. (The clergymember may also have the wording for a variety of original ceremonies—other than the standard—for you to examine.) Don't wait until the last minute. If there is a disagreement, it's much better to find out early on, when you can find another officiant if necessary.

honoring deceased relatives

- Include a moment of silence to honor a deceased relative.
- Print a tribute or dedication in the wedding program.
- Carry or wear a memento from a deceased relative (a favorite flower, a handkerchief, a strand of pearls).
- Select the person's favorite song as your processional, or have a soloist sing it during the ceremony.
- Ask the clergymember or officiant to mention him or her during the ceremony.
- Light a symbolic candle during the ceremony, and announce its significance to those assembled.
- Visit the relative's grave site after the ceremony and leave your bouquet.
- Make a donation to a favorite charity in the deceased person's name, on the occasion of your marriage.

two religions, one wedding: interfaith ceremony tips

- The clergymember at the house of worship where the ceremony takes place is the host. He or she is in charge of arrangements, has final service approval, and officially invites the other clergymember. You can pave the way by finding out if both are willing to participate (see Chapter 4, "Planning Your Wedding").

- The bride and groom should each feel their religion is respected equally. Intertwine religious symbols on your wedding program.

- Emphasize shared symbols— candles, wine, bread.

- Add prayers and music from each religion, praying and singing in unison.

- Select words and Scripture that emphasize what you both have in common. Have your sister read a Scripture from your fiancé's religion, while his brother reads a passage from yours.

- Have clergymembers alternate religious rituals (see Chapter 9, "Religious Rituals & Requirements").

- Ask clergymembers to explain religious traditions to guests. Explain traditions in program.

- Involve members of each family meaningfully in the ceremony (reading poems, Scripture, lighting candles).

- Compromise on traditions. Plan a garden wedding where your minister and his rabbi co-officiate under a floral *huppah* (see Chapter 9, "Religious Rituals & Requirements").

Incorporate old and new. It can be gratifying to use old, well-loved phrases and vows in addition to your own words. Some couples are fond of the traditional Protestant query, *"will you love her/him, comfort her/him, honor, and keep her/him . . . as long as you both shall live?"* and incorporate it into their own contemporary ceremonies.

Be personal. This is a perfect time to address what's unique about the two of you. If you have different backgrounds, promise to respect and honor both heritages while creating new traditions together. If this is a second wedding (see Chapter 11, "Remarriage"), talk about your faith in marriage and the miracle of new love. If you have children, acknowledge your commitment to your new family.

Ask yourselves questions. Your vows can address issues like, "What does marriage mean to me?" "Which promises are the most important to us?" "What can I promise to provide my fiancé?" "What do I want from him?" Contemplate what the words *love, trust, honesty, compassion, friendship, forgiveness, fidelity, faith, honor,* and *respect* mean to you.

Remember the solemnity of the occasion. Avoid overly cute or suggestive pledges (*"The bride will never leave her pantyhose hanging in the bathroom."*) Address child-rearing and financial issues privately. Very intimate thoughts and controversial political statements are inappropriate and likely to upset some guests.

Don't make your vows too long. Your spoken vows should be limited to one to three minutes. You don't need to deliver a sermon to the assembled guests on your views of marriage. Let some of your beliefs be expressed through readings, songs, and prayers read by family and friends.

Read your vows aloud in advance. Sometimes a sentence that looks fine on paper is difficult to understand when spoken. Change anything that trips your tongue or sounds awkward.

Make clear, legible copies of your vows and carry them with you on your wedding day. No matter how comfortable you feel with the words, nerves can wipe phrases from your memory—you'll want to be able to read the vows if you forget anything. The groom should carry two copies in a pocket. Give a copy to the clergymember as well. He or she can read the words, and you can repeat them.

Your Rehearsal

You, your groom, your clergyperson, and all members of the wedding, including ushers, readers, and musicians should plan to gather at the ceremony site (usually the night before the wedding) to go through the basics and answer last-minute questions. After the rehearsal, the groom's parents traditionally host a rehearsal dinner (see Chapter 3, "Prewedding Parties"). The entire wedding party, immediate families, and your clergy member and his or her spouse are invited. Out-of-town guests may be included in some cases. Some couples hold the rehearsal and rehearsal dinner a few days before the wedding so no one has to worry about rushing home for a good night's rest. If you decide to hold the rehearsal dinner the night before, make sure that you and your fiancé leave at a reasonable hour.

If your ceremony is simple and involves very few people or will be held in a public place such as a hotel, your clergymember may not schedule a rehearsal. Instead, brief instructions would be given to those involved before the ceremony begins.

Although superstitious brides once had someone stand in for them at the rehearsal, today a bride is urged to participate so she'll feel confident on her wedding day.

Remember these rehearsal basics:

Let your officiant take charge. He or she has handled many ceremonies and can tell everyone exactly where to stand, walk, and sit.

Resist making major changes or introducing new ideas. Time is short, everyone is excited, and a rehearsal is meant to calm and clarify, not confuse. Discuss ceremony ideas during your premarriage conference with your clergymember. Go over plans with bridesmaids, ushers, and honor attendants before the rehearsal to avoid upsets about assigned responsibilities at the altar (who stands next to each of you, who holds your bouquet, arranges your train, holds the bride's and groom's rings).

Review any special variations you've planned in the service. Although the entire marriage service will not be read, special variations will be reviewed, and key phrases that will act as cues for the honor attendant and best man will be noted.

Rehearse the roles of those assigned a special task. Anyone who will light a candle, read some Scripture, or sing a solo should run through his or her part. Go over whether or not the reading will be waiting on the lectern or carried by the reader on the wedding day, how to turn on the lectern light and adjust the microphone.

The clergymember or wedding consultant will brief ushers on protocol. They'll review the procedure for seating guests, including the bride's and groom's mothers, and

civil-ceremony tips

- The usual civil ceremony is an adaptation from the *Book of Common Prayer,* modernized at many city halls. It lasts not much more than a minute. (See Chapter 4, "Planning Your Wedding," for more on civil ceremonies.)

- Ask your judge or justice of the peace if you can add to the ceremony. Many officiants will add to the ceremony themselves.

- Feel free to read passages from your favorite poems, songs, and books. Or write personal vows (see "Writing Your Own Vows" section and Appendix, under Chapter 8, "Your Wedding Ceremony").

DO get enough sleep. You'll be on your feet through most of your exciting and demanding day, greeting, mingling, dancing.

DO take time to visualize each step of the day beforehand. This will calm you and give you a chance to anticipate any hitches.

DO leave enough time to bathe, dress, and reminisce with family. Take time to talk privately with your parents and tell them that you appreciate all that they've done for you.

DON'T bring along too many personal items to the ceremony; you'll just worry about them.

DO have a small meal or a snack of cheese or fruit before you leave for the ceremony. Don't risk feeling faint at the altar.

DO snap a few photos of the last hours at home.

DON'T panic if you fall behind schedule. The ceremony will wait for you. Remain flexible and calm. Guests want to see you smile. Looking and feeling your best is more important than starting on the dot.

assign special tasks, such as spreading the aisle runner or unrolling pew ribbons. Ushers should learn the layout of the site in order to direct guests to the water fountain, rest room, etc.

Take along dummy bouquets (a clutch of gift-ribbon bows from your shower). Then you and your honor attendant can practice passing your flowers. Also practice the necessary turns at the altar.

The officiant may review with your mother phrases that will lead to guest participation. Since her actions will cue everyone else, she will want to know at what points the clergyperson will say things such as "All rise."

Seating Guests

During the rehearsal, you should explain the seating positions to your ushers, who will be escorting the guests to their seats (see Chapter 6, "The Wedding Party").

In a Christian wedding, the bride's family and friends are seated on the left side (referred to as the Gospel side) of the church as you face the altar. (This will be the side of the church that the bride will be standing on as she faces the altar.) The right side of the church is reserved for the groom's family and friends. If the church has two center aisles, the bride's contingent sits on both sides of the left aisle, the groom's on both sides of the right aisle. The parents sit in the first few center rows.

In a Jewish wedding, the bride's guests sit on the right side. (This will be the side of the synagogue that the bride will be standing on as she faces the rabbi.) The left side of the synagogue is reserved for the groom's family and friends. All parents remain standing under the *huppah* throughout the ceremony.

If one family will have many more guests than the other, everyone may sit together. This will fill up the empty seats on one side and serve to introduce everyone earlier in the celebration.

Certain pew rows will be reserved for family members and special guests. Parents of both the bride and groom sit in the first pews on their respective sides, grandparents in the second pews (along the aisle) to ensure that they'll get the best view, alongside siblings of the bride and groom (in a Jewish ceremony, the bride and groom's parents stand under a *huppah;* grandparents and siblings sit in the first pews). You may reserve additional pews on each side for other honored guests and parents of the flower girl and ring bearer (their children may join them during the ceremony). If you have a blended family with stepsiblings, you may reserve additional pews. (Mark

The bride's family is seated on the left, the groom's family on the right, as you face the altar.

1. The bride's mother
2. The bride's father
3. The bride's siblings
4. The bride's grandparents
5. The bride's special guests (aunts, godmother, elderly relatives, parents of the flower girl)
6. The bride's father and his spouse (if divorced from the bride's mother). However, the bride's mother and her spouse take his seat if the bride's father is the custodial parent (which entitles him to sit in the front row).
7. (Optional) Close relatives and friends or elderly guests of the bride
8. The groom's father
9. The groom's mother
10. The groom's grandparents
11. The groom's siblings
12. The groom's father and spouse (if divorced from the groom's mother). Or the groom's mother and spouse if the groom's father is the custodial parent, which entitles him to sit in the front row.
13. The groom's special guests (aunt, godmother, elderly relatives, parents of the ring bearer)
14. (Optional) Close relatives and friends or elderly guests of the groom

these pews with flower garlands or ribbons.) Pew cards or "within the ribbon" cards may be sent to those guests you wish to honor with special seats (see Chapter 5, "Invitations & Announcements").

If your parents are divorced, your family situation determines the seating. For example, if neither parent has remarried and they are on friendly terms, they may sit side by side in the front pew. If this is not practical, the parent who raised you takes the front pew and the other parent should sit in the third pew with his or her spouse (if he or she has remarried). In a Jewish ceremony, their spouses sit in the second and third pews.

Seat all other guests from front to back as they enter the church. Late arrivals should slip into back rows, since no one should be seated by ushers after the bride's mother.

Ceremony Countdown

In some regions of the country, the groom's parents will stand in front of the house of worship to greet guests. Especially if it is a small, informal ceremony held at a non-religious site, the couple, as well as both sets of parents, may mingle with guests before the start of the ceremony. If this is the case, draw up your own timetable.

JEWISH-CEREMONY SEATING

The bride's family is seated on the right, the groom's family is seated on the left as you face the altar. All parents remain standing under the *huppah* throughout the ceremony. (If divorced, parents' partners will be seated in the second and third rows.)

1. The bride's grandparents
2. The bride's siblings
3. The spouse or companion of the bride's mother (if her mother is divorced from the bride's father)
4. The bride's special guests (aunt, godmother, elderly relatives, parents of the flower girl)
5. The spouse or companion of the bride's father (if the father is divorced from the bride's mother)
6. Close relatives and friends or elderly relatives of the bride
7. The groom's grandparents
8. The groom's siblings
9. The spouse or companion of the groom's mother (if his mother is divorced from the groom's father)
10. The groom's special guests (aunt, godmother, elderly relatives, parents of the ring bearer)
11. The spouse or companion of the groom's father (if his father is divorced from the groom's mother)
12. Close relatives and friends, or elderly relatives of the groom.

The sample timetable below is based on a large, formal wedding that will take place fifteen minutes from the bride's house. Adapt it to your own situation, allowing plenty of time—in traffic—to arrive at the ceremony site relaxed.

Three hours before the ceremony: If you're having your hair professionally done, allow an hour for the job (more if you're traveling to and from the salon).

Two hours before the ceremony: You, your mother, and your attendants begin dressing. (If you're getting ready at the ceremony site, arrive there at least an hour and a half before the service.) Your photographer arrives to set up for family pictures.

90 minutes before the ceremony: Any bridesmaids who have dressed elsewhere gather at your house (or at the ceremony site, if you're getting ready there) to pick up their flowers and pose for photographs.

One hour before the ceremony: Ushers arrive at the ceremony site and pin on their boutonnieres. They place wedding programs on seats or in pews (unless they'll be distributed at the door), then gather at the entrance to wait for the first guests to arrive.

Thirty minutes before the ceremony: The organist starts the prelude, while ushers escort guests to their seats. Your mother and attendants leave for the ceremony site.

Twenty minutes before the ceremony: The groom and his best man arrive, then meet with your officiant for any last–minute instructions. Meanwhile, you and your father (or whoever will escort you down the aisle) leave for the ceremony site.

Ten minutes before the ceremony: Your attendants arrive, as well as your mother, the groom's parents, and other family members. The bridal party and your parents wait in the vestibule (or hallway) while the relatives are seated.

Five minutes before the ceremony: The groom's mother is escorted to her seat. The groom's father follows a few feet behind, then takes his seat beside his wife, on the aisle. The head usher escorts your mother to her seat (unless she'll be escorting you). You and your father wait with the wedding party in the vestibule (or hallway).

One minute before the ceremony: Two ushers walk in step to the front of the aisle to lay the aisle runner, if there is one. It is on a spool or in pleats at the steps to the chancel. Each usher holds a corner of the aisle runner, and they both walk in step down the aisle, smoothing it in place behind them. The ushers then take their places with the other groomsmen. (The aisle runner, which protects the bride's gown, remains till all guests have left the sanctuary. After the ceremony is over and guests have departed, the church sexton or the maintenance crew of the synagogue, hotel, or banquet hall will remove it.)

Ceremony time: The minister, priest, or rabbi takes his or her place, followed by the groom and his best man. (In a Christian wedding, the groom and best man enter from the chancel door and stand facing the congregation—at an angle—with the groom next to the officiant, the best man one step behind the groom. In a Jewish wedding, the groom and best man are part of the procession.) As the procession begins, guests rise and turn to watch the bride enter.

The Procession

Some churches have two center aisles. In such cases, use the left aisle for the procession and the right aisle for the recession, or close off the second aisle entirely. Houses of worship with one center aisle are more common, however, and this aisle is used for both the procession and the recession.

The Protestant Procession

The ushers enter first from the back of the church, in pairs, by height—from shortest (first) to tallest. If there is an extra usher, the shortest leads, alone. Ushers walk slowly, in step, leaving three to four pews between each pair.

---

ceremony tips

- The congregation should be able to hear your voices. Anyone speaking should turn at a slight angle toward the congregation. Ask your clergymember if the house of worship has a sound system. If not, consider renting one for the day.

- Members of the wedding party, even those of different faiths, should realize that accepting the invitation to be an attendant means they will participate in the religious rituals: kneeling (in a Catholic ceremony), praying aloud, singing hymns, and wearing a yarmulke in a Jewish ceremony. People who feel uncomfortable should excuse themselves when first asked.

- If you are required to kneel or climb steps during the ceremony, your groom should plan to take your arm to help you up and down.

- The best man and honor attendants should have your rings handy (on her thumb, in his pocket), so that they can quickly give them to the officiant for the exchange of rings.

- After you two say your vows and the officiant has congratulated you, your groom should be prepared to lift your veil for the kiss.

- Afterward, your honor attendant should give your bouquet back (she has held it during your vows) and arrange your train as you turn to face the guests for the recession.

CHRISTIAN PROCESSION

1. The clergymember
2. The groom
3. The best man
4. The ushers
5. The bridesmaids
6. The honor attendant(s)
7. The ring bearer
8. The flower girl
9. The bride
10. The father of the bride

The bridesmaids walk down the aisle next, four to five pews behind the ushers. They walk alone if there are fewer than five; otherwise, they are paired according to height. If there is not an even number of bridesmaids, the shortest person leads, alone.

The junior bridesmaid precedes the honor attendant; if there are two junior bridesmaids, they may walk together.

The maid of honor or matron of honor precedes the child attendants (if there are any), or the bride (if there aren't). If there is both a maid of honor and a matron of honor, they may either walk together or separately. Whoever has the most duties walks last, directly before the bride.

The ring bearer walks alone or may be paired with the flower girl.

The flower girl precedes the bride (traditionally strewing rose petals in her path; today, practicality often rules that she simply carry a basket of flowers).

The bride and her father enter next, the bride on her father's left arm.

The pages (if there are any) end the procession, carrying the bride's train.

The Catholic Procession

The same order is followed, although the ushers may forgo the walk down the aisle and be met at the chancel door by the priest, groom, and best man.

The Jewish Procession

Orthodox, Conservative, and Reform Jewish processions vary according to local custom and the family's preferences.

In the most formal procession, the rabbi and cantor (walking on the rabbi's right) walk down the aisle first, followed by:

the bride's grandparents

the groom's grandparents

the ushers in pairs, by height: from shortest to tallest (last)

the best man

the groom on his father's right, his mother's left

the bridesmaids, individually by height (shortest first); if there are more than five, they may walk in pairs. If there is not an even number of bridesmaids, the shortest walks alone, first.

the honor attendant(s); the one with the most duties precedes the bride

the ring bearer

the flower girl

the bride on her father's right arm, her mother's left

In the most simple Jewish procession, the ushers walk down the aisle first in pairs, by height, followed by the bridesmaids in pairs, the best man, the groom, the honor attendant, the flower girl, the bride on her father's right arm. It's optional for the groom's parents and the bride's mother to join the procession.

The Informal Procession:

At very small weddings, such as simple civil ceremonies, the bride is preceded by one attendant and escorted into the room by her father. Or, there may not be a procession. The bride and groom might stand before the minister, with guests standing in a circle around them.

For a large civil ceremony in a ballroom or other formal setting, choose the procession that suits the site.

JEWISH PROCESSION:

1. The cantor
2. The rabbi
3. The bride's grandparents
4. The groom's grandparents
5. The ushers
6. The best man
7. The groom's father
8. The groom
9. The groom's mother
10. The bridesmaids
11. The honor attendant
12. The ring bearer
13. The flower girl
14. The bride's father
15. The bride
16. The bride's mother

CHRISTIAN CEREMONY POSITIONS:

1. The bride
2. The groom
3. The honor attendant
4. The best man
5. The officiant
6. The flower girl
7. The ring bearer
8. The bridesmaids
9. The ushers

Your Ceremony Escort

Traditionally, the bride is escorted down the aisle on her wedding day by her father. But some couples, regardless of religion, choose to follow the Jewish tradition of having both parents escort the bride and groom down the aisle. Here are some guidelines for nontraditional family situations:

If your father has died, you can walk alone. Or consider asking your mother, stepfather, brother, uncle, another relative, or a close family friend to escort you. Whoever takes the place of your absent father will sit in the front pew after the procession.

Your special escort may also respond when your clergymember asks, *"Who gives/supports this woman in marriage?"* Even if your mother has not walked you down the aisle, she may still respond *"I do"* from her place in the first pew, or she can be escorted to your side at the appropriate time by the best man.

If your mother has died, and you have asked an aunt or your grandmother to take your mother's place during the wedding, she should sit in the front pew with your father. She may even join your father in escorting you down the aisle.

If your parents are divorced and your mother is remarried, you could be faced with an awkward situation: Should your father or your stepfather walk you down the aisle? There is no single answer to this choice. Each family situation is different.

If you've remained close to your father, you may want him to fulfill his traditional role. There is no need for your stepfather to be completely left out, though. He can do a reading during the ceremony, propose a special toast at the reception, or dance the first dance with you.

If your father and stepfather are on good terms, you may ask both men to walk you down the aisle (one on each arm). Together, they respond *"We do,"* when the clergymember asks, *"Who gives/supports this woman in marriage?"*

Or your stepfather might walk you halfway down the aisle and then sit down in a front pew as you take your father's arm to the altar.

In a Jewish procession, many divorced parents still escort their son or daughter down the aisle together, on either side of him or her. They stand together under the *huppah;* their partners sit in the second and third pews.

When there is rancor over this issue, some brides simply choose to walk down the aisle alone or with their grooms.

When a marriage takes place during a worship service, such as during some Quaker meetings, the bride and groom are usually seated at the front of the sanctuary and simply step forward at the proper time.

Altar Procedures

Once attendants pass the first row of seats, they form one of these arrangements:

Diagonal lines. Each individual usher turns to the right to create a diagonal line behind the groom and best man, while each individual bridesmaid assembles in a similar line on the other side.

Single row or two rows. Each pair of attendants goes to an alternate side of the bride and groom. The pairs stand side by side or the bridesmaids stand one step ahead of the ushers.

A semicircle. The bridesmaids and ushers gather in a semicircle around the bride and groom, facing the congregation. (In some churches with a freestanding altar, the minister stands with his back to the guests, while the wedding party faces the congregation.)

Children. The ring bearer and flower girl may stand at the altar throughout the ceremony (the flower girl directly in front of the bridesmaids, the ring bearer in front of the ushers), if you think they are old enough to stay still that long. However, young children are usually happier if they are directed to slip into the second or third pew and sit with their parents for the rest of the ceremony.

A Protestant service. As the bride and her father reach the head of the aisle, the

remarriage-ceremony escorts

If this is a remarriage, there are several options for your walk down the aisle:

- Walk down the aisle with your groom; if you have children, they can precede you down the aisle together. The inclusion of children is a clear statement that "we are making this important step together."

- Walk down the aisle with one or all of your children (if there are more than two, have one escort you on each arm, any others walk before you, singly or in pairs). This is a meaningful, sentimental statement that shows how important your children are to you.

- Be escorted again by your father. There is no reason why your father cannot "bless you in your marriage" more than once. After all, he has stood by you through a first marriage and is now supporting your decision to marry again.

what's in a program?

Tell your guests what to expect. Include:

- The ceremony site
- The date, time, and place of the wedding
- The names of the bride and groom
- The names of the attendants and the officiants
- The names of the soloists, musicians, and pieces performed
- Your parents' names
- Tributes to deceased parents, relatives, and friends
- The words to readings, songs, prayers, and blessings (include sources)
- Foreign-language translations
- Explanations of religious or ethnic rituals, customs, and military traditions
- Thank-you's to parents

bride is on the left of the altar. Her father may remain standing between his daughter and her groom until the part of the ceremony where the minister asks, *"Who gives/supports this woman to be married?"* He replies, *"I do"* or *"Her mother and I do,"* then takes his seat next to the bride's mother in the first pew (or third pew, if he is divorced from the bride's mother—where he'll join his new wife or partner, or his relatives or friends).

Or the bride's father may kiss his daughter, take one step back, place his daughter's hand in her groom's, then take his seat. The honor attendant and best man take their positions on either side of the bride and groom, while the other attendants turn toward the altar. From his seat, the bride's father can respond to the minister's question at the appropriate time.

A Catholic service. The procedures are nearly the same as above. Most often, the bride's father simply places her hand in the groom's, pauses to give her a kiss (lifting her veil and putting it back down, if necessary) before joining her mother, as the couple ascend to the altar.

A Jewish service. The entire wedding party and the parents of the bride and groom stand under the *huppah* throughout the ceremony. The *huppah* may be made of greenery and flowers and may stand on its own. If it is a sheath of silk, satin, brocade, or velvet, or a prayer shawl spread across the top of four slender poles, these poles are held aloft throughout the ceremony by honored friends or relatives, often the ushers. (This is a strenuous task; assign it accordingly.) If the wedding is in a synagogue, the *huppah* is positioned on the pulpit.

The bride stands on the right side, facing the rabbi and cantor, who is on the rabbi's left; the groom stands on the left side. The honor attendant and best man stand one step diagonally behind the bride and groom, respectively; the parents of the bride and groom stand one step back diagonally behind the honor attendants. The bridesmaids and ushers form a diagonal line next to the parents, on either side of the couple. If the flower girl and ring bearer remain standing under the *huppah* (instead of joining their parents in a front pew), the ring bearer should stand to the right of the ushers; the flower girl, to the left of the bridesmaids. (For more information on Jewish-wedding ceremony procedures, see Chapter 9, "Religious Rituals & Requirements.")

The Wedding Program

A wedding program will help your guests follow your ceremony with ease, especially appreciated if it will be an interfaith or intercultural marriage, or if you are writing your own vows. Including the words of prayers or hymns will also help guests participate.

12 8 10 4 2 1 3 9 7 11

Printing styles. The program can be a single photocopied sheet or a professionally printed booklet in a style that complements your invitations. (See Chapter 5, "Invitations & Announcements.")

Consider programs personalized to coordinate with your wedding style (e.g., programs rolled up as scrolls and tied with ribbons in your wedding colors; a pen-and-ink sketch or watercolor of your ceremony site reproduced on the front cover).

Program information. Use your program to explain ceremony traditions to your guests and introduce the participants.

(Listing the names of your wedding party, officiants, and musicians is a way to say thank-you to them.) Printing the titles and words of readings, songs, or prayers, and the explanation of any religious or ethnic customs, will also make guests feel more a part of the ceremony. (See "What's in a Program?" box.)

Distribution. On your wedding day, the ushers should place a stack of programs at the end of each pew or put one on each seat. You could also have the ushers, a special friend, or a teenage relative pass them out to each guest at the door.

JEWISH CEREMONY POSITIONS

1. The bride
2. The groom
3. The honor attendant
4. The best man
5. The cantor
6. The rabbi
7. The flower girl
8. The ring bearer
9. The bride's parents
10. The groom's parents
11. The bridesmaids
12. The ushers

The Recession

When the organist sounds the triumphant chords of the recessional, the bride in a Christian ceremony turns around in place and takes her groom's right arm (centuries ago, once the marriage was official, it was deemed less likely that the groom would

CHRISTIAN RECESSION:

1. The bride
2. The groom
3. The flower girl
4. The ring bearer
5. The honor attendant
6. The best man
7. The bridesmaids
8. The ushers

have to use his sword to keep his bride from being kidnapped). In a Jewish ceremony, the bride turns and takes her groom's left arm. Then, the newlyweds walk back up the aisle together, leading the recession of the wedding party, in their first walk as husband and wife.

In a Christian recession, you will be followed up the aisle by the flower girl walking on the ring bearer's right. Each of your bridesmaids will line up with an usher as they file down the aisle: the honor attendant on the right arm of the best man, each bridesmaid on the right arm of an usher. (One usher may escort two bridesmaids if there is not an even number.) An extra usher walks alone; two extra ushers walk side by side.

When you reach the vestibule, ushers designated in advance return to escort the mothers of the couple and any other honored guests from the house of worship.

Then you, your groom, and both honor attendants will probably join your clergyperson in his or her chambers. There, you'll sign the marriage license, although this may be incorporated into your ceremony (as in a Quaker wedding, for example). This is when the best man will also hand the officiant a sealed envelope with his or her fee. (See Chapter 4, "Planning Your Wedding," under the "Ceremony and Officiant Fees" box).

The wedding party may return with you to the church or synagogue for more photos. Guests will wait in front for you to appear and receive their hugs and applause.

Form a receiving line in the church vestibule or on the steps. This is a natural time and place for this tradition, if you, the groom, and your honor attendants already signed the marriage license (perhaps at the rehearsal or before the ceremony). Then your officiant will just have to add his or her signature. (For large weddings, it might be more sensible to form the receiving line at the reception.)

The ushers will clear the church of personal items and direct guests to the reception. It is important that no guests be left stranded without rides to the reception site. Ushers might also distribute copies of directions to the reception.

The bride, groom, and bridesmaids dash into waiting cars to travel to the reception site. Once there, you'll be able to freshen your makeup, pose for pictures, bustle your train, and if you haven't done so already, form the receiving line before guests arrive.

In a Jewish recession, you and your groom will be followed up the aisle first by your parents (your mother on your father's left arm), the groom's parents (his mother on his father's left arm), the flower girl walking next to the ring bearer (on his left), your honor attendant on the best man's left arm, and the bridesmaids on the ushers' left arms. The cantor walks at the end of the procession, on the rabbi's left.

The yichud *traditionally follows the recession.* The bride and groom disappear for a few minutes of private time alone, symbolic of when the groom

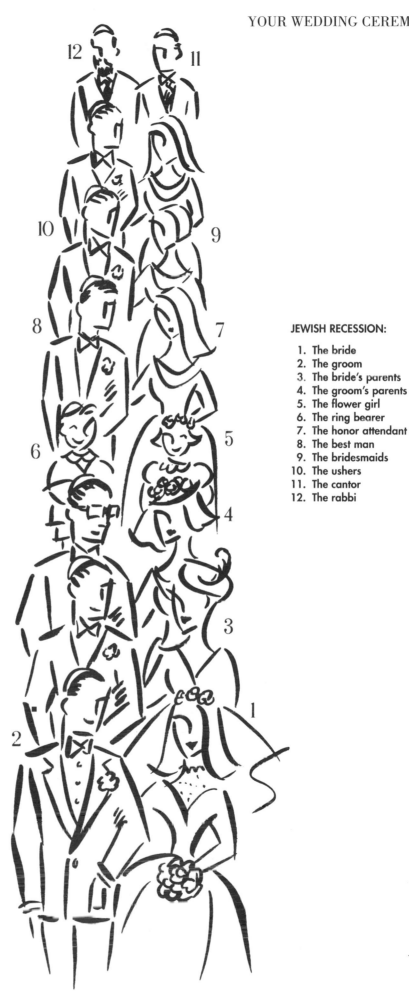

JEWISH RECESSION:

1. The bride
2. The groom
3. The bride's parents
4. The groom's parents
5. The flower girl
6. The ring bearer
7. The honor attendant
8. The best man
9. The bridesmaids
10. The ushers
11. The cantor
12. The rabbi

brought his bride to his tent to consummate the marriage and share their first meal together, thereby breaking their fast (see Chapter 9, "Religious Rituals & Requirements"). Today, the *yichud* is a time to let the reality of the marriage sink in. Two witnesses stand outside the door and when the couple emerge, the witnesses proclaim them husband and wife. They may be greeted by a toast or a shower of birdseed, even singing and dancing.

In the meantime, the ushers will direct guests to the reception site. Once the couple emerges, the wedding party may pose for photos, travel to the reception site with the newlyweds, and form the receiving line.

RELIGIOUS RITUALS & REQUIREMENTS

Today, wedding ceremonies reflect the very people they unite. They contain language about the equality of marriage partners and the importance of family support; they acknowledge the existence of interfaith marriages. And they recognize that some couples may choose to have a childless marriage. With much of the rigidity gone, couples now have the opportunity to arrange a wedding service that expresses their shared hopes and beliefs. Each religion has traditions associated with its liturgy. If yours is an interfaith ceremony, you can add significance by learning about the customs of each faith and incorporating something meaningful from both into your wedding service.

In reviewing this chapter, you'll notice that there are many similarities in the marriage ceremonies of religions practiced in the United States. At the same time, you may discover that within the same faith, local customs may influence the style of the wedding service. Discuss ceremony details with church or temple officials early in your engagement (see Chapter 4, "Planning Your Wedding," and Chapter 11, "Remarriage," for positions on religious remarriage for major U.S. denominations, and the Appendix, under Chapter 9, "Religious Rituals & Requirements").

Religious Marriage Requirements

Below is a summary of the doctrines, marriage rituals, and marriage requirements of the major religious denominations in this country.

Baha'i

Baha'i is an independent world religion started in Iran in 1844 by the prophet Baha'Allah, whose primary mission was to unite the world. Bahaists believe that there is only one God, though He may be called by many names. Together, the world's great religions are expressions of a single unfolding divine plan, "the changeless faith of God, eternal in the past, eternal in the future."

Parental Consent. Marriage in the Baha'i faith begins with the understanding that individuals are free to choose their own mates. In keeping with the primary teaching of unity in all realms, however, they must get the consent of all living parents. By seeking this unity within the immediate and extended family, the couple assures support for their marriage. The parental consents, presented in writing to the local spiritual assembly (nine elected individuals), state simply, *"I, John Smith, give approval for my daughter, Mary Smith, to marry John Doe."* The consents may also be presented as a more elaborate, personal letter.

Public Statement. All that's required for a Baha'i marriage is a simple public statement in the presence of two witnesses. The two individuals must say to each other, *"We will all verily abide by the will of God."* The witnesses will be chosen by the spiritual assembly unless the couple designate special persons. The marriage ceremony can be shared with family and friends anywhere, or with as few as just two attendants or your witnesses.

Ceremony Additions. A traditional wedding ceremony is also possible, as long as this public statement is included. There is no prescribed worship ritual in the Baha'i faith. If a couple choose to have a lengthier service, they devise it.

Since so much personal thought goes into the ceremony, there is usually an explanation provided for guests in the form of a wedding program or verbal commentary from one of the witnesses. Ceremonies might include readings from Baha'i Scripture and those of other faiths, since this religion accepts the teachings of all prophets. Other important elements: music, singing, secular readings including poetry, flowers, the recitation of the vow, and signing of the marriage certificate.

Attire. Wedding attire is up to the couple; many brides wear a traditional white wedding gown.

Buddhist

Sometimes, the wedding ceremony is set for an auspicious time, which may be determined by an astrologer, based on the bride's and groom's horoscopes. Be aware that different sects of Buddhism have different customs. Not all Buddhist wedding ceremonies follow the rituals mentioned below.

The *Poruwa*. A Buddhist ceremony takes place in a special structure known as a *poruwa,* symbolizing the establishment of the couple's new home. This platform has pots of flowers at the corners and a canopy of white flowers or white silk overhead.

Betel Leaves. After religious chanting by the officiant (an elder or a Buddhist priest), the couple share betel leaves (used in many festivals to show respect and thought to be a stimulant) with each other and with their parents.

Ceremony Customs. The couple then exchange rings and gifts. Finally, the officiant pours water over their fingers, which are bound with gold thread. There are closing chants and songs of blessing.

Eastern Orthodox

Eastern Orthodox Christendom, including Greek, Syrian, Armenian, and Russian Orthodox, is not Roman Catholic, but the liturgical services do share similarities with those of the Roman Catholic church. Interdenominational marriages are accepted when the non-Orthodox party is a baptized Christian. Banns of marriage may be proclaimed in accordance with the practice of the local diocese.

Timing. Eastern Orthodox weddings usually take place in the afternoon or early evening and may not be solemnized in church during Lent, on the eve of certain holy days, during the week after Easter, or in the two weeks prior to Christmas.

Ceremony Content. The Eastern Orthodox Marital Rite is rarely celebrated in conjunction with the Divine Liturgy. Because of the length of the ceremony, rich with symbolism and spirituality, it is expected that the couple shall have attended liturgy and received Holy Communion just prior to the wedding. Traditionally, the music of the Orthodox Church is that of a choir or the singing of ancient Byzantine and Russian chants.

Attire. Traditionally, a Greek Orthodox bride wears a face veil; a Russian Orthodox bride does not.

Wedding Party and Guests. Personal taste and local custom determine the size and arrangement of the wedding party. At some Russian Orthodox churches, guests remain standing during the ceremony, but in most Orthodox churches in the United States, they may sit.

Giving Away the Bride. The standard wedding procession in which the bride's father "gives her away" is customary in most Greek Orthodox ceremonies. In the Russian Orthodox ceremony, however, the clergymember meets the wedding party at the vestibule door and the bride is "given away" prior to the procession.

The Betrothal Ritual. An Eastern Orthodox wedding begins with a betrothal ritual, usually at the front or center of the church. This includes the blessing of the rings by the priest and the exchange of the rings, three times, between bride and groom to signify that the bethrothal is taking place among God: the Father, Son, and Holy Spirit. Wedding rings are worn by both bride and groom on their right hands, fourth fingers.

The Order of Marriage. After the close of the betrothal ritual, the celebration of the sacrament of marriage begins. Crowns are placed on the heads of the bride and groom and exchanged between them three times. In the Russian variation of the ceremony, the honor attendant and the best man hold the crowns above the couple's heads. The crowning of the wedding couple—the bridegroom first, followed by the bride—signifies their coronation into a new family realm; both are rulers, together, of their house.

The Dance of Isaiah. After the Gospel is read, the bride and groom partake three times from a common cup of wine, symbolizing the joys and the sorrows they will share together in marriage.

The *koumbaros,* or sponsor (traditionally the groom's godfather, but can be any person who will continue to have a significant relationship with the couple), then accompanies the bride and groom three times around a ceremonial table set with with sugarcoated almonds (symbolizing the bitter and sweet in life), candles, and icons. (The circling is a reminder that marriage is never-ending.) At the close of the ceremony, the congregation joins in singing—or wishing that—*"God Grant Them Many Years."*

Favors. In some Orthodox traditions, at the end of the reception, guests receive festive packets containing presents from the new couple. This custom has the same significance as the shower of rice tradition originated among the Chinese: *"May you always enjoy a life of plenty."*

Hindu

Before a Hindu wedding ceremony begins, a holy fire is lit to the fire god, Agni, who traditionally will bear witness to the wedding. The fire burns to symbolize purity and the eternal flame of love. A tree is planted (it was an ancient belief that plants and animals were representations of the gods, and this ensured their presence). Although marriages traditionally were arranged by the couple's parents, this is no longer a requirement. Neither bride nor groom need to be Hindu, but one should be a member of the temple. Note that Hindu marriage rites vary considerably throughout India. Consult a local temple for guidance.

Attire. The bride often wears a sari; the special colors of marriage are red and, depending on the region in India, yellow. She may wear a red veil; at the end of the ceremony, the groom might see the bride's face for the first time, reflected in the mirror she sits before. The bride's and groom's faces may be covered with red paint; their hands and feet may also be decorated the night before with *mendhi*, elaborate red swirled designs of vermilion henna. In certain regions, the bride's hair is parted and marked with red (vermilion), symbolic of the original blood covenant by which she was introduced into her husband's sect.

Giving Away the Bride. Customs during the service are both religious and cultural. The bride's father gives her hand to the groom, then sprinkles her with holy water to indicate his ties with her are washed away. Garlands are exchanged between the couple and hung around their shoulders. A consecrated cord is hung around their necks, uniting them, accompanied by prayers.

The Bride's Jewelry. A *tali*, a gold ornament threaded on a gold string, is tied on the bride's neck by her mother (who has been collecting gold jewelry for her since her birth) and the groom's sisters. The bride will wear the *tali* throughout her married life; its three knots remind her of her duty to serve her parents, husband, and sons. During the wedding ceremony, the bride receives a nose ring, a symbol of married life, removed only if she becomes a widow.

Circling the Flame. The ceremony concludes when the couple circle three times around the sacred fire walking seven steps per rotation, throwing offerings of rice and flowers into the air. The seven steps, or *sapta padi*, symbolize everlasting friendship.

Islamic (Muslim)

A Muslim man may marry a non-Muslim woman, providing she is Christian or Jewish (people of the Book or Bible), but a Muslim woman may not marry out of the faith. The two witnesses and the bride's counsel—a close friend or relative—may be of any faith.

The Betrothal. In traditional arranged marriages, the Muslim groom would not cast his eyes on his bride until the wedding. This is not usually the case in today's Islamic marriages. The bride's consent to the union is required, however, before the wedding can take place.

Two witnesses and the bride's counsel ask for her consent, then communicate it to the groom, who is waiting in a separate public place or registry. The representatives say to him: *"Assalam o alaikum warehmatullah"* or *"God's peace and blessings be upon you."*

There is no formal clergy in Islam, so any religious leader, registrar, or person may be authorized to conduct a wedding. The registrar asks the groom if he is prepared to accept the bride, then has him present his *dower* to his fiancée. The *dower*, similar to a bride's dowry, may be given immediately or deferred and is in any amount agreed to between future husband and wife. The largely symbolic exchange allows the woman to maintain her economic independence when she comes to her new home and serves to boost her self-esteem. Although the couple are now legally married, Islamic marriages can't be conducted in secrecy, and a public announcement or wedding must follow.

Ceremony Site. The ceremony is held in a magistrate's office in an Islamic country but may be conducted in a mosque or any public place in the United States. Men and women, including the bride and groom, are seated separately.

Ceremony Customs. An old custom—rarely practiced today—is to henna the hands of the bride and groom with *mendhi*, (elaborate patterns of swirls, hand–painted with a vermilion dye) at festive gatherings the night before the wedding.

At the wedding, the couple join hands under a white cloth, while an officiant may lead them in reciting their vows. The officiant gives an address or *khutba*, noting that both husband and wife should treat each other with respect and compassion. Then he offers *dua*, a prayer to God to bless the bride and groom and the wedding, and the couple vow to live and die as Muslims.

The bride and groom may be enthroned for the reception, although many Muslims emphasize simple weddings with no music or dancing. At least one day after the marriage is consummated, the groom throws a feast, called *walima*, for family and friends.

Jewish

No single set of rules applies to all Jewish weddings, for there are differences among the Orthodox, Conservative, and Reform branches of the faith. Individual rabbis and synagogues are likely to have their own interpretations of the marriage ceremony, so verify all procedures with the officiating rabbi before plans are finalized (see Appendix, under Chapter 9, "Religious Rituals & Requirements"). As a rule, Orthodox and Conservative rabbis will not perform interfaith marriages. Some, but not all, Reform clergy will participate in interfaith ceremonies (see "The Interfaith Wedding" section).

Timing. According to Orthodox law, Jewish weddings may take place at any time except on the Sabbath (from sundown on Friday to sundown on Saturday), on Holy Days, during a three-week period in mid-summer, and during almost all of the time between Passover and *Shavuot*.

Most weddings are on Saturday evening after sundown or on Sunday.

Ceremony Site. Jewish weddings may occur almost anywhere, and many are not performed in synagogues or temples. It is more usual in some locales for the ceremony to take place at a club, hotel, or catering hall where the centuries-old splendor of the wedding feast and dancing may follow.

Attire. Conventional wedding attire, including a face veil for the bride if she is Orthodox, is generally worn. In a prewedding Orthodox ritual, the bride is "veiled" by the groom as a sign that she is, indeed, his betrothed. In Conservative and Orthodox ceremonies, all the men are required to cover their heads with either yarmulkes or silk top hats; the women, with hats or kerchiefs. If planning a Reform ceremony, ask the rabbi if there are any head-covering requirements.

Prewedding Traditions. The bride and groom may not see each other before the "veiling" (if there is one), which occurs just before the ceremony. The bride and her attendants may wait, in wedding attire, in a separate room, where they receive guests beforehand. In some places, there may be a brief cocktail–and–hors d'oeuvres reception preceding the ceremony, while the prewedding rituals are carried out.

Seating. At the appropriate time, the bride's family will be seated on the right side of the hall or temple, the groom's family on the left, before any other guests are ushered to their places.

The Procession. The order of the procession and positions during the ceremony are set by local custom, with Orthodox and Conservative processions usually including the groom, the bride, both sets of parents (who walk them down the aisle), both sets of grandparents, bridesmaids, ushers, and child attendants (see Chapter 8, "Your Wedding Ceremony").

The *Huppah*. Jewish marriages are traditionally performed under a *huppah*, a heavily ornamented canopy symbolizing the ancient bridal chamber of consummation; shelter from the open sky in nomadic times; and the home the couple will share together. The *huppah* may also be embellished with—or woven entirely of—fresh flowers. It is usually placed in front of an attractive background at one end of the room, or in front of the Ark in a temple. Each person in the procession takes a prearranged position under or near the *huppah* (see Chapter 8, "Your Wedding Ceremony").

Under the *huppah*, the rabbi and cantor stand next to a small table covered in white, set with one or two goblets for ritual wine.

The Ceremony. As the bride arrives under the *huppah*, she may walk three (the Bible mentions betrothal three times; a husband has three obligations to his wife —food, clothing, conjugal relations) or seven (the number of completion—the number of days it took God to create the universe) times around the groom in an Orthodox ceremony.

The service begins with a betrothal ceremony, followed by an introductory blessing. Next, the groom sips from a goblet of wine and passes it to the bride. After the couple have spoken their vows, the groom recites a marriage proposal in English and in Hebrew and places a plain gold band on the bride's right index finger in the Conservative and Orthodox ceremonies; on her left ring finger in the Reform ceremony. Conservative, Orthodox, and some Reform rabbis read aloud the *ketubah*, or traditional marriage contract, detailing what the groom promises to provide for the bride. The *ketubah* is then given to the bride and groom, who hang it in their new home.

The ceremony ends with the traditional reciting of the Seven (the number of completion) Blessings by the rabbi, or others given the honor. The blessings cover the creation of the world and humanity, the survival of the Jewish people and of Israel, the marriage, the couple's happiness, and the raising of the family. They are a reminder that life's goals are not selfish, but designed for the betterment of the world, the glory of God.

Breaking the Glass. At the close of the ceremony, a wine glass is wrapped in a cloth napkin or handkerchief and placed on the ground. The groom stamps down, smashing it not for good luck, nor for the symbolic loss of the bride's virginity (as is commonly believed), but as a reminder of the destruction of the Holy Temple in Jerusalem, and of other calamities that befell the Jewish people that should not be forgotten, even during this most joyous occasion. The breaking of the glass generally signifies the close of the marriage ceremony and may be greeted with shouts of *"Mazel Tov!"* or "Good Luck!" from guests.

The *Yichud*. Traditionally, the bride and groom spend fifteen minutes alone together in *yichud*—seclusion. This is symbolic of ancient days when a groom brought his bride to his tent to consummate the marriage. This has not been the literal custom for centuries. These private moments, however, are a symbolic consummation, a demonstration of the couple's right to privacy.

The Wedding Feast. The reception feast is traditionally begun with a blessing (by the fathers, the rabbi, or the couple) over a *challah* (a braided loaf of egg-rich bread). It then is cut and distributed to each table for good luck.

Protestant

There are a wide number of denominations within the Protestant church. One may be liturgical, another Pentecostal in spirit. The Protestant wedding is a worship service, and guests are both participants and witnesses; there may be standing, singing, and praying aloud. A homily or sermon by the officiant is common.

Almost all Protestant churches use a variation of the standard *("Dearly Beloved . . .")* wedding service, and most request that the congregation stand during part of the ceremony. Many Protestant clergy are reluctant to perform wedding ceremonies on Sundays and religious holidays, but this is dictated by preference rather than canon law. (There is a growing trend among some congregationally governed churches toward Sunday weddings. In these cases, if the wedding follows the Sunday-morning service, an open invitation is often issued to members.)

Rules about music vary; it's wise to get prior approval from a church authority for the use of secular music, especially any modern popular songs. There may be guidelines, rather than rules, about decorations and attire for the sanctuary. It's possible that bare-backed or strapless gowns will require a jacket or wrap until the reception. (Many dresses for brides, bridesmaids, and mothers come with coverups for this very reason.) Discuss any questions about the appropriateness of the bride's and bridesmaids' gowns with the clergymember.

The following variations can be found among some of the Protestant faiths:

Amish

The Amish service is quite simple. There is no instrumental music, nor does the couple enter to a wedding march. Weddings take place after the harvest is completed, on Tuesdays or Thursdays. The choice of day assures that the whole community will have time to prepare, participate, and clean up, leaving the weekend free for church activities.

Assemblies of God

The minister counsels the couple and must be convinced of their "forethought, wisdom, and sobriety" in seeking marriage. While the church leaves the decision to marry interfaith couples to each individual minister, it is preferred that both partners be committed, born-again Christians.

Baptist

In Southern Baptist and American Baptist congregations, the local church sets the policy—from marrying only members of the church, to marrying people of any religion. Consult your local clergymember.

Christian Scientist

The Church of Christ, Scientist, is a church of lay members and has no ordained clergy. When members marry, they are free to choose a minister ordained in another denomination or a proper legal authority to perform the ceremony. The ceremony's format is determined by the bride and groom in collaboration with the officiant.

Episcopal

At least one partner must be a baptized Christian to be married in the Episcopal church. A couple must give thirty days' notice of their plans to marry and sign a declaration of intention for a lifelong union. The priest is required to conduct premarital counseling and be sure that there is a serious commitment to marriage. Clergymembers of other faiths sometimes co-officiate.

A Nuptial Mass may be included in the service. The church usually discourages formal weddings during Lent.

Lutheran, Methodist, Presbyterian

Weddings are performed at the discretion of the clergymember after counseling the partners to determine their commitment. Each faith has a service book, worship guides, and other resources for planning weddings.

Mormon

The Church of Jesus Christ of Latter-Day Saints recognizes two kinds of marriage.

The first is for the faithful found worthy (by the head of the local congregation) of marriage in one of the church's holy temples—of which there are fifty-one. Such couples are wed in a *sealing ordinance* "for time and eternity" (instead of "until death do you part"), with both man and woman wearing white to symbolize purity. Their children are believed to potentially belong to them for all eternity as well—contingent on worthiness (how the couple live their lives according to the teachings of Jesus Christ).

The second is a civil ceremony performed by bishops of the church or other legal authorities. These couples are sometimes re-wed in a temple at a later date, "sealing" their marriage for eternity. A Mormon and a non-Mormon may be wed in such a civil ceremony.

Society of Friends (Quaker)

A wedding under the care of a Friends meeting may require prior approval (which may take up to three months) from the monthly meeting of the Religious Society of Friends. A letter requesting approval is written by the couple and sent to the meeting under whose care they would be married. (See Appendix, under Chapter 9, "Religious Rituals & Requirements.")

Traditional: The marriage itself takes place during a meeting for worship, where those in attendance meditate quietly. The bridal couple enter the meeting together and join the circle of Friends already seated. (A traditional procession, including the couple, their parents, honor attendants, and the committee members, is another option). There is usually no music. The bridal party takes seats on benches facing the entire meeting.

In the midst of the traditional Quaker silence, the bride and groom rise, join hands, and say their vows. The groom and bride speak their promises in whichever order they choose. The bride is not given away, nor does a third person pronounce the couple married, for the Friends believe that only God creates such a union.

The marriage certificate is then brought to the couple to sign, after which it is read aloud by a member of the meeting. The gathering may continue until the bride and groom feel ready to leave. The ceremony usually lasts one hour. All guests sign the marriage certificate before departing, a custom that couples marrying in other faiths may choose to incorporate. Further details of the Quaker wedding are usually worked out in advance between the couple and an appointed group of meeting members. It is this group that oversees the wedding.

Contemporary: Today, a Quaker couple may design a highly personalized service with attendants, flowers, music, or readings. The wedding still remains a simple one—very much in the Quaker tradition. Although neither a bridal party nor the exchange of rings is necessary, both are commonly seen. It is the custom for bridesmaids to dress quite simply. In some areas of the country, the meeting will have a pastor, who naturally would take part in the ceremony and in the prewedding discussion.

Unitarian-Universalist Society

This religion incorporates tenets from all faiths into its worship, and wedding ceremonies are no exception. There is no set liturgy. The minister and couple work together to fashion a service that fits the beliefs and ideals of this unique marriage. There may be Christian or Jewish symbols or readings, but the interpretation is as likely to be humanistic as religious. This pluralistic religion is a comfortable meeting ground for couples of different faiths and beliefs, where a thoughtful, reverent service can be worked out.

United Church of Christ (Congregational)

Although not a requirement for marriage, couples are expected to participate in two to three sessions of premarital counseling with a pastor. The bride and groom are often encouraged to compile their own wedding service from a menu of prayers, Scripture, readings, and hymns (with the pastor performing the service), so that they invest something of themselves into the ceremony. Increasingly, today, either one or both of the prospective spouses is expected to be a member of or a participant in the congregation where the wedding ceremony is held.

Roman Catholic

The easiest marriage to arrange in the Roman Catholic church is one between two never-married adults who grew up as Catholics in the same parish. Every other scenario requires more paperwork. (See Appendix, under Chapter 9, "Religious Rituals & Requirements," and Chapter 11, "Remarriage.")

The Banns. Before a couple wed, it's customary for the banns (intentions to marry) to be published in the parish churches of both the bride and groom (some parishes, however, may waive this practice). These announcements may be made from the pulpit at the principal Mass on three consecutive Sundays before the wedding, or be published in the church calendar or bulletin. (The banns originated as a way for the church to make sure that each party was free to marry.) The banns are not usually proclaimed for an interfaith marriage, nor for the marriage of an older couple (it is assumed that any encumbrances to the marriage will already be known by the couple's priest).

Permissions. A Catholic wedding ceremony can take place in the parish of the bride or groom. If another parish is chosen, permission is necessary. The officiating priest will need proof of baptism for baptized persons (a baptismal certificate) and evidence of freedom to marry (divorce and nullity decree, as well as the sworn declaration of witnesses; death certificate).

Co-officiating. Catholic weddings are rarely conducted outside a church building, although interdenominational marriages are sometimes performed in the church of the non-Catholic. In such cases, a Roman Catholic priest may pronounce a prayer or blessing over the couple. (If the ceremony is an interfaith one, it is more common for it to be performed in a secular place, such as a hotel ballroom.) When someone other than a priest (or bishop or deacon) is to officiate at a wedding, a dispensation from canonical form is requested. The Catholic party must make this request through his or her parish priest.

An interfaith or interdenominational wedding with two clergymembers participating may also be held in a Roman Catholic parish, in which case a Roman Catholic priest will officiate (including the exchange of vows) while the non-Catholic minister may address and bless the couple. The host clergymember is always the principal officiant.

The non-Catholic bride or groom in a mixed marriage need not be baptized but must be free to marry in a Catholic church. The Catholic party will first have to obtain a dispensation from the bishop of the diocese. It is easy to secure if you've never been married before; the priest who will marry you will most likely handle the procedure. However, the Roman Catholic partner must promise to baptize and raise as Catholics any children of the marriage.

Additionally, both the bride and groom, even if they are both Catholic, must be free to marry in the church. This means that they cannot have been previously married, unless widowed. If either was married before, they must receive an annulment before they can officially be wed again.

Prewedding Counseling (Pre-cana). Couples planning to marry in the Catholic church attend a series of prewedding sessions with the priest, an Engaged Encounter weekend, or some other marriage-preparation weekend or sessions (see Appendix, under Chapter 4, "Planning Your Wedding") before they wed. The couple will be asked to discuss practical issues (such as money management), as well as spiritual issues.

The Procession. In a Catholic wedding, the bride may be escorted down the aisle, but is not "given away." Many options are open to the couple in the new marriage rites. Each couple may discuss these with the priest before the wedding. The two most popular options are:

Option 1: The bride's father, another person she chooses, or her father *and* mother, escort(s) her to the steps of the altar, where the groom and the priest are waiting. Many couples at this point exchange a greeting with the priest and with the bride's father, mother, or whomever escorted her down the aisle. Then, in a gesture of recognizing the groom, the person escorting the bride places the bride's hand in the groom's hand. He or she may lift the bride's veil and kiss her before taking a seat.

Option 2: Some couples choose to be greeted at the vestibule door by the priest, then be led by him to the altar.

Music. Certain popular music may not be allowed in some Catholic dioceses, as it is not seen as appropriate for worship. (See Chapter 14, "Wedding Music," and consult your priest.)

Timing. During Advent, Catholic marriages may be performed and Nuptial Masses celebrated; they may also be performed during Lent, but some parishes may discourage it. Most churches have no flowers during Lent, but if they allow weddings, they will not legislate your choice of blooms.

Nuptial Mass. A Nuptial Mass may be arranged for almost any Catholic wedding, with the brief wedding ceremony being incorporated into the Mass, after the homily. Non-Catholics at a Nuptial Mass (including the bride or groom, if it is a mixed marriage) do not take Communion. Many churches have hymnals and worship books so guests may follow the ritual of the Mass. Non-Catholic guests needn't give the responses or kneel, but should sit quietly while others kneel. All guests should stand at the proper times in the ceremony.

Because a non-Catholic partner and guests will not be able to receive Holy Communion, some Roman Catholics choose to attend a Mass earlier in the day with family, rather than exclude others from participation.

Ceremony Participation. There are many opportunities to include friends and relatives in the service—readings, presenting the bread and wine for the Eucharist, and attending the priest at the altar. Remember to give altar servers a gift—the best man can pass it along (see Chapter 17, "Wedding Gifts").

Flowers for the Virgin Mary. During or following the marriage ceremony, a Catholic bride may leave her flowers before a statue of Mary, the Blessed Mother, who is the patron saint of family life, with a prayer for her own new family.

Shinto

With its strong cultural roots, the ancient Shinto religion practiced by many Japanese seems to be more a matter of custom than the manifestation of deeply held religious beliefs. There is little conflict between the religious doctrines of Shinto and other sects, allowing them to coexist with Christian beliefs.

Ceremony site. The ceremony may be held before a Shinto shrine, in the innermost shrine building (or, outside Japan, in a Christian chapel).

Attire. The bride and groom may wear traditional, colorful, ceremonial kimonos, but either one or both may change later to Western-style wedding attire. During the reception, the bride exits and reappears up to three times in different outfits. Kimonos may be rented for the occasion, but the fee may be high.

Ceremony Rites. Ancestors are honored in the ritual through the bowing and offerings of food before family ancestral shrines and the ringing of bells. Prayers are recited by the officiating Shinto priest, and, traditionally, only close relatives are invited. There are no vows, but the couple exchange rings and share nine sips of sake, the *sansan kudo* (three sips from three cups of sake—a rice wine)—which is the essence of the ceremony. Later, sips of sake are exchanged with the couple's parents, both to honor them and to mark their formal acceptance of the marriage.

A Western-style reception, often held in a hall adjoining the shrine or a hotel, follows the religious ceremony. The wedding guests make speeches, and the wedding cake is cut and served.

The Interfaith Wedding

When the bride and groom are of different faiths, it is possible for them to be married in a ceremony that combines the rituals of both religions. The content of your interfaith wedding, sometimes known as the ecumenical service among Christian groups, will depend on your own wishes and those of the clergymembers involved. The ceremony can be performed almost entirely by an officiant of one faith, with the other one giving a short blessing at the end. For example, the couple might be married by a Catholic priest according to the ritual of the Mass, and have a rabbi present to offer the Hebrew Seven Blessings after the vows are exchanged.

Or the service can be divided equally between the two faiths, with a minister and priest perhaps alternating religious readings, then joining together for the exchange of vows and the ring ceremony.

Emphasize what you have in common. At a Jewish/Protestant wedding, you might use only Scripture from the Old Testament. To demonstrate your respect for each other's faith, have your sister read a Scripture from his faith; his brother, a passage from yours. (See Chapter 4, "Planning Your Wedding," and Chapter 8, "Your Wedding Ceremony," for more on finding officiants for and planning an interfaith wedding, and the Appendix, under Chapter 4, for sources).

Religious Wedding Variations

Almost all religions allow certain variations in their ceremonies; many even have several services from which you might choose. You and your fiancé should discuss the standard vows with your clergymember. Is this what you want your wedding to express? If you want to make changes—and they can be accomplished without offending anyone's sensibilities—alterations in the wedding service can greatly enrich this day in your memory. (For more on personalizing your ceremony and writing your own vows, see Chapter 8, "Your Wedding Ceremony," and the Appendix, under Chapter 8.)

SPECIAL WEDDINGS & NEW WAYS TO WED

Weddings today make personal statements about the couple—their careers and interests, their ethnicity and backgrounds, their relationship. Floral arrangements, for example, may highlight the bride's Texas roots with bluebonnets—the state flower. Or the cake may be topped with seashells, instead of bride and groom figurines, symbolizing the couple's love of the sea (see Appendix, under Chapter 10, "Special Weddings and New Ways to Wed").

Today's celebrations also reflect new situations facing couples and their families: Men and women are marrying at a later age. They may have grown up with different cultures and religions. Friends and relatives are often scattered around the country, even the world. And for most women, marrying the boy next door—or even in the next town—is rare. Today's etiquette balances their needs and wants with tradition, consideration for others, and, above all, good taste.

The Long-Weekend Wedding

You might have grown up in Chicago, your groom may be from San Francisco, and you may have met in Boston. In these transient times, friends and relatives will be converging from all parts of the country, and sometimes from around the world, to celebrate your wedding. A long-weekend wedding, packed with activities and parties that will add incentives for far-flung guests to attend—as well as more opportunities for you to spend time with them—may be the perfect way to bring everyone together.

long-weekend wedding tips

- Sketch out a plan of the weekend—events, guests, ages, and interests. Offer activities for all age groups.

- Find out who can put people up in their homes and who would be willing to host parties.

- Send out save-the-date cards or a newsletter or announcement of events (well in advance of the wedding invitation, to allow guests to make their plans). When invitations go out, include a tentative schedule, maps, suggested attire, and separate R.s.v.p. cards for each event (unless party hosts prefer to send their own separate invitations).

- Reserve blocks of hotel rooms.

- Have guests met at the airport or train station by attendants, family, or friends. Set up transportation to each event.

- Provide welcoming touches—a list of all long-distance guests and where they're staying; hosts' phone numbers; guest baskets with fruit, candy, and homemade cookies. Also, contact the local convention and visitors bureau for free maps, guides to local attractions, and postcards.

- If you've invited children, either plan to include them or provide (and pay for) childcare.

- Attend every event, although you needn't stay from beginning to end. Greet all guests and thank party hosts.

- Give thank-you gifts to all who host parties (see Chapter 17, "Wedding Gifts").

Friends and relatives on both sides of the family may host parties and get-togethers in your honor—an open-house breakfast, a backyard barbecue, an ice-skating party—with the wedding and reception as the central event of the weekend. This approach doesn't have to cost more than a traditional one-day wedding. Guests usually pay for their own travel and lodging, and hosts (parents of the bride and groom, grandparents, friends, and other relatives) pick up the tab for the event they plan. Some activities, such as swimming at the beach or a volleyball game at the park, may be free or cost very little. Here are more ideas:

Get-Acquainted Tea/Cocktail Party. Once long-distance guests arrive in town, invite them for an informal gathering. A buffet dinner with a local theme, such as Cajun food and music for a New Orleans wedding, can help break the ice and get everyone acquainted. Or consider hiring a dance instructor to help get people up on their feet.

Saturday Tours/Museum Visits. Hire a bus to introduce visitors to the wedding town or nearby area. Include tours of museums—appropriate to each age group. Historic sites might appeal to older guests; hands-on science exhibits could interest children. Organize a hike, a visit to the zoo, or a day at the beach.

Barbecue/Pool Party. A country club or neighbor's backyard could accommodate this gathering, suitable for all ages. Brew up some iced tea, stoke the grill, and crank up the CDs. Get a game of volleyball or lawn croquet going.

Softball Game. Divide guests into the Bride's Team and the Groom's Team to encourage mingling and camaraderie. Touch football, volleyball, basketball, or a tennis or golf tournament are other possibilities. Consider printing up team T-shirts or baseball caps to help introduce guests to each other. And don't forget to present silly prizes to winners or MVP's.

Dinner for Out-of-Towners. Be sure guests who aren't included in the rehearsal dinner aren't left stranded in an unfamiliar city: Ask for a friend or relative to host an event for them during that time. Or consider having the rehearsal dinner on Thursday—there's no rule that says it must be the night before the wedding—so you can have a party for all long-distance guests on Friday night.

Wedding-Day Breakfast. A casual breakfast buffet at the bride's home, or at the home of a close relative, provides a place for out-of-towners to gather, savor private moments, and finalize plans for the main event. Plan a simple menu of coffee, tea, juice, muffins, eggs, and fruit. Feel free to excuse yourself at any time.

Day-After-the-Wedding Brunch. A relaxed late-morning or noontime picnic in a neighbor's yard, or a hotel buffet, is a final get-together for the newlyweds, their families, and friends. Informal foods, such as barbecued ribs, corn on the cob, and sandwiches help guests relax after the long weekend. You might set up badminton or lawn croquet. Guests will have a chance to take last-minute photographs, reflect on the weekend events, and say their good-byes to each other and the honeymoon-bound couple.

The Moveable Wedding

When guests can't all travel to one location to celebrate, the bridal couple can bring the wedding to them. The bride and groom and their close relatives and friends take the celebration, called a moveable wedding, on the road, traveling to predetermined spots, such as his and her hometowns, for parties hosted in the newlyweds' honor. This can be the perfect solution for couples with large groups of friends and family scattered in different locations or with divorced parents who are not attending the wedding. Here's how to schedule a moveable wedding.

Marry in the town you live in now. Planning the actual ceremony from your current residence makes the details, such as obtaining the marriage license, and finding an officiant, much easier. Local friends and out-of-town relatives who can travel will be there to share the celebration with you.

Travel to your parents' hometown. Your parents may host the next wedding celebration by having a formal, seated dinner/wedding reception, following your arrival from the out-of-town ceremony. Form a receiving line, drink champagne, and serve cake—much as you would at any reception. You may want to wear your wedding dress; your groom, his formalwear. Otherwise, choose a dress that is appropriate for the style and formality of the party.

Progress to your groom's hometown. The party at this stop—a day or two later—may be hosted by his parents. It can be as formal as the first wedding reception, or a casual open house for well-wishers. You may wear your gown again and at subsequent formal celebrations, but most brides choose to wear a cocktail dress instead.

Move to other relatives' towns and/or friends' towns. These next events may be smaller and less formal—such as cocktail parties or brunches—and may be held at individual homes.

Move on to your private honeymoon. You deserve the time alone—to relax, unwind, and simply enjoy being newlyweds.

moveable-wedding tips

- Choose cities and towns closest to where most of your guests live.

- Appoint someone at each site to make arrangements with vendors—such as caterers and florists—for you.

- Send out invitations to guests in each city for each party (you can include more than one event on an invitation to inform guests of all your plans). Enclose the correct number of reply cards—one for each get-together.

- Work with a travel agent; he or she may be able to organize special airfares.

- Have receiving lines at each party to enable guests to meet you and thank the hosts.

- Box pieces of the original wedding cake to bring to each host on the trip. You may wish to serve bottles of the champagne you poured at the wedding reception.

- For favors, give guests who attend follow-up parties souvenirs from the city where the wedding was held (e.g., small pieces of pottery from Albuquerque, New Mexico).

- Show a videotape of the out-of-town ceremony at subsequent parties and receptions. (One couple had their marriage broadcast by satellite into the living room of the groom's parents, thousands of miles away, where a reception was being held in the newlyweds' honor. The couple then traveled on to see the groom's family a few days later.)

- Consider how many people will be able to fit at your sentimental journey site. If the area can't accommodate more than your immediate family, research nearby lodges, hotels, and inns, for adequate space.

- Assemble a slide show of events you fondly remember: shots from your college days or summers at the camp you attended as a child. Enlist the help of friends and relatives.

- Organize a touch-football game and give each player a scarf or bandanna with school or camp colors, or a college T-shirt in two team colors. Include activities for those guests not inclined or able to participate in group sports.

The Sentimental Journey

This new way to marry is similar in style to the long-weekend wedding, except that it takes place at a spot with special meaning and memories for the couple (for example, your college campus, the seaside resort town where you first met). The sentimental journey is also a nostalgic alternative for couples who may prefer not to marry in the bride's hometown. Although no one in either family may live at the site, it should have enough of an attraction that a substantial number of your wedding guests will want to make the trip. Below are a selection of sentimental journey locations:

A college campus. Return to your alma mater to relive good times. Perhaps plan the wedding celebration around your class reunion and include already-scheduled events so college friends, who are guests, can enjoy their own sentimental journey. Rent out one wing or dorm so everyone can stay together, but consider getting a special hotel suite for yourself to prepare for the ceremony. Hire the school's chamber quartet to play during the ceremony; a band to accompany you, the bridal party, and guests from the chapel to the reception.

A summer home or family vacation spot. Return to the beaches of your childhood summers. Plan a rerun of past pleasures—clambakes, volleyball games, sand-castle and fishing competitions—as well as nostalgic visits to childhood haunts, such as an amusement park or zoo.

Summer camp. Rent cabins for the returning and visiting campers, and arrange to have meals catered in the dining hall. Invite friends to sing old camp songs—provide the words and sheet music for all—and stage a canoe race or a midnight swim.

The Destination Wedding

Couples can combine a romantic wedding ceremony with a fantasy vacation by transporting the whole celebration directly to the honeymoon site. Possible options include islands or beach resorts, ski resorts, cruises, or even foreign cities.

This new way to wed is a good option for couples who no longer live in their hometowns, or whose families are far–flung. It is also especially well suited to couples with children from prior marriages; it allows the two merging families to spend time together just prior to and after the wedding. Guests may find this the perfect way to combine the vacation they need with the family reunion they've anticipated. And though getting married in paradise may sound expensive, that doesn't have to be the case. Many all–inclusive resorts don't charge for the ceremony, and since your guest list will likely be smaller, you can opt for a more intimate terrace reception instead of a ballroom blowout.

After the festivities, the newlyweds should go off on their own to another locale for some private time. Guests have the option of staying on and continuing their vacation at their leisure. The destination wedding, which can combine the features of a long-weekend wedding, is often a smaller, more intimate celebration for immediate family and close friends. Although most guests will be responsible for their own airfare and hotel costs, you and your family may want to pay for younger siblings or elderly grandparents who wouldn't be able to afford the trip otherwise. More planning tips:

Select the site. Choose a location the same way you would a honeymoon spot. Contact tourist boards and travel agents, research travel magazines, the Internet and ask friends for recommendations. Find out about typical weather for the season you plan to go—Bermuda is coldest in December and Madrid is hottest in August. You can also make this a sentimental journey and return to a vacation area you've enjoyed previously as a couple. If you both met while working one summer at a theme park, a wedding there will be great incentive for all of your guests to join you while visiting the park with their families.

Check legalities. Contact the consulate or tourist board where you plan to marry to learn about local rules and residency requirements. Also write to the appropriate U.S. Embassy if it's a foreign site. Allow plenty of time—at least three months—to comply with rules and compile proper documents, once you know what's needed. For example, France has a forty-day residency requirement prior to the wedding.

Check customs regulations. Many countries require that you declare any prescription medications or other pharmaceuticals upon entering. Alert guests that they should bring along all prescriptions and keep drugs in the bottles in which they were sold. Having to make a court appearance in a foreign country will put a damper on your celebration.

Hire an on-site consultant. Ask your hotel or the tourist board (or check the website of the destination or resort) for names of local wedding planners to help organize and oversee your celebration, and find an officiant, caterer and florist. Some hotels offer wedding packages: Find out what they include and what fits your plans. (For more information, see Appendix, Chapter 10.)

Decide where the wedding will take place. Do you envision a simple beachside ceremony and reception, or a lavish affair at a nearby historic mansion? Consult the tourist board, your resort and/or consultant, as well as local websites for ideas.

Send save-the-date cards. Your friends and family will need plenty of time to make travel arrangements, so send a save-the-date card, then follow up with a phone call. Getting a rough estimate of your guest list means you'll be able to block off rooms and plan accordingly.

Send invitations to all. Although some may not be able to afford the extra time and expense involved, all will appreciate your thinking of them with an invitation. Some may surprise you by jumping at the chance to fly to an exotic site for your wedding.

destination wedding tips

- If foreign regulations and paperwork are too complex, marry legally at home, then travel to your honeymoon spot for a festive reception or reaffirmation.

- Host a second reception closer to home—to celebrate with those who can't make the destination wedding.

- Check with guests you want at your wedding *before* finalizing plans.

- Keep guests' budgets in mind when choosing hotels—look into group rates or suggest hotels for a range of budgets.

- Arrive a few days early to finalize paperwork and details and meet with the officiant, caterer, florist, and wedding planner.

- Encourage guests to mail gifts to your home or to your parents' home.

- Bring the dress box on the plane or carry the gown in a garment bag. Let the flight attendant know what your cargo is, so it can be stowed carefully or hung.

- Take advantage of local customs, food, music, and style (include ukulele players at a Hawaiian party, for example). Wear the traditional attire.

- Favor guests with take-home gifts native to the wedding locale—music tapes, cookbooks of regional cuisine, or paintings or crafts by artisans from the area.

rush wedding tips

- Be realistic. Set priorities and make some compromises in order to come as close as possible to your dream wedding, given the short notice. You may have to settle for your second-choice reception site to get the earlier date you prefer.

- Delegate wedding tasks and research to friends and family; you'll be amazed at how quickly wedding and reception plans can come together.

- Consider having a civil ceremony, which can be arranged in most states in a matter of days (see Chapter 4, "Planning Your Wedding"). You can follow up with a more traditional reception later on, giving you time to plan—and to make sure that guests you want to see will be able to attend.

- If you elope, make it festive by wearing a pretty new dress and carrying flowers. Toast each other at your post-wedding celebration, and again at a reception when you return home.

- Take pictures at the ceremony and on your honeymoon to share with friends and family at a party later on.

Choose an appropriate officiant. Do your research so there are no eleventh-hour surprises. Make sure your officiant is licensed to perform a wedding ceremony at your location. (A ship's captain, for example, cannot legally marry you on a cruise unless he or she is also a minister or judge. You *can* be married by a clergymember while on board ship. Check with the cruise line to learn if one may be coming aboard.)

Dress to suit the site. Consider the climate and ambience of the site when choosing wedding attire. A formal gown with a high neck and long sleeves is out for a tropical celebration; breezy, looser fabrics, such as chiffon and organza, are better choices. Many fabrics pack and travel well, but others—linen and silk taffeta, for example—wrinkle easily and will require ironing.

Don't forget to pack wedding essentials. Many tropical islands will not have the wedding accessories you envision, so assemble your groom's and ushers' formalwear, your garter, and so on.

The Rush Wedding

While most engagements are at least a year long, sometimes outside forces speed up the process. But even if you're getting married quickly, etiquette still plays a role—for example, your guests should receive an invitation *at least* two weeks before the wedding. If time is tight, your parents may send handwritten notes or invite guests personally by telephone, telegram, overnight mail, fax, or e-mail. Be sure that all the information that would be included on a printed invitation—who's getting married, where, when, the style of the service, the location of the reception, R.s.v.p. address, and a return address (so that people will know where to send gifts)—is passed along to guests, however you spread the word. If you will be handling the telephoning personally but want to indicate that your parents are hosting the wedding, say, "Mom and Dad wanted you to be with us." Here are some reasons for a quick wedding:

Illness. A serious health problem, such as an impending operation, whether it involves a close relative, a bridal-party member, or the bride or groom, may dictate moving up the date.

Pregnancy. Depending on how the couple handle this issue—and on their families' attitudes—a small, quick wedding may be the most comfortable approach for everyone. Most bridal shop owners can suggest gowns that camouflage a pregnant shape.

Job transfer. You or your fiancé may be scheduled to move away from family and friends, to start a new job. Instead of relocating and then dealing with complex wedding plans long-distance, you could opt to complete your plans quickly, marry now, and leave together as a married couple.

School. One of you may be moving away from home to start school; a quick, local celebration now may be easier to plan than a long-distance one later.

Military service. A sudden call into combat or a change in job assignment may spur a couple to hastily arrange a marriage prior to departure. They may decide to marry prior to long-term, foreign duty for military or other career purposes, rather than wait for a partner's return. For example, if the non–military prospective spouse chooses to go along, married status may be required for the pair to live together, especially for overseas assignments.

Insurance benefits. If your fiancé has better health coverage than you, you may move up the wedding date to avoid any anticipated, major health expenses.

The Military Wedding

A dramatic way to salute your military status, a Military Wedding is dictated more by tradition than strict laws. The military considers weddings to be "unofficial," social occasions. Both bride and groom, if each is in the military, have the option of wearing a military uniform or traditional wedding attire. Many choose to wed in very traditional military style by wearing a uniform, wording the invitation in proper military form, and including the arch of sabers or swords. Below are more tips:

Site. Choose your own church or synagogue or use the chapel at your military base. You can also marry at a military academy if you are a graduate (active or retired), a child of a graduate, or a member of the faculty or staff.

Attire. The full ceremonial dress uniform of the service and rank is often worn including white gloves and swords (for the navy and coast guard) or sabers (for the army and marines). Military decorations replace boutonnieres on men's uniforms, although a bride in uniform can carry a bouquet. Most servicewomen prefer to wear a traditional wedding gown. Nonmilitary ushers dress in formalwear.

Invitations. Gold-braided edges or an ink drawing of crossed swords add a military flourish. The wording differs only in that the groom's and/or bride's rank and service are indicated (see Chapter 5, "Invitations & Announcements").

Protocol. When their rank is captain or higher in the army, or lieutenant senior grade or higher in the navy, a guest's, bride's, or groom's title appears *before* the name. A lower rank would be listed *after* the name: *Max White, Ensign, United States Navy* (see Chapter 5, "Invitations & Announcements"). *Mr.* is never used to refer to an officer on active duty. Contact the protocol officer at the nearest base or a military chaplain for more information (see Appendix, under Chapter 10, "Special Weddings & New Ways to Wed").

military wedding tips

- Verify your plans well in advance with the proper military authorities. Get permission for flowers, music, and photography from the chaplain as each academy and military base has its own guidelines.

- If members of the honor guard are also wedding attendants, they must wear military dress. Only someone who is wearing the full-dress uniform can carry a sword or saber.

- For an overseas wedding on- or off-base, determine what papers are required before a spouse-to-be leaves the U.S.

- Contact the chaplain early if you wish to marry at a military academy chapel. Since undergraduates may not marry, back-to-back wedding ceremonies may be the norm following graduation.

- If the bride will not be in uniform, she should complement the very formal style of the military uniforms by wearing a long, elegant dress with a flowing train and veil (for a second wedding, omit the train and veil; see Chapter 11, "Remarriage"). Bridesmaids and honor attendant wear equally formal long dresses.

wedding tips for clerics

- Choose a style of gown that suits the formality of the wedding and fits the customs of your religious denomination. Low-cut necklines or backs, or strapless dresses may not be acceptable or appropriate.

- Discuss choice of music, decor, and order of events with church or synagogue officials before finalizing plans. Clergymembers may be expected to adhere to traditions specific to their place of worship, if that's where the ceremony is held.

- Consider adding special blessings to address congregants and guests, and thank them for sharing the occasion with you.

Decorations. It's common to display the American flag and/or the standards of the couple's military units during the ceremony, in addition to flowers.

Procession/Recession. The military procession follows standard procedure, but the recession is dramatized by the traditional arch of steel—swords or sabers. The arch is formed by an honor guard (made up of commissioned officers), and symbolizes a safe passage into marriage. The arch may be formed outside the church or synagogue, in front of the chapel, or both, depending on church rules, branch of service, and personal preference. On command, swords or sabers are raised with cutting edges facing up. The couple enter the arch, kiss, then pass through. The newlywed(s) in uniform salute(s) the honor guard. Officers then sheath the swords or sabers and return them to the carry position.

Reception. You might feature regimental decorations and music, including miniature flags and the theme song of the groom's and/or bride's branch of service. At a seated reception, military guests are shown to their places in order of rank. The highlight of the celebration comes when the bride and groom cut the cake using a sword or saber.

Wedding of a Clergymember

Today, either the bride or the groom may be a member of the clergy. The couple's wedding ceremony, reception, and rituals are largely the same as for nonclerics, with a few additional traditions expressly for clergymembers.

Site. When the groom is a clergymember, the ceremony still usually takes place in the bride's church or synagogue. When the bride is the clergymember, the ceremony is held at her place of worship.

Attire. A cleric, whether the bride or the groom, has the choice of wearing clerical garb or traditional formal attire. The groom also has the option of dressing in formalwear with a clerical collar. The customs of the couple's denomination and the formality of the wedding will determine specific details, such as the style of the wedding gown.

Officiant. The clergymember at the bride's house of worship officiates when the groom is a clergymember. If the bride is the groom's parishioner, then her fiancé's superior, or another member of the clergy of equal rank, might perform the ceremony, frequently with the entire congregation involved. The bride chooses the officiant when she is the clergymember.

Parent as Officiant. If one of the couple's parents is a clergymember, he or she may officiate at the ceremony. If it's the bride's father, another male relative may escort her down the aisle and her mother may step forward to give her away or "support her" in marriage.

The Double Wedding

Sisters, close relatives, or good friends may wish to express their mutual fondness for each other by sharing their wedding day and planning a Double Wedding. A Double Wedding, in the long run, is a savings. At the time, however, a Double Wedding can be quite an extravaganza to plan and coordinate, with twice the number of attendants, more guests, and a lavish outpouring of food and drink. A joint reception always follows a double wedding.

Site. Select a facility large enough to accommodate a joint reception and possibly a joint bridal-party table.

Attire. Brides wear differently styled wedding dresses with trains and veils of about the same length. Attendants of both brides dress with the same degree of formality, and in the same color or complementary shades (deep plum and pale lavender for bridesmaids). For a formal wedding, ushers all wear traditional black-and-white formalwear (with different but complementary bow ties and cummerbunds for the grooms and best men) or, for a ceremony before 6 P.M., cutaways.

Invitations. The two brides may wish to issue a joint invitation, particularly if they are sisters or very close friends (see Chapter 5, "Invitations & Announcements," the "Wording Invitations" section). List the elder bride's name first on an invitation for a double wedding. (If the brides are twins, list their names alphabetically.) It is also appropriate to send separate invitations if the two brides are not sisters.

Procession. If the church or synagogue has two aisles, the processions may take place simultaneously—one on each side, with each set of parents in the first pew on either side of their couple's aisle. With a single aisle, one couple may lead the procession and the other the recession. If the brides are sisters, the elder one usually leads with her set of attendants. Both grooms walk in together, behind the clergymember, and take their places side by side. The fiancé of the first bride stands nearer to the aisle.

Procession Order. Both sets of ushers, paired by height, lead the procession. The bridesmaids, honor attendant, and flower girl of the first bride come next, followed by the bride on her father's arm. The second set of attendants and second bride follow in similar fashion. Or the attendants might walk two by two, one sister's maid of honor paired with the other's honor attendant, and so forth. At the head of the aisle, attendants usually separate so those of the first bride are on the left, those of the second bride are on the right.

The Brides' Escorts. If a father walks one sister down the aisle, a brother or other male relative may escort the second bride. Or the father may walk his elder daughter down the aisle, then return to escort his younger daughter. Other options: The mother escorts the younger daughter, or the father walks down the aisle with one bride on each arm, space

double-wedding tips

- Discuss each couple's ideas for the celebration—style, formality, menu, decor, and entertainment—before planning a double wedding. The pair's tastes and visions should be similar enough to allow compromise.

- Keep communication open among members of the bridal parties by meeting or phoning on a regular basis, or using e-mail and faxes to update each other about plans (see Appendix, under Chapter 4, "Planning Your Wedding)".

- Consider the size of the guest list if four sets of relatives are involved. You may want to invite fewer guests than you normally would for a "single" wedding to make the event more manageable.

- Issue invitations jointly with both sets of hosts and couples noted. If the brides are sisters, the elder bride and her groom are usually mentioned first. Separate invitations may be sent if the brides are not sisters.

- Order napkins and imprinted favors with the names of both couples and the date. (These may also be ordered separately.)

- Order two guest books, two journals to record gifts, two cake-cutting knives, and two ceremonial wine goblets, so each couple will have keepsakes. You may wish to hire two photographers—to assure no special moments are missed, especially with all the activities and guests at the joint celebration.

outdoor-wedding site tips

- Consult the local chamber of commerce, museums, historical associations, and travel guides—to find suitable outdoor locations in your area.

- Ask all attendants and immediate family members if they have any allergies relating to the outdoors, and the season. Select a site accordingly.

- Arrange for necessary permits and rentals (see Chapter 4, "Planning Your Wedding," under the "Reception Rental Tips" box). Sign contracts.

- Check out parking availability. Notify local police about traffic increase, need for public parking. Arrange for transportation by bus or "shuttle cars" from the nearest large parking area.

- Create an aisle trimmed with garlands of greens. Consult your florist for more ideas. If your dress has a train, spread out a canvas to protect it.

- Send a map to the site with your invitations.

- Post signs to direct guests to the exact ceremony location.

permitting. That might be possible at an outdoor wedding or banquet site where aisle widths can be adjusted. In a Jewish ceremony, the mother and the father walk the elder daughter down the aisle, then return to escort the younger daughter.

Altar Proceedings. The two couples stand side by side in front of the wedding officiant, the first bride on the left. The father of two sisters stands behind the elder bride until he "gives her away," then moves over to give his younger daughter away before he takes his seat.

Ceremony. The ceremony may be divided into sections, with each couple completing each part in turn: First one couple speak their vows, then the other. However, the final blessing may be given to both at the same time. Then each pair kiss and turn to face their guests.

The Recession. The recession is led by the two newlywed couples, one preceding the other, followed by the two sets of honor attendants, then the bridesmaids and ushers in pairs. When the brides serve as each other's honor attendants, the best men escort the bridesmaids up the aisle, and the extra ushers bring up the rear.

The Receiving Line. Sisters receive guests in the same line, with the elder bride and her husband preceding the younger. Honor attendants may participate in the receiving line, but bridesmaids and ushers should circulate—to keep the line to a manageable length. When the brides are not sisters, each family may form a separate receiving line, including maids, if they wish.

The Reception. Available space and size of the bridal party will determine whether to have a joint table or two separate head tables. Each bride may wish to have her own cake, to be cut at the same time. Other traditions, such as tossing the bouquet, may be carried out simultaneously or one after the other, depending on the brides' preferences.

The Outdoor Wedding

Choosing to marry outdoors can provide a wide array of possibilities to personalize your day. It can also be a more convenient and affordable option for many couples. As with any wedding, the degree of formality is determined by the site, choice of attire, time of day, and type of menu. (For outdoor weddings at home, see also "The Home Wedding".)

Ceremony site. The possibilities include a large outdoor garden, a state park or meadow, a beach or public forest. Consider your needs for handling food, restroom facilities, and the ceremony itself. An altar table and kneeling bench or a *huppah* or floral canopy can be brought in if needed. You may have to arrange spraying for insects and clearing away of debris just before the wedding.

Weather. Prepare for inclement weather by renting a large tent or having an alternate indoor site. You might even enclose a small card with the invitation with the following information: *"In the event of rain, the wedding will be held at Somerset Town Hall [or a private residence or other location]."* Scorching sun can also be a problem, so many outdoor weddings include a tent, rain or shine.

Tents. As a safety precaution, arrange for a tent to be set up a night or two before the wedding (before the ground can be wet by a rainstorm). Reserve your tent early; tents are in high demand during peak wedding months—May through October. Raise a canopy or awning over serving tables to protect food.

Wedding Consultant. Although it is generally a less expensive option, having an outdoor wedding is no small undertaking. It is a good idea to work with a wedding consultant who can help you determine what rental items will be necessary (tables, chairs, altar, etc.) and then hire all the required vendors, including caterer and florist, etc.

Permits. Check to see if a permit is required for your chosen site, and if you must reserve the area with the local parks and recreation department. Also ask if you need a permit for the increased noise level a band or disc jockey will create (the music may have to stop at 10:00 P.M.) And find out whether you need permission to have cooking fires if you're planning to prepare or heat food there. You may be asked to leave a deposit to guarantee cleanup.

Contracts. Sign and countersign a contract that specifies what time your caterer, florist, and band can arrive at a public site to set up. Also note the length of time that your party can go on, whether or not you are allowed to serve food and alcoholic beverages (liquor use may be restricted in public parks), who's responsible for setting up and cleaning up, and precise fees and payment timing.

Food. For any outdoor reception, place food—especially the cake—in a shaded area out of traffic. Waiters might circulate with trays of hors d'oeuvres and/or you can set up a buffet meal. Finger foods work best if guests are standing—plates, forks, and glasses are hard to handle all at once.

Furniture. Rental agencies can provide everything from chairs, tableware, and table linens to sound equipment (see Chapter 4, "Planning Your Wedding"). Many also offer planning services to help organize the event.

Parking, Restrooms. Make sure you can accommodate whatever number of guests you invite with the necessary facilities. Hire a valet or ask a friend to help direct guests to parking areas. This lowers the risk of accidents and damage to your property. Warn the local police department about the increased traffic and parking in the area that day. Rent portable latrines, if necessary.

Music. Ask the bandleader to visit the site to make sure the proper acoustics and sound system will be on hand. He should arrange for an extra generator to be there the day of the party—just in case one doesn't work.

Lighting. Make sure your photographer and videographer visit the site in advance of your wedding day—to test the lighting before and after dark. Be sure that you arrange for adequate outdoor lighting (Japanese lanterns, candles) if your celebration will continue after sundown. Nothing will make guests think of leaving faster than a sudden realization that they can no longer see the face of the person with whom they are speaking.

Greetings. Ask a relative or a close friend to greet guests at the entrance of your site and direct them to the wedding area and restrooms. Your honor attendant (or your wedding consultant) may be responsible for greeting the wedding officiant and showing him or her where to change, if necessary.

Ceremony. The procession can be modified a bit, with the bridesmaids, honor attendant, and bride and her father making their entrance across a lawn, for instance. The bride also may enter alone with her father meeting her at the entrance to the ceremony space; he would then escort his daughter to her groom's side. You may choose to forego the recession and, instead, you and the groom can turn to form a receiving line to greet guests as soon as the ceremony is finished. Ushers can lead the way to the reception and refreshments.

home-wedding planning tips

- Start planning early: Delegate responsibilities to friends and family; hire a wedding consultant.

- Stick to a detailed, realistic timetable to eliminate added prewedding stress.

- Plan home renovations and major landscaping far in advance of the wedding.

- Invite neighbors, since there will be increased noise and congestion.

- Set up several bars outside and inside. Hire enough bartenders, waiters, and waitresses.

- Arrange for necessary rentals (see Chapter 4, "Planning Your Wedding," under the "Reception Rental Tips" box).

- Post signs to direct guests to your home.

The Home Wedding

Marrying at your own home or that of a close friend or relative adds a warm, personal touch to the celebration. It may also be the most appropriate and affordable way for a couple to host their own event. (However, be aware that you will have to rent tables, chairs, glassware and every other item usually available at most wedding locales.) Home weddings may be inside or outside, perhaps under a rented tent. (For more information, see "The Outdoor Wedding".) The level of formality is determined by your choice of attire, time of day, and type of menu.

Ceremony site. At home, an attractive fireplace or a large, floral screen provides an appropriate backdrop for an indoor religious ceremony. An altar table and kneeling bench or a *huppah* or floral canopy can be brought in if needed. In your own backyard, pick the prettiest garden spot for the ceremony: before a trellis of fragrant roses, in a latticed summerhouse by a garden path, or under a gazebo.

Weather. If the ceremony and/or reception is planned for outdoors, prepare for inclement weather by renting a large tent or having an alternate indoor site.

Wedding Consultant. Consider hiring a wedding consultant to handle arrangements for flowers, caterer, etc., and also to put the finishing touches on everything such as making sure guest towels are available and any wedding gifts are stored safely. Having a large wedding in your home is entertaining on a grand scale. You and your family should be free to enjoy the day.

Furniture. Make sure you have enough chairs for everyone to sit down. Check local Yellow Pages or websites for the names of rental agencies. You may also want to move some furniture out of your home for the day to provide more space for guests to circulate.

Ceremony. The procession is a modified form of the traditional one, with the bridesmaids, honor attendant, and bride and her father making their entrance from an adjoining room, or down a staircase. The bride also may enter alone with her father meeting her at the foot of the stairs or at the entrance to the ceremony room; he would then escort his daughter to her groom's side. You may do without the recession and, instead, you and the groom can turn to form a receiving line to greet guests immediately after the kiss.

The Candlelight Wedding

Marrying by candlelight adds beauty and drama that's unmatched by any other decorative effect. A late afternoon or evening ceremony or a winter wedding after sunset is an ideal setting. Candles also may take on symbolic meaning at the ceremony if, for example, the couple carry separate candles to light one Unity Candle after the clergy pronounces them husband and wife. This graphic joining of families is especially touching for an interfaith wedding or in the creation of a new, blended family of two previously married parents (see Chapter 11, "Remarriage").

Regulations. Local fire ordinances may dictate the number and placement of candles; check with a church authority and local building or fire-safety inspector for details.

Placement. Candles can be situated to shine throughout the church. Large candles on stands, perhaps decorated by the florist, may be placed at the end of each pew. Another group of candles can define the area where the bridal couple will exchange vows. Votive candles can be placed on windowsills. To create a romantic mood, candles may also outline the steps of the church or synagogue or line the walk from the ceremony site to the reception.

Candle Lighting. Acolytes, a pair of boys or girls who are either special friends, relatives, or regular assistants at the church, proceed slowly up the aisle, lighting the pew candles before the procession is to begin. They usually wear white vestments and take their instructions from the officiating clergymember. (Thank them for their help with a small gift; see Chapter 17, "Wedding Gifts.") A less ceremonial but practical approach is for the best man or head usher to light the candles as guests arrive.

Candle Bearers. Attendants can carry lighted candles with sprigs of flowers at the base, as they make their way down the aisle to a very slow wedding march. The florist can provide holders that are easy to grip. A charming and safer option for maids is to carry hurricane lamps or lanterns with a soft glow.

candlelight-ceremony tips

- Decorate the candle stands or pedestals at each pew with a seasonal theme—green boughs and pinecones at Christmas—or with classic white flowers and satin bows. Majestic silver candelabra add an elegant accent, and can be rented in sufficient number to use in the church. (Some churches may have their own; be sure to ask.)

- Consider carefully the building's structure before you set out candles. You'll want to keep them out of drafts caused by air-conditioning or heating, and natural breezes.

- Arrange to spotlight the altar if electric lighting is dimmed, so the clergymember can see to perform the ceremony.

- Save the Unity Candle to rekindle the flame on each anniversary.

- Thank acolytes with a tip or gift.

- Make sure fire-safety equipment, such as fire extinguishers and sprinklers, are in working order. Ask a caretaker for the church to check for you.

Close of Ceremony. Once the recession has occurred and before ushers direct guests to depart, the acolytes may slowly make their way back to the altar, snuffing the candles row by row. This creates a meditative close to the ceremony. Or, the church lights may be raised gently before guests file out or people may walk out under the candles' glow.

The Unity Candle. Two lighted candles, one each on the bride's and groom's sides, represent the pair's two separate lives and families. After the clergy's pronouncement of their union, the bride and groom carry their respective candles to light the taller, unlit Unity Candle, which symbolizes that their two lives are now becoming one (see Chapter 2, "Wedding Customs," and Chapter 8, "Your Wedding Ceremony").

Candles of Peace. Ask ushers to distribute candles to each guest as he or she is seated. After lighting the Unity Candle, the bride and groom walk to the first pew on their respective sides of the church or synagogue; with their individual candles, they each light the candle of the person seated in the first seat of the first pew. Each guest, in turn, lights the candle of the person sitting next to him or her, until all of these Candles of Peace are lit throughout the room. The officiant may acknowledge the symbolic flame of love and peace that all share, then ask guests to extinguish their flames (see Chapter 8, "Your Wedding Ceremony").

Reception. Candles at the reception are usually used to impart a mood or style to the celebration. Votive candles placed along a path in sand-filled bags create a southwestern ambience. Candles for both the reception and ceremony may be all white or match your wedding colors.

Theme Weddings

Put a spin on a traditional wedding by giving it a theme. The dress, flowers, decorations, and entertainment are limited only by your imaginations. Here, some ideas (See also Appendix, Chapter 10):

Nautical

- Site: a yacht, yacht club, or beach
- Decorations: colorful signal flags spelling your names
- Dress: a straw boater instead of a veil; blazers and khakis for the men
- Centerpieces: piles of seashells
- Food: seafood, of course

Brazilian

- Food: *feijoada* (black beans, rice, and meats); platters of shrimp
- Drink: *caipirinha* (cane liquor, sugar, and lime)
- Music: a samba band
- Dress: everyone—even the guys—in ruffles

Spring

- Bouquet: a hand-tied clutch of freesia, lilacs, cornflowers, peonies, and roses
- Centerpieces: flats of tulips
- Favors: seed packets
- Hors d'oeuvres: elaborate crudités

(wild asparagus, stuffed pea pods, marinated fennel)

- Entrée: roast lamb

Medieval/Renaissance

- Invitations: Scrolls, tied with gold cord
- Dress: Period costumes
- Entrée: Carving board, featuring a variety of roasts and other hearty fare
- Special touch: Add a traditional medieval "handfasting" ritual; bride and groom face each other, cross arms and hold hands. The best man then binds their hands with ribbon or cloth so that they form the sign for infinity, while reciting their vows.

Victorian

- Invitations: Period valentines
- Dress: Turn of the Century–style bustled high–neck lace gown
- Music: String quartet
- Bouquets: Tussie mussies

Provençal

- Food: French bread and cheese; bouillabaisse
- Drink: red and white wine
- Favors: lavender sachets
- Special touch: a sunflower arch

Midnight

- Ceremony: walk down the aisle at the stroke of twelve
- Reception site: an all-night diner
- Drink: champagne and coffee
- Favors: bagels and the newspaper at dawn

Viennese

- Music: waltzes
- Dress: ball gowns and white tie and tails
- Food: caviar, elaborate desserts, including a Sacher Torte
- Getaway: horse-drawn carriage

Luau

- Food: pu pu platters
- Drink: mai tais
- Decor: tiki torches; orchids; flowering ginger; palm fronds
- Music: traditional Hawaiian music (with ukelele)
- Favors: flower leis

Derby Day

- Drink: mint juleps
- Dress: fabulous hats for all the ladies
- Music: bluegrass
- Favors: paper fans
- Getaway: horse–drawn carriage

Harvest

- Bouquets: autumn flowers, leaves and sheaves of wheat
- Centerpieces: cornucopias overflowing with fruits and vegetables; carved pumpkins and gourds holding flower arrangements
- Colors: cranberry, pumpkin, deep greens and sable
- Food: A bountiful Thanksgiving–style buffet

New Orleans

- Music: jazz or zydeco band
- Food: cajun gumbo, jambalaya, crawfish, and an oyster bar
- Drink: hurricanes
- Special touch: a "second line" parade from the church to the reception site, led by the bride and groom carrying a big white flower–covered umbrella, and accompanied by a small brass band and guests, waving white handkerchiefs

Politically Correct

- Invitations: on recycled paper
- Centerpieces: tree saplings

ethnic-wedding planning tips

- Wear wedding attire that reflects the traditional dress in your country of origin.

- Select authentic foods, drinks, and desserts.

- Ask the band to play ethnic music.

- Plan your wedding color scheme around the colors in the national flag of your country of origin.

- Design centerpieces with your florist that include mini national flags or flowers from those countries (such as tulips, if you're from Holland).

- Choose favors to reflect your heritage (cowrie shells from Africa, mini perfume flasks from France, chocolates from Switzerland).

- Include wedding customs from your country of origin (present guests with colorful handkerchiefs if you're from Belgium or tree saplings if you're from Bermuda; set aside time for "The Dollar Dance" if you're from Poland; jump the broom if you're African-American).

- Getaway: on bikes
- Special touch: donate leftovers to a homeless shelter

Art Deco Wedding

- Invitations: gold, black, and white
- Bride's gown: knee-length silk chemise with silver and crystal beading, plunging back
- Music: pianist playing 1920s tunes

Valentine's Day Wedding

- Invitations: Heart-shaped; escort cards for guests on Victorian-style valentines
- Bride's gown: blush-colored silk sheath overlaid with white lace; subtle pink or red accents
- Petticoat: bright red
- Bridesmaids' gowns: ruby velvet, rose chiffon, or pink satin
- Bouquets, centerpieces: red, white, and pink blooms—sweetheart roses, ranunculus, calla lilies, stephanotis, gardenias, orchids, cyclamen, stock, peppermint-striped parrot tulips
- Favors: heart-shaped chocolates or long-stemmed red roses at each place
- Heart-shaped groom's cake topped with a cupid

- Bridesmaids' gifts: heart-shaped lockets or earrings

Fourth of July Wedding

- Site: historic site connected to the Revolutionary War
- Music: fifes and drums
- Bridesmaids' gowns and accessories: red, white, and blue
- Food: all-American barbecue
- Dessert: ice cream cake served with sparklers on top
- Linens: red, white, and blue

Christmas Wedding

- Bride's attire: white velvet gown, red cape, white fur muff
- Bridesmaids, child attendants: dressed in red or green velvet
- Favors: tree ornaments with your names and wedding date at each place setting
- Music: festive holiday songs played during the cocktail hour; children pass out song sheets and carol at the reception.
- Flowers: holly and pomegranates painted gold for the bride; holly wreaths with tiny silver bells for the bridesmaids; table centerpieces of poinsettias and pinecones

Ethnic Weddings

Ethnic touches, which celebrate the couple's various cultures and traditions, add another important dimension to wedding celebrations today. Plan a wedding that includes traditions, food, music, and perhaps clothing from both of your heritages. (See Chapter 2, "Wedding Customs," and Appendix, Chapter 10, for more specific ideas.)

More Ways to Wed

There's more than one way to get married. In addition to the ideas outlined in this chapter, you might consider a *Surprise Wedding*, in which guests are invited to a party but aren't informed it's a wedding (this can relieve the pressure of gift giving, particularly for second marriages or when the couple have already formed a household). *All-Night Weddings* are nonstop parties for diehard night owls. Looking to have a more traditional, yet still creative wedding? Choose a surprising site: a botanical garden, historic mansion, winery, train station, orchard, bird sanctuary, ferryboat, theme park, aquarium, and lighthouse are all options with built–in theme possibilities.

surprise-wedding tips

- Invite guests to a cocktail or costume party.
- Once guests have assembled, announce the surprise: That evening, a wedding will take place—yours!
- Announce that in lieu of a wedding gift, guests might make a contribution to their (or your) favorite charity.

all-night wedding tips

- Invite guests for 9:30 P.M.
- Begin the ceremony at 10 P.M.
- Follow it with cocktails and hors d'oeuvres, then supper and dancing.
- Hire two bands, so that the music continues till dawn. (And make sure you have all the necessary permits and clearances ahead of time.)
- Serve a breakfast buffet.
- Give guests a morning newspaper and bagels as they leave.

REMARRIAGE

11

Today, second marriages are viewed as a happy new beginning. No matter whether it is you, your groom or both of you marrying for the second time, many of the traditions that are part of a first marriage can be celebrated again. Yes, you can wear white. Yes, you can have a bridal shower. Yes, you can make this wedding everything you've always wanted a wedding to be. You have the freedom to be as creative as you please and to embrace timeless traditions. What's important is not your age or what has happened before—it's the unique and personal way you celebrate the love you share. This chapter is designed to help you and your fiancé consider your options and choose just the right ceremony and reception for your style, your families, and friends.

Announcing Your Engagement

Many people in both your lives will be affected by the news of your impending marriage (see Chapter 1, "Your Engagement"). When announcing your engagement, follow this order.

Children from previous marriages. Tell them the news that you will remarry first. Consider their ages and their relationship with your fiancé. Speak with them privately, then arrange time together with your fiancé to discuss the future of the new family. Every child will have questions and concerns about how the marriage will change his or her life.

Your parents and his. Give them the news once your children know. Speak with them as a couple, so that you both can answer any questions they may have.

- Great Outdoors Shower. Gifts: (his and hers) gardening tools, deck chairs, or a gas grill.

- Night-on-the-Town Shower. Gifts: tickets to the theater or symphony, or dinner at an elegant restaurant.

- Wine-Cellar Shower. Gifts: corkscrew, ice bucket, wine rack, wineglasses, and an assortment of wines.

- Self-Enrichment Shower. Group or individual gifts can include: lessons for ballroom dancing, cooking, furniture refinishing, scuba diving, cross-country skiing; memberships to a health or swim club, book-of-the-month club, museum; ticket series for art-history lectures, the opera, the ballet; or gift certificates for a spa or a personal trainer.

second wedding sites

Couples planning a second wedding often feel less pressure to meet family or social expectations. Then, as now, however, the key is finding the space that best reflects your shared tastes and the tone of the ceremony you're planning. (See also, Chapter 4, "Planning Your Wedding," under the "Where—Choosing the Site" section.)

- an art gallery

- a loft

- a museum

- a vineyard

- a yacht

- a botanical garden

- a rooftop terrace at night

Your former spouse(s) and his/her parents (if you had children together). They can be notified once your children and parents know of your engagement. If you feel uncomfortable phoning, write notes.

Friends and relatives. Let your family and friends in on the good news. As you would for a first-time marriage, don't hesitate to show off your engagement ring. Or call close friends and relatives; tell others your news as you see them.

The outside world. If you are recently divorced or widowed, it is traditional to hold off announcing your engagement and announce just the wedding, later on. Otherwise, feel free to spread the word in your hometown newspaper(s). (Check with the lifestyle editor(s) about format and deadlines.) Your parents may officially make the announcement—whether this is your first marriage and your fiancé's second or even if this is your second marriage. It's also appropriate to announce your engagement yourselves (see Chapter 1, "Your Engagement").

Prewedding Parties

A second-time bride doesn't usually receive quite as lavish a round of parties as she did before her first marriage. However, a dinner in your honor, hosted by your parents or other close relatives or special family get-togethers are wonderful ways for everyone to get better acquainted.

If you want to have a shower, hosted by your family or friends, clue the hostess or hosts in on the style of your wedding; discuss whether a large traditional shower would make you uncomfortable. (While such a shower is appropriate, you may prefer a small couples' party.) Send flowers to each hostess before the party, and a written thank-you note afterward. For more ideas, see Chapter 3, "Prewedding Parties."

Planning Your Ceremony

Plan a celebration that reflects your personal style. Think back on the previous wedding you planned and how you want this one to be different or similar. Ask yourself:

What things do I want to do differently? If you eloped the first time, you may want the church wedding you missed, complete with attendants and a floor-length white dress. (If you are worried that any of your more conservative relatives might find this inappropriate, tell them of your plans in advance and ask for their support.)

Did someone else run the show the last time around? This is your chance to have the wedding *you* want. Talk through each aspect with your fiancé—Scripture, vows, menus, music—and decide what will make you both happy.

Did I feel overwhelmed by the size of my last wedding? This time, consider an intimate ceremony—just family and close friends at the wedding followed by a reception that's as large as you'd like. You might plan a small religious ceremony at a chapel, rabbi's study, or friend's home.

Did the style of my first wedding reflect my tastes? If so, feel free to celebrate in a similar way. Do not, however, return to the same reception site or repeat any unusual personal touches from your first wedding. This is a time for looking forward, not back.

Do I want to invite more than fifty guests to the ceremony? If so, you should choose attendants and ushers (at least one usher to seat every 50 guests). You can marry in a church, synagogue, large hall, restaurant, mansion, or club. (For more ideas, see "Second Wedding Sites" box.)

What special role(s) can my children play? If either of you have children, including them in the ceremony will make them feel part of the celebration. Teens can be junior bridesmaids or junior ushers. Young girls can be flower girls; little boys can be ring bearers or pages. If you are planning a very small ceremony, you might simply have them walk you down the aisle, stand with you at the altar, or read a special poem. If your children express a preference not to participate, respect their wishes. (It is also a good idea to let your ex-spouse know of plans involving children whose custody you share.)

Is it okay to include my former in-laws and my ex-spouse? If you are close to your in-laws, you may want to invite them, though you are not obligated to do so, nor are they expected to attend. An ex-spouse would rarely be invited—consider the feelings of other relatives, your children, and your fiancé. If you do invite an ex-spouse, you leave him or her the choice of refusing the invitation, and perhaps *looking* bad, or accepting the invitation, and perhaps *feeling* bad. It may be wiser to invite your ex-spouse to dinner with your family after the honeymoon, so you all can get acquainted.

Would I feel more comfortable with a civil ceremony? You can be married at city hall, in a judge's chambers, or at your own or your parents' home. (See Chapter 4, "Planning Your Wedding," for more on civil ceremonies.) Remember, just because you have a small wedding ceremony doesn't mean that you can't have a large celebration. Many couples plan a hotel reception later that evening, or a large, informal party several weeks after their honeymoon, when they will be able to fully enjoy the festivities.

Visiting Your Officiant

As soon as you've decided on the size and type of ceremony you'd like, make an appointment to visit your minister, rabbi, priest, or other ceremony official. Bring your fiancé with you. This is the time to discuss:

who pays for what?

If this is a second marriage for both you and your groom, you'll probably handle wedding expenses yourselves. You may divide the costs, based on the financial status of each partner. Options:

- Assign expenses in advance—you pay for your dress, the flowers, and the cake. He pays for the church, the reception, and the honeymoon.

- One person pays for the ceremony expenses; the other, the reception expenses.

- One person pays for the ceremony and reception; the other for the honeymoon.

- Both pay bills as they come up and total the receipts after the wedding. If one partner paid more, he or she pays less of the household expenses till the difference is evened out.

- Open a joint bank account for wedding expenses.

- The groom gives the wedding to his bride as a gift.

- The bride's parents may offer to pay for the wedding if she is a very young widow or divorcée, or if this is her first marriage.

- Both sets of parents pay for the wedding if the couple is not in a financial position to pay for it themselves.

Your chosen date and time for the wedding. Also bring up your plans concerning the music, flowers, attendants, and so on. Some houses of worship have very specific rules about secular vs. religious music, or the use of an aisle runner, candles, etc.

Your ceremony officiant's suggestions and concerns. He or she may suggest the use of the chapel rather than the main church, for example. If, as discussions go on, you find that your clergymember has problems performing the ceremony you want, you may want to look for another officiant, or even another church. If you find yourself in a jam, call local churches, talk with college chaplains, or call the church headquarters in your state for ideas (see Appendix, under Chapter 9, "Religious Rituals & Requirements"). Or, you may choose to marry in a civil ceremony (see Chapter 4, "Planning Your Wedding").

Your faith's view of your previous marriage. If you belong to a faith with its own divorce laws (Jewish or Roman Catholic, for example), you may have problems remarrying within your house of worship, even though you have obtained a legal civil divorce. Expect the clergymember to bring up your first marriage during your conference. While many restrictions in the remarriage of divorced persons may have eased in recent years, you may still need not only your own clergymember's permission but, in some cases, permission from higher religious authorities as well. (See Appendix, under Chapter 9, "Religious Rituals & Requirements," for the phone numbers of national offices of some major religions. Some will recommend contacting a local clergymember.) In almost all denominations, the ceremony officiant will want to meet with you for premarital counseling (see Appendix, under Chapter 4, "Planning Your Wedding").

Below are the basic positions on religious remarriage for some of the largest U.S. denominations:

Amish

The wedding vow *"Til death do you part"* is taken very literally by the Amish; divorce is not recognized, and remarriage in an Amish church is not possible unless the spouse dies. The person leaving the marriage is excommunicated; if the partner left behind remarries, he or she is excommunicated.

Assemblies of God

Two acceptable reasons for divorce and remarriage are recognized by the church's general constitution and bylaws: infidelity by a partner and divorce of the Christian partner by an unbelieving partner. A local minister may agree to remarry a divorced person under these "exceptional" circumstances, after counseling the engaged couple.

Baha'i

The Baha'i religion recognizes civil divorce and does not require couples to obtain any special annulments, dispensations, or other church procedures before remarrying. The religion does, however, strongly discourage divorce, and, in fact, requires that a couple wishing one first undergo a year's separation (to attempt to work out the problems) before legally dissolving the marriage. After that time, the person is free to divorce and remarry.

Baptist

There is no churchwide policy; Southern and American Baptist congregations have local autonomy. Some ministers permit no second marriages; others recognize valid reasons for divorce.

Buddhist

A couple may remarry in the Buddhist religion after one or both partners have been divorced. The Buddhist priest may wish to meet the couple prior to the wedding to get a sense of their commitment. If the divorce is final and legal, and if the priest has no reservations about marrying the couple, the wedding can be performed.

Christian Scientist

There are no specific guidelines limiting or governing remarriage.

Eastern Orthodox

Civil divorce is not recognized because of the sacramental nature of marriage that places it under the jurisdiction of Divine Law. If reconciliation attempts fail, a spiritual court must be convened to consider the granting of a church divorce, after which the bishop must write a letter of special dispensation sanctioning the second marriage. The marriage partner of the petitioner must be a Christian baptized in the Holy Trinity.

Episcopal

There is no churchwide policy on remarriage after divorce. Rectors review each case on its own merits (they ask the divorced person to discuss their previous marriage to determine if both parties are marrying freely or if there are issues lingering from the first marriage that may spill over into the second). Dispensations may be needed; rectors make recommendations to their bishop, who makes the final determination. The process takes one to two months. There is some variation on what bishops recognize as valid grounds for divorce; consult your local church rector.

Hindu

Remarriage is recognized and accepted, but Hindu Scripture describes required codes of conduct to be followed, and community leaders must approve both divorce and remarriage. A person cannot dissolve a marriage against their spouse's will. The divorce is completed and remarriage possible only after the ex-husband returns to his former wife all property that was given to him by her. The ex-wife must cut off all claims to her former spouse's property.

Islamic (Muslim)

Remarriage is permitted in the Koran (the Holy Book) but is not desirable. After the divorce is completed and the required time to wait has expired—three menstrual cycles (to be certain the divorced woman is not pregnant)—a Muslim may marry again, but not to the same partner. The person who was married before must have evidence (legal documents) to support the claim the divorce is final.

Jewish

Reform Jews require only a civil divorce. Orthodox and Conservative Jews must obtain a *get* (a Jewish divorce decree) from a rabbinical court before they can remarry. Customarily, women delay remarriage for at least three months after receiving a *get*.

Lutheran, Methodist, Presbyterian

A single, lifelong marriage is stressed, but the validity of divorce is recognized when marriage fails. The local minister counsels the engaged couple and may marry them without seeking permission from any denominational office.

Mormon

The Church of Jesus Christ of Latter-Day Saints recognizes the validity of legal divorce. Couples who were married in a Mormon temple, however, were believed to marry for eternity. Such a sealing must be canceled before a second temple marriage can take place.

Quaker

Quakers do recognize civil divorces, and there are no special church-directed requirements that must be fulfilled by those remarrying. However, the couple (like any couple marrying for the first time) must get approval to marry in the church from the church's monthly meeting of the Society of Friends. In the case of a remarriage, the "committee" would, for example, judge whether you are deemed to be free of entanglements (i.e., the divorce is legal and final).

Roman Catholic

The belief is that a marriage can be dissolved only by death. You can, however, be free to remarry if you receive an annulment (a judgment that the marriage was never valid in the eyes of the church). The petitioner must submit questionnaires and statements from witnesses to a diocesan tribunal, which will determine if the first marriage was entered into by two adults capable of lifelong commitment. Decisions take eight to twelve months. Call your local parish priest for more information.

Shinto

Remarriages for those who believe in Shinto (the "Way of the Gods") are permitted at Shinto shrines. All Shinto weddings take place in the innermost shrine building.

Unitarian Universalist Society

Local ministers set their own criteria; most will perform a second marriage if a couple demonstrate a readiness for long-term commitment.

United Church of Christ (Congregational)

Remarriage is not prohibited by the church, but the decision to grant a second marriage is at the discretion of the church's pastor.

Invitations and Announcements

When it's time to invite or announce, follow these guidelines:

DO make a careful and thoughtful guest list. Older couples—especially those paying for the wedding—may wish to invite more of *their* friends than their parents' friends. Professional colleagues may be among your closest friends, but you need only invite colleagues with whom you socialize, and/or those from your own department. You may also decide that you want to invite former in-laws and friends from a first marriage. This is fine if everyone feels comfortable with this decision.

DON'T forget to ask both sets of parents for names of close friends they'd like to invite, even though you may be paying for the wedding yourselves.

DO feel free to personalize your invitations and announcements. They may have a traditional look or a unique design. Some couples and their children jointly issue the invitation complete with a photo of bride, groom, and their respective children.

DON'T feel that formal invitations are necessary for a small, informal wedding. A brief note or phone call can take the place of a printed invitation when fewer than 50 guests are invited.

DO mail printed invitations for more than 50 guests (see Chapter 5, "Invitations & Announcements").

Typical remarriage invitation wording:

*The honour of your presence
is requested at the marriage of
Marcia Maureen Craig
to
Nathan Randolph Carter
Saturday, the second of May
at four o'clock
Hotel Mark Hopkins
San Francisco*

*R.s.v.p.
1053 Foster Lane
Oakland, California 12345*

DON'T shy away from more traditional wording on the invitation if this is what you feel most comfortable with. The bride's name can be written *Marcia Maureen Craig*, or, in the case of widowhood, *Mrs. Albert Brendon Craig*. (If your parents or both sets of parents are issuing the invitation, use the appropriate wording found in Chapter 5, "Invitations & Announcements.") The invitation may be issued in the names of the parents whether or not they make a financial contribution to the cost of the wedding.

DO send formal reception invitations to guests if you are inviting a large number of people to the reception but only a few to the ceremony. You can also insert handwritten ceremony cards for those who are invited to both the reception and the ceremony.

DON'T neglect to announce your marriage to those who were not invited to the wedding. Formal announcements sent after the ceremony are an excellent way to notify friends. Your parents may have "the honour" of announcing your marriage, or you may send your own announcements:

*Marcia Maureen Craig
and
Nathan Randolph Carter
announce their marriage
Saturday, the second of May
Two thousand and three
San Francisco*

introduction etiquette

Remarriages merge new family relationships with old. Here are suggestions for how to gracefully introduce your guests to each other and to members of your new family:

- Introduce a former in-law as a "friend" rather than as an ex-sister-in-law.

- Introduce your ex-mother-in-law as "Cindy's grandmother."

- If your new husband's children refer to you as their stepmother, introduce them the same way: "This is my stepson, Rob."

- Introduce your new husband's son or daughter as your child's stepbrother or stepsister, so that the children will understand what they are to each other. Introduce your husband's parents as their stepgrandparents.

- Especially if you already have children, make a point of establishing how your ex-husband will refer to your new husband. Since they may be partners in raising your children, the relationship between them should be polite and firmly established early on.

your name change

To let your friends and colleagues know your preference:

- Enclose a name card with your announcement: *Barbara White Redford will be changing her name to Barbara Redford Smith following her marriage June 18, 2003*

- Announce it on an at-home card: *Barbara Redford Smith Malcolm Ross Smith After the fourth of July* (See Chapter 5, "Invitations & Announcements.")

- Add a line to your newspaper announcement: *"The bride will retain the name Barbara Lynn White after her marriage."*

DO let newspapers know of your marriage. Check with the lifestyle editor for announcement requirements (see Chapter 16, "Photography, Videography, & Publicity"). Such an announcement might read:

Marcia Maureen Craig and Nathan Randolph Carter, both of Oakland, were married Saturday, May second, at the Hotel Mark Hopkins in San Francisco by Justice James Howard of the California Supreme Court. The bride is the daughter of Mr. and Mrs. Daniel Ackerman of Los Angeles. She is a professor at the University of California. Mr. Carter is the son of Mrs. Leon Ball Carter and the late Mr. Carter of San Francisco. He is an accountant with the firm of Richardson and Level. Mrs. Craig's previous marriage ended in divorce. The couple will reside in Berkeley.

The Question of Names

Once you remarry, what name will you use? Review your options, below. (See also, Chapter 4, "Planning Your Wedding" under "The Name Decision" section.)

1. Barbara Lynn White

Your first, middle, and maiden names only.

2. Barbara Lynn Redford

Your first and middle names and former married surname only. If you have already established a professional reputation, or have the same last name as your children, you may not want to add on to or change your new married name (*Smith*). Some women use both names, for different aspects of their lives. For example, you could remain *Barbara Lynn Redford* for business, but use *Barbara Lynn Smith* socially.

3. Barbara Lynn Smith

Your first, middle, and new married names. You've decided to drop your former husband's surname in favor of your new husband's surname.

4. Barbara White Redford

Your first name, maiden name, and former married surname. Similar to Example Number 2, you already may have an established identity with this name professionally, and as the mother of your children.

5. Barbara Redford Smith

Your first name and former married surname, followed by your new married name. Some women drop their middle name and retain their first married name with their married name, to help retain an identity similar to their children's.

6. Barbara White Smith

A combination of your first name, maiden name, and new married surname.

7. Barbara White-Smith or Barbara Redford-Smith.

Your maiden name and new married name joined by a hyphen. Or your former husband's name hyphenated with your new husband's name. The latter choice may help identify you with your children.

Your Remarriage Wedding Dress

No matter how you envision this special occasion, the remarrying bride has many choices in a wedding dress today—from classic lacy, long and white, to chic, elegant, street-length and pastel. The only requirement is that you find a dress you love. Mothers and attendants should be guided by your choice of dress; men and children should wear traditional formal clothes appropriate for the wedding style and time of day (see Chapter 7, "Wedding Clothes"). The following true/false quiz will help you separate the truth from the myths surrounding wedding dresses for the second-time bride.

Bridal white is for virgins.

FALSE: Bridal white is widely recognized as a symbol of joy and celebration, not virginity. If white is important to you for a second-time wedding, wear it. Pastels are popular, too; consider silvery gray, café au lait, or other light shades that flatter your skin tone.

Bridal shops are for first-time brides.

FALSE: Bridal shops also cater to the special needs of the remarrying bride. They will have many dresses just right for a second wedding, from a floor-length antique lace sheath to a satin cocktail-length suit in platinum.

A long train and veil are for the first-time bride.

TRUE: The long train and veil are still considered symbols of youth and innocence. The train, which creates a larger-than-life aura, is generally considered the prerogative of the first-time bride only. However, if you haven't worn a veil and train before and want to this time, go ahead. A sweep or fishtail train are the best options. Complete your outfit with a hat, a small tiara, delicate ornaments, or flowers in your hair.

The second-time bride should wear a short dress.

FALSE: You can wear any length you want, depending on the formality of the ceremony and the time of day (see Chapter 7, "Wedding Clothes"). You can choose anything from a graceful, floor-length ball gown in white or your favorite color, to a short and sexy skirt. For a nighttime wedding, wear a cocktail-length or floor-length dress; for daytime, select a dress that is any length, from long or high-low to ballet-length or short. Be guided by the location and climate. Remember: The degree of orthodoxy determines what you wear or do in any religion.

A bridal dress must be traditional to be tasteful.

FALSE: Rather than traditional lace, taffeta, and satin, you can opt for crepe, chiffon, charmeuse, or silk. You needn't wear a voluminous dress, either. Sleek, body-hugging sheaths or gently flared skirts create a slender silhouette. Many second-time brides also prefer sophisticated beading and pearl embroidery to traditional ruffles or lace. Another option is a beaded strapless corset with a small jacket paired with a long skirt.

ceremony roles for children

- Ask each to escort you or participate in the ceremony— as a flower girl, ring bearer, bridesmaid, usher, or honor attendant.

- Assign them a special seat and have them escorted there just before the seating of the bride's mother.

- Order special flowers for them to wear—a wrist corsage or boutonniere.

- Mention their names in a special prayer.

- Include their names in the ceremony program.

- Ask them to pass out hymnals or programs before the ceremony begins.

- Ask your teenager for a list of songs for the band.

- Give each child a gift to commemorate the day—an engraved locket or a camera, for instance.

- After you have exchanged rings, have the children join you at the altar for an affirmation of the family unit. Many children subsequently refer to the wedding date as "the day we all got married."

The Ceremony

You'll want the wedding ceremony to be an appropriate expression of the way you and your groom feel about one another. Some topics that should be discussed by the two of you, as well as with your officiant and your families:

Being "given away." Your father may escort you to the altar and when asked by the officiant, *"Who supports this couple in marriage?"* he can say, *"Her mother and I support and bless this union."* If you have older children from a previous marriage, you can walk up the aisle with them at your side. At the altar, your children might respond to the officiant with, *"We support and love Mom and know she'll be happy with Jim."* Or perhaps you and your groom will choose to walk down the aisle together.

The procession and recession. Discuss the procession and recession with your officiant. At a small wedding you may want to skip the procession down the aisle and enter through a side or vestry door in the house of worship to meet your groom and best man, already waiting at the altar. After the ceremony, simply turn to greet your guests.

At a civil ceremony—in a judge's chambers, perhaps—there will be no formal procession or recession. The bride and her attendant should enter the room to find the groom and his best man waiting for them.

Honor attendants. It is appropriate for a remarrying bride to have attendants who can serve as legal witnesses. Being surrounded by people who love you and support your new marriage is very important. Some brides and grooms ask the ushers and bridesmaids who supported them at their first marriage to fill the same role again.

Exchanging rings. Will this be a two-ring ceremony, or will you be the only one to receive a ring? The double-ring ceremony is considered to be symbolic of a marriage that will be based on equality.

The role of your children. Your children may escort you down the aisle, act as attendants, as mentioned before, as altar servers (See Chapter 6, "The Wedding Party"), or readers. When children are a part of your life together, they should participate in the wedding unless they feel uncomfortable. Your vows to each other might be followed by a family prayer, with each person in the family adding a phrase. Light a Unity Candle, a symbolic ritual for families (see Chapter 10, "Special Weddings & New Ways to Wed"). For more ideas, see the "Ceremony Roles for Children" box, and the "Helping Your Children Adjust" section.

Vows. To express your feelings about this new marriage, you may choose to write your own wedding vows (see Chapter 8, "Your Wedding Ceremony").

Readings and responses. You might prefer an alternate Scripture reading, prayer, or response. Your clergymember can explain the options to you (see Chapter 8, "Your Wedding Ceremony"). You can also visit bookstores or log on to the Internet to find appropriate and meaningful selections.

Decorations. Express yourself with music, flowers, and decorations—within the acceptable bounds of the ceremony site. A Victorian mansion may restrict the use of candles as a fire hazard, for example. If you carried a nosegay for your first wedding, consider a cascade of spring flowers. Let the florist know this is a second wedding so he or she can create an arrangement with which you're comfortable.

Helping Your Children Adjust

As the wedding day grows nearer, your children may be hit with a wave of insecurity. A parent should take time to offer extra emotional support in the days preceding the wedding (see Appendix, under Chapter 11, "Remarriage"). Answer any questions your children have about living space, lifestyle, or visits with their father or mother. On your wedding day, ask a grandmother or aunt to sit nearby for reassurance and emotional support during the ceremony. Young children also need physical supervision; on the wedding day, put someone in charge of looking after your children so you won't be distracted or worried about their whereabouts or safety.

The Reception

Your reception can include the same formalities and traditions as a first-time wedding, including receiving lines, dancing, a traditional wedding cake, a groom's cake, and champagne. You and your groom may head up the receiving line yourselves while your parents circulate among the guests. You might—but don't have to—omit such first-wedding customs as tossing the bride's bouquet and removing and tossing the bride's garter, as well as exiting through a shower of rice, flower petals, birdseed, or bubbles. Your reception may follow all the first-time wedding customs, including the first dance, the ceremonial cutting of the cake, and rounds of toasts from your parents, honor attendants, children, and friends. Don't expect gifts at a second wedding—especially from those who attended your or your partner's first wedding (many *will* send gifts, though, to mark your new beginning). (For more on gift etiquette, see Chapter 17, "Wedding Gifts.")

reception roles for children

Make a special effort to include your children and the children of your groom in the reception fun:

- Schedule an afternoon wedding, so they'll be awake.

- Offer them special seats of honor at the bride's table.

- Make sure the photographer takes lots of family candids.

- Take family portraits: your groom with his children, you with your children, the whole new family together.

the if-you-have-children honeymoon

- Plan a two-part honeymoon. Make arrangements for a family trip following your private honeymoon. With their sights set on "their honeymoon" (a trip to a theme park or white-water rafting, for example), the kids will likely be content to stay behind while you and your groom first go off by yourselves.

- Go over the itinerary with your children, explaining where you'll go and who will take care of them while you're away.

- Send postcards.

- Call often.

- Bring back souvenirs and photos to share.

The Second Honeymoon

Don't make the mistake of believing that a honeymoon isn't necessary "this time around." Make sure you get away—even if it's just for a few days. You'll need some rest and relaxation after the exciting—and nonetheless exhausting—events surrounding your wedding. And some time spent together—just the two of you, away from family and friends and responsibilities—is a perfect way to begin a new marriage.

For your honeymoon destination, choose any location *except* where you went last time. With so many wonderful vacation places to choose from, you should have no trouble picking a gorgeous spot that will be new to both of you.

STICKY SITUATIONS, UNEXPECTED SITUATIONS

Despite all of your planning, chances are that something unexpected will occur on your wedding day. There could be a blizzard. Your dress might tear. Or your caterer might show up with the wrong cake.

Don't panic. Assess your options and choose an alternative plan quickly. How you handle each dilemma will determine how serious it becomes. Keep in mind, friends and relatives can help. For example, send a cousin to pick up the organist whose car broke down. Ask all of your guests to send you photographs as a backup in case the photographer who arrives to cover the wedding is *not* the one whose work you've previously seen. Forget the vows you wrote? Your clergymember will help you through the ceremony.

Of course, the best way to protect yourself financially is to specify all terms in a signed and countersigned contract with each wedding professional hired. Below, a range of situations that could happen to you . . .

Crisis Control: Handling Wedding Dilemmas

My father is not in good health. What should I do if he is too sick to attend my wedding? When a parent is too ill to attend, there are several options. Hook up a special telephone line—or perhaps even a closed–circuit television—to let your parent listen from a hospital bed. Ask a close relative to stand in for your parent during the service. Be sure you pay tribute to the absent person during the ceremony (the officiant or person reading a Scripture might dedicate it to your parent and ask for everyone's prayers). Capture your wedding on video; at a later time, you'll be able to view it as well as share wedding photos with your parent.

One of my bridesmaids will be eight months pregnant on my wedding day. What will I do if she can't attend? The show must still go on. It is really not polite to ask someone else to stand in at the last minute. Remember, it isn't essential that you have an even number of ushers and bridesmaids. Bridesmaids can walk down the aisle in pairs or alone; one usher can escort a bridesmaid on each arm during the recession. Share the video and photos with your absent friend after the wedding.

My fiancé's brother, who was to be his best man, was recently killed in a car accident. My fiancé and his parents are completely devastated. Should we postpone the wedding? The decision is up to you and your fiancé. If a sibling or parent should pass away immediately before the wedding, you might decide to proceed with the wedding and reception if you feel that individual would have wanted you to. As a gesture of respect, however, you might modify the celebration, canceling the band or orchestra, for example. Close family members and friends who may be traveling long-distance to pay their respects to the deceased may also want to help mark the start of your new life together. This new beginning that you make together can be a statement of faith and hope for the future.

At the reception, guests might make toasts that bridge the gap between the two events (*"Jim would want life to go on. We feel his presence with us today."*) Your clergymember will be particularly helpful with such situations and sentiments.

What if someone faints at the altar? Anyone who feels faint should sit down immediately and put his or her head between the knees until the feeling passes. The ceremony should continue unless there is a serious medical emergency.

My uncle has very high blood pressure and has had two heart attacks. How can we prepare in case he feels ill at our wedding? If someone becomes ill during the ceremony or reception, the normal activities should be interrupted until medical assistance arrives. The guest should be removed only by medical personnel. Consider hiring a nurse for the day or having a doctor on the premises with medical equipment nearby. Make sure that a family member carries a cellular phone in case it is necessary to call 911.

If there is a medical emergency during your ceremony, remember that if you have already said your vows, you are legally married, whether or not the entire ceremony is completed. If you have not yet said your vows when the illness occurs, continue with the service after medical personnel leave.

We live in an area of the country that has unpredictable winter weather. What can we do if there's a blizzard? If a snowstorm threatens your plans, make arrangements with a snowplow operator to clear out the church or synagogue parking lot and your own driveway. You might also rent four-wheel-drive vehicles to ensure you'll have reliable transportation and be able to pick up guests at the airport.

Weather can turn nasty in any season. Since no one can guarantee cloudless blue skies or moderate temperatures, have a backup location for anything planned outside. A ceremony in the garden of a museum might move to a room inside. A relative's car might substitute for a horse-and-carriage getaway. Torrential rain? Have oversized umbrellas on hand for ushers to use when escorting guests from the house of worship to their cars.

We live in Arizona. What can we do if there is a particularly brutal heat wave? Provide plenty of extra water for the guests and the flowers and have lots of nonalcoholic drinks on hand (alcohol dehydrates). If the electricity at the ceremony and reception sites can handle the extra strain, borrow air conditioners or electric fans. (Otherwise, buy inexpensive handheld fans of paper or bamboo and place them in each pew.) Be sure that the site has a backup generator, or arrange for one to be there.

The organ in my church is in very bad shape, and the new one won't be delivered until after our wedding. What can we do? Other instruments (trumpet, flute, strings) can also provide beautiful wedding music. A piano or portable organ can be rented or even moved from your home. Really desperate? Ask a talented friend or relative to bring a guitar.

If you find you are without an organist at the last minute, try to hire someone from another church or synagogue to play at your ceremony. Or check with the house of worship to see if a qualified relative or friend would be permitted to play the in-house organ. The best solution may be recorded music. CDs or tapes of wedding music should be available in most music stores or on the Internet (see Appendix, under Chapter 14, "Wedding Music"). Ask a church member who is familiar with the church's sound equipment to control the sound and the length of play.

What if my wedding gown becomes dirty or damaged on my wedding day? Anything can go wrong with clothes—zippers stick, trains get stepped on, hats blow away, dresses get spotted and shrink mysteriously. Follow these tips:

wedding-day emergency kit

- pain reliever
- antihistamines
- threaded needle
- safety pins
- hairpins
- white masking tape
- tampons
- tissues
- makeup
- comb and brush
- cellular phone
- scissors
- nail file
- hair dryer
- clear nail polish
- extra hosiery
- cotton swabs
- antacid
- hand lotion
- white chalk
- breath freshener
- perfume
- a snack to keep you going
- a small bottle of water

wedding-contract musts

All contracts should list:

- dates

- times

- locations

- prices, including taxes and gratuities, plus details of the agreed-upon payment plan (remember: never pay 100% of the cost of a service until it has been delivered)

- a protective clause, including refund policies

- names of professionals hired

- expected attire of professionals hired

- overtime fees

Ask your bridal salon in advance for emergency cleaning tips. The consultant there should be able to give you suggestions for your particular fabric when you buy the gown.

Be ready for emergency repairs. Bring safety pins, needle, thread, tape, glue (see "Wedding-Day Emergency Kit" box) to the ceremony site for last-minute repairs. Hold the bridal bouquet in a position that hides a spot or tear, if possible.

Try on your wedding clothes one week before the wedding. Try standing and sitting. If prewedding parties have added extra pounds, return for a final fitting. (A steady exercise regimen will help you look better and feel calmer.)

Practice walking, sitting, rising, in your gown at home. Most women aren't used to walking in a long dress or negotiating a train and veil. Show your honor attendant how to arrange your train so that it is not wrinkled as you stand at the altar, and so that your father or groom won't trip over it and rip it. Also be sure she knows how to bustle your train, so you can maneuver at the reception.

What if something happens to the ring? Follow these precautions:

Sew a faux ring onto the ring bearer's pillow. Give the real one to the best man.

Ask the best man to keep the bride's ring in his pocket, after checking for holes. It's best for him not to slip it onto his finger; it might slip off or get stuck.

Suggest that your honor attendant wear the groom's ring on her thumb, which she should keep securely bent around her bouquet.

The bride and groom should rub their ring fingers with baby powder or a dab of petroleum jelly before the ceremony. Warm weather and tension make hands swell, so that the rings may not go on.

If your ring gets lost or is forgotten at home, borrow one from a parent or attendant. In a pinch, turn your engagement ring so the stone faces the inside of your hand. Later, your clergymember can bless the real wedding ring.

I'm concerned that an unwelcome guest might show up at our wedding and cause a scene. What can I do? Most reasonable adults know that an invitation is a prerequisite to attending a wedding. If your ex-mother-in-law or your ex-spouse does come and sits unobtrusively in the rear of the house of worship, their motivation might simply be to share your happiness. Greet them cordially at the end of the ceremony if you come face to face. Warn ushers beforehand if you are concerned that an uninvited guest might attend and create a disruption. Show them the person's photograph; they will then be prepared to turn this person away at the door. If safety is an overwhelming concern, hire a professional security guard.

If a cat or dog wanders into the house of worship, just let it sit and watch. If its behavior is potentially disruptive, an usher or family member should lead it quietly out of the building.

What if the band that shows up isn't the one I hired? Popular bandleaders may have several groups playing under their name. Read your contract carefully. Does it say that you have booked the company or a particular band? If you want the exact musicians you auditioned, you must list their specific names and their group name in your contract, along with the wedding date, exact times, length of breaks or continuous music, overtime rates, total price and payment schedule, and any other special arrangements you have made verbally.

My reception is at an out-of-the-way place. How can I make sure the florist, caterer, and other service providers find it on my wedding day? Some of the most romantic weddings take place at old mansions tucked into the countryside or in private gardens. The danger of getting lost on unfamiliar roads is very real. Even if your wedding is in a well-known spot, follow these steps:

Give professionals written directions and a map. Also give them phone numbers for your home, the reception site, the wedding consultant or banquet manager, and another family member or friend who will be reachable (and who knows the way) if they get lost. Call the ceremony site to make sure guests won't be detoured by construction or road work.

Confirm all plans by telephone one week before the wedding and the day before the wedding. If you are too busy, ask a friend or attendant to make these calls for you; ask someone to be on hand to check on and receive deliveries. Any mistakes in orders should be caught and rectified immediately, not hours later—when it may be too late!

My caterer seems overextended by many events. What if my order gets mixed up with another? Keep checking with the caterer throughout your planning months, calling at least once a week the month before the wedding. Verify your order, date, time, and site. The arrival time of your guests cannot be postponed on your wedding day—neither can the arrival of your food. If liquor or food goes astray, or the wrong order is delivered (sandwiches for 50 instead of hors d'oeuvres for 200), call the store or caterer at once. If the mix-up cannot be rectified quickly, send ushers or family members to delicatessens, bakeries, liquor stores. Once you have made additional purchases, do *not* accept a late delivery from your caterer. In this case, as in all cases of diminished services, a protective clause in your contract is essential. Never pay 100 percent of the cost of a service until it has been delivered.

I ordered my wedding dress seven months ago from a local bridal store, but it still hasn't arrived. My wedding is four weeks away. I keep calling the store, and they keep telling me it should be in anytime. I'm nervous the dress will never arrive. What can I do? If you ordered the dress from a reputable store, relax. They're not in the business of stiffing clients. However, if the dress still isn't in within a week, devise a back-up plan. Order another dress from a manufacturer who can produce it in a week or two, or take a sample dress from the bridal salon that's already in stock. The store may put your deposit toward this new dress.

It's a week before my wedding and the reception hall we booked has closed down because of a fire. It won't reopen in time for our wedding. Help! Enlist your family, attendants, and friends to start calling hotels and restaurants in your area to see if any has available space for your reception. Look for a place that's already equipped with chairs, tables, linens, dishes, and glassware, rather than an empty space that you'll have to furnish from scratch.

I sent all my out-of-town guests detailed maps to the church, but it's just a day before my wedding and a construction crew has ripped up and blocked off the main road. I was told the road will be closed off for weeks until the work is completed. My guests will have to take a detour, and I'm worried some will get lost. Post someone familiar with the area near the detour to give alternate directions to guests (verbally or via a simple map) as they drive by. Have him or her hold up a sign, such as "Schulman-Matthews Wedding" so guests will take notice.

I asked my stepfather to walk me down the aisle, but now my biological father says he won't attend the wedding if he doesn't give me away. What should I do? Have both men give you away. Or split up the father-of-the-bride duties. Have one give you away and the other dance first with you at the reception.

I'm afraid I may have botched the seating plan. I have nightmares that 10 guests will be placed at table 14 (or 6 or 11) when only 8 should be there. What should I do if I notice a commotion? Alert the banquet manager or host and ask them to set two more place settings.

For information about what to do when unexpected situations occur on your honeymoon, see Chapter 19, "Going Away."

How to Avoid Problems with Vendors

Ask for referrals from friends and family members. Talk to recent brides who have used the service you are considering. Ask for their pros and cons. Interview at least three different firms before committing. Don't accept a banquet hall's recommendation without first checking out the firm. Don't accept an absolute (*"On tables, we always put carnations in bud vases."*). Insist on reviewing sample books of florists' and photographers' work.

Hire a company with a successful track record. A firm that has been in business for years has proven itself to hundreds of customers. Although this is not a guarantee (management can change), it is a positive sign.

Check with the Better Business Bureau in the city where the business is located or with your state's Department of Consumer Affairs (see Appendix, under Chapter 12, "Sticky Situations, Unexpected Situations"). Ask if there are complaints filed against the company. If a complaint was resolved successfully, it is not necessarily a bad sign. A series of unresolved problems, however, is a red flag. *Warning:* Some disreputable firms skirt around the records kept by the Better Business Bureau by changing their names after complaints have been filed. (Old complaints may not appear under a new name.) If the company's history is unavailable, be wary.

Trust your feelings. A wedding-service professional who seems haughty, patronizing, overly rushed, or resistant to your suggestions in an initial interview is unlikely to change over the next several months. If simple conversation is uncomfortable, go elsewhere. Avoid anyone who asks for an initial deposit that is more than 50 percent of the total price of the service. Withholding full payment is your only leverage if the service is not provided or if it is substandard.

Be suspicious of any professional who refuses to sign a contract. Anything that has been promised verbally must be spelled out in writing. If a company says they do not have standard contracts, ask for, or provide, a letter of agreement. Both you and the service provider must sign any document to make it legally binding.

Write in all services you have agreed upon (see specific chapters for points to be included in contracts with each wedding-service professional). Verbal agreements are often unenforceable in court (it's your word against theirs), and even honest people can forget things they've said. Specify in writing that you want white roses; list a backup color. If you want candid photos instead of posed shots, include that.

Never be pushed into signing anything. Give yourself time to fully understand the document. Ask as many questions as are necessary. An ethical professional whose services are in demand should courteously answer all questions and never pressure you for a quick decision or deposit. For example, never cave in to pressure to put a deposit down on a gown before the store closes that day. If this means that you must return another day to finalize the deal, do that. If you were made to feel uncomfortable about delaying your decision, rethink buying from the store or hiring the firm.

Keep tabs on the professionals once you've put down a deposit. Bands, in particular, may break up or re-form during your engagement months. Market changes may make it impossible for your florist to deliver a particular flower. Stay in touch.

if you've been ripped off

If you don't receive the services for which you've contracted:

- **Withhold final payment.**

- **Write a letter to the company** explaining your position and ask for a return of your deposit.

- **Take the company to small-claims court** (if the disputed deposit doesn't exceed the maximum—$3,000 in some states; check in yours).

- **File a complaint with the Better Business Bureau** in the state where the company is located (see Appendix, under Chapter 12, "Sticky Situations, Unexpected Situations") and let them contact the company. (Results rest with the firm's willingness to cooperate. Your letter will remain on file to warn future brides who check on the provider.)

- **Report the case to your state's Department of Consumer Affairs.** (If they receive similar complaints, they may investigate.)

- **Hire a lawyer and sue** to recover your deposit. (Your contract should stipulate a full refund for nondelivery of services.)

Sticky Situations

Weddings bring out the best—and worst—in people. You'll have to bring up tense topics like money and delicate issues like where a divorced parent sits. You'll have to diplomatically handle bridesmaids who are making you crazy and friends who are concerned about how your marriage will affect your relationships with them. When anxieties run high, tempers get short. Here, how to handle some sensitive matters:

Out-of-Control Bridesmaids

• **Dress debacles.** If your bridesmaids are giving you grief about the dress you've picked out for them, hear them out. Yes, a bride is entitled to have her wedding party look the way she wants it to, but no one should be forced to wear a dress that makes her look unattractive or feel uncomfortable. See if you can agree on a compromise. Or give your attendants some guidelines (a color, such as navy, or a style, such as a sleeveless ankle-length sheath) and allow them to choose their own dress.

• **Hair-raising problems.** If they're reluctant to wear their hair in the style you've chosen for them—say, a chignon—ease up. Bridesmaids don't have to look identical, and forcing a woman to coax her hair into a style that's unflattering isn't bound to win you friends—or great wedding pictures.

Divorced Parents

No matter how bitter the split, your wedding will probably bring divorced parents together—at least for a few hours. To ease tension and sidestep problems, you'll need a plan. Some guidelines:

• **For your walk down the aisle**, ask your father to do the honors if you're close to him. If you have a better relationship with your stepfather, ask him to escort you. (For more ideas, see "Crisis Control: Handling Wedding Dilemmas.")

• **Who sits where during the ceremony?** That depends on your family situation. If your parents have remained friendly and neither is remarried, they may sit together in the first pew. If there's tension between them or one or the other has remarried, seat the parent who raised you (and his/her spouse) in the first pew, your other parent (and his/her spouse) in the third pew.

• **Who gets photographed with whom?** Using index cards, write each posed photo you want your photographer to take and who should be in it. If you will be doing shots with both parents together, inform them beforehand, so no one is caught off-guard.

• **Traditionally, fathers do not have to stand in the receiving line**, so just have your mom receive guests. If you do want your father in the line, don't position him next to your mother.

Friends Who Fear Losing You to Your New Husband

Without a doubt, marriage changes a friendship. You may have less time for friends, find you have different interests, or feel conflicted about making your spouse a priority. Yet while marriage changes things, it doesn't have to end them. Reinvent your friendships into something that's comfortable for everyone. Even if you don't want to hit the single's scene with friends, you can still go shopping, see movies, and have dinner. If time is tight, use the phone, or e-mail. Ask them if they want to do errands together, like grocery shopping.

Money Matters: Seeing Red over the Green Stuff

Money is the number-one thing couples argue about, so don't feel alone. Instead of accusing, blaming, or ignoring, open up the communication by scheduling monthly money summits. Review your wedding budget, upcoming expenses, and where you both think things can be tightened or loosened. Don't interrupt or dismiss a concern. Each person should feel free to air any thoughts or feelings. Be honest about how much money you have and how much money you've been spending. Even when it comes to your wallet, honesty is the best policy. If you think you need to develop and adhere to a tighter budget, make sure it's a mutual effort. When only one of you is making sacrifices, resentment creeps in.

YOUR RECEPTION 13

The vows have been said and the rings exchanged. It's time to celebrate! Your reception should be as special—and memorable—as your ceremony. It can include a sumptuous seated dinner and dessert buffet with a ten-piece band or just you two, your parents, and a few close friends around a big table at your favorite inn or restaurant. As long as the celebration gives those who love you an opportunity to wish you happiness, a reception can be either of the above—or anything in between. All you really need is the opportunity and the space to gather everyone together; serve a sparkling beverage for the toast and a cake for a sweet ending. (For more information on selecting a site and a caterer, see Chapter 4, "Planning Your Wedding.")

Reception Timetable

The following is a sample schedule for a three-hour reception. (If your celebration will be longer, allow more time between events, or keep to this timetable and enjoy the dancing *after* dinner.) Once you've filled in time estimates for your reception, give your timetable to an attendant or your wedding consultant and ask her to make sure the caterer, photographer, and bandleader or DJ stick to it. They should be directed to discuss any scheduling problems with this person, rather than with you.

receiving-line etiquette

- A day or two before the wedding, go over the guest list with your groom and parents so names are fresh in your mind.

- Remind receiving-line participants beforehand to keep comments brief.

- Position the line in a convenient spot near the entrance or exit, where guests can move down it easily, directly into the refreshment area (if the receiving line is at the reception site).

- Ask waiters to pass food and drinks to those in line; keep chairs accessible for those who might need them.

- Provide musical entertainment, a photo display of old family wedding pictures, or snapshots of the bride and groom growing up, around the cocktail area.

- If you don't know a guest, simply introduce yourself—he or she will offer his or her name in return.

- It's friendly to remove gloves for handshaking.

- Bride and bridesmaids should hold bouquets in their left hands, or set them aside.

The reception:

You, the groom, and the wedding party should arrive at the reception site before the guests begin to gather, if possible.

The first half-hour:

If you did not have a receiving line immediately after the ceremony, assemble one now to greet guests as they arrive. The band or DJ starts playing music. Drinks are poured and hors d'oeuvres are served (these can also be offered to guests as they wait in the receiving line). Photographs of you, your groom, and the bridal party may also be taken during this time if the receiving line was at the ceremony site.

The second half-hour:

Guests mingle and pick up their place cards. You and the groom start making your way around the room. The photographer begins shooting the pictures you requested of relatives and friends.

After one hour:

Dinner is announced; the wedding party is seated. Your officiant or parents may say a blessing. Guests line up for the buffet or sit for table service. The wedding party is served.

The best man and/or maid of honor offers a toast to the couple, and the bride and groom may follow with their own thoughts and thanks.

After one-and-a-half hours:

The first course is cleared from the head table, then from the guests' tables. The couple dances their first dance as husband and wife, followed by the father–daughter dance, and so on. (These dances may also take place before dinner begins, or after the entrée; consult with your bandleader or DJ.) Everyone then sits down for the main course.

After two hours:

Tables are cleared; the cake–cutting ceremony takes place. Dancing resumes, while the cake and any other dessert are cut and served.

The last half-hour:

The single women gather as the bride tosses her bouquet, then the groom throws her garter to a group of bachelors.

The couple may slip away to change and say good-bye to their parents before leaving, but most stay and dance until the very end.

The Receiving Line

After the ceremony, your guests will be eager to hug you and congratulate you. A receiving line is an efficient way for you and your parents to receive these good wishes and give a warm welcome to friends and family who have come to share this special day. At large weddings, it may be the only chance you get to speak to each guest.

When does a receiving line take place? The receiving line should form after the ceremony, but before the reception. If you aren't going directly to the reception site

1 2 3 4 5 6 7 8 8

1. The mother of the bride
2. The father of the bride (optional)
3. The mother of the groom
4. The father of the groom (optional)
5. The bride
6. The groom
7. The bride's honor attendant (optional)
8. The bridesmaids (optional)

(because you'll be taking pictures, for example), set up the line at the ceremony site. If you'll take bridal-party pictures at the ceremony site, form a receiving line at the reception site.

Who stands in the line? The wedding hosts head the line. If your parents are hosting, your mother would greet guests first, followed by your father, to her left; the groom's mother, then his father to her left; the bride; the groom; the maid of honor; and the bridesmaids. (It is optional for fathers and attendants to stand in the line; you may prefer that they circulate among guests.)

If you do not have a mother or stepmother to receive your guests, your grandmother, a sister, or an aunt might head the line with your father. If the reception is hosted by persons other than your parents, they are the first in line to greet guests. If you and the groom are the wedding hosts, you would head the line.

What about divorced parents? If your parents or your groom's parents are divorced, it's often easiest to have fathers circulate among the guests rather than have them stand in the line. Even if divorced parents are friendly, having them stand together is confusing to guests who might then assume they are married.

If your parents are divorced and your father is hosting the party, you may want him to head the line anyway—just don't position him next to your mother. If you are close to your stepmother, you might want her to stand in line, too. In this case, position your mother at the head of the line, followed by your groom's parents, the bride and groom; your stepmother and father stand to the left of the groom.

What should you say? Thank guests for coming, tell them how happy your are to see them, and introduce them to your groom or other members of the wedding party they

guest-book tips

- Set your guest book on an attractive table in a prominent place at the reception site—at the end of the receiving line or near the reception-hall entrance.

- Provide several ballpoint pens (avoid felt-tip pens, which may run if the book accidentally gets wet).

- Ask the last person in the receiving line to point guests in the direction of the book.

- Later, ask your bandleader to remind guests to sign—or have an usher or another friend or relative circulate with the book.

reception seating tips

- Start as soon as your R.s.v.p. cards are in. Determine the number of tables, location, and seats at each.

- Make up a chart outlining table positions; fill in guests' names. Don't seat older guests near the band or kitchen; it may be hard for them to hear.

- Consider interests and personalities. Seat friends who share hobbies or occupations together, as well as single guests and teens. Mix shy personalities with outgoing ones. Arrange a children's table with books, favors, and a chaperone.

- Seat divorced parents separately, each hosting their own table of family and friends. Or seat the parent who raised you with the groom's parents, the other with the officiant.

- Include spouses, girlfriends, and boyfriends of attendants at the head table—if the bridal party is small. Or seat attendants at the head table, their spouses and dates separately.

- If there is no head table for the wedding party, the bridal couple can sit alone or with parents and siblings.

- If not at the head table, seat parents, grandparents, aunts, uncles, with the clergymember.

THE PARENTS' TABLE:

1. The mother of the bride
2. The father of the bride
3. The father of the groom
4. The wedding officiant
5. The mother of the groom
6. The wedding officiant's spouse or assistant, or another honored female guest

may not know. When introducing them, try to give a small fact that will help them remember each other—*"Mary was my college roommate,"* for example. If your groom or another receiving-line participant knows them, on the other hand, he or she can introduce them to you. Keep comments brief; otherwise the line may become too long (you can chat later, during table visits).

The Guest Book

A wedding guest book is a keepsake that preserves the names of friends and relatives who were present at your wedding. You can buy one at most stationery stores, choose an elegant leather album, or make your own, which you can decorate with pictures from your childhood or courtship (make sure to leave space for congratulatory comments and addresses). Consider how many guests plan to attend, and make sure there's enough space for them to write personal remarks and good wishes.

Reception Seating

When planning reception seating, consider the style of the food being served. Cocktails and finger foods don't require formal seating. Buffets, since they are full meals, do. All seated meals should have a seating plan; guests will appreciate the fact that you have thought of each one of them and specified a place.

THE HEAD TABLE:

1. The bride
2. The groom
3. The bride's honor attendant
4. The best man
5. The bridesmaids
6. The ushers

If you're designating seating at the reception, write out table (or escort) cards with guests' names and table numbers. (You might hire a calligrapher to write out these cards.) The cards may be on solid-colored paper or might be accented with the names or initials of the bride and groom, or a dried flower that echoes a flower in the table centerpieces. To create a friendly atmosphere among guests, address placecards informally. (*Janet Riley* or *Mrs. Riley* instead of *Mrs. John P. Riley.* If two people have the same last name, however, be sure to include first names or initials.) Check your cards against a master guest list to make sure you haven't omitted anyone.

Set the cards in alphabetical order on a separate table near the doorway. Or, post a seating chart with each guest's name and table number.

Place cards mark each seat at the bride's and parents' tables, but are optional elsewhere. At very formal weddings, and if you want to introduce specific guests to each other at each table,

you might specify in which seat they will sit at their tables; set place cards on the folded napkin, which rests on each service plate (or above the dinner plate). Write first and last names on both sides of the place card—to make it easier for guests who don't know one another to strike up a conversation.

Decide if you'll have a head table. Traditionally, the focus of the reception is the bride's (or head) table, where all the members of the bridal party sit on one side, facing the guests. The table is often elevated on a large platform called a dais and covered with a long cloth of lace, damask, or linen. Keep decorations low—bouquets and candles or simple garlands of flowers, greens, and ribbons—so guests get an unobstructed view. You and your groom sit in the center of the table (groom on the bride's left, best man on her right). The matron or maid of honor sits to the groom's left. Bridesmaids and ushers sit in alternating seats on either side.

Attendants who are married needn't be seated with their spouses at the same table, if the bridal party is large. If the

head-table etiquette

All eyes will be on you; set a good example.

• Keep voices low—especially during reception announcements and rituals (e.g., the cake-cutting ceremony or the toasts).

• Men should keep jackets on; women, shoes on—for the entire celebration.

• Women should not comb their hair or apply makeup at the table.

• Smoking looks out of place in bridal attire. No one should smoke when seated, posing for pictures, or standing in the receiving line. (Slip outside.)

• Avoid having too much to drink. Have someone escort a drunk attendant outdoors for a while.

• Remember to eat. You'll need energy for dancing, toasting, and mingling.

wedding party is small, however, you might have the husbands and wives of attendants, your parents, siblings, clergymember and his or her spouse join the head table; or, arrange a few seated tables for the bridal party and their partners.

Plan special parents' tables if parents won't be seated at the head table. Traditionally, your mother and father, as hosts, sit at opposite ends of the parents'

table. The groom's father sits at your mother's right, the wedding officiant to her left, the groom's mother to your father's right, and the wedding officiant's spouse or assistant, or another honored female guest, to his left.

Or you might arrange two parents' tables, one for your folks and one for his. That will seat more guests at special tables. If parents are divorced, they can individually host tables.

Blessings

When all the guests are seated for the meal, your clergymember, a member of your family, or another honored guest may say a prayer. Be sure to arrange this ahead of time, since not everyone is comfortable speaking spontaneously in public. At Christian weddings, the clergymember may rise to say grace. At Jewish weddings, a special blessing called the *hamotzi* is given over a large braided loaf of egg-rich bread called *challah* by the rabbi or two fathers, or any other honored guest. Pieces of *challah* are then passed to guests.

Wedding Toasts

Traditionally, the best man makes the first reception toast to the bride and groom—anytime after the receiving line is over and everyone has been served a glass of champagne or other sparkling drink. The band can get everyone's attention with a drumroll or fanfare. The groom rises to thank the best man, then toasts his bride and both sets of parents. The bride may then rise to make a toast, followed by parents, relatives, members of the wedding party, and friends. The best man can act as toastmaster and might prepare a list of the order in which each person will make a toast (see Appendix, under Chapter 13, "Your Reception").

toasting tips

- Prepare and rehearse. The toast should sound spontaneous yet well thought-out.

- Write the toast on index cards. Look at them if you need to, yet *don't* read the toast.

- Don't exceed three minutes; keep it short and sincere.

- Stand to give or to drink a toast; stay seated to receive one. The person being toasted does not raise his or her glass or drink to him or herself.

- Mention those whom you're toasting by name, mention your relationship to them, and add a thought about their future good fortune.

- Tell a personal story involving the couple, to turn the attention away from you and on to them.

- Don't be lewd or suggestive.

- Cite a favorite poem, quotation, joke, Scripture, or song lyric that seems relevant or meaningful.

Sample best man's toast:
"Here's to Sharon and Gary. I wanted to come to their wedding so much, I introduced them! May their lives be full of the kind of happiness we are enjoying here today."

Sample groom's toast:
"Thank you, Paul. You've been my best friend for twelve years, and I can't tell you how much it has meant for me to have you by my side through every major milestone. I thank you for introducing me

to my beautiful bride; I'm eternally grateful. I toast you, Sharon, for coming into my life and agreeing to share your own life with me. And I toast, and thank, your parents, for welcoming me into their family, and for giving us this incredible wedding. I also toast my own parents and family for their support and love over the years. And I thank all of you for coming to share this day with us."

Sample bride's toast:
"To my husband, the most wonderful man in the world. To my new family, with thanks for raising such a loving and supportive person. And to my parents, for all the love and strength they've given me. May we all have many, many more memorable days together."

cake innovations

- lace-like icing with a cascading bow
- handpainted marzipan fruits, flowers, and birds
- almond cake with raspberry-marmalade filling and apricot glaze
- handpainted sugar cameo portrait, wreathed in wildflowers
- pearl-like piping that outlines the different tiers
- chocolate cake with white or colorful flower decoration
- flowing pastilliage ribbon with gold leaf highlights
- gum paste sugar bouquets of symbolic or favorite flowers
- cakes inspired by Mediterranean mosaic tiles, Greek columns, or Shaker boxes
- brightly colored cake decorated with gum paste polka dots, faux gems, and stars
- retro designs with mod and pop-art motifs like daisies and hearts
- basketweave design with fresh flowers scattered on each tier

The Wedding Cake

Since Roman times, when a thin wheat cake, representing bounty, was crumbled over the bride's head to ensure her fertility, cake has been an important feature of the wedding celebration (see Chapter 2, "Wedding Customs"). In Victorian times, cakes became as frilly and elaborate as the bride's attire, decorated with roses, cupids, and garlands, often in the shape of romantic gazebos and cupolas. Today, bakers are creating innovative cakes that taste like fine desserts (see Appendix under Chapter 13, "Your Reception"), by varying the traditional white bride's cake with favorite flavors (orange, cherry, banana, chocolate, spice, carrot, hazelnut, mocha, marble, Amaretto, cheesecake), fillings (chocolate mousse, apricot, orange liqueur), and icings (white chocolate, mocha, vanilla, hazelnut). Today's wedding cake shapes—and toppers—reflect hobbies, occupations, and personal interests (a violin and sheet music, snow board, castle, a motif from the wedding gown). Create a special setting for the cake that coordinates with the reception decor and protects it from jostling. Consider creating a special tablecloth, different from the ones on the dining tables, or adding tulle and bows, or a garland of flowers. Below are tips for cutting the cake.

Cut the cake just before dessert at a luncheon or dinner reception; just after guests have been greeted at a tea or cocktail reception.

Use a ribbon-tied silver knife—a Heritage Cake Knife just received from your registry, with your initials newly engraved is a good choice, as is an heirloom knife (the one used by your parents at their wedding).

The groom places his right hand over the bride's, and together they cut into the bottom layer.

Traditionally, the bride and groom feed each other a taste of the first slice as a symbol of their willingness to share a household. (Don't smash cake in each other's face.)

creative cake toppers

- an antique floral teacup filled to overflowing with flowers that match the couple's china pattern

- a menagerie of origami birds, fish, and other animals made with colored and metallic paper

- a jewelry box brimming with faux pearls; more pearls scallop each tier of the cake

- a heart-shaped silver picture frame holding a photo of the two of you

- a tiny model of the Eiffel Tower, Leaning Tower of Pisa, or some other memento from a memorable trip together

- a small topiary tree

- antique bride-and-groom cake toppers from the 1940s and 1950s (check out flea markets or ask your baker for a source)

- a small basket stuffed with fresh flowers

- a miniature framed watercolor (placed on a small gilded easel) of anything meaningful—the first flowers he sent you; the beach where you met

- a hand-carved birdcage or a bird's nest made of spun sugar

- an arrangement of pinecones and gilded walnuts on a bed of leaves for an autumn wedding

- silver snowflakes for a winter wedding

- toy cars

- sugar seashells—appropriate for a beach wedding

- handblown ornaments for a holiday wedding

- miniature musical instruments with sheet music

- china and crystal figurines that become a keepsake

The bride serves her new in-laws their pieces, then the groom serves his new in-laws slices.

The rest of the cake is cut by the catering staff (this is best done in the kitchen) then served to all guests. (It is considered bad luck for a guest to leave the reception without tasting the cake.)

According to custom, the top tier of the wedding cake is saved and eaten on the couple's first anniversary (the groom's cake may also be used for this purpose). Wrap cake carefully so it is airtight, and freeze. Or to ensure it will still be tasty, freeze it to share on your one-month anniversary. Re-create a miniature version of the original cake for your first anniversary.

A charming old tradition says a piece of bride's cake under a single person's pillow will lead to dreams of a future spouse. (The groom's cake may also be used for this purpose.) The couple might ask the caterer to pack slices of any leftover wedding cake in small decorative boxes to send home with guests.

Cake Toppers

Plastic bride and groom figurines have been replaced by personalized, whimsical cake ornaments depicting a couple's occupations, hobbies, or how they met. Some examples: a miniature T-bird (representing a passion for antique cars), a pair of tennis racquets. Also popular: fresh flowers, especially at country or outdoor weddings, pulled sugar flowers (in cool weather), heirloom toppers from parents' or grandparents' cakes, or an accent that echoes the cake's decorative motif.

The Groom's Cake

Traditionally, the groom's cake is a single-layer dark fruitcake that accompanies the bride's cake, which is white (see Chapter 2, "Wedding Customs"). Groom's cakes today are often baked in the groom's favorite flavor, such as chocolate, and may be in a shape that's symbolic of his favorite interest or hobby—a mountaintop, football, or vintage car.

The groom's cake can be sliced and served at the reception and boxed for guests to take home as favors. It also might be saved for the couple's first anniversary. (To preserve a fruitcake, wrap it in a brandy- or rum-soaked cheesecloth, seal it in a tin, and store it in a cool place until you're ready to eat it.)

Reception Dancing

Guests can swing to an orchestra, waltz to the sounds of a string trio, or rock to the tunes played by a DJ. At a hotel or club reception, the area in front of the bride's table is usually cleared for dancing; at home, you might set aside one whole room or have a temporary dance floor laid down at the end of a large living room. For a garden reception, guests may dance on the terrace or on a temporary floor set up under a tent.

The first dance. The bride and groom's first dance as husband and wife is most often scheduled immediately after the first course, before the entrée is served. Guests can still be invited onto the dance floor as soon as they have been through the receiving line and passed into the reception banquet room. The bandleader will announce your first dance to clear the dance floor. (Although some couples opt to put all dancing off till after the entrée course, this can put a damper on the celebratory mood that guests are eager to express.)

Ballroom-dance lessons. In preparation for the first dance, which will put you two at the center of attention, many engaged couples are taking ballroom-dance lessons and practicing dancing to their favorite song. For your reception, you'll want to learn the basic steps of the waltz, fox-trot, and swing. (For fun, also learn the cha-cha, rumba, and tango.) Begin classes six months before the wedding; aim for two classes a week. And definitely practice.

To find a dance studio, look in the Yellow Pages under "Dancing," and ask friends for recommendations. Visit the studio, observe a class, and check out the studio's reputation with the local Better Business Bureau before signing up. Inquire about instructors' credentials (are they members of Dance Masters, Dance Educators of America, or the Imperial Society of Teachers of Dancing?). Rent or buy dance videos for home practice.

Ethnic dances. To get everyone onto the dance floor, many couples are asking their bands to play songs that reflect their heritages (see Chapter 14, "Wedding Music," for the "Music for Your Ceremony and Reception" chart). Many disc jockeys and bandleaders will play a recognizable line or circle dance such as the *horah* and encourage everyone to join in. If a band doesn't know a particular song, taped music can be used. These lively dances can be done by young and old alike:

The Mizinke: Usually performed to the Yiddish song *"Die Mizinke Oysgegeben,"* this song is played at a wedding when the last child in the family marries. Originally played to honor a Jewish mother whose last daughter wed, today the custom is extended to the last son *or* daughter. *Both* parents are seated in the center of the dance floor and presented with bouquets, while guests swirl around them in a lively circle dance.

The Dollar Dance ("The Bride's Dance"): This is derived from an old Polish custom in which the men who dance with the bride fill her pockets with

first-dance order

Here is one possible dance order to follow. Remember that it is not necessary to dance through an entire song before switching partners.

1. The bride and groom circle the floor to their favorite song.

2. The bride's father cuts in and dances with the bride, while the groom dances with his mother-in-law. (If the bride's parents are divorced and it is awkward to choose between dancing with a father or stepfather, all guests may be invited onto the floor.)

3. The bride dances with the father of the groom while the groom dances with his own mother.

4. The bride dances with the best man, while the groom dances with the honor attendant.

5. The bandleader invites the other members of the wedding party onto the dance floor.

6. The bandleader invites all guests onto the dance floor.

Before the evening ends, you should try to dance with each usher, and your groom with each bridesmaid. It's also customary for the ushers to dance with many of the single women present, and to request a dance with each bridesmaid and both mothers.

creative activities

- hire a fortune teller, tarot-card reader or handwriting analyst

- arrange for a performance by professional dancers; a special group dance lesson (for example, if you've hired a swing band to play at the reception, it might be a good idea to offer a group lesson, to help get people up and dancing); or a limbo contest

- hire a magician, mimes, or some other performer

- a creative guest–book alternative: ask guests to contribute to a large blank memory book; leave pens, pencils, crayons and see what happens (works best if you ask one of your more creative pals to make the first entry)

- outdoors, a fireworks display; indoors, sparklers (obtain required permits from fire department; check insurance with banquet manager). (See Appendix, under Chapter 13, "Your Reception," for source.)

- ask your videographer to visit each table and film guests who want to offer their personal wedding wishes and greetings

- place disposable cameras on each table, so guests can pose or snap their own candids and then leave them for you to develop later

money or pin bills to her veil. The money may be given in lieu of a gift, or a dollar (or more) may be given for a turn around the dance floor. The bride today puts the money in a bridal purse.

The Greek Handkerchief Dance: The groom is linked to the bride by a handkerchief; others hold shoulders; the dancing weaves around the room.

The Horah: This Israeli folk dance is performed in a circle while holding hands. Dancers lift the bride and groom, who hold a linen napkin between their hands, up on chairs in the center.

The Tarantella: This lively Italian folk dance in 6/8 time is often danced by couples at weddings. It has quick hops and tapping foot movements.

The Grand March: Newlyweds at Italian weddings may link arms and lead attendants and guests in a lively march around the room, sometimes outside and around the building. They then form an arch with their arms. Two by two, the guests pass under their arms, then form another arch to continue the "bridge" longer. When all the guests have followed suit, the bridge disbands with the last two in line passing all the way back through to kiss the couple who started it all. All come back through until the bride and groom head the line.

Following the Grand March, a second receiving line may be formed beside a table laden with *bomboniere*—cake boxes, porcelain boxes, cookies, candied almonds, cigars, or other favors (see Chapter 2, "Wedding Customs," under "Italy"). This receiving line is a chance to say good-bye to the couple, who will dance their last dance and then depart.

Guests may also form a circle to watch the couple's last dance. The bride and groom pass through and say good-bye at the song's conclusion.

Reception Entertainment

Some couples elect to provide entertainment for their reception guests. You might feature a slide show of your childhood and romance; friends might stage a scene from a play, read suitable poetry, or perform a special song for you, your college choir might sing a rendition of "your song" or school song. You or your groom might even perform or write your own wedding song, with humorous lyrics, and sing it to a familiar tune. Or you could hire a professional entertainer, such as a magician, comedian, or caricaturist to sketch portraits of guests. Some couples even arrange for fireworks or a laser show. If you hire an entertainer, be sure to review the entire act beforehand to make sure it is in good taste and likely to be appreciated by the many ages and personalities at your party. And no matter who's performing, don't let it run too long. Guests need a chance to eat, dance, and mingle on their own as well.

Favors

Though favors are by no means mandatory, think of them as a token of affection, something that will give your guests a lasting memory of your day. Choose gifts and themes reminiscent of the unique style and regional location of your wedding.

Theme Weddings. Create breakaway table centerpieces of small, individually potted poinsettias for a holiday wedding. A country theme? Set small dried-flower arrangements at each place. Getting married at the beach? Give your guests miniature potted palm trees, or mini sand pails filled with saltwater taffy. At a surprise wedding, have guests break a piñata to release a grab bag of tiny treats.

Food Favors. Opt for a few pieces of elegant chocolate–dipped fruit, such as long-stemmed strawberries. Or give guests a taste of your ethnic cuisine: English fruitcake, Italian *confetti* (candy-coated almonds), German chocolate cake, cookies, or French pastries— wrapped in tulle, or placed in small special containers.

Personalized Favors. Order monogrammed mints and set them at each place, in porcelain keepsake cups. Or, create a custom CD, stamped with your names and wedding date (see Appendix, Chapter 13). Another innovative idea? Write fortunes for each table of guests and either order or bake fortune cookies to tuck them into. Another meaningful keepsake? Place simple frames embossed with your monogram and/or wedding date at each place. Then ask the photographer's assistant to snap an instant photo of each guest or couple as they enter the reception room, and hang them on a "Photo Tree." Throughout the reception, or when leaving, guests can take their picture and put it in the frame to keep.

Ecologically and Socially Aware Favors. Give guests packets of seeds or tree saplings; they can plant them at home. Use found objects, native to the area, such as colorful shells, miniature pinecones, or unique stones. With a drop of clear glue, attach a line of special poetry, along with your names and the date. Or, leave a note written in calligraphy on each table stating that "In honor of George and Sue's wedding, a donation has been made to their favorite charity."

Floral Favors. Give each guest a small mini wreath made of a symbolic herb (rosemary for remembrance). Set a long-stemmed red rose at each place. Wrap linen napkins in floral rings. Position votive candle holders with floating magnolia blossoms at each place.

Collectible Favors. Give delicate crystal bud vases or unique decorative boxes. Or, near Christmas, select ornaments engraved with the year.

Ethnic Favors. For a Japanese wedding, give each guest a pair of laquered chopsticks. If you have Irish ancestry, give them an Irish linen handkerchief. Those who are Scandinavian can give boxes of marzipan candies. If you're British, con-

wedding favors

Below are just a few ideas.

- tulle-wrapped candied almonds
- decorative paper boxes filled with chocolates
- chocolates personalized with the couple's initials
- bottles of wine or sake with the bride and groom's own label
- a stack of small wrapped favors on a raised cake plate makes a festive centerpiece and saves on flower costs
- breakaway centerpieces
- a cluster of small bud vases filled with fresh blossoms
- lottery tickets
- decoupage flowerpots
- miniature wedding cakes
- hand-painted Easter eggs personalized with the couples' initials
- bags of bagels and copies of the Sunday newspaper distributed at the end of a Saturday evening wedding
- let your favors do double-duty as place cards: for example, attach personalized tags on each favor, or place names inside individual picture frames

tossing tips

- The bride turns and throws the bouquet over one shoulder. If you'd like to aim at a sister or close friend, face the group as you throw. (Tradition holds that the woman who catches the bouquet will be the next to marry.)

- The groom removes the bride's garter and tosses it over one shoulder to the bachelors at the reception; in some regions, the bride may toss the garter. (The man who captures it is destined to be the next to wed.)

when you're on a budget: reception cost-cutters

- Limit the number of guests. Think twice before inviting all your co-workers and the friends you no longer keep in touch with.

- Choose an off-season month (i.e., January on the East Coast; August in the Southwest).

- Investigate the possibility of using business-district restaurants for a Saturday-night wedding.

- Borrow punch bowls, linens, chairs, and dishes, so you won't have to rent these items.

- Instead of serving a full-course meal, have food stations set up.

- Offer red and white wine, punch, and a champagne toast instead of an open bar.

- Order a small wedding cake that's displayed; have the kitchen staff cut up a larger sheet cake in the back, then serve it to guests.

- Use in-season flowers in your bouquets and centerpieces.

sider small pieces of English china. For a Chinese wedding, opt for beautiful folding paper fans.

Favors They Can Use Again. Put escort cards inside small picture frames or pewter or china card holders. Wrap candied almonds in lace or men's handkerchiefs, sashed with ribbons. For a Jewish wedding, order velvet or satin yarmulkes that men can wear on future holidays; inside, personalize them with the names of the bride and groom and the wedding date.

Wedding Pranks

Part of the fun of a wedding is planning decorations for the couple's car, a "ribbing" sung to the tune of your college song, a funny telegram sent to the honeymoon hotel, or a groom who kneels at the altar to reveal the words "Help Me!" scrawled by his ushers on the soles of his shoes. But sometimes, in all the excitement, good judgment goes out the window. There is nothing funny about having your reservations changed from a double to a single room, your plane tickets canceled, or your car's paint job ruined by whitewash lettering. And no one likes an elegant country club reception to be interrupted by a rowdy group of friends determined to throw the groom into the pool. The best man should pass the word to the ushers: Play all the tricks you want at the bachelor party, but keep the fun under control at the reception.

The Bouquet and Garter Toss

Just before you leave to change into your going-away clothes, your bandleader, musician, or disc jockey may ask your bridesmaids and other single women to gather at a convenient spot for the throwing of the bouquet. If you want to keep your bouquet, to be dried as a keepsake, you might have your florist make up a breakaway bouquet, a small arrangement that separates from the main bouquet for you to toss. Or, ask your florist to make up a separate token bouquet for tossing.

The groom may next remove the bride's garter and toss it to a gathered group of single men. The bachelor who catches it may then slip the garter onto the leg of the single woman who caught the bouquet (see Chapter 2, "Wedding Customs").

Personalizing Your Reception

Your wedding reception—like your ceremony—should be a unique reflection of your love and commitment. Here, ways to personalize it.

1. Incorporate the food of your romance into the menu. Did you meet over the tomato bins at a farm stand? Start your meal with a salad of sliced heirloom tomatoes. Were root-beer floats an important part of your courtship? Set up a soda stand. You could even create a meal based on tastes you discovered together on vacation: freshly shucked oysters in honor of summer at the beach or Peking duck from a weekend in San Francisco. Menu cards can list each course and its significance to your relationship.

2. Acknowledge family milestones. If your Uncle Joe recently turned 80, ask guests to toast his health. You could announce the birth of a new baby, a sibling's graduation, or your parent's anniversary—just make sure you stop at one or two meaningful highlights.

3. Include a memory card with your invitations, along with a request that each guest write down a special memory of you, your fiancé, or the two of you and return it with the response card. You can glue them into an album and place it near the guest book for everyone to look through.

4. Show a short video (no more than 10 minutes) that follows both of you from childhood to courtship to the wedding. Incorporate videotapes, home movies, snapshots, and interviews with friends and relatives.

5. If your families serve particular foods at special occasions, include them in your menu. But rather than ask your mom to spend your wedding day whipping up multiple batches of her famous veal piccata, see if your caterer is willing to work with her recipe. If not, they can probably suggest a substitute that will at least approximate the original. Note the dish's originator on the menu card.

6. Ask guests to bring a photo of themselves with one or both of you. Put someone in charge of attaching them to a large board. It's a great conversation piece at the reception and will be a wonderful keepsake for you to take home.

7. Order special labels for the wine. You could design them yourselves and include the wedding date as well as your names. You can give half bottles as favors; be sure to save one or two for future anniversaries.

8. Place a letter of introduction on each guest table. It can outline who the table-mates are and what their relationship is to the bride and groom.

9. Recruit testimonials. Each of you asks a friend from grade school, another from high school, and yet another from college to share a brief anecdote about their relationship with the bride and groom.

10. After your own first dance, request the first dance from your parents' wedding reception. Make sure your bandleader or DJ is aware of the significance of any special song so that he or she can make the appropriate announcement—and so that they will be prepared to either perform the song, or play a recording.

WEDDING MUSIC
14

Your wedding music should reflect the style of your celebration and the personalities of you and your groom. Take the time to hire musicians and/or a DJ who will be responsive to your wishes and help to create a truly harmonious day.

Religious Ceremony Music

Inquire about the music policy at your house of worship. You may be surprised: Some churches and synagogues will not allow musicians other than their organist or permit secular (nonreligious) music to be played during a wedding ceremony. That sometimes includes "Wedding March (Bridal Chorus)," from Wagner's *Lohengrin*, which was composed to mark an ill-fated operatic union, and Mendelssohn's "Wedding March," from *A Midsummer Night's Dream*, which was written for the pagan wedding of the Duke of Athens to the Queen of the Amazons. Some religions will permit classical music and contemporary songs while others do not. (See Chapter 9, "Religious Rituals & Requirements.")

Protestant Weddings. It is acceptable to have both popular and religious music. It can be performed by the church organist, soloist, or choir, who will be familiar with wedding procedures and can offer a wide variety of selections from which you can choose. If you request something obscure or unusual, give the musician enough time to learn and practice the piece.

Roman Catholic Ceremonies. Some Catholic clergy may ask that you refrain from playing popular music and instead choose religious selections and the hymns sung at regular Masses. A choir or, more often, a soloist may sing. Schubert's "Ave Maria" is a favorite ceremony selection; other possibilities may include César Franck's "Panis Angelius" and Mozart's "Ave Verum."

Jewish Ceremonies. Many Reform and Conservative weddings permit secular music, including the usual wedding

ceremony music timetable

- Prelude—soft instrumental music and vocal solos performed during the thirty minutes when guests are being seated
- Vocal solo or choir piece—performed after the mothers are seated
- Processional—majestic pieces played while the wedding party and bride walk down the aisle
- Ceremony—vocal or instrumental solo, hymns, or folk songs performed after the vows
- Recessional—triumphant piece played as the newlyweds walk up the aisle as husband and wife, followed by the wedding party
- Postlude—lively selection played as guests file out

marches. Orthodox rabbis, however, may prefer that couples use only traditional Hebrew music. The cantor traditionally chants the Seven Blessings and may perform other solo pieces, if requested. Ask the rabbi and cantor for suggestions on both traditional Hebrew songs and contemporary Israeli music.

Eastern Orthodox and Greek Orthodox Ceremonies. Eastern Orthodox and Greek Orthodox faiths allow only vocal music at wedding ceremonies.

Quaker Ceremonies. Some groups allow music and others don't. Check to find one that suits your needs.

Ceremony Choices

Ceremony music is usually performed by an organist and/or string quartet (two violins, a viola, a cello); a trio (a violin, a flute, a harpsichord); or a brass ensemble (trumpets, a trombone, a French horn, a baritone). Think about the songs you prefer and the mood you want to create (see Appendix, under Chapter 14, "Wedding Music").

Consult with the music director of the church or synagogue. He or she will be familiar with standard and popular wedding music. Ask about the use of an organ and other keyboard instruments, as well as the policy of hiring a professional organist. You may have to pay the church organist whether or not you employ him or her (see "Hiring Musicians" section).

Add your own personal touch. Choose from current love songs, show and movie theme songs, folk and country ballads, classical works, or even the song played when you two first danced. (See "Wedding Ceremony Music" chart.)

Include the people you love. If friends' or relatives' talent is on the *professional* level, and they've performed in public before, ask one to play the prelude on the piano, another to offer a solo after the vows. (Some couples prefer to invite guests to perform at the reception, where the mood is lighter.) Thank these talented performers with a gift at the rehearsal dinner or another prewedding event.

Think twice before singing yourselves. Even the most seasoned performers get wedding-day nerves. Consider whether you want the stress of performing musically, in addition to walking down the aisle.

Hiring Musicians

Whether hiring musicians for the ceremony, cocktail hour, or reception, realize that some orchestras, bands, and soloists may be booked a year or more in advance. Begin your search as soon as the wedding date is set.

Choose ceremony instruments and musicians. Ask the organist or clergymember about the acoustics in the house of worship where you will be married. Ask that person to refer you to local musicians—particularly those who have performed for other weddings held there. A string or woodwind quartet, a group of madrigal singers, a harpist, or a trumpeter are some options. You might have them perform alone or in conjunction with an organist. Select instruments and tunes that are neither too soft nor too overpowering, and make sure the selections work with the instruments. For example, Pachelbel's "Canon in D" was written for strings and will sound different should you have an organist perform it.

Get other referrals for ceremony musicians from friends, relatives, and other newlyweds. Call local music schools, colleges, and symphonies for the names of string quartets and soloists. Consult the Internet, or contact the local musicians union (listed under "Musicians" in the Yellow Pages); union offices may provide videotapes of bands and direct you to musicians who meet the description of the style you prefer. If you want to include a band in your ceremony, ask your caterer, photographer, and florist for the names of those with whom they've enjoyed working. Ask for and check references from couples who have recently hired the musicians for their weddings.

Listen to the musicians perform. If you choose to hire a band, try to see a live performance or watch an audition tape. This will help you evaluate the band's stage presence and will give you an overall feel for their style of music. Make sure you like the quality of instrumental and vocal performances, that the sound is not overpowering, and that it seems appropriate for a ceremony.

Give the ceremony musicians your musical requests. If you plan to include a contemporary or original song, provide the group with sheet music early enough so that they have time to learn it well.

Ask friends and relatives for reception-band referrals. Follow the same process detailed above when searching for reception musicians. Attend a wedding or other large party where the band is playing. At the very least, view a videotape. Notice how loud the sound is (it should not be overpowering), the dress and demeanor of the band members, the style of the bandleader when introducing songs, guests, or reception activities.

Discuss your tastes for dance music. Since your reception music should appeal to all guests, a versatile band is essential. Meet with the bandleader to discuss the type of music you want played—be it pop, jazz, Motown, or reggae. Be as detailed as possible; if you like jazz, specify swing, familiar, or progressive jazz.

Give the bandleader a list of any special songs you want played. If songs are unusual, provide sheet music and lyrics, and allow sufficient time for the group to

music-contract tips

Specify the following points in a signed and countersigned contract:

- the ceremony and reception's date, time, and place

- equipment provided; rental fees

- the names of the specific musicians, vocalists, and DJ to perform (you may pay a premium for "stars")

- a backup system if any band members become ill: Who will perform?

- the hours the musicians will play

- when, specifically, during the wedding the musicians will play (i.e., prelude, ceremony, cocktail hour, and reception)

- all fees and overtime rates

- late-arrival penalties

- the number and length of breaks

- if music will be continuous (ask for taped music or a soloist during breaks)

- the musicians' attire

- if meals will be provided

practice. Also prepare the bandleader with any introductions you'd like him or her to make ("This is the song that the bride's parents danced to at *their* wedding, thirty years ago"). Let the musicians know how and when the wedding party will be introduced; when you want the first dance, father-daughter and mother-son dances played; when the best man will make his toast; and if you'll throw the bouquet and garter.

Tell the bandleader what you do *not* want played. Some couples specify that they do not want a particular song played ("YMCA" or "The Macarena").

Ask if the musicians will bring their own sound system. If they will, check to see if the equipment is electrically compatible with the reception site, and where electrical outlets are located. If they won't, ask what they will require and find out the total cost for providing it. An extra generator is a must; more than one wedding has gone without music simply because a generator has blown or failed to work. Plan where in the reception hall the band will perform and test the acoustics. (It's best to position a band at one far end of a tent or room, so sound isn't overwhelming.) If you want the band to provide continuous music, ask if they will also have a guitarist, a violinist, a piano player, or bring taped music—compact discs (CDs) or cassettes. Do they own this equipment? If not, how much are rental fees?

Get all the specific instructions for the ceremony and reception musicians in writing. In a contract signed by you and countersigned by the band, specify all details (see "Music-Contract Tips" box). Expect to pay a 50 percent deposit up front, with the balance due on your wedding day. Your only leverage if the vocalist or "star" of the orchestra whom you thought you booked does not show up, or the group deviates in any way from the service promised in the contract, is to decrease the balance due accordingly. Bands do not expect tips or the same meal that is being served, but since the average reception is four hours, you should offer them snacks and sandwiches.

Look for a harmonious working relationship. If the bandleader isn't responsive to your needs during the initial negotiations, look elsewhere.

Hiring a Disc Jockey

With their wide choice of music and ability to control volume and play continuously, many couples are hiring a DJ to provide taped music for their ceremony and/or reception. DJs are often skilled at sensing what style of music will get each group of guests out onto the dance floor. (To help your DJ make sure the dance floor fills up as soon as the reception begins, enlist a group of friends or family members in advance to get up and dance immediately. It will encourage others to join in.)

Is a DJ appropriate for a wedding? Unless your wedding will be very formal, the answer is yes. The tapes, CDs, and records played by a DJ are viable alternatives to live music—especially appropriate when the reception site does not have a dance floor, yet you would like to provide background music. A DJ can play quality recordings for all segments of the wedding—prelude, ceremony, processional, recessional, postlude, receiving line, cocktail hour, and reception.

Don't DJs show up at parties in jeans and leather jackets? As with any wedding-service professional, including musicians, you should list all of the points that will be a factor on your wedding day in a signed and countersigned contract (see "Music Contract Tips" box). Simply specify that you would like the DJ to wear formal attire.

How expensive is a DJ? In most cases, hiring a DJ will be less expensive than hiring live musicians. Most charge a set fee for a party. Specify this amount, as well as overtime rates, in your contract. Also allow for a (10 to 15 percent) tip at the end of the evening.

Will a DJ be familiar with wedding protocol? Maybe, but not necessarily. Ask for the names and phone numbers of couples who hired the DJ for their weddings. As when interviewing or auditioning wedding bands, ask to see videotapes of the DJ in action, or attend an event where he or she will be working. Is the DJ's manner of speaking pleasing to you? That's important considering he or she will be your announcer for all wedding events and introductions. Always specify in your contract that the DJ you saw *will* be the DJ you get at your wedding. Never pay in full in advance; you will have no leverage if a different DJ shows up. Specify in the contract who will be the backup if the DJ becomes ill.

How can I be sure the DJ is experienced? Anyone can buy equipment, tapes or CDs, and call himself or herself a DJ. That is why you must ask for referrals from friends, relatives, and other wedding professionals who may have worked with DJs in the past. Ask the DJ just what kind of experience he or she has. If the DJ you're considering only has experience playing proms and sweet sixteens, keep shopping. You may find DJs listed under "Disc Jockeys and Entertainment" in the Yellow Pages or on the Internet, but be sure to check references before signing a contract.

Will the DJ bring his or her own equipment? Yes. Otherwise, why hire one? (You could borrow or rent the equipment and music tapes and ask a friend to stand at the controls throughout the celebration.) You *should* ask the DJ about his or her equipment, and ask if he or she has worked at your site. If not, ask him or her to visit beforehand to check electrical outlets and acoustics. As with a band or orchestra, have an extra generator.

Will the DJ play what I want? DJs pride themselves on knowing what to play when— to get the crowd onto the dance floor. Although you want your DJ to have creative lee-

disc jockey pluses

- variety of music
- original songs played as guests remember them
- minimal space needed for equipment
- continuous music
- skilled announcer

way, give him or her a list of songs to be played for the first dance, father-daughter dance, mother-son dance, cake cutting, bouquet and/or garter toss. Include bands or singers, as well as specific songs that you want to hear during the reception.

The Ceremony

The Prelude. The musical prelude, which takes place as the guests are seated, should last between fifteen minutes and a half hour. Wedding musicians (as well as the musical director at your house of worship) have a broad repertoire of beautiful classical pieces from which to choose: Ask to hear several possibilities and then pick your favorites. You might consider Bach fugues, preludes, inventions and chorales, as well as slow movements from concertos or sonatas by 19th-century composers such as Brahms, Chopin, Schubert, and Mendelssohn. Baroque chamber music for instrumental groups is also appropriate.

The Processional. A majestic selection is played while the wedding party walks down the aisle, followed by a regal piece played as the bride and her father proceed. (Some processionals, if especially uplifting, may be used instead for the recessional.) If you'll be walking down the aisle to something different than your bridesmaids, make sure the two selections are in an identical—or at least related—key.

Hymns and Solos. Today, pop songs are often blended with Broadway show tunes and religious hymns—performed with lyrics or as instrumentals. Check with your clergymember for any restrictions. Hymns are a great way for everyone to participate in the ceremony. When selecting hymns, remember to read through all the verses and eliminate the inappropriate ones. Your clergymember can lend you hymnals and offer suggestions.

The Recessional. The triumphant first notes of the recessional are heard shortly after the newlyweds kiss and begin to walk back up the aisle as husband and wife. The piece selected should be joyous and uplifting—in celebration of the new marriage.

The Postlude. Triumphant music continues as guests file out. (See the "Music for Your Ceremony and Reception" chart for suggestions for each part of the ceremony.)

The Reception

Reception music may range from jazz for cocktails to classic rock for after-dinner dancing. Variety is essential (see "Music for Your Ceremony and Reception" chart).

The Cocktail Hour/Receiving Line. Unobtrusive background music is most appropriate at this time. Consider soft piano music, a string quartet or jazz ensemble. Jazz by Duke Ellington, Miles Davis, Wynton Marsalis or Diana Krall, or piano music by George Winston are all good selections.

Special Dances. Throughout the reception, you may request special dances (the first dance; the father-daughter dance; the mother-son dance), ethnic line and circle dances, specific songs from various decades, and current hits. Give the bandleader a list of your requests at least two weeks before the reception.

Music for Your Ceremony and Reception

THE PRELUDE

- "Adagio," Albinoni
- "Bénédiction Nuptiale," Saint-Saëns
- "Chant de May," Jongen
- "Largo," *The New World Symphony*, Dvořák
- "O Perfect Love," Burleigh
- "Siciliano for a High Ceremony," Howells
- "Songs Without Words," #48, Mendelssohn
- "The Lord's Prayer," Malotte
- "The Wedding Song," Stookey
- "Wedding Day at Troldhaugen," *Lyric Pieces*, Grieg

THE PROCESSIONAL

- "Air" and "Bourrée," *Water Music*, Handel
- "Allemande," G-Major Suite, Pachelbel
- "Apotheosis," *Sleeping Beauty*, Tchaikovsky
- "Coronation March," *Crown Imperial*, Walton
- "Fanfare," *Te Deum*, Charpentier
- "Intrada," Sibelius
- "Music for a Royal Occasion" ("March"), Handel
- "Prince of Denmark's March," Clarke
- "St. Anthony Chorale," Haydn
- "Spring," *The Four Seasons*, Vivaldi
- "Trumpet Voluntary," Clarke
- "Wedding March," *A Midsummer Night's Dream*, Mendelssohn
- "Wedding March," *The Marriage of Figaro*, Mozart
- "Wedding March," ("Bridal Chorus," aka "Here Comes the Bride"), *Lohengrin*, Wagner

THE RECESSIONAL

- "Benedictus," Simon and Garfunkel
- "Bridal March," Hollins
- "March No. 4," *Pomp and Circumstance*, Elgar
- "Priests' March," *The Magic Flute*, Mozart
- "Radetzky March," Johann Strauss, Sr.
- "Rondeau," *Fanfares for Violins, Oboe, Bassoon, Trumpets, and Percussions* (*Masterpiece Theatre theme*), Mouret
- "Toccata," Organ Symphony No. 5, Opus 42, Widor
- "Trumpet Tune," Stanley

THE FIRST DANCE

- "A Kiss to Build a Dream On," Kalmar, Ruby, Hammerstein (Louis B. Armstrong)
- "As Time Goes By," Hupfeld
- "A Whole New World," Rice and Menken (Peabo Bryson and Regina Belle)
- "Can You Feel the Love Tonight?" John and Rice (Elton John)
- "Can't Help Falling in Love (With You)," Creatore, Peretti, and Weiss (Elvis Presley)
- "Caught Up in the Rapture," Glenn and Quander (Anita Baker)
- "Cheek to Cheek," Berlin
- "Crazy for You," Bettis and Lind (Madonna)
- "Crazy Love," Young (Van Morrison)
- "Fever," Davenport and Cooley (Peggy Lee)
- "Fields of Gold,"Sting
- "Fly Me to the Moon," Howard (Frank Sinatra)
- "Groovy Kind of Love," Wine and Bayer Sager (The Mind Benders, Phil Collins)
- "Happy Together," Gordon and Bonner (The Turtles)
- "Have I Told You Lately," Wiseman (Van Morrison, Rod Stewart)
- "I Got You Babe," Bono (Sonny and Cher)
- "I've Got You Under My Skin," Porter
- "I Only Have Eyes for You," Dubin and Warren (The Flamingos, Art Garfunkel)
- "I Say a Little Prayer," Bacharach and David (Dionne Warwick)
- "I Will," Lennon and McCartney (The Beatles)
- "In My Life," Lennon and McCartney (The Beatles)
- "It Had to Be You," Jones and Kahn (Frank Sinatra)
- "It's Not Unusual," Mills and Reed (Tom Jones)
- "Let It Be Me," the Everly Brothers
- "La Vie en Rose," Edith Piaf
- "Let's Hang On," Crewe, Linzer, and Randell (The Four Seasons)
- "Let's Stay Together," Green, Jackson, and Mitchell (Al Green)
- "Looking Through the Eyes of Love," Hamlisch and Bayer Sager (Melissa Manchester)
- "Love Will Keep Us Alive," The Eagles
- "Love Will Keep Us Together," Sedaka and Greenfield (The Captain and Tennille)
- "L.O.V.E.," Gabler and Kaempfert (Nat King Cole)
- "Never Knew Love Like This Before," Lucas and Mtume (Stephanie Mills)
- "Night and Day," Porter
- "Our Love Is Here to Stay" Gershwin
- "So Glad You're Mine," Green (Al Green)
- "Someone to Watch over Me," Gershwin
- "Stand by My Woman," Kravitz, Hirsch, Pasch, and Krizan (Lenny Kravitz)
- "Still Crazy After All These Years," Simon (Paul Simon)
- "Thanks Again," Rushing (Ricky Skaggs)
- "This Magic Moment," (Jay and the Americans)
- "Unforgettable," Gordon (Nat King Cole)
- "What a Difference You've Made in My Life," Jordan (Ronnie Milsap)
- "What a Wonderful World," Douglass and Weiss (Louis Armstrong)
- "Wink and a Smile," Shaiman, McLean
- "Wonderful Tonight," Clapton (Eric Clapton)

THE FATHER-DAUGHTER DANCE

- "How Sweet It Is (to Be Loved by You)," Holland, Holland, and Dozier (James Taylor)
- "My Girl," Robinson and White (The Temptations)
- "My Heart Belongs to Daddy," Porter
- "Sunrise, Sunset," Harnick and Bock (from *Fiddler on the Roof*)
- "Thank Heaven for Little Girls," Lerner and Loewe (Maurice Chevalier, from Gigi)
- "Thanks for the Memory," Robin and Rainger
- "The Times of Your Life," Lane and Nichols (Paul Anka)
- "The Way You Look Tonight," Fields, Kern (Frank Sinatra)
- "Through the Years," Dorff and Panzer (Kenny Rogers)
- "Turn Around," Belafonte, Greene, and Reynolds (Harry Belafonte)

THE MOTHER-SON DANCE

- "I Get a Kick Out of You," Porter
- "Summer Wind," Mayer and Mercer (Frank Sinatra)
- "Wind Beneath My Wings," Silbar and Henley (Bette Midler)
- "You Are the Sunshine of My Life," Wonder (Stevie Wonder)
- "You're the Top," Porter

WEDDING FLOWERS 15

Flowers bespeak love and romance, and no wedding would be complete without them. Brides have worn or carried flowers since the earliest days. Garlands, blooms, and petals have graced wedding altars, decorated wedding tables, and lined wedding pathways for centuries. Flowers were believed to symbolize bounty and fertility, while their heady aroma was believed to ward off evil spirits (see Chapter 2, "Wedding Customs"). Whether you're planning a formal wedding with all the trimmings or a small, quiet affair, let love bloom with beautiful floral flourishes.

Your Floral Agenda

Your wedding-day flowers should have the same creative touch as every other detail of your wedding (see Appendix, under Chapter 15, "Wedding Flowers"). Coordination of all the floral elements, including centerpieces and bouquets, is the key to a sophisticated look. Think of the bouquets as accessories; appropriate to the season, style and location of the wedding, as well as the proportions and fabrics of the dresses. Not surprisingly, the true path to satisfaction is to hire the right florist and establish a solid working relationship.

1. Know yourself. Are you a flower aficionada with definite ideas, or could you not care less—as long as they're pretty and arrive on time? Your personality will guide your needs.

2. Compile ideas and photos you like. Consult flower, party-planning, and decorating books, as well as bridal magazines, which frequently feature stories on bridal flowers.

cost-cutting tips

- Avoid wired, labor-intensive—and more expensive—bouquets. Opt instead for a few full-blown peonies or a single hydrangea, simply bound with ribbon.

- Find your own antique or unusual ribbon or lace (at flea markets or in antique stores). Some florists have only a standard supply; your bouquet can look more elegant with special touches.

- Avoid scheduling your wedding on or near a flower-giving holiday; flowers can be much more expensive near Valentine's Day and Mother's Day.

- Utilize seasonal (more plentiful) and local (less costly) blooms and flowering branches. Vases of fresh-cut garden rhododendron or magnolia are magnificent in spring.

- Consider blossoming bulbs as table centerpieces: Trim small pots of miniature daffodils or hyacinths with a tulle bow.

- Select wedding and reception sites that need minimal decorating—a flowering garden or ornate room.

- Check to see if ceremony flowers can be shared with the bride whose wedding is before or after yours in your house of worship.

- Use ceremony arrangements at the reception site.

- Keep in mind that a single majestic arrangement is more impressive than a dozen minimal clusters.

Visit parks and botanical gardens. Put together a scrapbook of information—photographs of your dress, your site, favorite colors, flowers, and decorative elements.

3. Choose a florist carefully—and early in the planning process. Most florists have experience planning parties and can offer valuable advice, even suggesting reception sites and caterers. Visit shops. Ask recent brides and friends who frequently use florists for recommendations. Also look on the Internet, and in the Yellow Pages under "Florists," and write down names from local bridal magazines and bridal newspaper supplements.

4. Make an appointment. Don't expect to walk into a busy flower shop and start discussing ideas. Choose a time that will give you a chance to interview the florist. Is she open to your ideas? Does she have interesting suggestions? Is the florist comfortable with your budget? Has she handled a wedding your size before? Is the shop able to service more than one wedding in a day? Do you feel comfortable with the florist and other staff members' attitudes?

5. Judge a store by its look and its staff. Are the flowers presented in an appealing manner? Do they appear healthy? Look for design flair. The shop decor will clearly signal the existence of a creative, inspired owner.

6. Ask to see photographs of flowers created for other weddings. You need to see examples of their work in order to accurately judge a florist's skills, and to assess whether or not she will be able to create the type of designs you envision.

7. Determine the mood and style of your wedding. You'll want your floral plans to match your wedding. Will it be grand or casual? A holiday celebration or a summer fête? Will the ceremony be at a religious site with a reception elsewhere, or will the wedding and reception be at the same location? Describe the style of your gown and your attendants' gowns; bring along swatches of fabrics or photos taken during your fitting, as well as swatches of linens for the tables at the reception. Before ordering, be sure no one in the wedding party is allergic to any particular flower or greenery (see Chapter 4, "Planning Your Wedding").

8. Establish a budget. Be realistic—it will eliminate wasteful replanning. Inquire about specific costs. Every good florist can work within any budget, so even brides planning to spend very little on flowers can make a splash. Save even more by enlisting the help of creative friends or marrying in a garden that's in full bloom. (See "Cost-Cutting Tips" box.)

9. Reserve your date early. To avoid disappointment, book the florist up to a year in advance, especially if the florist or your wedding date is popular. If you have a large budget for flowers, start specific floral planning at least three months in advance;

you'll want time to refine all the details with your florist. Less formal weddings are easily managed in eight weeks or less.

10. Sign a contract. A signed and countersigned contract or bill of sale should outline the services you expect from your florist (see "Flower-Contract Tips" box). Be reasonable. Flowers are perishable and not always available as requested. In an emergency, a florist should make only comparable substitutions.

Questions for Your Florist

What are some wedding-flower trends? Is color for the bridal bouquet in or out? Are bouquets in holders more or less popular than those that are hand-held? A good florist should be able to tell you this and more.

How will my bouquet complement my dress? Once you've picked out your gown, show a picture of it to your florist. She should be able to design a bouquet that will highlight the best features of your dress, yet still be in proportion to your height, weight, and gown. For example, a if you're wearing a sheath, the bouquet should be small, so it won't overpower the simple lines of your dress. If your gown uses delicate fabrics such as chantilly lace or chiffon the flowers should be tissue–light, such as ranunculus or sweet peas. If your dress is very detailed in front, the bouquet should be constructed so that's it's comfortable to hold from the side.

Can you create a sample bouquet? This could help cut down on miscommunication and prevent wedding-day disappointments. Expect to pay a fee.

How will the centerpieces coordinate with the bouquets? How can I use flowers to enhance my wedding site? A formal wedding in a traditional setting like a hotel ballroom cries out for a structured centerpiece. One or two flowers used in the bride's bouquet could be the focal point of a traditional arrangement. If your florist is unfamiliar with the reception site, ask her to visit it beforehand (same goes for the ceremony site). Or send her pictures along with details, such as the color of the draperies and carpeting, table linens, etc. As with the bouquet, ask the florist to show you a sample centerpiece.

Will the flowers I'm interested in be available at the time of my wedding? If you have your heart set on flowers that will be out of season on your wedding day, ask him or her to recommend other choices that will give you the look you want.

Will the flowers I've chosen hold up throughout my wedding? If you're getting married outdoors under the blazing sun or want your flowers to arrive hours before the

Include:

- the date, time of deliveries, and sites (your home for the bouquets, the house of worship for corsages, the reception site for table arrangements).

- the amount and color of each type of flower (e.g., ten red roses) in each bouquet, corsage, boutonniere, and arrangement.

- the acceptable substitutes within your budget if first choices are not available that week. (State that you must be notified to approve substitutions.)

- the unacceptable substitutes (e.g., *no* carnations, *nothing* purple).

- the numbers and sizes of altar and table arrangements.

- the decorative items (garlands, wreaths, pew markers).

- the expected condition of flowers (fresh and in bloom, not wilted).

- the style and color of ribbons, candelabra, vases, and other accessories.

- the name of the person responsible for on-site setup that day (and backup person in case of emergency).

- the total cost and payment schedule; deposit made.

- the refund or cancellation policy.

ceremony so you have plenty of time to take pictures, ask your florist for hardy blooms that can stand up to time and Mother Nature.

Prayer Book Flowers

In a formal or semiformal wedding, the bride may choose to carry a flower-covered prayer book instead of a bouquet. This prayer book is often an old family Bible or a new book purchased for the occasion by the bride's or groom's parents. Cover the book in white silk or satin (to complement your dress). Choose any flowers to adorn the prayer book; white orchids, with a few smaller blossoms or ribbon streamers (to match the proportion of a long gown), are timeless options.

Bouquet Glossary

Bouquet—The classic bridal accessory. A cluster of blooms either handtied or anchored in a water-saturated oasis and sunk inside a plastic bouquet holder. Available in a wide variety of sizes and shapes.

Nosegay—A round, densely packed burst of flowers gathered in a bouquet holder or handtied with ribbon; almost any flower can be used. A small nosegay is a posy. In Victorian times, nosegays were always carried to social events.

Biedermeier—A small tight cluster featuring concentric rings of varied colors and blooms; each of the rings in a Biedermeier is usually composed of a single type of small blossom.

Tussie mussie—A handtied bouquet in which stems are cut to a uniform, convenient-to-carry length and trimmed with ribbon. Often they're inserted into a silver, cone-shaped tussie-mussie holder,

popular in Victorian times. Tussie mussies of colorful herbs and flowers were once carried to ward off bad smells and disease.

Wired—Each individual bloom is wired to stand upright, or each bloom may be attached to a slender filament of wire with green tape to simulate a stem. These flexible stalks are manipulated to create a bouquet.

Cascade—A bouquet commonly anchored in an oasis, which acts as the support base. Blooms and greenery gracefully spill downward from the oasis along the front of the gown.

Composite—Individual petals of a flower or a cluster of individual blooms are wired or glued together to create a fuller, fanciful blossom on a single stem. A "glamelia" is a bloom handmade by a florist: Dozens of split gladiola florets combine, one inside the other, to create a camellialike blossom. Another option: Create a lush oversized rose with rose petals.

Pomander—A plump, blossom-covered globe that is suspended and held from a satin ribbon; an easy-to-carry option for a petite bride or child attendants.

Boa—A luxurious length of wired blossoms and greenery worn as a stole in lieu of a bouquet.

The White Bouquet

All-white or all-cream bouquets have been traditional for weddings since Queen Victoria wed in white in 1840.

Classic. For texture, mix flowers in different hues of white and in various stages of bloom: tiny rosebuds newly picked, past-peak roses, or those in full bloom; diminutive snowdrops with full peonies. Add ivy, a symbol of fidelity, and other greens.

Modern. Today, in addition to combining white and near-white blooms (in ivory, champagne, creamy white, ecru, pure white) and varying textures, bridal bouquets may have small blossoms layered inside each other, creating one large, composite, new bloom. For a fall bouquet, create a clutch of rich-hued blooms; a bright, garden palette would look pretty in spring. Cluster single flower stems of the same variety of flower (a mass of tulips, for example) to create the appearance of one lush blossom.

Floral Headpieces

Brides and bridesmaids have traditionally worn floral wreaths or crescents of orange blossoms or other light, symbolic flowers, such as stephanotis. These headpieces fit across the top of the head or in a circle that rests on the crown. They are held in place by small combs or hairpins; a veil may be attached. *At the reception*: The bride may remove her traditional veil and headpiece and replace them with a fresh floral wreath, which is easier to wear while dancing. Bridesmaids may wear a single bloom in their hair, held in place with a comb or hairpin (each bridesmaid should wear the flower on the same side of her head).

Bridesmaids' Blossoms

The bouquets that your attendants carry don't have to all look alike. Select one flower that will appear in each arrangement, with accent flowers varying. The honor atten-

classic white bouquet choices

- amaryllis
- astrantia mixed with freesia
- camellias
- Easter lilies
- gardenias
- hyacinths mixed with stephanotis
- lilacs
- lily of the valley
- orange blossoms
- orchids
- Queen Anne's lace
- roses
- stephanotis
- stock mixed with peonies
- tulips
- white violets

modern white bouquet choices

- apple blossoms with blush tulips, peonies, lilacs
- dendrobium orchids
- hydrangea
- jasmine
- Serena roses
- wild sweet peas
- lilies of the valley, hostas, ivy, and grasses.

colorful accents

Add touches of color to an all-white bouquet:

- blue violets
- gloriosa lilies
- irises
- ranunculus
- stargazer lilies with red centers

bouquet trends

- Mix the classic with the unexpected—a bouquet favorite like lily of the valley looks fresh with lavender or other herbs.

- If your dress is modern and spare, consider a simple bouquet of large graphic blossoms, such as tulips.

- Blend hard and soft (lotus pods with sabrina roses); vivid color with pale shades (warm corals with cool purple).

- Keep everything in one tone, blending shades of apricot, peach, and ocher, for instance.

- Or, stick to the very same hue, but mix and match textures, as in the classic white bouquet.

- Bursting with warmth and color, the all-red bouquet is perfect for a holiday wedding.

- Repeat a design detail from your dress in your bouquet (if the lace trim at the bodice uses rosettes, include tiny roses in your bouquet).

- A smaller, rounder bouquet makes a more modern statement.

- A hand–tied bouquet looks just-picked from the garden.

- Remember to keep the color palette harmonious. Including very dark flowers with light-toned ones will cause the bouquet to stand out too much in photographs. (FYI, very dark colors can also create dark holes in your photos.)

dant may carry a bouquet in the same size as the bridesmaids, but in a different shade or contrasting color. Below, other tips:

Shape and style. The bridesmaids' bouquets should be smaller than the bride's, complement her bouquet, and also be in proportion to each woman's stature. The flowers should either match or contrast with the color of their dresses.

Classic choices. Anemones, chrysanthemums, freesia, dried herbs mixed with flowers, holly, hydrangea, larkspur, lilacs, peonies, roses, sweet peas, tulips, and wheat sheaves.

Innovations. If each attendant is wearing a different-colored gown, select tulips in contrasting colors, tied with matching ribbons. For a Victorian wedding, opt for tussie mussies or nosegays. Order each bridesmaid's bouquet made of her favorite flower or birth-month flower.

Accessories. Additional flowers may be ordered for attendants to pin in their hair.

Children's Blossoms

The flowers that your child attendants will wear or carry should charm them and enchant adults. Although traditionally little girls tossed rose petals as they walked down the aisle, these petals may cause guests (or those in your wedding party) to slip. Order a miniature basket of blossoms or a nosegay instead.

Shape and style. Order easy-to-hold arrangements. Add colorful ribbon streamers that will complement the wedding color scheme and the children's outfits.

Classic choices. Biedermeier bouquets of Serena roses and miniature grape hyacinths, French roses, lily of the valley, rosebuds, Victorian nosegays, and violets.

Innovations. Select mini nosegays, tiny basket arrangements, garlands of flowers and greens that will drape over children's shoulders as they walk down the aisle. Also consider floral balls, pomanders, floral hoops—to loop over little arms.

Accessories. For flower girls, headbands, hair wreaths, or single blooms for barrettes; pocket posies for the jacket pockets of ring bearers.

Boutonnieres

The groom's, ushers', and fathers' boutonnieres are worn on the left lapel. To distinguish his position of honor, the groom can wear a type of flower that appears in the bride's bouquet. Boutonnieres should be small in scale, tailored and not too feminine in appearance. They can also be symbolic in meaning (see "The Language of Flowers" section). Consider a bud or tiny floret with greenery.

Classic choices. For ushers and fathers: White roses. For groom, best man: stephanotis, lily of the valley, and freesia with greenery.

Innovations. Ranunculus, calla lily, phlox, gloriosa lily, bachelor's button, one red rose (love) paired with a white rose ("I am worthy of you").

The Language of Flowers

Indulge in the sentimental tradition of flowers. The very reserved Victorians coined the following romantic meanings of blossoms, so that a clever pairing of blooms translated into a passionate "hidden" message between lovers.

amaryllis—splendid beauty, pride
bachelor's button—celibacy, single
    blessedness
blue violet—faithfulness, modesty
bluebell—constancy
camellia—perfect loveliness,
    excellence
daffodil—regard
daisy—"Share your feelings,"
    innocence
forget-me-not—true love, do not forget
hibiscus—delicate beauty
holly—foresight
honeysuckle—generous affection,
    bonds of love
ivy—fidelity, marriage
jasmine—grace, elegance, joy,
    amiability, attachment
jonquil—"I desire a return of affection"
larkspur—levity
lilacs—first emotions of love
lily—gaiety
lily of the valley—return of happiness

mimosa—secret love, sensitivity
morning glory—affection
myrtle—love, remembrance
orange blossoms—bridal festivities,
    fertility, purity
peony—bashfulness
red carnation—"Alas, my poor heart!"
red chrysanthemum—"I love you"
red rose—"I love you"
red tulip—declaration of love
rosemary—remembrance
sweet pea—delicate pleasures,
    departure
sweet William—gallantry
sunflower (dwarf)—adoration
thyme—activity
water lily—purity of heart
white camellia—perfect loveliness
white daisy—innocence
white lily—purity, youthful innocence
white rose—"I am worthy of you"
wood sorrel—joy, maternal tenderness
yellow tulip—hopeless love

The flowers in *your* bouquet can be selected for their specific meanings, or the first letter of each one can together spell out a word (his name, a message). Give your moth-

aromatic flowers

The aroma of fresh flowers can help add warmth and atmosphere to your wedding. Flowers that are sure to leave a fragrant memory in your path:

- freesia
- gardenia
- grape hyacinth
- iris
- jasmine
- lilac
- lily
- magnolia
- rose
- stephanotis
- violet

More fragrant tips:

1. Add a drop of flower oil in a fragrance that matches your bouquet on pew bows.

2. Blend fragrant herbs—thyme or rosemary, for example—into arrangements.

3. Place a bowl of fragrant potpourri on an entry table.

Note: As a general rule, fragrance should be used only as an accent, as it can easily overwhelm a room. Keep in mind any allergy sufferers, as well as those guests who may be extremely sensitive to smells.

Flowers in Season

SPRING	SUMMER	FALL	WINTER	ALL-YEAR
anemone	bachelor's button	bouvardia	amaryllis	alstroemeria
azalea	bells of Ireland	celosia (cockscomb)	cyclamen	baby's breath
camellia	blue lace flower	China aster	eucalyptus berries	calla lily
dianthus	blue salvia	dahlia	heather	carnation
garden rose	clematis	euphorbia fulgens	helleborus	chrysanthemum
hyacinth	cornflower	grape ivy	(Christmas rose)	cymbidium orchid
hydrangea	delphinium	hydrangea	holly (ilex)	daisy
Iceland poppy	eremurus	statice	Juniper pine gardenia	dendrobium orchid
jasmine	honeysuckle	viburnum berries	narcissus	freesia
lilac	joe-pye weed	yarrow	(paper-whites)	gardenia
mimosa	larkspur		pepper berries	gerbera
pansy	lysimachia		poinsettia	gladiolus
peony	phlox		santolina	iris
primrose	Queen Anne's lace			ivy
ranunculus	rosemary			lily
sweet pea	sedum			lily of the valley
tulip	sunflower			nerine
viburnum	sweet William			phalaenopsis orchid
violet	zinnia			rose
tuberose	hydrangea			September aster
	tuberose			snapdragon
	cattleya orchid			stephanotis
				stock

ers small white bellflowers (gratitude) on the wedding day; send them wood sorrel (maternal tenderness) from your honeymoon destination. Order your attendants blue periwinkle (early friendship) bouquets. Be creative and use flowers to make a personal statement. (See Appendix, under Chapter 15, "Wedding Flowers," for books with more on the language of flowers.)

If you select flowers that are in bloom during the month of your wedding, they will be less expensive, more readily available, fuller, and hardier. Because of new, improved nursery operations worldwide, many varieties of seasonal flowers are now available for longer periods of time or year-round. Consult your florist.

Ceremony Flowers

Discuss what altar decorations are permitted with your clergymember before you place your order. You may find that a simple chapel needs more decorations than an ornate cathedral. Ask if another wedding will take place the same day in your house of worship. You may be able to share the cost of altar flowers with the other bride. Also ask your florist to visit the site to generate ideas. The following floral tips range from inexpensive to "the sky's the limit." (If the flowers are just for your wedding, consider designating one or two family members, or your florist, to move flowers to the reception site.)

Have at least one vase of flowers on each side of the altar. Add several other arrangements if budget permits.

Attach dramatic sprays of flowers to aisle posts, instead of, or in addition to, pew ribbons. Place them on every second or third pew, or on those pews reserved for special guests or relatives. Fasten nosegays of fragrant blossoms, such as freesia, or paper cones filled with flowers. Drape garlands of white tulle tied with large bows.

Place an eye-catching arrangement of flowers on each windowsill. This is especially lovely if the house of worship has plain windows.

Position a bank of ferns, palms, or potted flowers to mark the section of the church needed for the ceremony. Use ropes of flowers mixed with ivy, laurel, or boxwood to partition the church or drape the altar rail.

Repeat the bridesmaids' flowers in the altar arrangements. It will create a unified theme.

Inquire about other altar decorations. For the sides of the altar, consider large urns filled with elaborate garden arrangements set on pedestals or columns. Rent ficus trees in wicker baskets or an arch fashioned of twigs, metal, or fabric, laden with twisting vines, and fresh flowers. For an evening wedding: Rent tall candelabra to stand on each side of the wedding party.

Ask your florist to visit an outdoor ceremony site in advance. Don't overdecorate if it's already lush. Include cuttings from the site's bushes and plants in floral arrangements. Liven up dull shrubs with bright blossoms, such as magenta azaleas, in clay pots. Set flowering branches of cherry blossoms and forsythia in large urns or vases.

Floral Styles

Formal—The bridal party's flowers are usually white, maybe finished with a gilded ribbon or petals. Complementary bouquets are carried by every bridesmaid. The bride's blooms are a grander version, featuring just one to three types of flowers, such as a lush clutch of lily of the valley. A lavish splash of flowers decorates all important areas of the wedding and reception sites, following a simple, elegant color scheme.

personalizing your ceremony and reception site with flowers

- Deck the door—surround the front door of your church or synagogue with an arch of greens and flowers. For a winter wedding think about pine or boxwood mixed with baby's breath, lilies, and gilded pinecones. In the spring use forsythia branches combined with ivy, lilacs, and roses. A less expensive option is a floral wreath.

- For a bit of sparkle and style, add crystals or faux gems to your bouquet, or tie it with a special heirloom ribbon

- Use fresh garden flowers for an outdoor wedding; bright colors for a beach wedding.

- Honor your family—give your grandmothers special bouquets; pin boutonnieres on your grandfather's lapels. Have your florist work a small breakaway bunch of flowers into your bouquet; give it to your mother right before you reach the altar.

- Create floral settings—place a single long-stemmed rose on each napkin and tie it with ribbon.

- Swag the tables—attach a tussie mussie to each of the gathered folds.

- Dress up the chairs—attach nosegays or bunches of fragrant herbs to the back of each chair.

- Give your guests flowers— have your florist provide containers of the same flowers that appear in your bouquet; at the end of the reception, each guest receives a stem as a farewell.

centerpiece trends

- flowers blooming from terra-cotta pots
- small topiaries
- mix-and-match vases
- tree saplings
- flats of bulb flowers like daffodils or tulips for a spring wedding
- the addition of seasonal elements—kale and peppers added to a centerpiece for a fall wedding; herbs mixed into a floral arrangement for a summer wedding

new ideas for centerpieces

- Silver bowls of fruit—try a citrusy combination of lemons and limes or a crisp assortment of red, yellow, and green apples.
- A collection. If you collect seashells or even snow globes, think about incorporating them into your table scheme. Delicate items can chip, so use your judgment.
- Photographs. For a small wedding, use clusters of inexpensive silver picture frames with photos of you two as children or posing with friends, relatives, or each other.
- Wedding icons. Search flea markets for vintage bride-and-groom cake toppers; center several on each table.
- Unusual candlesticks. Look for hand-painted ceramic candlesticks, dramatic wooden pillars, or curvy hurricane lamps. For added impact, use an array of tapers in pastels or brights instead of cream or white.

Semiformal—A wide range of bouquet options are favored. Hand-tied bouquets or baskets of colorful blooms—a potpourri of garden roses or vibrant striped parrot tulips—needn't be identical, merely compatible. Attendants may be garland-bearing children. An arch of garden blossoms marks the wedding site; a wreath hangs on the door, welcoming guests.

Informal—A posy or alternative floral accessory—a breast pocket filled with tiny blossoms, a hat brimming with blooms, a flower boa worn around the shoulders—are good bridal choices. The groom may opt for a pocket square in lieu of a boutonniere. A single, wonderful table arrangement or flowering plant is appropriate for intimate weddings.

Reception Flowers

Floral arrangements may be as simple or elaborate as your budget allows. Echo the wedding's color scheme by repeating the flowers in your bouquet, as well as your attendants'. Place centerpieces on dinner and refreshment tables, as well as on the cake table. Select anything from a few sprigs to arrangements of mixed blossoms. Repeat a few signature blooms throughout the wedding celebrations.

Make sure centerpieces don't obstruct conversation or views. At the head table, the wedding party will want to be able to see guests, and vice versa. Similarly, centerpieces on all reception tables should be low enough to make it easy for guests to meet and talk across the table. Tall centerpieces are appropriate in a high-ceilinged room but should be in proportion to the scale of the space. They are usually arranged, or lifted, on narrow columns, so that all the flowers and greenery are above the heads of the guests. Long-stemmed flowers, such as roses or lilies, accentuate height.

Be creative. Decorate the tables with a few large-scale flowers such as hydrangea, peonies, and lilies arranged in vases covered with organza. For a twist on classic wedding flowers, such as roses, add unexpected elements to the mix, like lavender or herbs. An inexpensive option is to use clay pots of in-season flowers like tulips or daffodils in spring, or amaryllis and paper-whites in winter.

Create a tropical paradise. Decorate tables with mini pineapples (nonedible), pink dendrobium orchids, waxy red anthurium, large split monstera leaves. Choose flowers with sentimental meaning: the white roses he brought on your first date; red tulips like those from the park where he proposed.

Make blossoms twinkle. Brighten the reception with tiny, Christmas-style lights that are intertwined among the flowers, in matching colors.

Consider small topiaries in amusing shapes (animals, bicycles), for a garden wedding site.

Consider the color of table linens. Cream-colored linens offer the most flexibility. Stark white linens may wash out pastel flowers.

Consider a breakaway centerpiece. Guests may each take home a small potted plant or a bud vase as a favor.

Decorate the cake table with garlands or other small floral arrangements. You might also top your cake with fresh flowers that match your bouquet.

Use floral screens or banks of ferns as backdrops for the receiving line. Flowers and greenery warm a room and create an inviting environment.

Florists may also rent other room or tent decorations. Inquire about draperies, statues, paintings, columns, large potted plants, etc.

Your Floral Keepsakes

Fragrant, beautiful mementos of your wedding day can be the legacy of your bridal bouquet and your groom's boutonniere.

Order a second mini-bouquet to toss at the end of your wedding. Dry yours to create aromatic, sentimental potpourri. Or have an expert dry, preserve, and frame your bouquet and perhaps the groom's boutonniere (see Appendix, under Chapter 15, "Wedding Flowers").

Press petals from your bouquet. Use them to decorate thank-you notes and stationery personal.

Order thank-you arrangements for your parents. Have your florist deliver them the day after the wedding.

Arrange to have flowers sent to mark your first anniversary. It will be a sentimental reminder for you and your husband one year later, to receive a duplicate of your bridal bouquet.

floral dos & don'ts

DO create a visual backdrop for your wedding vows. Rented plants and columns instantly transform nondescript rooms.

DON'T overdecorate. Tasteful, well-placed table arrangements impress without cluttering or overwhelming the view.

DO opt to carry a manageable bouquet. Heavy, awkward bouquets are impossible to clutch gracefully.

DON'T consider heat-sensitive blooms for summer weddings. Quick-to-wilt gardenias, lily of the valley, and wildflowers look limp before the "I dos" are done.

DO have flowers delivered before the ceremony well misted and boxed with cellophane, or waxed paper wrappings, to maintain moisture.

DON'T forget to assign a reliable friend to double-check flower arrivals and their condition.

PHOTOGRAPHY, VIDEO-GRAPHY, & PUBLICITY

16

You dream of your wedding for years, you plan it for months, then the ceremony and reception fly by in a blur. That's why it's important that your mementos—bridal portrait, photographs, videotape, and newspaper clippings—capture the spirit of your day. Here's how to ensure that you, your groom, and your families are left with enduring keepsakes you'll treasure for years to come.

Your Bridal Portrait

This formal, posed wedding photograph is the one that will be displayed in your home, as well as the homes of relatives, and is often the picture that is published in the newspaper. For this portrait, you may want to use the person who will shoot your wedding—particularly if a prewedding portrait session is included in their package of services (see "Wedding Photography" section), or you can hire a photographer who specializes in portraits. Select an unobtrusive background for results that will stand the test of time. This is also a good opportunity to have a dress rehearsal for your wedding hairstyle; bring your headpiece to your hairdresser on the day your portrait is taken. Since precise makeup application is the key to a flawless look, consider hiring a makeup artist for your bridal portrait and for your wedding day. The combination of knowing you look your very best, and the great photographic results will be well worth the extra cost.

When should I have my bridal portrait taken? Most newspapers require that wedding photographs be submitted at least ten days before the scheduled publication date. Talk with the photographer to find out how much time they will need to develop and print your photographs. To allow enough time, plan on having your portrait taken one to three months before the wedding (depending on when your gown arrives).

wedding-portrait trends

- Portraits of the bride and groom: Most newspapers now print engagement and wedding photos of *couples*. These photos are often taken during pre–wedding lifestyle shoots (see below), with couples dressed in street clothes. Formal portraits of the couple, both dressed in their wedding clothes, are taken the day of the ceremony, and supplied to newspapers that will be running announcements after the fact.

- Color photos in newspapers: Many papers can print color portraits.

- Lifestyle shoots: Many couples are spending an afternoon with a photographer, posing on the beach, riding horses, playing golf.

- Lifestyle photos displayed at the wedding: Some couples have enlargements made of their lifestyle shoot, then display a few at the reception—in the entry area, near the cake table, or on the way to the restrooms.

- Lifestyle photos in wedding albums: Today, albums become "this-is-your-life" reviews. Many couples begin and end their albums with shots from their lifestyle shoot.

camera-ready makeup

Color film intensifies bold shades. Makeup should look natural.

- Apply foundation for an even skin tone.

- Use neutral eye colors, such as grays and browns; avoid frosted and pastel shadows.

- Try a smoky shade of liner all around the eyes for definition.

- Tweeze stray eyebrow hairs. Brush brows into place with clear mascara.

- Highlight your cheeks with a soft blush that enhances your skin tone.

- Wear a neutral lipstick shade.

makeup for black-and-white photos

Black-and-white film whitens pale shades and darkens rich, vibrant colors.

- Avoid red lipstick; it photographs black.

- Choose neutral hues that enhance natural skin tone.

- Blend all makeup, eliminating any harsh lines.

Where should I go? If the proper facilities are available, you can arrange to have your portrait taken at your bridal salon during your final fitting. Ask your photographer to join you there. Otherwise, make certain that your dress will be ready in time for you to make a prewedding trip to the photographer's studio, where you'll be assured of the proper lighting and background.

What should I bring with me? Your bridal portrait should look as if it were taken on your wedding day, so bring along all accessories—shoes, slip, gloves, jewelry, headpiece (and prayer book, if you'll carry one). If you want to be photographed with your bridal bouquet, order a replica from your florist.

Should I pose any particular way? In general, it's best to work with a photographer who has experience with portrait photography. Your photographer will take several different shots of you in a variety of poses, then supply you with proofs. Choose one look for publicity purposes (some newspapers will work with color if it's sharply focused, though most require a 5×7-inch black-and-white glossy for their wedding columns). You might select a different pose for the portrait you'll keep for yourselves and give to you families. Order at least one black-and-white print for yourself, too; color may fade over the years.

Your Wedding Announcement

It's customary to publish the details of a formal wedding in your hometown newspapers. A morning wedding is sometimes written up in an evening paper the same day, but most wedding stories are published the day after the ceremony. Ask if your newspapers will print announcements the week after the wedding. You may have time to send in an actual wedding photo.

Decide on the publications to which you'll send your announcement. Many couples send the news of their wedding to their hometown papers, college alumni magazines, professional societies and clubs, and the newsletters of their church or synagogue.

Meet the deadline. Check with the lifestyle editor to learn exact requirements and deadlines. Some papers ask brides to fill out a standard form; others offer guidelines for writing the notice, requesting that information be submitted to the lifestyle editor ten or more days before the wedding. (Some papers may accept announcements two months in advance.) Still others want telephoned confirmation that the wedding has actually taken place before they'll publish the news. Some papers charge a fee; others will print your announcement free of charge. Many times, a paper's guidelines are printed with the weekly wedding announcements, or posted on their website.

Follow the appropriate style. If your paper does not supply wedding-announcement forms, type up the announcement, using a double-spaced format, and print it on white paper. In the upper-right corner, list your name, address, and telephone number(s)—or those of someone in your family who can be called for verification and additional details. The date you'd like the announcement published should appear, as well. Keep a copy of the information you send.

Decide how much information to include. Read several announcements published by the paper to get a sense of the amount of information they publish (see "Traditional Announcement Wording" section). Decide if you will include your ages, parents' occupations, stepparents' names and occupations, dress descriptions, names of attendants, whether or not you're keeping your name, and any unusual details of the wedding day (*The couple left for their honeymoon in a hot-air balloon,* or *The bride was walked down the aisle by her stepfather, James Connelly*).

Include a photograph. Make sure it's a 5×7-inch or 8×10-inch glossy black-and-white print of your bridal portrait, or a shot of the two of you together. Again, some papers will accept a color photo. Tape a typed line of identification to the photo's back, in case it gets separated from the story. Don't expect the picture to be returned. If you send photos to more than one local paper, you may want to submit different shots to each.

Package the photo and announcement carefully. Enclose the picture, announcement, and a piece of stiff cardboard in a manila envelope and address it to the lifestyle editor. Mail it or drop it off.

Handle errors tactfully. If you discover an error in one of your published announcements, first check your copy to see if the mistake was yours, then call the paper. Most can't rerun a whole announcement, but if it's a major error—it says you've married your brother-in-law—request that a correction be printed.

Traditional announcement wording:
Patricia Clark Butler, the daughter of Mr. and Mrs. Clifford Marion Butler of Atlanta, was married this afternoon to Mitchell Sullivan, a son of Dr. and Mrs. Paul Sullivan of Philadelphia, Pennsylvania. Msgr. Patrick Flynn of Birmingham, uncle of the bride, performed the ceremony in Trinity Church in Atlanta.

Ms. Butler is a teacher at Woodrow Wilson Elementary School in Atlanta. She graduated from the University of Virginia. Her father is a senior vice president at the advertising agency Glenn & Howard in Atlanta. Her mother is an art director at Sun Graphics in Atlanta.

Mr. Sullivan is an associate at the Atlanta law firm of Cody & Wallace. He graduated magna cum laude from Princeton University, where he was elected to Phi Beta Kappa, and received his law degree from Georgetown University. His father is a pediatrician in Philadelphia. His mother is a partner at Wales & Mulloy, a law firm in Philadelphia.

news tips

- Ask two people to proofread the announcement before sending it out. Make sure names and locations are spelled correctly.

- Keep a copy of the announcement in case it's lost in the mail or a question arises.

- Don't expect the newspaper to mail you a copy when your announcement appears. Check newsstands and purchase one.

- Don't be surprised if your announcement doesn't appear right away. Wedding notices are often only printed in weekend editions.

- Don't be disappointed if your announcement is abbreviated. If there is a major news event, or many other weddings have recently taken place, space may be tight.

photo trends

- Photojournalism—a style of photography that emphasizes candid, spontaneous, unposed photos—is increasingly popular at weddings.

- Placing a full-page shot next to one with quarter-page images can give an album a modern, magazine-layout look.

- Black-and-white prints are making a comeback in wedding albums. They add a timeless, yet dramatic and more artistic tone to your photos.

- Disposable cameras, left at each guest's table, invite everyone to snap candids.

- Some brides request brown-toned sepia prints or black-and-white photos that are handpainted after printing.

- Photo portfolios of oversized black-and-white prints are now often selected, instead of the traditional smaller albums.

If couples want careers emphasized:

Patricia Clark Butler, a teacher at Woodrow Wilson Elementary school in Atlanta, was married this afternoon to Mitchell Sullivan, an associate at the Atlanta law firm of Cody & Wallace. Msgr. Patrick Flynn of Birmingham, uncle of the bride, performed the ceremony in Trinity Church in Atlanta.

Ms. Butler graduated from the University of Virginia. She is a daughter of Mr. and Mrs. Clifford Marion Butler. Her father is a senior vice president at the advertising agency Glenn & Howard in Atlanta. Her mother is an art director at Sun Graphics in Atlanta.

Mr. Sullivan graduated magna cum laude from Princeton University, where he was elected to Phi Beta Kappa, and received his law degree from Georgetown University. He is the son of Dr. and Mrs. Paul Sullivan of Philadelphia. His father is a pediatrician in Philadelphia. His mother is a partner at Wales & Malloy, a law firm in Philadelphia.

If the bride is keeping her own name:

The first paragraph remains the same. Then add:

Ms. Butler is keeping her name. She graduated from the University of Virginia, and is a daughter of . . .

If dress descriptions are included (50 words or less):

The first three paragraphs remain the same. Then add:

The bride, escorted by her father, wore an ivory dress of organza trimmed with Venise lace. Bands of matching lace edged her chapel train and veil. She carried a cascade of white roses.

If attendants' names are included:

The first three to four paragraphs remain the same. Then add:

Carla Butler, sister of the bride, was maid of honor. Bridesmaids were Gloria Geller and Linda Kerr of Atlanta, Gina DeGeorgio of Savannah, and Francis Demery of Buffalo, New York.

Arthur Clay of Birmingham served as best man. The ushers were Neil Butler, brother of the bride, Nathan Freeman of Short Hills, New Jersey, and Harvey Lyons and David Chan of New York, New York.

If both sets of parents are divorced and one parent is remarried:

The first paragraph remains the same. Then add:

Ms. Butler graduated from the University of Virginia. She is a daughter of Clifford Marion Butler and Jane S. Butler, both of Atlanta. Her father is a senior vice president at the advertising agency Glenn & Howard in Atlanta. Her mother is an art director at Sun Graphics in Atlanta.

Mr. Sullivan graduated magna cum laude from Princeton University, where he was elected to Phi Beta Kappa, and received his law degree from Georgetown University. He is the son of Dr. Paul Sullivan of Pittsburgh and Elizabeth S. Mason of Philadelphia. His father is a pediatrician in Pittsburgh. His mother is a partner at Wales & Malloy, a law firm in Philadelphia. The bridegroom is a stepson of Jonathan Mason of Philadelphia.

If a parent is deceased:

The first paragraph remains the same. Then add:

Ms. Butler graduated from the University of Virginia. She is a daughter of Jane

Marion Butler of Atlanta and the late Clifford Marion Butler. Her mother is an art director at Sun Graphics in Atlanta. Her father was a senior vice president at the advertising agency Glenn & Howard in Atlanta.

If a bride or groom is remarrying:

To the first two paragraphs, add:

Mr. Sullivan is an associate at the Atlanta law firm of Cody & Wallace. He graduated magna cum laude from Princeton University, where he was elected to Phi Beta Kappa, and received his law degree from Georgetown University. His father is a pediatrician in Philadelphia. His mother is a partner at Wales & Malloy, a law firm in Philadelphia. The bridegroom's previous marriage ended in divorce.

The bride's (or groom's) parents have divorced, and the bride (or groom) has adopted a stepfather's name:

Patricia Clark Butler, a teacher at Woodrow Wilson Elementary school in Atlanta, was married this afternoon to Mitchell Sullivan, an associate at the Atlanta law firm of Cody & Wallace. Msgr. Patrick Flynn of Birmingham, uncle of the bride, performed the ceremony in Trinity Church in Atlanta.

Ms. Butler graduated from the University of Virginia. She is the daughter of Mr. and Mrs. Clifford Marion Butler of Atlanta. Her stepfather is a financial consultant with Shearson Lehman Brothers in Atlanta. Her mother is an art director at Sun Graphics in Atlanta. She is also the daughter of Mr. Jeremy Wade of Dallas, Texas, an attorney.

Wedding Photography

Shoot for the best. A wedding is a once-in-a-lifetime occasion that good photos will preserve forever. (An insurance policy called Weddingsurance will reimburse a couple for the cost of reassembling the wedding party to retake wedding photographs if they do not come out or the film is stolen. See the Appendix, under Chapter 4, "Planning Your Wedding," for more information.) Though it may be tempting—and inexpensive—to enlist a talented friend or relative for the job, hiring a professional is the best insurance that you'll end up with quality wedding photos. Professional wedding photographers should have top-of-the-line equipment, correct lighting, as well as experience in quickly posing people for traditional portraits. He or she should also have a quick eye for spotting a good candid shot; unexpected photographs are often the best mementos of your celebration.

Find a professional. Soon after you've set the date, start asking around for referrals (some photographers book a year or more in advance). Caterers, hotel managers, recently married friends, the Internet and the Yellow Pages are all good sources. Also, visit bridal shows where you can see samples of photographers' work. Then, set up appointments; meet with the person who would actually photograph your wedding. Remember, your photographer will be by your side

photo secrets

Meet with your photographer two weeks before the wedding to review details.

- Give him or her a list of attendants, guests, and family members who you want to have included in formal portraits.

- List not-to-be-missed photos (e.g., your grandmother with all her grandchildren and great-grandchildren).

- Appoint someone from both the bride's and groom's families to cue the photographer in to whom you want photos of (bosses, cousins, college roommates, etc.)

- Brief your photographer about special or sensitive family relationships (divorced parents, stepmother with whom you don't get along, gay siblings attending the wedding with partners).

- Discuss special events that will take place—religious customs, ethnic dances or a dance with your grandfather, for example.

- Review site/clergy regulations. Some churches and synagogues don't allow flashbulbs or altar shots during the ceremony. Some country clubs don't allow wedding couples on golf greens.

photo contract tips

Include the following in a signed and countersigned contract:

- the name of the professional whose work you've seen, who will photograph the wedding

- the name of the photographer's backup (in case of emergency)

- a guarantee that they will carry backup equipment in case of equipment failure

- the number of assistants, and any related costs

- the photographer's—and, if applicable, assistant's—attire (tuxedos, suits)

- the number of rolls of film to be shot

- all locations (the bride's house, church, reception site) and addresses and arrival times

- the date, time, hours to be worked (11:30 A.M. to 6:30 P.M., so he or she is there for the cake cutting)

- what's included in the package (e.g., set-ups, developing, prints, proofs, etc.)

- the total cost and overtime fees

- the cost for extra albums, prints, and proofs

- the time frame for delivery of proofs, prints, and albums

- the deposit and payment schedule (when balance is due)

for most of the wedding, so choose someone who makes you feel at ease, and whose work you admire. Look at sample wedding albums. Ask for references if you haven't been referred to the photographer by someone you know (see Appendix, under Chapter 16, "Photography, Videography, & Publicity").

Invite guests to snap candids. Photographs taken by family and friends are often the perfect supplements to your professional shots. Relatives, especially, may have the chance to capture unusual candids (such as the bride having breakfast on the wedding morning). Leave disposable cameras in a basket outside the reception room or on each reception table. Post a sign asking guests to drop the cameras in baskets after the festivities.

Take some posed shots. Posed shots are how you'll make sure you have pictures of the most important people at your wedding—your families and wedding party. Give your photographer a list of "must take" group shots.

Request candid shots. Your photographer should also capture spontaneous

action (the flower girl waltzing with her brother, or a smile shared by you and your groom). If this style especially appeals to you, choose a photographer who specializes in a photojournalistic or documentary approach.

Schedule reception time for photos. Whatever you do, don't make your guests wait around while you and your wedding party take endless formal portraits. It will make every detail of your reception late. Have your posed shots taken as quickly and unobtrusively as possible. If you want to be photographed with your parents or bridesmaids, for instance, take these shots at home as soon as you finish dressing or arrive at the wedding site an hour to an hour and a half early. Then go directly to the reception site after the ceremony, before the receiving line, and pose for formal photos with your husband and the wedding party.

Get everything in writing. Your photographer should countersign a contract with you that gets on paper everything you've discussed (see "Photo Contract Tips" box).

Wedding Videography

Videography captures the sights—as well as the sounds and activity—of your wedding day. To ensure a quality videotape, don't rely on a well-meaning relative or friend who offers to bring his video camera.

Hire a professional. Start your search for a videographer several months before the wedding (as with photographers, the best ones are booked early). Ask your photographer, wedding officiant, and friends for recommendations. Look in the Yellow Pages for videographers who specialize in weddings, or consult websites, such as www.weva.com, the official site for the Wedding and Event Videographers Association. Contact candidates to learn about their packages, prices, and how you can review their sample tapes. (Some will mail tapes to you, others might ask you to visit their studio.) When reviewing videotapes, note whether the sound is clear, with voices audible; the colors bright, not muddy; the images clear, not grainy; the camera close-ups and pans smooth; the editing professional. For the most honest assessment of video quality, turn off the sound; it's surprising how musical soundtracks can sometimes help to mask editing flaws. Be sure the tape you're watching has been shot by the same professional you will hire, and plan to note this in the contract, as well (see "Video Contract Tips" box).

Ask about the videographer's equipment. Depending on the type of video you want, and how much you choose to spend, one or more cameras may be required. However, make sure the equipment does not interfere with the day's events. Does your videographer use a camera light consistently directed at eye level? If you feel this will be distracting, ask if it's possible to bounce a light off the ceiling, instead. Also ask about technique. Will the videographer walk around with a hand-held camera or simply set it on a tripod for the entire wedding? What format will the video ultimately be available in (VHS or DVD, for example)? Videographers with digital production capabilities can produce DVD's, which provide the best and most lasting image quality. Does your videographer have any special effects capabilities, and if so what are they? Given the technology available today, it's not unrealistic to expect an extremely polished, professional end result.

Find the right package. Your videographer will work with you to choose the style of video that suits your budget. Whatever you plan to spend, focus on image and sound quality first; special effects should be secondary. Typically, packages include recording and editing the master tape and perhaps a second copy. (The number of cameras used, as well as the length of the ceremony and reception—longer than four hours, for example—can affect the price.) State exactly what you want. In addition to basic wedding coverage, many couples choose to include an opening photo sequence (of childhood or engagement pictures, for example), a highlight montage at the end of the video, a listing of wedding party and family members in the credits, and/or rehearsal dinner coverage. Also, be specific about what you don't want (the interviewing of guests). Will you have access to outtakes, or the edit master tape? Ask about special effects, such as freeze-frames and strobe techniques, and familiarize yourself with the editing styles available:

Romance/Nostalgia

This style may be the most costly, since it includes extensive editing and camera work. Accompanied by the couple's favorite songs, the video begins with childhood pictures of the bride and groom from family albums, then segues into a sequence of courtship and lifestyle shots of the couple together. After video footage of the ceremony and

video-contract tips

List the following in a signed and countersigned contract:

- the name of the professional whose work you've seen, who will videotape the wedding

- the name of videographer's backup (in case of emergency)

- a guarantee that backup equipment will be on site, in case of equipment failure

- the number of assistants and cameras

- the attire (tuxedos, suits)

- the depth of coverage, and number of tapes to be shot

- all locations (e.g., bride's house, church, reception site) and addresses, arrival times

- the date, time, and hours to be worked (e.g., 11:30 A.M. to 6:30 P.M., so he or she is there for the cake cutting)

- editing techniques (credits, music, etc.)

- what's included in package

- the total cost and overtime fees (including any extra charges, such as assistants, wireless microphones, or travel time)

- the cost for extra tapes

- the time frame for delivery of wedding video

- the deposit and payment schedule (when balance is due)

budget-conscious tips

Talk to your photographer about ways to keep photo costs within your budget. Ask if:

- traveling to your home before the wedding will add to the cost. (If so, consider dressing at the ceremony site.)

- the photographer can bring a backdrop to the reception and shoot your formal portrait there.

- paying an hourly fee will be less than a package rate.

- you can buy proofs and prints without albums. (Order portraits to frame; use guests' candids for albums.)

- choosing fewer photos for an album will lower the cost.

- ordering smaller prints lets you afford more shots.

- the photographer will keep your negatives for several years. See if you may order additional prints in the future. Will the photographer contact you when he no longer needs your negatives?

photo gift ideas

- extra albums for parents
- 5 × 7-inch wedding portraits for your home and office
- 8 × 10-inch prints for your parents
- a copy of the wedding video for those unable to attend
- extra prints for parents
- framed prints of attendants (give as thank-you gifts)
- wedding candids slipped into holiday cards

reception, the video ends with photos of the couple leaving.

Documentary

This video style features the wedding day, alone, beginning with behind-the-scenes shots (the couple getting dressed, guests arriving). There may be extra editing costs, since videographers may shoot with two cameras. The groom may wear a cordless microphone, so that vows can be recorded and conversations captured. At the reception, guests may be asked to make a toast to your future, or may be interviewed by the videographer for their advice on marriage and family or anecdotes about your childhood or college days.

Straight-shot Formats

Generally the least expensive option. The ceremony and reception are shot with one camera; there is no editing. The videotape is ready for your VCR at the end of the reception.

Animated Titles

During the introduction, the couple's names and wedding date are added to the tape with a character generator for a minimal (or no) fee. For a nominal fee, a sixty-second musical animation can be added to the introduction of the video, featuring the couple's names and wedding date.

Plan in advance. Check with your officiant regarding policies on cameras and lighting equipment. Also, let your videographer and photographer know that they'll be working together so they can compare schedules and avoid clashes. Request that they both attend the rehearsal to discuss where cameras will be set up. As with the photographer, you should create a detailed list of reception events (like the wedding party's introduction, the bride's dance with her father), and inform the videographer of any special events (your groom's dance with his mother). Ask a close friend to let him know who key guests are; you may even want to ask, in advance, that some of those special people prepare a few words to say on–camera.

Get everything in writing. As when hiring any wedding professional, you should put all details in a contract signed by you and countersigned by your videographer. If there are additional charges (for an assistant, a wireless microphone, or travel time), make sure they're clearly stated. (See "Video Contract Tips" box.)

17

WEDDING GIFTS

The time-honored custom for those attending a wedding is to send a wedding gift to the bride and groom. Gifts help the couple furnish their home, mark the joyous occasion of their marriage, and are lifelong symbols of the givers' affection.

Gifts may begin arriving at the bride's and groom's home(s) as soon as their engagement becomes public knowledge. Although engagement gifts are optional (see Chapter 1, "Your Engagement"), many friends and relatives will want to give you a present during this happy time. Shower guests will also be selecting gifts—for either a traditional women-only shower, or for a co-ed shower, to which the groom is also invited (see Chapter 3, "Prewedding Parties"). Wedding gifts will arrive throughout your engagement, and may be sent up to a year after the wedding.

If you've ever shopped for a wedding gift, you know how much time and thought can go into it. As a bride, you can make the gift giving experience easy and fun for your guests—*and* get what you want and need in the process.

The Wedding Gift Registry

Because you've selected everything yourself, registering for wedding gifts—at a department or specialty store, museum shop, with a catalog or via the Internet—is a surefire way to receive the things you really want. Guests can request a printout of

gift-receiving etiquette

- Register for your gift preferences with your fiancé.

- Ask relatives, attendants, and friends to spread the word about where you registered.

- Suggest that your maid of honor send out a "wedding newsletter" to other attendants, and shower guests, updating them on wedding details and listing where you are registered.

- Never print where you are registered on wedding invitations. It is acceptable, however, for shower hostesses to list where you're registered or enclose printed registry cards in shower invitations.

- Keep all enclosure cards and accurate gift records. Buy a wedding-planning notebook or gift-record book from a bridal salon, stationer, or bookstore as soon as you get engaged.

your registry and select a gift in person, or call and have the list mailed or faxed to their home or office; the purchase can then be made over the phone. Today, most stores offer online registries, as well, where the entire process can take place with just a few clicks of a mouse.

Register early. Make registry choices before prewedding parties or showers—about 6 to 12 months before the wedding. Since certain items, such as linen patterns, might be discontinued seasonally—and because guests will be purchasing items from the list continually—be sure to update the list closer to your wedding day, especially in the last two weeks, when the majority of people will do their shopping.

Ask how long your registry list will be kept in the store's computer. The time frame may range from three months to two years. Many couples find that they continue to receive items from their registry for anniversary and birthday gifts. If available, you may also want to take advantage of a store's discount "completion program," which will allow you to purchase any selections you don't receive as gifts.

Do some preliminary shopping. This is the shopping trip of a lifetime! Both you and your fiancé should look through bridal and home magazines together, and browse in stores, and online. Make some basic decisions before registering. With china, for instance, narrow down the colors you both like. Decide if you want white, ivory, or a colored background. Consider border styles—do you prefer geometric patterns, floral motifs, or solid color bands? In stores, set up sample place settings with china, crystal, and silver to see how they blend. What type of entertaining do you enjoy—grilling outdoors for a crowd, or candlelit, intimate dinner parties? Your entertaining style will determine whether you need casual or formal tableware—or both. Today's lifestyle lets you mix and match, so be sure to include interesting accent pieces in your registry selection. Keep in mind that even if you plan to register with an online service, it's best to select your china crystal, silver, and linens in person to ensure proper quality, size, and coordination of pieces.

Make an appointment with a registry consultant, if one is available at the store you've selected. Try to shop during off-hours; call ahead and ask when the bridal department is least crowded. Evenings and Monday mornings tend to be best; avoid one-day sales, holiday weekends, and lunch hours. Some bridal–registry consultants will make appointments with brides in the morning, before the store opens. Set aside one or two hours for the consultant to guide you through the registry, help you coordinate table patterns, and suggest other gifts to suit your lifestyle. She can also tailor the size of your gift list to "fit" the number of guests invited, and provide information on manufacturers' warranties, as well as use and care instructions on the patterns you select. Later, she may notify you if your selections go on sale or will be discontinued. (For this reason, always notify the registry of a new phone number, address, or e–mail address.)

Using online registries. Today, you can register for anything your hearts desire, quickly and easily, and at your convenience. Online registries can streamline the entire process for you and your fiancé, as well as your guests, by offering one-stop shopping access to large and small retailers, as well as specialty stores. Familiarize yourself with what's available by first looking at a "supersite" registry, such as *WeddingChannel.com*, then let your imagination run wild. Once you've narrowed things down, it's still best to make a trip to your local retailer to see tabletop and linen items in person, to be certain of colors, quality, size and coordination of pieces, before signing up online. Be sure to look for the locked padlock or unbroken key symbols on homepages; these indicate that the site is secure for financial transactions. For those guests who don't use the Internet, make sure that your chosen site(s) offer a number (preferably toll-free) which they can call to place phone orders, if they prefer. Also, insure that the site(s) will fax your registry list to guests upon request.

Don't register in a day. Take your time choosing gifts. Preview tabletop items (china, crystal, silver), domestics (sheets, towels, bed linens, tablecloths, napkins), and kitchenware (cookware, appliances) choices, then return to actually register in person (or do so online) after you've had time to decide what you would like. Another option: visit the registry department alone to narrow down choices, then return with your fiancé to make final selections.

Use your imagination. Take this opportunity to create your ultimate wish list. Today, in addition to formal and casual dinnerware, couples register for everything from gas grills to computers, luggage to gardening tools, stereo equipment to DVD players. Some travel agencies offer the option to register for your honeymoon using a gift fund. Registries are also available at many art galleries, museum stores, hardware and home specialty stores, record and video stores, sporting-goods stores, and even some antiques shops and banks (for a mortgage or down payment on a home). Some mail-order houses also have national registries (see Appendix, under Chapter 17, "Wedding Gifts"). In general, it's wise to register with a single store or Internet site for china, crystal and silver (to help eliminate double-orders and mistakes), as well as one or two other retailers for non-traditional gifts.

Register for a variety of gifts in a wide price range. List high-priced items for guests who can afford them or who want to pool funds for group gifts. Also include less-expensive items—wine, kitchen gadgets, place mats—for showers and guests on a budget.

Make sure you've registered for the things you want. Today, virtually all registry information is computerized—even when registering in person. Most stores will give you a hand-held scanner that will transfer all the necessary information into the store's computer when you pass it over an item. When you have finished "shopping", be sure to examine your list before leaving the store. Since mistakes may be made

your gift record

When a gift or special-order notice arrives, record the following information in a wedding-planning notebook or gift-record book:

- name and address of sender
- gift description
- your feelings about it to help you write a more thoughtful thank-you note
- store
- date of arrival
- date thank-you note is sent

Save card, paperwork, tags, mailing labels, and gift box.

If a store you like does not have a registry, speak to the manager; she may be able to create one for you.

inputting information, request that the store also send you a printout of your registry list; keep your own notes to compare for errors.

Avoid overlap. Don't register for the same items (such as place settings of your tableware) in different stores. You'll be much less likely to receive duplicates or end up with "gaps" in your silver pattern, for instance, if you register for it at just one store, where you can accurately keep track of purchases. Keep in mind that returns can be expensive, since you will be responsible for postage.

Don't include registry or gift preference information in your wedding invitations. Also, stay away from e-mail guest notification services offered by many of the online registries. Both of these actions imply that a gift is expected. However, relatives, attendants, or close friends can spread the word to other guests in person or over the phone. If someone asks you what you and your fiancé need, mention where you are registered. Some stores may issue registry cards, which are appropriate enclosures for shower invitations (since the very reason for a shower is to "shower" the bride with gifts).

Keep an accurate gift record. When you receive a gift, first check the attached paperwork to be sure you've received all the boxes and pieces sent. Save enclosed cards, invoices, tags, mailing labels (often the only proof of purchase, which you'll need to make exchanges), and gift boxes (which have the store's logo). Devise an easy-to-use system—a notebook, a wedding-planning book, or a computer spreadsheet—to record gifts and notices that items have been special-ordered or back-ordered. This will facilitate writing thank-you notes.

Follow up with your consultant. Contact her every few weeks (more often as your wedding day gets closer) so that your list can be updated. Definitely call after every prewedding party. If you're not using a consultant, be sure to monitor your list closely, particularly in the weeks just before your wedding. Visit the store or check online once or twice to view your current list and correct any disparities. If most of your choices have been purchased, go ahead and add more. Keep in mind that the majority of registry purchases will take place in the two weeks preceding your wedding. Make sure there are plenty of selections available, in a variety of price ranges. It's always better to register for more items than the number of guests you have invited.

Common Gift Questions

Will we have to tell guests how to use the wedding gift registry? Most guests have purchased wedding gifts often enough that they generally know what to do. When they visit (or log onto) the registry, they will receive a copy of your gift list, complete with current prices. With increasing frequency, long-distance or time-pressured guests are doing the entire transaction online, or are calling to request that the printout be mailed or faxed to them. They can select a gift at their leisure, bill it to their credit card, and have it sent to you and taken off your list.

If a guest calls for my list, must he or she purchase the gift in that store? It's easier if the guest does, but he might prefer to shop at a store more convenient to his home. Keep in mind that it's your responsibility to let your registry consultant know which items should be crossed off your list if you receive them from other stores. Today, however, many stores don't actually deliver your gifts until you review what was purchased for you. Anything that you decide you don't want or need (such as duplications, purchased elsewhere) can become a "credit" that you can spend on other things.

We'd like guests to make a donation to our favorite charity instead of giving us a gift. Is that appropriate? Some couples today are spreading the word that they would prefer contributions to a particular charity instead of wedding gifts. This is especially common among older and remarrying couples, and can often be arranged online, via sites such as *helping.org, idofoundation.org* and *americaspromise.org*. Remember: *Don't* print your gift preference on your wedding invitation. Some guests will prefer to give you a present anyway; accept it graciously.

Where, when, and how is a gift display set up? A gift display is not necessary, but is traditional in some parts of the country. It's often easier to leave your wedding presents out than to unpack them each time friends and relatives visit and ask to see them. You might arrange a gift display as soon as you start receiving presents, and leave it up until after the wedding, when you start to use them. Select a central location, where most guests will be visiting—most likely your home or your parents' home. (In some regions, brides display their gifts at the reception. Only do so if you can provide security.)

Set gifts up on cloth-covered tables accented with flowers or greenery. Don't display gift cards next to presents, and avoid positioning a very costly item (sterling tea set) next to an inexpensive gift (picnic plates and cups). Arrange gifts according to category (silver bowls with silver candlesticks, for example), or create attractive groupings that mix textures and colors. Set out only one single place setting of china, crystal, and silver, or one of a specific gift if there are duplicates. Similar items, such as votive candles, can be scattered over the table. *Never* display broken items or gifts of money.

What should we do with the money we receive at the reception? Carry a white purse to collect checks given to you at your wedding, or have the groom put them in a

---

gifts for remarriage

Technically, gifts are never *required*, and in the case of a guest who was also at your first wedding, a present should not be expected. However, most people will still want to mark the occasion with a gift. Register:

- at specialty stores (e.g., antique or sporting goods stores)
- gourmet or wine shop; travel agency
- for a new china pattern (start fresh!)
- for small or state-of-the-art kitchen gadgets

Send thank-you notes for each gift.

gift-display tips

- Don't display cards next to gifts.
- Set out one sample tableware setting.
- Group gifts by category.
- Don't display duplicates.
- Don't display monetary gifts.
- Don't display broken gifts.

pocket. When you leave the reception, endorse the checks, and on the back of each write, "For deposit only," along with your bank account number. Keep a list of givers and the amount of each gift. Then give all checks and a filled-in deposit slip to a trusted relative or attendant so they can be taken to the bank while you're on your honeymoon.

What should we do with gifts brought to the wedding? Arrange in advance for a safe place for gifts at the reception site—perhaps an attended coatroom, or a closet or other room that locks. Set up a table where guests can place gifts as they arrive; have two friends man it, then store and lock up everything once the reception begins. *Don't* open the gifts then and there; you could easily lose the cards, and guests who didn't bring gifts may feel uncomfortable. Arrange for someone to transport the gifts home safely after the reception is over.

At a Long Weekend Wedding (see Chapter 10, "Special Weddings & New Ways to Wed"), it's best to open gifts after the reception. If possible, open them in private (not in front of other guests). If you do open gifts in front of close friends or attendants, temper your reactions so individual feelings aren't hurt. When you receive a gift of money, do not openly acknowledge the amount.

Present Problems: Handling Typical Wedding-Gift Dilemmas

As with everything wedding–related, there are bound to be some awkward gift moments and situations about which you have no clue what to do. Fortunately, there are guidelines for every dilemma.

Telling guests about the registry. You want guests to know where you're registered, but you're not sure how to tell them. Don't announce it yourself or include the information with your wedding invitation—that implies that a gift is expected. Instead, ask your bridesmaids, close friends, and relatives to spread the word. If someone asks, it's okay to mention where you're registered.

Cash vs. gifts. You prefer money over presents, and you're wondering about the best way to let guests know of your wishes. Again, it's inappropriate to tell them yourself. Rely on your network of attendants, friends, and family to discreetly fill guests in about what you'd really like.

Feeling awkward about your "wish list"? Many brides feel a bit uncomfortable "asking for gifts" when they begin registering. However, it's good to keep in mind that you're actually being thoughtful—and at the same time, getting a great headstart planning for your new life together. Specifying what you'd like can make things easier for guests, especially those who don't know you well or are unsure about your needs or tastes. Some guests will send gifts of their own choosing, regardless, but think of the registry as a helpful reference that's there for any guest who needs it.

The taste factor. Someone sent you a brightly colored set of table linens that don't coordinate with your pastel china. Do you exchange it? Not before you consider the giver's feelings. If it comes from a close friend or relative who will be visiting your home and expecting to see the gift in use, it's probably a good idea to keep it, and use it when the giver arrives. Think about your future needs, too. Those placemats and napkins can be the base of a linen wardrobe as your tableware collection grows. That brass door knocker? Apartment dwellers who have no use for one today may move into a house within a couple of years, when they'll be able to put the gift to good use.

Two's a crowd? What about duplicate wedding gifts? Should you keep them, or is it okay to return one? Depending on the gifts, you may want to consider keeping some of them. You'll need extras of items like sheets, towels, and anything breakable, such as wineglasses. When you entertain a large group for dinner, you'll want to set the table with more than just one pair of candlesticks and salt and pepper shakers. But if there are some items you really don't need two of, like a vacuum cleaner, don't tell either guest about the exchange (or mention it in the thank-you note). Never ask the giver where a gift was purchased so that you can exchange it.

A gift from a nonguest. Mrs. Feldman, who lives down the street from your parents, sent you a wedding gift. You weren't planning to invite her to the wedding. Are you obligated to now? No. Send her a warm note of thanks and accept the gift for what it was intended to be—a thoughtful acknowledgment of your upcoming marriage.

Damaged goods. Crystal arrives in pieces. Linens have pulled threads. What can you do about gifts that arrive at your home in less-than-tip-top shape? Check the box to see whether a store shipped the gift or if it was mailed by an individual. If it was sent by a store, or from a mail–order or online location, call the customer-service department to arrange for a replacement to be sent to you at no charge. In this case, there is no need to tell the giver about the damage. If the present was mailed by the giver, check the package for a post office insurance stamp, indicating that the contents are insured against breakage. If there is one, return the package to the giver with a note of explanation. He will be reimbursed by the post office and will probably send you a replacement gift. If the gift was not insured, don't mention the damage, the person may feel obligated to buy another gift for you. If you can tell where the gift was purchased from the wrappings, you may be able to exchange it yourself. Don't mention the damage in your thank–you note, and don't display a broken gift in your wedding gift display (see Appendix, under Chapter 17, "Wedding Gifts").

A postponed or canceled wedding. If the wedding is on hold, send an announcement to the guests (see Chapter 5, "Invitations & Announcements"), and keep the gifts you've received. If the wedding is canceled, however, each gift—even those that have been monogrammed—must go back to the person who sent it. Send a note with each, expressing gratitude and explaining that the wedding will not take place. You don't have to give any further explanation.

No-show gift. You haven't received a gift from a close friend. You know she wouldn't let your wedding go by without sending a present, and you're tempted to call her to make sure it didn't get lost in the shuffle. Don't. Assume that if she sent a gift and hasn't heard from you, she will eventually ask if you've received it. At that point, she can follow up if the gift appears to be missing. Also remember that, traditionally, a guest has up to one year after your wedding takes place to send a gift; she may just not have gotten around to it yet.

Rough around the edges. You've chipped a bowl—now the person who gave it to you is coming to visit. Do you stash it or set your table with it? Display the bowl if the chip is minor, but also offer an explanation rather than try to cover up the damage. Honesty is the best policy—and in this case, the sincerest form of flattery. Simply tell your guest that you're very upset that the gift got chipped, but it just goes to show how much you have loved and used the item. Keep in mind that things like chips, clean breaks, and spotted or scratched silver can often be repaired. Ask your store for recommendations, or look in the Yellow Pages, or on the Internet, under "Repairs" or "Restoration."

Protecting Your Presents

During your engagement, the number of valuable personal possessions and pieces of jewelry that you own will increase—probably dramatically. It's a good idea to meet with your insurance agent to be sure that you are adequately covered for theft or loss. If you find that you're not, look into taking out a policy that will cover all your wedding gifts—and even the wedding itself. Of course, no one wants to dwell on what could happen, but you're better safe than sorry.

Take out wedding insurance. Wedding insurance, such as that offered by R. V. Nunncio & Associates (see Appendix, under Chapter 4, "Planning Your Wedding") protects against wedding-day disasters and disappointments. Among other things, the policy will reimburse you if your wedding attire is damaged or if your wedding gifts are stolen or broken at the reception.

Take inventory of your new possessions and ask your insurance agent about adding more coverage. To protect against loss or theft of wedding gifts and wedding rings, pearls, watches, and other items, purchase an *endorsement* (additional coverage added to your homeowners's/renter's policy). Or, purchase a *rider* (a separate policy offering additional insurance). Both are usually good for the term of the contract—often one year.

Don't print your exact address in your newspaper engagement or wedding announcement. This will alert potential burglars when your home will be unattended.

Arrange for someone to guard wedding gifts at the reception. Don't leave them piled, unattended, in a corner of the reception-site lobby or banquet room. Plan in advance for the coat-check attendant to watch gifts, or for friends to store them in a locked room or closet after everyone has arrived.

Ask friends to safely transport gifts home. Since you will be leaving on your honeymoon, you'll want to be certain that gifts are not inadvertantly left behind.

Consider leaving gifts with your parents or close friends until you return. This may be the safest, and simplest, option, especially if you're going to be away for more than a few days.

Tell police the dates you will be away. If you do have your gifts delivered to your house, ask them to patrol the neighborhood more frequently in your absence. Or alert neighbors or local crimewatch groups of your absence, giving them your honeymoon departure and return dates. They can also keep an eye on your house and notify the police if anything seems suspicious.

Consider getting a burglar alarm. Or use light timers that turn on and off at different times. Other tips to make your home seem lived in: Stop delivery of mail, newspapers, and packages. Ask a neighbor to collect circulars and restaurant menus. Finally, don't leave your keys under a mat, over the door, or in the mailbox. Thieves know where all the common hiding places are.

thank-you-note tips

- Enlist your groom's help. He might write notes to his friends or family for items he's more familiar with (tools, coffee-maker, etc.).

- It's acceptable to write one thank-you note for a gift given by a large group. Thank each individual giver in person when you see them.

- Acknowledge gifts received before the wedding within two weeks of their arrival; after that, within a month of receipt.

- Send printed gift-received cards (see Chapter 5, "Invitations & Announcements," for wording) if you expect to receive many more gifts than you can acknowledge during the expected time period. These *must*, however, be followed promptly by handwritten notes.

Thank-You Notes

Even if you've already verbally thanked your guests, you must send a personal note of appreciation for each gift you receive. The only exceptions to this rule are gifts received from your groom and your parents, although they would surely treasure a written expression of your love and appreciation. Follow these guidelines:

Send notes early. The most important thing about writing thank-you notes is to do it promptly. Acknowledge a gift received before the wedding within two weeks; within a month if it is received after that. Traditional thank-you notes are written in black ink on folded ecru or white notepaper. Today, however, many couples choose colored or decorated paper. Your names or monogram may be embossed on notes sent after you're married; you might order another set of notes

three-step guide to writing thank-you notes

- Name the gift. *"Thank you for the place setting of china."*

- Describe how you'll use the gift. *"John and I are nervous about throwing our first dinner party, but now at least we know the table will look terrific no matter how the food turns out."*

- Add a personal thought or two about your wedding or your relationship with the giver. *"I've known you all my life. It meant to much for me to have you there to share my wedding day."*

to send before the wedding (you would use your maiden name or monogram), or simply use plain ones.

Don't use cards with a preprinted message, don't type them, and do not e-mail them. All three are too impersonal. If you feel you can write only with the help of a computer, draft your ideas on a computer first, and then handwrite or print the actual notes themselves.

Keep careful records. As each gift arrives, jot down a description and your thoughts and feelings about it, along with the name and address of the sender. Be aware that the computerized tracking systems used by most stores and registry sites *can* sometimes make mistakes.

Categorize. Ideally, you should acknowledge gifts in the order you receive them. If a pile is forming, however, divide it into groups: your family, his family, mutual friends. Next subdivide these into smaller, manageable stacks (college friends, work friends, etc.). It's acceptable to send one note for a present given by a large group of co-workers or roommates. Be sure to thank them individually when you see them, as well.

Write the hardest notes first. Start with notes for gifts that are a bit out of the ordinary, or to distant relatives and others you don't know well. Or alternate between difficult responses and those you're looking forward to dashing off.

Write notes together. Divide and conquer. Perhaps write five notes each morning as you sip coffee together.

Set up writing space. Put out all pens, paper, and supplies you'll need, clear a desk or table, and reserve the area for writing thank-you notes. This kind of organization will allow you to write a few notes any time you have a little time, without having to hunt for a pen or your gift list. Also consider taking some note cards, pens, and addresses with you each day. You may be able to squeeze in a few notes during your lunch break or in a doctor's waiting room.

Create a routine and an award system for yourself. A suggestion from time–management experts: Set a goal and give yourself a reward for reaching it. Agree to write five notes each weekday, ten notes each Saturday and Sunday. If you stay on schedule all week, treat yourselves to dinner or a movie.

Devote yourself to at least ten minutes a day. If a set number of notes seems tedious, then set aside just ten minutes for thank-yous each day. After you've written that long, decide whether you're feeling inspired enough to continue for another 10 minutes— and so on. You'll find that you'll accomplish more than you might expect.

Remember that writing is just the process of putting your thoughts on paper. It may help to close your eyes and imagine using the gift. (For example, serving your first Thanksgiving turkey on the platter sent by your aunt.) Or think about the giver and all the memories you have of him or her.

Wording Thank-You Notes

Some of your notes will be easy to write; others will be more of a challenge. Each note should be warm and personal. Start by mentioning the gift and how you plan to use it. Add at least one thought besides "thank you" to the note. You might include an invitation to visit, a comment about the wedding, or a word about your new apartment. Always be gracious in your note—even if you're less than enthusiastic about the present.

While the person who writes the note is traditionally the one who signs it, you should mention your husband (and he you) in the body of the message.

You may sign notes to relatives and close friends with your first name only, but use your full name when writing to people you don't know well. After the wedding, you may include your maiden name whenever necessary for identification (e.g., sign your name *Ann Smith*, *Ann Brown Smith*, but never *Mrs. John Smith*). If you will keep your maiden name after marriage, take this opportunity to let everyone know by signing your notes *Ann Brown*. Below are some examples:

Note to married couple. Traditionally, a note to a married couple is addressed to one person—most often, the wife, alone. The husband is referred to in the body of the note. (Today, however, it's common to address both partners, such as *Dear Mr. and Mrs. Smith*. Still, only one person signs the note.)

Dear Mrs. Smith:

Thank you so much for the beautiful crystal bowl you and Mr. Smith sent. Ann and I keep it on our table filled with apples.

We are both so glad that you were able to share our special day with us.

Sincerely yours,
Steven Jones

Thank-you for a monetary gift. Acknowledging a gift of money or a savings bond or stock certificate, is easy if you mention how you plan to use the money.

Dear Uncle Ed,

Thank you so much for your very generous wedding check. Steve and I have added it to savings earmarked for a car—and thanks to you, we're almost there!

We'll be driving down to see you soon!
Love,
Ann

Thank-you for a mystery gift. Clueless about what an item is? Describe it.

Dear Mrs. Martin:

Thank you for the beautiful crystal piece you and Mr. Martin sent. What a unique design! We've already found the perfect place for it in our apartment, and I know it will always remind us of you.

We're glad you could share our wedding.

Sincerely,
Steve Jones

Thank-you for a gift you're lukewarm about. There's no need to rave about a gift you don't like, but you should still be kind and say something positive.

buy thank-you gifts for:

- bridesmaids and ushers
- honor attendants
- child attendants
- prewedding party hosts
- ceremony readers and soloists, as well as musicians who are friends
- reception helpers (guest-book attendant, program and rice passers, spotter for the photographer)
- friends who lodge or drive out-of-town guests
- parents

Dear Larry,

Steve and I would like to thank you, sincerely, for the humidor. It's already holding some cigars Steve bought on our honeymoon. We'll think of you each time we see it.

Thank you again for traveling to our wedding and sharing our special day.

Love,

Ann

Note when you haven't met the giver.
Dear Ms. Robbins:

Thank you for the lovely crystal vase. Right now it's holding some beautiful roses Steve brought home for our first-month anniversary.

I look forward to meeting you soon and thanking you in person.

Sincerely yours,

Ann Brown

When you don't care for a gift and can't return it. Find something nice to say about it or about the senders, anyway. You can always bring the gift out just when they visit.

Dear Bob and Jan,

Thanks so much for the gum-machine lamp! It is one of the most unusual gifts that we received—and we're sure it will be a conversation piece whenever we have guests.

Please come visit us soon!

Fondly,

Steve

Thank-you when you receive a group gift. If the gift came from a large group (five or more), one thank-you note addressed to the group is sufficient. (Thank each sender in person, as well.)
Dear Jane, Jim, Susan, Bill, and Fred:

Thank you for the place setting of china. Now Steve and I have service for seven—just the right number to have you all to dinner!

We appreciate your thoughtfulness. I can't wait to show you our honeymoon snapshots.

With much affection,

Ann Smith

Monogramming Gifts

Monograms are initials, embossed or embroidered on silver, linens, or other items to give them a personal stamp. There was a time when almost every wedding gift bore a monogram when it arrived. However, you probably won't want gifts to be monogrammed until after the wedding. This will give you time to decide if you will keep your maiden name after the marriage, or to design a contemporary monogram that includes both your husband's and your own first initials. *Also note:* Since most stores have a no-return policy for monogrammed items, you might want to request on your Wedding Gift Registry list, *"Please do not monogram."* Here's how to go about monogramming gifts:

Ask your registry consultant or wedding stationery resource to help you choose **an appropriate style.** Options: A single initial (usually your husband's last name); your first and last initials *and* your husband's first and last initials; your first initial *and* your husband's first initial; the initial of his last name, large, in the center, with each of your first initials on either side.

Take into account the style and size of the gift, and the space that will be filled by the monogram. A towel, sheet, or table cloth has ample room for any monogram. Silver flatware, serving pieces (such as serving spoons and forks, cake knives), on the other hand, will need a simplified or reduced monogram.

Consider the appearance of your joint initials—particularly if they spell out a word. If your initials spell out a word such as *JAR, FUN, BAD, ICK*, etc., choose a monogram in which the last initial is in the center, larger than the other two: *jRa, fNu, bDa, iKc.*

Gifts for Attendants

It is customary to give each of your attendants a small gift as a memento of your wedding, as well as a token of appreciation for all their help and support. These don't have to be expensive, but they should be items that will have lasting or special meaning. Traditionally, each bridesmaid and usher get an identical gift, but honor attendants usually receive something more distinctive. Or you may break with tradition and give each attendant a unique gift chosen just for him or her. Consider their hobbies and lifestyles.

Gifts to your attendants are distributed before the wedding, usually at the rehearsal dinner. However, some couples may prefer to present the gifts at another prewedding event, such as a bridesmaids' luncheon. (See Chapter 3, "Prewedding Parties.")

Attendants may receive something to wear for the wedding (that might be monogrammed and engraved with the wedding date). Everyone in the wedding should receive a thank-you gift, including flower girls, altar boys, pages, ring bearers, and junior bridesmaids. When buying their gifts, consider items that they'll enjoy using in the future, as well as things which commemorate your wedding day.

Gifts for Bridesmaids. Pearl earrings, bracelet or necklace in a keepsake pouch; vintage locket; hand-made perfume bottle; crystal picture frame; ornamental hair accessories, silver compact, or a vanity set for a dresser; music box; bead–trimmed gloves or satin gloves with hand embroidery; certificate for a massage, facial, manicure, pedicure or makeup lesson; photo album filled with photos of the two of you; manicure set and polish; leather backpack or briefcase; silver or leather business-card case.

Gifts for groomsmen. Engraved money clip, business-card case, pewter mug or key ring; fun cuff links (in the shape of champagne bottles for example); vest or cummerbund to wear at the wedding;

Swiss Army knife; silver razor, comb-and-brush set or bookmark; all-expenses-paid day of skiing, golfing, etc.; binoculars; bottle of vintage wine or scotch; monogrammed bathrobe; sports-team memorabilia (a team sweatshirt).

For Either. Two tickets to a concert, play, or sporting event; weekend bag; personalized stationery; leather address book or day planner; fountain pen engraved with initials; coffee table book (on a sub- ject of interest to him/her); gift certificates for movie theaters, video/DVD rentals, or restaurants; membership to a wine-, beer-, or flower-of-the-month club.

For children. Bride and groom dolls; teddy bear; charm bracelet or heart locket; classic children's book; computer-game software; autographed baseball; Mickey Mouse watch; wedding-day accessory (shoes, vest, bow tie).

Thank-You Gifts

It is appropriate to give or send both sets of parents a gift to thank them for all they have done during your engagement. Also thank any friend or relative who graciously hosted a prewedding party by giving them a gift. You might arrange for flowers to be delivered to parents the day after your wedding (prewrite the cards). Also consider sending flowers to a host/hostess the day of the party, or present a gift as you leave.

Gifts for Party Hosts/Hostesses and Other Wedding Helpers. Flowers; wine, fruit baskets; flowering plants; scented soaps, candles, and bath products; gourmet gift baskets; notepaper; votive candles; Christmas ornaments; collectibles (teacups, thimbles).

Gifts for Mothers. Flower arrangements; perfume bottles; porcelain figurines or miniature handpainted porcelain boxes; silver or gold compacts.

Gifts for Fathers. Cuff links; key chains; tie clip; paperweights; a boxed set of videos or CDs; bookends; a case of great wine.

Gifts for Both. Picture frames with wedding photos or photos of them with you as a baby; framed wedding invitations; monogrammed leather photo albums; engraved silver bowls or plates; clocks; champagne bottles and champagne flutes; spa gift certificates.

Gifts for the Bride and Groom

Although optional, it is traditional for the bride and groom to give each other a wedding gift in addition to the wedding rings. A wedding is also the time many parents pass down heirlooms—gifts with sentimental meaning.

Gifts from Parents to Newlyweds. Heirloom jewelry; a favorite rocking chair; a bottle of cognac or case of wine purchased the day the bride was born; a family Bible or crèche; furniture; a set of flatware; money for buying a home, car, or some other longed-for item.

Gifts for the Groom from the Bride. Watch; classic gold or enamel cuff links; diamond studs; wallet; attaché case; sterling picture frame with wedding photo; camera; favorite CDs, videos, and DVDs; sterling-silver belt buckle; leather stud box; first edition books; skis; golf clubs; fishing gear; luggage, bike rack; leather passport holder; hand-blown champagne glasses; the diary you kept of your courtship or engagement.

Gifts for the Bride from the Groom. Pearl necklace or earrings; 3–stone diamond necklace, representing the past, present and future; South Sea pearl pendant; gold, silver or diamond initial pendant; leather handbag or luggage; porcelain tea set; puppy; bicycle; diamond eternity band; sterling-silver compact or hairbrush and comb; ring holder; skates; skis; golf clubs; snorkeling gear; canoe; silver-plated key to new home; locket engraved with a love note; music box; antique chest to hold heirlooms.

Ultimate Personalized Gifts. Fortune cookies with personal messages; framed love poem delivered on your wedding morning; tape of your favorite love songs from your courtship; postcard from your honeymoon sent to your home address with the message: "I love you!"; on your wedding morning, request that a special song be played on his favorite radio station (make sure he's listening); honeymoon booklet with coupons for "one back rub," "bubble bath for two," "breakfast in bed," "dancing under the stars"; shadow box filled with courtship memories: matchbooks from restaurants, ticket stubs, pressed flowers from park where he proposed.

Gifts That Reflect Your Heritages

A wedding gift can celebrate your love, but sometimes it can also celebrate your cultural, ethnic, or religious background. Here, some gift traditions you or your family, friends, and guests may choose to follow or adapt.

Australian
Couples receive congratulatory telegrams from faraway friends and relatives, reading them aloud at the wedding. Guests bring gifts to the reception.

Austrian
Brides received wooden tubs with the words *"Be Happy and Industrious"* painted on the sides. The tubs were to transport possessions to their new home.

Chinese

The bride's mother fills a pocketbook with gold, jewelry, money, and valuables. Wedding gifts from guests are typically practical; money is the most popular. Gifts of gold and silver are considered ostentatious; white, funereal. Red (the color of joy) wrapping paper is used.

England

Brides received brass warming pans inscribed *"Love and Live in Peace."* In Hertfordshire, England, a pig was a traditional gift from a father to his newly married daughter.

Fijian

The groom may give the bride's father a whale's tooth, or something of great value.

Filipino

The groom's family may give old coins, symbolizing prosperity, to the couple.

French

Friends or family present a special two-handled cup (the *coupe de mariage*) for drinking wedding toasts (have it engraved with your initials). Guests still send gifts to the bride's parents—with a note of congratulations *and* flowers to the bride on her wedding day.

Hopi

Community members give cotton to the groom's father, to weave cloth for bridal garments.

Iroquois

The bride and her mother brought maize cakes to her future mother-in-law's home, and the mother-in-law presented them with venison. This gift exchange constituted a marriage ceremony.

Italian

Guests receive candied almonds wrapped in tulle or presented in porcelain boxes (guest favors, called *bomboniere*) as a symbol of good fortune.

Japanese

The bride receives clothing, accessories, and food—in pairs (two measures of tea, two pairs of sandals). Her family gives identical presents to the groom—down to the exact number of fish in a picnic basket. Guests give money envelopes with gold and silver coins, and receive gifts in return.

Jewish

The bride's mother may give the groom a *tallit* (prayer shawl) of silk; the groom's mother may give the bride Sabbath candlesticks or a tablecloth. The act of espousal is sealed when the groom gives his bride something of value, usually a plain gold wedding ring.

Korean

Ducks and geese mate for life, so friends may give a live goose and gander, or a figurine of the birds, as a symbol of fidelity.

Mexican

Godparents participate in the wedding ceremony, often giving the couple rosaries, prayer books, or kneeling pillows.

Muslim

The bride and groom may give guests candy or eggs, representing a sweet and fruitful life. Guests may give crystal, silver, or china—*after* the wedding. They don't expect thank-you notes.

Nigerian

After marriage, a bride may give her family members old clothing. She wears the new garments and jewelry given to her by her husband.

Pennsylvania-German (Amish)

Neighbors give the couple practical items (such as a *schrank*—a handpainted storage piece) for their new home.

Polish

To mark the bride's married status, her mother and grandmother may replace her wedding veil with a *babushka* (a triangularly folded kerchief) and an apron.

Scottish

Grooms may give their bride a silver teaspoon (a *wedding spune*), engraved with their initials and wedding date.

Southern Indian (Hindu)

The groom may present his bride with a jeweled string or necklace, called a *thali,* to wear throughout the marriage.

Swiss

Junior bridesmaids may lead a procession with handfuls of colored handkerchiefs. Guests "buy" handkerchiefs, with the money going to the couple.

Welsh

The bride may give her bridesmaids sprigs of myrtle from her bouquet. The maids plant them; the one whose sprig takes root will marry soon.

Anniversary Gifts

Picturing the years of marriage ahead, you may be thinking of anniversaries—and the gifts you will give each other to celebrate. If you request, your wedding gift registry may keep your list of gift preferences current, for years of gift giving from your spouse, parents, or relatives. You may want to hold a reaffirmation ceremony to celebrate an important anniversary (five, ten, or twenty-five years), or to mark a recommitment of your love. Here is a list of traditional and contemporary anniversary gifts:

Traditional

1st: paper
2nd: cotton
3rd: leather
4th: linen
5th: wood
6th: iron
7th: wool
8th: bronze
9th: pottery
10th: tin, aluminum
11th: steel
12th: silk
13th: lace
14th: ivory
15th: crystal
16th: peridot (a deep yellowish-green gem)
17th: watch
18th: cat's eye (a semiprecious stone)
19th: aquamarine
20th: china
25th: silver
30th: pearls
35th: coral, jade
40th: rubies
45th: sapphires
50th: gold
55th: emeralds
60th: diamonds

Contemporary

1st: clocks
2nd: china
3rd: crystal, glass
4th: electrical appliances
5th: silverware
6th: wood
7th: desk sets
8th: linens, lace
9th: leather
10th: diamond jewelry
11th: fashion jewelry, accessories
12th: pearls or colored gems
13th: textiles, furs
14th: gold jewelry
15th: watches
16th: silver hollowware, sterling or plate
17th: furniture
18th: porcelain
19th: bronze
20th: platinum
25th: sterling silver
30th: diamonds
35th: jade
40th: rubies
45th: sapphires
50th: gold
55th: emeralds
60th: diamonds

These are, of course, suggestions. Use your imagination and build on the traditional and contemporary gift choices listed. For example, a first-anniversary gift of paper could mean a magazine subscription, engraved stationery, a stock certificate, or a deed to a house. Silver on the twenty-fifth anniversary could easily be a silver ice bucket or plane tickets to Los Angeles—and Hollywood—land of the silver screen. Feel free to interpret the traditional suggestions in a contemporary way: leather for a third anniversary could be anything from a cool black leather jacket to an antique leather-bound book. A gift from the heart that reflects the love you've shared for another year is what matters.

18 WEDDING GUESTS

Wedding guests are invited to witness the wedding ceremony, wish the bride and groom happiness and prosperity at the reception, and join them in celebrating their new life as husband and wife. Each wedding style—whether a formal evening ceremony followed by a seated dinner or a surfside ceremony followed by an afternoon beach barbecue—calls for a particular kind of invitation response, gift, and style of dress. Here, a guest's guide to enjoying the festivities (see Appendix, under Chapter 18, "Wedding Guests").

Receiving an Invitation

Wedding invitations are typically mailed four to six weeks before the wedding date (eight weeks before if the wedding is near a holiday or requires most guests to travel). Whatever the R.s.v.p. date, it's considerate to reply promptly, in writing, so the seating plan can be worked out as early as possible and the final head count can be given to the caterer. How the guest responds depends upon the formality of the invitation.

An R.s.v.p. card acceptance/regret:
Today, most invitations include a printed response card with a stamped, self-addressed, printed envelope. To help the wedding host keep track of replies efficiently, guests should fill out the card and return it promptly.
Mr. and Mrs. Joel Kageyama _____will _____will not attend.
Another alternative: a blank response card, for guests to write their own acceptance or regrets message. A guest may also slip a separate note in with the R.s.v.p. card, in the enclosed envelope, to add a more personal explanation or message of congratulations.

A formal acceptance:
A traditional, engraved invitation to a wedding ceremony and reception may

invitation dos and don'ts

Here are etiquette points for wedding guests:

DO let hosts know if an unexpected complication (an illness or out-of-country business trip, for example) will make it impossible to attend the wedding as planned. Write, telephone, or fax regrets to the hostess with an explanation as soon as possible.

DON'T assume that children and others who live with you are invited *unless* their names appear on the inside envelope (see Chapter 5, "Invitations & Announcements"). If the hosts address the invitation "Miss Marx," then they expect only that person to attend the wedding—not every member of her household.

DO bring young children if they are invited, but only if you or someone else can watch them closely during the ceremony and reception (ask the hosts if a baby-sitter will be present). Otherwise make arrangements to leave them at home.

DON'T ask the bride if you can bring a date or special friend along to a wedding unless the bride has requested a specific name or address for her invitation guest list (see Chapter 5, "Invitations & Announcements"). Space might be tight and your request could put the bride in an awkward position.

arrive without a printed R.s.v.p. card. The guest is expected to send a written response to the wedding host promptly. It should be written on plain white or cream-colored notepaper in blue, blue-black, or black ink.

> *Mr. and Mrs. Joel Kageyama*
> *accept with pleasure*
> *the invitation of*
> *Mr. and Mrs. Ernest Carr Burke*
> *for Saturday, the fourth of April*
> *at half after four o'clock.*

It is not necessary to repeat the name of the bride and groom, but including the date and time indicates that they have been correctly understood. Including the location is optional. Wording and spacing should duplicate as closely as possible that of the invitation.

A formal regret:

> *Mr. Jean-Jacques DeLille*
> *regrets that he is unable to accept*
> *the kind invitation of*
> *Mr. and Mrs. Ernest Carr Burke*
> *for Saturday, the fourth of April.*

A regret does not repeat the time or the place, merely the date. It is not necessary to give a reason, but the guest may enclose a separate informal note to explain why he or she cannot attend the

wedding and to offer the bride and groom congratulations.

An informal acceptance:

A handwritten, contemporary, or personalized invitation, with no printed R.s.v.p. card, calls for an informal, handwritten note on the guest's favorite stationery.

> *Dear Stephanie,*
> *Rick and I are delighted to be included among the guests at Rochelle's wedding on the fifteenth of June at 11:30 a.m., at Central Methodist Church. We are looking forward to both the ceremony and the reception.*
> *Affectionately,*
> *Becky*

An informal regret:

> *Dear Stephanie,*
> *Charlotte and I regret that we will be away on the fifteenth of June, as my younger sister will be graduating that day. You know that nothing but a family celebration of our own could keep us from attending Shelly and Norman's wedding.*
> *Please give Shelly and Norman our best wishes for their future happiness.*
> *Fondly,*
> *Gary*

Receiving an Announcement

A wedding announcement does not obligate a recipient in any way; neither a gift nor a personal acknowledgment is necessary. When close friends are involved, however, it is a thoughtful gesture to send a personal note of good wishes to the couple, and perhaps to their parents as well. If announcement recipients *do* want to mark the news of the wedding with a gift, they can check with a parent or close friend to see where the newlyweds are registered.

Out-of-Town Weddings

Most invitations to out-of-town weddings include a map or other written directions to the wedding site. If they are not included, guests can request them from the bride's or groom's family. To avoid missing the ceremony, double-check the instructions received by consulting a road map, or a website, such as *maps.com*.

Wedding hosts have certain obligations to guests who are traveling long distances to attend a wedding. (In return, guests should keep track of whoever entertained them and send thank-you notes, and perhaps a small gift of appreciation.) Here are some traditional responsibilities.

Wedding accommodations. The bride's family should recommend places to stay and may reserve a block of rooms in a hotel for out-of-town guests (often at a reduced group rate). The bride's family is not expected to pay for the accommodations of out-of-town guests but should enclose printed information about available hotels with the wedding invitation. Guests can then call the hotel to make their own reservations.

Entertainment. Family or friends will probably host a welcome cocktail party or dinner for out-of-town guests (often the same night that the bride's and groom's families and the wedding party will be at the rehearsal dinner). Or, out-of-town guests may be invited to a get-acquainted breakfast the day of the wedding, or to a postwedding brunch the day after the wedding. At a long-weekend wedding, there will most likely be several gatherings hosted by friends and family members of the bride and groom. Some couples host a barbecue and pool party or a softball game: bride's team vs. the groom's team. If an itinerary of all of these outings is not included with the invitation, the wedding hosts should leave a schedule in each guest's hotel room, along with a welcome basket of fruit, candy, cookies, etc. It is also a thoughtful gesture to leave each guest a list of all other out-of-town guests staying in the same hotel, as well as the name and phone number of someone (a friend or relative) who lives in that town or knows it well, and can answer any questions about the planned activities and logistics.

Sight-seeing arrangements. The wedding host(s) may also arrange a bus tour of a large city, a trip to a museum, or perhaps an afternoon of boating or skating. Or, they may leave a list of what-to-do suggestions in each out-of-town guest's hotel room, should guests want to explore on their own. The bride's and groom's families will appreciate being left free the day before the wedding, to finalize last-minute details.

Transportation. It is considerate for the wedding hosts to arrange transportation around town, or at least back and forth to the ceremony and reception sites, for all out-of-town guests. Some couples arrange for a bus or vans to transport all guests. Others arrange for limousines or ask wedding attendants and other close friends to provide rides.

gift-giving etiquette

- Find out where the couple are registered. The items listed in their wedding gift registry are things they want and need, so you know that a gift selected from among these items will always be used and appreciated.

- *Bring* a shower gift to a shower. *Send* a wedding gift before or after the wedding.

- Send a wedding gift within one year of the wedding (within one month, though, is best). Keep in mind that most store and online gift registries remain available and are kept current for up to a year after the wedding, sometimes longer.

- Ask the store to enclose a receipt for the item, omitting the price, in case it needs to be exchanged or returned. Wedding gift registries generally do this automatically, simplifying the entire process—for the sender and the recipients.

- If sending a gift that you purchased on your own, be sure to wrap it in a box with the store's name or logo, so that the couple will know where they can exchange or replace it, if necessary.

- If mailing the gift yourself, insure the package so that you are covered for the possibility of loss or damages.

- The gift should be sent to the address on the registry information, or to the return address on the wedding invitation.

- Make monetary gifts payable to the bride or groom before the wedding; to *both* on wedding day or after.

- If you don't receive a thank-you note, wait at least one month after the gift was sent to ask if it was received.

when wedding gifts may be optional

Guests may choose to send a wedding gift as a token of congratulations and affection. It is not, however, absolutely necessary if you will not be at the wedding or reception, or if it is a second wedding. Optional gift situations include:

- When a group invitation to the ceremony is extended to members of the church congregation.

- When a wedding invitation must be refused because of a previous commitment.

- When the guest is attending the second wedding of the bride or the groom just a few years after attending the first. (If you wish to give something, remember the couple are combining homes, not creating one, and choose items they would not buy themselves. See Chapter 17, "Wedding Gifts.")

The Wedding Gift

Always plan on sending a gift when you accept a wedding invitation (see "When Wedding Gifts May Be Optional" box). The best—and easiest—way to shop for the "perfect" gift is to consult the couple's wedding gift registry, since these are the items they want and need to begin their new life together. (See Chapter 17, "The Wedding Gift Registry.") Below, some etiquette pointers for guests:

How much time does a guest have to send a gift? Traditionally, a gift may be sent up to a year after the wedding, but it's best to shop nearer to the event (within one month after the wedding), so the occasion isn't forgotten. Keep in mind that most wedding gift registries are kept current for up to a year or longer following the wedding.

Where should the wedding gift be sent? When you purchase a gift from the couple's registry, it will automatically be sent to the correct address. Non-registry gifts are traditionally sent to the bride at her home, or to the R.s.v.p. address on the wedding invitation. However, if the guest is a close friend of the groom's parents and wants them to see the gift, it is acceptable to send the gift to their home. Also consider the address that will be most helpful for the couple. If they already live in a city other than the site of the wedding, sending the gift to that address will give them one less item to transport. Check with the couple's wedding gift registry information for a preferred delivery address.

Can't a guest just bring the gift to the reception? In some geographic regions, this is the custom. However, making sure that the gift arrives at the appropriate home address before or after the wedding is traditional and *wise*. Otherwise, the bride and groom will have to worry about security (gifts can be lost, damaged, or stolen, and cards often get detached), as well as having the gifts transported home by their wedding party, family, or friends. If the gift is sent directly to the parents' or couple's home, it can be safely stored.

Should a guest order an item on the couple's registry list if it is out of stock, or a special order? If an item is not immediately available, the store or website will place an order with the warehouse. The bride should then receive a card telling her what was purchased, the name of the sender, and the date it will be delivered. If the item ordered is discontinued, the bride should also be notified, and asked to make an alternate gift selection.

Is a monetary gift appropriate? To whom should it be made payable? Money is a suitable and always–appreciated wedding gift. Guests may give a check, cash, gift certificate to a favorite store, contribution to a travel (honeymoon) or mortgage registry fund, U.S. Government Bond, or stock certificate. Before the wedding, checks are made out to the bride *or* groom (if the bride, for example, is a close relative or friend, make it out to her; if the groom is family or a good friend, make it out to him) and are sent—in a wedding card—to that person's home. On the wedding day or after, make the gift payable to *both* the bride and groom; if you wish, present it personally to the couple at the reception.

When can guests expect to receive acknowledgment of their gift? For gifts received before the wedding, thank-you notes should be sent by the bride or groom within two weeks of their arrival. For gifts received on or after the wedding, thank-you notes should be sent within a month of the honeymoon (see Chapter 17, "Wedding Gifts"). If a few months have passed since the wedding and the couple still have not acknowledged receiving the gift, contact the store or online registry service from which the gift was purchased to make sure it was actually delivered. Or ask the post office to trace the package (always keep insurance receipts for any gifts mailed). If the gift seems to have been lost or damaged, replace it, enclosing a note of explanation to the couple. If all appears to be in order, you may ask about the present's arrival; it may be awkward to check on the gift's status without implying to the newlyweds that their manners are amiss. A casual remark made during conversation with the couple (or their parents), such as, *"Have you had a chance to use that silver serving tray yet?"* may bring you exactly the reassurance you need. This should also prompt the couple to send a thank-you note.

Are guests expected to send other prewedding gifts, in addition to a wedding gift? Engagement gifts are optional, even if a friend or family member receives an invitation to an engagement party (see Chapter 1, "Your Engagement"). Many guests do, however, choose to give the couple a present to congratulate them. If a guest accepts an invitation to a shower, however, a gift is expected. After all, the purpose of a shower is to shower the bride and groom with the items needed to set up a home together.

Dressing for the Wedding

General guidelines. Wedding guests dress as they would for almost any other social event held at the same hour and season (see Chapter 7, "Guide to Wedding Clothes" chart). Traditionally, it has been taboo for women guests to wear black (perceived as too funereal) or white (the color reserved for the bride). Today, however, it is acceptable for a woman guest to wear a black cocktail or evening dress to a formal evening reception— it might include colored accessories, such as a red shawl, shoes, or handbag. So as not to draw attention away from the bride, women guests wearing white should use colored accessories, such as a bright, patterned scarf around her shoulders.

Very formal and formal evening. Traditionally, an engraved invitation to an evening wedding indicates very formal (white tie) or formal (black tie) attire for the wedding party. Although this does not mean that all male guests must dress at the same level of formality, many hosts today will print "black tie" on the invitation, to let guests know that the wedding will be formal and that black tie (tuxedos) are expected. Although "white tie" is seldom printed on the invitation, you can let guests know that the wedding will be *very* formal and that white tie (tails) will be appreciated, by spreading the information via word of mouth. At a *very* formal evening wedding, women are expected to wear long dresses; at a formal evening wedding, long dresses or very dressy cocktail clothes are called for.

Formal daytime. If the ceremony begins before 5 P.M., women guests wear dressy daytime dresses or elegant cocktail suits. Men wear dark suits.

Informal (daytime or evening). Traditionally, women wear street-length dresses or suits, depending upon the time of day. Men wear suits or a blazer and tie. Keep in mind that "informal" doesn't imply wearing casual work attire; guests should always make an effort to dress up, in honor of the bride and groom. At a nontraditional wedding, perhaps one held in a meadow with a barbecue afterward, "casual clothes" might be specified, particularly if the reception will include an activity such as square dancing. When in doubt, call the bride, her mother, the groom's mother, or anyone involved in the wedding preparations. Then help spread the word by telling other guests what kind of dress is expected.

Ceremony Procedures

When should guests arrive at a wedding? Guests without pew cards should arrive at the site of the ceremony thirty minutes before the time printed on the invitation, even earlier for a very large wedding, to allow ample time to be seated by the ushers. People with reserved seats (pew cards) should arrive about twenty minutes before the ceremony begins. Guests arriving later than ten minutes before the ceremony should seat themselves quietly in the rear if ushers are no longer seating guests. If the wedding procession is already under way, guests should remain in the rear of the church or synagogue until the wedding party reaches the altar, then seat themselves (unless an usher is stationed at the back to seat latecomers). Allow extra time for inclement weather, traffic delays, and finding an out-of-the-way church or synagogue.

On which side should guests sit? When guests arrive at the church, synagogue, or ceremony site, they'll be met in the vestibule by an usher who will ask if they are a friend or relative of the bride or the groom. In Christian weddings, the groom's relatives and friends are seated on the right side of the altar (the same position the groom will be in as he faces the altar); the bride's relatives and friends on the left (where the bride will be). The reverse is true for Jewish weddings: the groom's relatives and friends are seated on the left side of the altar; the bride's on the right. A friend of both bride and groom is seated in the best available spot. The usher will extend his right arm to a female guest and escort her down the aisle to her seat; if she has a male escort, he walks a few steps behind. Sometimes the usher will simply say, *"Please follow me,"* and lead the way down the aisle, so a couple can walk together. He may let guests know that the families of the bride and groom are sitting together in a spirit of unity; in this case, he will show the guest to the best available seat.

Is it appropriate for guests to talk before the ceremony? It is customary for guests and ushers to talk in a low tone as they proceed down the aisle (see Chapter 6, "The Wedding Party"). Once in their seats, during the playing of the prelude, quiet talk with other guests is accepted until the wedding procession begins.

Are guests expected to participate in all religious ceremony rituals? A printed wedding program explaining all religious customs or details may be distributed by ushers to guests as they enter the church or synagogue (see Chapter 8, "Your Wedding Ceremony"). It is not necessary for guests to carry out unfamiliar rituals, especially if they are of a different faith and feel uncomfortable doing so. It is polite, however, to follow the lead of the families seated in the front pews. Guests stand when the families stand (in some religions, when the bride proceeds down the aisle) but may remain seated when others kneel. In Orthodox or Conservative Jewish congregations, all men cover their heads; married women may also choose to do so. It would be polite for a Christian man to accept the yarmulke (skullcap) and a married woman, the lace handkerchief with hairpin, distributed at the door. Women may also wear a hat; check with the bride's relatives to determine what's proper.

The bride and groom may request that certain personalized rituals be a part of the ceremony—such as congregational hymn singing, handshakes, or a brief greeting with the guests seated nearby. Guests should take part, in the spirit of the occasion.

Is there a proper way to exit the sanctuary after the wedding party walks up the aisle? After the recession, guests remain in their seats until the ushers have escorted the families of the bride and groom, including the grandmothers and other close relatives, out of the church or synagogue. Frequently, the ushers will indicate the time to leave by returning to stand at the sides of each pew, beginning at the front of the sanctuary, signaling guests to file out row by row. Should you need directions to the reception site, restrooms, and so on, the ushers are the best people to ask. If the receiving line is scheduled for right after the ceremony (often positioned in the vestibule of the house of worship or in the hallway of the hotel or banquet hall), guests will file out in an orderly manner, moving down the receiving line and greeting the newlyweds, their parents, and attendants (see Chapter 13, "Your Reception").

guest ceremony tips

- Arrive 30 minutes before the ceremony begins.

- Tell the usher whether you are a friend or relative of the bride or groom.

- Take the usher's right arm (if you're a female), or follow behind (if you're a male), to the pew indicated by the usher.

- Wait until ushers direct your pew to file out of the sanctuary after the recession.

- Pass through the receiving line—if it is directly after the ceremony—introducing yourself and stating your relationship to the couple.

*guest reception
tips*

- If at the reception site, pass through the receiving line introducing yourself and stating your relationship to the couple.

- Introduce yourself to guests at your table, talking briefly to the person on your right and left, then to others at the table.

- Join other guests on the dance floor when invited to dance by the bandleader, or by friends.

- Rise and drink to each toast made to the couple at the reception.

- Dance and participate in the bouquet or the garter toss—if you are single.

- Try to thank hosts before leaving the reception, or write a thank-you note the next day.

Reception Rituals

Must all guests walk through the receiving line? Yes. This is an excellent opportunity for each guest to greet and hug or shake hands with the newlyweds and their families (fathers and attendants may circulate), wishing the couple well and sharing the joy of the occasion (see Chapter 13, "Your Reception").

Is there any receiving-line etiquette of which a guest should be aware? If a guest does not personally know those in the receiving line, he or she should introduce himself or herself to each person. It's customary to make some remark about the wedding, the bride, or the newly married couple, depending on how well the guest knows the people involved. An example: *"Hello, Mrs. Atkins. I'm Indira Shakib, Glenda's old friend from music camp. I particularly enjoyed the violin solo."* It was once traditional to congratulate the groom and to wish the bride happiness—since the groom "caught" the bride. Today, however, both husbands and wives will be happy to receive congratulations from their guests.

It's considerate to move quickly down the line so that others are not kept waiting.

When should guests sign the guest book? Once past the receiving line, guests sign the guest book (or Bride's Book), which may be positioned near its end. Sometimes, the bride may position the guest book on a table in the room where the cocktail hour is held or near the cake table in the reception room. Or a bridesmaid or friend of the bride or groom may circulate throughout the cocktail hour and reception, asking guests to sign the guest book (see Chapter 13, "Your Reception").

Where do guests go after the receiving line? If there is a cocktail hour, guests go directly to that area. Or, the receiving line may be positioned in a corner of the room where cocktails are being served. If the receiving line was held in the church or synagogue vestibule or on the steps, the guests move on to the reception site.

How will guests know when to take their seats in the reception room? Usually, the banquet manager or waiters will approach guests and ask them to make their way into the reception room. At a seated luncheon or dinner (buffet or waiter service), guests should proceed to the table indicated on their escort card. At that table, place cards may indicate where they are to be seated. If the celebration is buffet service with unspecified seats, guests may proceed to the buffet line, then choose a seat at one of the unreserved tables. At a tea or cocktail reception, guests may serve themselves and continue to circulate.

When is it appropriate for guests to begin dancing? At a very large reception, the father of the bride may see to it that dancing is well under way before the couple appear on the scene for their traditional first dance with each other and with their parents. At most weddings, however, the bride's father, a member of the wedding party, or the bandleader introduces the newlywed couple for their first dance, which takes place after the receiving line and the cocktail buffet are over and the couple have entered the room where the dinner will take place (see Chapter 13, "Your Reception"). After several stanzas of the song, the bride and groom may dance with their parents; next, the wedding party may step onto the dance floor, and finally, all guests will be invited to join in the celebration. The band may wait, at the couple's request, to begin the music and dancing until the main course has been served, although this is not the best way to get guests on their feet and mixing.

What is the appropriate etiquette for guests' participation in the best man's toast? After the wedding party take their places at the bridal (or head) table, the best man will make the first toast, followed by a thank-you toast from the groom and, often, the bride. Then other relatives and friends (probably the fathers and mothers first) may stand to make a good-natured toast to the couple. Every guest should rise and drink every toast (but not necessarily finish the glass), whether his or her beverage preference is champagne, iced tea, or ginger ale.

What is expected of a guest at a wedding? Guests should enjoy themselves, which will make the party a success. They should talk to the people seated at their table (splitting their attention equally between the people seated to their left and right, then talking to others at the table, and introducing themselves when necessary). If they are invited onto the dance floor for an ethnic dance or a conga line, they should give it a try; they should also clear the dance floor for the cake-cutting ceremony, as well as for special dances for the bride and her father, and the groom and his mother. Single female guests should participate if asked to catch the bride's bouquet; single male guests should gather if asked to catch the bride's garter, which is removed and thrown by the groom.

When is it acceptable for a guest to leave the reception? Wedding receptions have no specified length, although four hours is about average. Traditionally, guests remain until the bride and groom leave the reception. Today, however, most brides and grooms are choosing to stay until the party ends. (After all, many wedding guests travel from all over the country to see them, and the couple want to visit with them as long as they can.) If the couple do not seem to be in a rush to leave, it is acceptable for guests to depart any time after the cutting of the cake. (It is considered bad luck if a guest does not have at least a *taste* of the wedding cake.) Before leaving, guests should find a member of the bride's immediate family and thank him or her. (A guest might say, *"Thanks for a really enjoyable evening, Mrs. Atkins. It was a beautiful wedding."*) If a guest is not able to personally thank the wedding hosts, he or she should write the next day (or perhaps phone if it's a close relative or friend) to say that he or she had a wonderful time. Eventually, the wedding hosts will signal the end of the reception by ending the music (a last dance will be played), closing the bar, and preparing to leave themselves. (For more tips, see Appendix, under Chapter 18, "Wedding Guests.")

GOING AWAY
19

Traditionally, the bride and groom are the first to leave the reception; their departure signals to guests that it is appropriate for them to leave, too. However, today many couples live far from the town in which they grew up, and guests may have traveled long distances to be part of the festivities. Because of this, newlyweds frequently stay till the end of the reception, continuing to dance and celebrate with their guests.

If you do decide to linger, have attendants pass the word to your guests that the bouquet toss is not a sign of your imminent departure. If you do not make a dramatic exit, it is appropriate for guests to begin to leave any time after the cutting and serving of the cake (see Chapter 13, "Your Reception").

Leaving the Reception

Following tradition, the bride and groom leave the reception about a half-hour before it ends. Shortly after the bride throws her bouquet and the groom tosses the bride's garter, the newlyweds leave the room with their honor attendants to change into traveling outfits and dash out amid a shower of rice, birdseed, or flower petals (see Appendix, under Chapter 2, "Wedding Customs") The couple depart in a getaway car, which has often been "decorated" by the ushers. Guests usually leave shortly after. Below, a going-away timetable:

Enjoy a last dance, about a half-hour before you leave (after cutting the cake). Begin saying good-bye to your guests.

Ask the bandleader to announce your bouquet toss. Single women should gather in an open space—under a balcony or at the bottom of a stairway.

With your back to the group, give the bouquet a good toss over your shoulder. Or, you may face the group and throw the bouquet to your sister or a special friend. Tradition says that the woman who catches the bouquet will be the next to marry.

Stage a garter toss, if desired. The groom removes the garter from the bride's leg and either the bride or groom tosses it to the assembled group of single men. The recipient (who, legend has it, will be the next to marry) may then place it on the leg of the woman who caught the bridal bouquet.

Leave the room with your honor attendants to change into your going-away outfits. Your maid or matron of honor, or another friend or relative, should help— by seeing that your wedding dress and accessories are safely stored while you are on your honeymoon. (The best man should assist the groom and take responsibility for returning his formalwear.) Your going-away outfit can be a suit, dress, or pantsuit appropriate for your destination. Even if you're just going camping, wear something more stylish than jeans.

The best man will make sure all honeymoon luggage is safely stored in the getaway car. He will keep practical jokers away from the car and make sure that no decorations obstruct the driver's vision or hamper his hearing. He will also hand the groom the car keys and plane or train tickets. While you're on your honeymoon, he and the maid or matron of honor can also assist by depositing endorsed gift checks.

Say a special good-bye to parents. Have attendants notify them that you are about to leave, so you have a chance to thank them for all their help and support.

Dash to your getaway car under a shower of rice, seeds, or flower petals. Your child attendants and younger guests can distribute packets of rice, millet seed, safflower seed, birdseed, or flower petals, or small bottles of soap bubbles for guests to toss or blow in your direction. (Rice and grains are symbols of fertility and bounty and have been used in weddings for centuries; see Chapter 2, "Wedding Customs".)

When your parents are ready to leave, they will signal the band to stop playing and the bar to close. Guests take the cue and begin to leave. *Note:* Some families decide to pay the band overtime and keep the celebration going an extra hour. That's why it's important to write the overtime fee into your contract.

Staying at the Reception

Many brides and grooms choose to remain at the reception until the end, just as they would if hosting a dinner party. Following are some ideas to help signal your plans to your guests, since many of them may feel they have to stay until you make a tradi-tional departure:

Have attendants pass the word that you will be staying until the reception ends. Guests will then know they need not wait for your departure before leaving.

After the cake cutting, make a thank-you toast. Thank your guests for coming, and tell them that you two will be the last to leave because you are staying to visit longer with all of them.

When the party is over, you can slip away in your gown and formalwear or change into something more comfort-able, depending on your plans. Some couples enjoy arriving at their wedding-night hotel in wedding attire; others pre-fer to arrive discreetly.

car-decorating tips

Ushers must decorate carefully so they don't damage the car or obscure vision for driving:

- Use masking or floral tape or shoe polish. Avoid using glue, cellophane tape, rubber cement, and paint, which can cause damage to the car's paint finish.

- Don't write or drape streamers or balloons across windows; obstructed views are dangerous.

- If it looks like rain, steer clear of colored crepe paper, which might bleed.

- Be sure it's the right car!

Attending Postwedding Parties

If you have organized a Long Weekend Wedding, with several parties scheduled throughout the weekend for long-distance guests, your wedding will probably not be the last occasion where you will see your friends and relatives. If this is the case:

Plan to leave the wedding reception whenever you wish, but plan to attend all other parties during the weekend. Pre-and postwedding parties during the weekend will allow you time to visit with all your guests. You may not wish to stay for the entire length of time, but do at least make an appearance at each get-together. The postwedding brunch (the morning after the wedding) is often when the newlyweds say a final good-bye before leaving for their honeymoon.

Decorating the Car

It's part of wedding lore: The bride and groom drive off in a car festooned with stream-ers, crepe paper, tin cans that clatter against the pavement, old shoes, flowers, and "Just Married" written in big letters on the back (see Chapter 2, "Wedding Customs"). Exactly how—and when—is the newlyweds' car decorated? The lighthearted task of decorating the car belongs to the ushers, who do this job while you are enjoying your reception. If you will leave on your honeymoon in a borrowed or rented car, be sure that your groom passes this information to the ushers, so that they will be careful. Fol-lowing are some simple decoration suggestions:

Start with a "getaway kit" from party stores. These kits include crepe paper, signs, balloons. Wrap the car up as a gift with a big bow on top. Paint the newly-

creative getaways

Here, other unique ways to exit:

- hot-air balloon
- dogsled, skis
- horse and sleigh
- horse and buggy
- horseback
- ski gondola
- rowboat
- motorboat
- riverboat
- bicycle built for two
- motorcycle
- in-line skates
- antique car
- cable car
- helicopter
- taxi
- golf cart
- rickshaw
- seaplane
- ferryboat
- scooter

weds' first names and "Just Married" on a sign or write it with white shoe polish (which washes off with water—test it on a small area, first) on the hood.

Check with limousine companies before the wedding. If you've hired a limousine, ask if they provide decorations.

Ask your florist to bedeck the car in advance. Many will provide special floral tape that won't mar the body of the car and metal clips for stringing garlands. Consider encircling the car with a garland of inexpensive flowers, such as carnations or the more flamboyant dendrobium orchids. Or form a rainbow-style arc of colorful blossoms across the top of the windshield, leaving a clear view; a train of flowers and streamers trail behind.

Renting a Limousine

For many couples, the stylish getaway vehicle of choice is a chauffeur-driven limousine. Contact an established, reputable limousine firm—your wedding is one day you can't afford a reckless or late driver or a dirty or unsafe car.

Book a limousine six months before the wedding. Ask friends, your caterer, photographer, and other wedding professionals for recommendations; or find companies in the Yellow Pages, or on the Internet, under "Limousine Service" and ask them for references. To be sure you're dealing with a reputable firm, call the National Limousine Association (NLA) (see Appendix, under Chapter 19, "Going Away") and ask if the company is a member. You can check their website at www.limo.org for members near you. (The NLA requires members to have proper licensing and insurance.) Call the local Better Business Bureau and Consumer Affairs Department to see if any complaints have been registered against the companies you're considering.

Visit several companies. Read their insurance policy; is it valid and up-to-date? Does it include personal injury insurance? Ask to see their license and NLA logo.

Examine the cars. Are they in good condition? Are there seat belts in the back and front seats? How many people can they accommodate? Are they equipped with the amenities you want (i.e., a TV, bar, or phone)?

If there are few cars, or you're told cars are out, it may mean the company doesn't own their vehicles. If they're renting them from other firms, this may increase your chance of not getting what you ask for or being left waiting on your wedding day.

Ask the company if they have an official chauffeur training program. Some include video or classroom training, testing behind the wheel, and apprenticeship programs. Choose a provider that places a high value on the caliber of their chauffeurs.

Decide how many cars you'll need. Traditionally, one limousine transports the bride and her father to the ceremony site, while one or more limousines (or sedans, which seat two in back comfortably, one in front) transport your bridesmaids and mother. Additional cars can drive members of the groom's family, and ushers. After the ceremony and reception, the bride and groom ride in the limousine in which the bride and her father arrived. (A *formal limousine* seats four people, so the maid of honor and best man *could* join the newlyweds. A *stretch limousine* allows for six to ten people.)

Cost-cutting tips: Most companies have a one- or two-hour minimum. Don't keep a limousine on call; you'll just pay for the driver's waiting time during the reception. Instead, hire one limo to take you to the ceremony and reception; another for leaving the reception. Or just hire two limousines: one each for the bride's and groom's families. Ask attendants to drive their own cars to the ceremony; later, the two limousines can shuttle attendants from ceremony to reception and back. Also ask about special wedding packages, the different cars available (e.g., a luxury stretch limousine costs more to rent than a corporate stretch limousine). Are extra amenities—sunroof, bar, tinted windows, VCR, TV—necessary after the reception? Finally, let companies know you're comparison shopping; ask if there are any considerations they can extend.

Sign a contract or letter of agreement. Once you choose your limousine company, get the details in writing, either in a standard contract or a letter you write and have the company manager sign. Read the fine print. The bill may be based on a minimum number of hours and may or may not include the standard 15 percent gratuity; ask. Put down the smallest deposit possible (20 to 25 percent) to minimize loss if the firm goes out of business or provides inadequate service. If the balance is due on your wedding day, assign an attendant to deliver it. (Allow extra cash for gratuities—if service is great.)

limousine-contract tips

Include the following:

- total cost—deposit; balance (is gratuity included in fee?); payment schedule; extra fees for tolls, parking, travel time, overtime, cleaning up (rice, spills)

- date and times

- pickup locations, destinations, whether drivers should wait at each site or return

- make, model, year, color, license-plate number of car

- amenities—decorations, TV, DVD player, VCR, stereo, FM-radio, bar, air conditioner, champagne, sunroof, phone, umbrellas

- cancellation and refund policies (what happens if the car breaks down? if features contracted for are missing? if you or they must cancel?)

- driver's name; backup driver in case of emergency

- driver's attire (suit and tie, tuxedo, or uniform?)

- driver's duties—buff car before reception, assist elderly guests

- insurance coverage, and safety guarantees (e.g., the car will be steel-sided, not fiberglass)

Having Your Friends Drive

Friends can help drive out-of-town guests, elderly guests, or the wedding party to the wedding and ceremony sites if you choose not to use a limousine company. Thank your drivers by paying for a tank of gas and a car wash, and perhaps even give them a small gift.

Contact local rental-car firms. Consider renting cars for friends to drive. If they'll be used to transport wedding party members, several cars of the same model and color will create a more uniform look. Be sure to familiarize your drivers with times, passengers, and destinations.

Think about renting a minivan to

transport the wedding party, or an English double-decker bus for out-of-town guests. Inquire about renting sports cars or antique cars for yourselves and the wedding party. Remember, however, that sports cars may lack trunk space. Antique cars may not be able to travel at highway speeds, so budget in extra time to get from home to the ceremony, and from the ceremony to the reception!

Keep in mind that in most states, you must be twenty-five to rent a car. A driver's license is required, as is a major credit card (the number will be taken as insurance that you'll return the car and pay the fee). For exotic cars, a loss/damage waiver—which says the renter will pay for any damage done to the car—may be mandatory; standard auto insurance won't cover damage to a very expensive car. (Some credit cards do cover auto insurance when the card holder rents a car; ask if this is true for your card.)

The First Night

Years ago, weddings were in the morning, followed by a simple lunch or even breakfast, giving the newlyweds a chance to get a good start on honeymoon travels. Now wedding receptions are later and longer, and many couples stay till the end. Since most newlyweds leave on flights the next morning, they spend their first married night together in a hotel room or at home. If you and your groom have been living together, the idea of returning to the comforts of your own apartment before leaving on a trip can seem appealing and practical months before the wedding day. Still, you are likely to want to make your first night of marriage special. Even if you are in familiar surroundings, be carried over the threshold (as brides have been for centuries; see Chapter 2, "Wedding Customs"), and surround yourselves with flowers, candlelight, and champagne.

Sexpectations

It may be hard to face the most meaningful sexual encounter of your lives right after the emotional roller coaster of your wedding. If something wonderful happens the first night, great. If you just collapse into bed and pass out, that's okay, too. Realize that this is just the first of many nights together or the continuation of what is already a satisfying relationship.

Also try not to put pressure on each other to perform once you hit your honeymoon spot. You may be exhausted from months of wedding preparations and/or work, just as would be true on any vacation. You may also find yourselves preoccupied with exploring everything your honeymoon site has to offer, hiking, tennis, beach walks, sailing, sightseeing, sumptuous buffets, and dancing. Great sex—or even any sex at all—may elude you until you begin to unwind and relax.

Traveling Together

You may envision your honeymoon as nonstop bliss, but like any trip it can have its ups and downs. If you anticipate some quiet or tense moments and handle them with humor and understanding, your honeymoon will flow much more smoothly.

Different styles. You have two bulging suitcases loaded with every possible outfit; he's packed only a tote bag with a few shirts and changes of underwear. You insist on getting to the airport at least two hours before your flight leaves; he prefers to dash in shortly before departure. While these travel-style differences may drive you crazy, don't criticize: compromise. Maybe you can make do with one sweater instead of three; perhaps getting to the airport with time to spare—especially when dealing with security—isn't such a bad idea.

Scheduling standoffs. He always wants to be doing something: golf, tennis, windsurfing. You treasure long walks holding hands or two-hour lunches. A honeymoon doesn't mean you have to be together constantly. Now, and in the future, you won't always want to do the same things at the same time. Talk things out and improvise: He might windsurf while you shop. Afterward, you'll meet for lunch to share your experiences.

Disappearing dialogue. What if you're at a romantic meal and can't think of anything to talk about? Don't worry. Quiet companionship is fine, too. At home, you're apart most of the day, so there's catching up to do. After a few days and nights together, you may not have dozens of things to tell each other. Why not invite another couple you meet to join you for a meal or drink? Remember that this is the beginning of married social life.

Honeymoon Travel Plans

It's never too early to start planning your honeymoon—the best travel buys go quickly, and many popular destinations are booked a year in advance. Shortly after your engagement, start discussing your time frame, your budget, and, of course, your dream destination. Compile travel articles from magazines, consult the guidebooks at the nearest mega-bookstore, review newspaper travel sections and travel websites. Once you've narrowed your destination choices to two or three, it's time to call or visit a travel agent (at least six months before the wedding). He or she can guide you through the rest of the planning—from buying the plane tickets and making hotel reservations to booking a rental car.

How do we find the right travel agent? Your best bet is a personal recommendation. Also scan the Yellow Pages for members of the American Society of Travel Agents

honeymoon tips

- Purchase the lowest refundable fare if plans are tentative.

- Opt for a paper ticket instead of an e-ticket, even if you have to pay an extra fee. If you do book an e-ticket, keep a printout of the computer confirmation with you.

- Do not put film in checked baggage. High-tech scanning machines can erase photos.

- Book *nonstop* flights—no stops or plane changes (*direct* flights land at airports along the way; *connecting* flights require plane changes—more chance for missed flights, lost luggage; *charter* flights are a bargain but are more likely to be delayed, or canceled).

- Tightened security means bigger delays, so leave yourselves plenty of time to make that connection or catch that cruise ship.

- If renting a car, reserve early for the model of choice; specify *automatic* or *shift*; ask about hidden expenses (rate per mile, insurance, tax, gas, one-way rental). Will your own car insurance policy or credit-card limit cover rentals?

- On a cruise, ask about cabin sizes and prices, and whether beds are doubles or bunks.

- When making hotel reservations, be sure to mention that you are honeymooners. Hotels often treat newlyweds to free champagne and room upgrades.

honeymoon-budget tips

- Investigate off-season rates.

- Find out why any special rate is being offered (because the hotel is under construction, it's hurricane season, etc.).

- Consider package tours.

- Book hotel, airfare/cruise, car rental at the same time—and early.

- Turn in frequent-flier miles early; leave time to receive discount coupons.

- Check exchange rates.

- Use travel discounts available through professional memberships.

- Look into credit-card perks. Use a certain credit card to book your room or pay for plane tickets, and you may get a free upgrade and other bonuses.

- Watch out for offers that seem "too good to be true."

(ASTA), or contact ASTA (see Appendix, under Chapter 19, "Going Away"), for a list of members near you. Remember that some agencies have specialties: cruises, ski packages, adventure trips. Look for someone who is experienced, will listen to your needs, and shop around for the best rates.

Can we just leave everything to the travel agent? A travel agent can simplify things for you, but she or he is not a mind reader. You have to do some brainstorming of your own. Ask yourselves what you want from the trip: Outdoor adventure? A week on the beach? Then meet with the agent in person, set the budget, and tell her what you're looking for. Once you decide where to go, the next step is to choose the style of your accomodation. If you're a conservative couple, you probably wouldn't be happy at the trendiest hotel in London, and if you're seeking seclusion, don't stay at the biggest resort on the island. Common sense can go a long way toward avoiding honeymoon disappointments. Whatever you decide, try to make decisions early enough to take advantage of lower airfares and packages. The agent can book airline, cruise, or train tickets, accommodations, car rentals, sight-seeing tours, and package deals, often charging a small fee for her service. Once your trip is booked, you should ask the agent for a honeymoon itinerary, as well as paper confirmations from the rental car company and hotel (which you should carry with you); reconfirm your own flights before you leave and before you return.

How do we develop a travel budget? After you decide how much you can spend, make a list of what you'll have to pay for: plane tickets, hotel, meals, rental car, cocktails, tips, gifts. Research all costs before you go, from the price of a taxi between the airport and hotel to the cost of a helicopter ride, sailboat rental, tennis lessons, and admission fees to museums or clubs. If you're honeymooning at an all-inclusive resort, remember that spa treatments, tee times, and motorized watersports may be considered extras. In many cases, you will save time and money by working with a travel agent.

Will we need special travel documents? Ask your travel agent to fill you in on the requirements for your destination. If you're traveling within the U.S. (including Hawaii, Alaska, Puerto Rico, and the U.S.V.I.), you won't need anything more than a government-issued photo I.D. to get on the plane. Technically, Canada, Mexico, and some non-American Caribbean islands also require only a photo I.D. for entry; however, when traveling outside the U.S., carrying a passport is always wise. Passports are universally accepted, and less cumbersome than hauling around loose papers that can't be replaced abroad if lost. So if you don't have a passport, get one, and if you do have one, double-check the expiration date. New applicants need proof of citizenship (such as a birth or naturalization certificate), proof of identity (like a driver's license), two passport photos, and $60. Go to *travel.state.gov/passport_services.html* to download application forms and get information on where to apply. It usually takes about a month to receive your new passport. In addition, your travel agent may inform you that you'll need travel visas to visit your destination. He or she can advise you on the easiest way to go about procuring the necessary documentation. And lastly, always make copies of your I.D.s and keep them in a separate location, just in case you lose the originals.

Which name should I use when booking my honeymoon? Even if you're planning on changing your name, book your plane or cruise reservations under the name listed on your passport and driver's license. With airport security tighter than it's ever been, any discrepancy may be enough to bar you from boarding your flight. Hotel reservations, however, can be booked under your married name. Carry a copy of your marriage license with you to avoid any questions. For instance, in some countries, a couple traveling together may not be allowed to share a room without proof of marriage. Mention this to your officiant if you will have to arrange to photocopy the marriage certificate after the ceremony.

What can we do to protect our health during our trip? Carry a supply of any medications you are taking (in their original containers), as well as duplicate prescriptions (that goes for contact lenses, too). If you're traveling abroad, call your health insurer to see whether you're covered for illness or injury outside the United States. Still concerned? Fill in the gaps with travel insurance; comprehensive plans typically include coverage for care (as long as you begin treatment while you're abroad) and for evacuation to the nearest hospital. Check with the Centers for Disease Control and Prevention (*cdc.gov/travel/#geographic*), and the World Health Organization (WHO) at (*who.int/home/map_ht.html*), for a list of vaccines and medications recommended for your particular destination. Many immunizations take time to take effect, or must be administered in several steps, over the course of months or weeks, so make an appointment with your doctor as soon as you determine your destination. Have him or her record the shots in a WHO booklet, and bring it along as proof of inoculation.

Should we buy trip insurance? It can be a good idea. If your flight is delayed because of bad weather, and the ship sails without you, you'll be reimbursed. If a broken bone sidelines you from a white-water rafting adventure, you'll also be glad you bought trip insurance, which covers you against trip delay or cancellation, as well as for lost, stolen, or delayed luggage. It also provides emergency assistance—even medical evacuation. First, confirm the coverage provided by your home-owners' or renters' policy and through credit cards. Then, contact your travel agent or a reputable insurance company if you need additional insurance (see Appendix, under Chapter 4, "Planning Your Wedding"). Be sure to ask plenty of questions. Not every policy covers injuries due to high-risk activities like diving and rock-climbing, or cancellations due to travel advisories, terrorism, or "mass" events.

How do we turn frequent-flier miles into a honeymoon trip? If you've been stockpiling frequent-flier miles (a minimum of 25,000 miles on any one carrier), at least one

once you get there: 10 cost cutters

1. Use public transportation instead of taxis.

2. Visit restaurants outside tourist areas.

3. Read the fine print; sometimes tips and service charges are included in hotel rates and restaurant bills.

4. If you're going to make calls from your room, use a calling card, or better yet (if you're in the U.S.), a cell phone with a nationwide calling plan. In European cities and towns, call home from the post office.

5. Compare exchange rates at banks before changing your money at your hotel (look, too, for commissions—banks and exchange counters often charge them, hotels usually don't).

6. Steer clear of the minibar, brimming with high-priced snacks.

7. Buy a youth-oriented travel guide before you go (it can help you locate low-priced hotels and restaurants).

8. Pack all the film, sunblock, and other toiletries you think you might need—to avoid making a pit stop in notoriously expensive resort gift shops.

9. To make sure you're really getting a duty-free bargain, check items at home before you leave to get an idea of prices.

10. This trip is for you; don't load up on presents for everyone else.

of you can probably fly for free, perhaps with a discount on a rental car or hotel, too. Better yet, trade in 20,000 miles to upgrade two domestic coach seats to first-class. Ask your airline or travel agent about blackout dates and other restrictions.

Is it true we can save money in the off-season? In the off-season, hotels discount their rates by as much as 40 percent and may offer off-season bargain packages (with meals, sight-seeing excursions and a rental car, for instance) that are unavailable at other times. In the Caribbean, Mexico, and Florida, the low season is summer (generally April 15 to November 15). Even though these tropical resorts can be delightful in June, it's in winter (high season) that travelers will pay top dollar for the sun and sand. In subtropical Bermuda, where winters can be cool, low season extends from fall until spring. *Note:* Hawaiian honeymoons are in demand year-round; resorts there generally do not offer seasonal rates. Going to Europe in March or October may be less expensive than in July. Ski resorts, off-season, provide great horseback riding and mountain climbing; contact chambers of commerce to inquire about regional events and arts festivals.

How can we cut costs when planning our honeymoon? Consider a travel agency with a wedding registry; then guests can make gift donations toward your trip (gift cards will not list monetary amounts). There are also honeymoon registry sites on the web, such as *honeyluna.com*, and *thehoneymoon.com*. Ask your travel agent about prepackaged tours, which include airfare, hotel, food, and sightseeing. With so many hotels vying for your business, there are often special rates that may be available at any time. Cruises are also a good value; they include food, entertainment, and several destinations (see Appendix, under Chapter 19, "Going Away"). Decide early and take advantage of early-booking bonuses (cash discounts, free rental cars, extra land tours). Traveling off-season will also stretch your budget (see "Honeymoon-Budget Tips" box). For greater discounts, look for packages that include airfare, rental car, and hotel. Also check your organization memberships, which may lower your car and hotel rates; tell your travel agent which alumni groups, professional organizations, groups such as the American Automobile Association (AAA), you belong to. Turn in your frequent-flier miles early, since it can take up to four weeks to receive ticket coupons. And wherever you travel, tell hotel management that you're honeymooning; they may upgrade your room, or offer champagne, chocolates, or a fruit basket.

Ask yourselves these questions: Is it vital to be right on the ocean, or could you be just as content staying in a hotel with a short walk to the beach? Could you save money by renting a condo with a small kitchen and having some of your meals there? If you go the resort route, find out whether continental breakfasts are included in your room rate. And get to know your meal plan acronyms: CP (Continental Plan) means breakfast only; AP (American Plan) includes two meals daily; and EP (European Plan) offers no meals. A la carte your only option? Try to eat off-property as much as you can. Also have your travel agent ask if the hotel is offering any special rates.

Often, if a resort is under construction, it will offer lower rates during the duration. If you don't mind the inconvenience, it can be a cost-effective way to honeymoon.

If you travel abroad, check exchange rates first. Change only a small amount of money before you go; you'll get a better exchange rate at a bank once you arrive. (*Note:* Hotels offer the *least* favorable rate of exchange.) Check with your bank for the locations of ATMs at your destination. They'll have the best exchange rate of all.

Honeymoon Countdown

One year before. Start making inquiries. Top accommodations in U.S. national parks and the most popular country inns can fill up a year in advance. You'll also need to get a move on if you'll be honeymooning over any major holiday.

Nine months before. With your fiancé, create a wish list. Start researching your dream destination on the Internet, in guidebooks and the travel sections of newspapers and magazines. Contact the tourist offices of the places you're considering (many international destinations have offices in major cities, as well as toll-free numbers) to request brochures and information.

Six months before. Firm up your budget and the amount of time you can be away, then ask friends and family to recommend a good travel agent. If you don't have a major credit card, apply for one now. Many hotels and rental companies require that you have one. Still, go easy on the plastic. Incurring major debt is no way to start off your marriage.

Five months before. Meet with your travel agent to discuss budget, destination, and possible itineraries. Once you've made your decision, have your agent finalize bookings.

Four months before. If you're traveling to a foreign country, you'll need passports or some proof of citizenship, usually notarized copies of your birth certificates. (For the phone number and location of your local passport office, call the Federal Information Center at 800-688-9889, or go to *iafb.travel.state.gov*). Some destinations require a visa; ask your travel agent for information. If you're traveling overseas, check with the tourist boards or the consulates of the countries you plan to visit about necessary inoculations.

Two months before. Check out your wardrobe. Do you need a new bathing suit? Ski pants? Take stock of your luggage, too. Will your old bags do the job, or is it time to invest in a new set?

One month before. Fill any prescriptions you'll need (including birth control).

Two weeks before. Do you have airline tickets and seat assignments? Your hotel and rental car confirmations? If not, call

portable medicine chest

Drugs made overseas may vary in strength and quality from those back home. Pack your own:

- prescription medications in original bottles (to avoid customs hassles). Pack in carry-on for safety; take all prescriptions with you.
- cold remedies
- antiseptic
- anti-itch ointment, anti-bacterial ointment
- extra birth control
- pain relievers
- bandages
- thermometer
- spare eyeglasses and contact lenses
- bug spray
- remedies for diarrhea and upset stomach

your travel agent (or airline and hotel) and alert him/her. Arrange for your transportation from the reception to your wedding-night hotel, and then from the hotel to the airport.

One week before. Buy traveler's checks. Purchase enough foreign currency (at a bank or currency broker, such as Amer-ican Express) to pay for taxis, tips, and perhaps your first couple of meals. Begin packing.

One day before. Finish last-minute packing. Leave copies of your itinerary with your family or friends. Confirm your outbound flight and transportation to the airport. Bon voyage!

Honeymoon Health

It's your worst nightmare: getting sick on your honeymoon. Fortunately, most travel-related illness are short-lived, and many can be prevented.

Don't drink the water. To head off trav-eler's diarrhea and the nausea, cramps, and other symptoms that go along with it, avoid tap water and ice in certain tropical areas (such as Mexico), and in the rural areas of many foreign coun-tries. Stick with bottled water and bev-erages, and hot coffee or tea. (Forgo the ice, and watch for condensation on cans, bottles, and glasses.) Bring along an anti-diarrhea medicine, such as Imod-ium or Lomotil, just in case.

Make sure meals are served piping hot. Since contaminated food can trigger stomach problems, be sure meals are served hot. It's fine to eat breads and fruits that you peel, but avoid melons—which may be filled with water to increase weight—and also raw vegeta-bles, salsa, guacamole, and dairy prod-ucts. To stave off digestive disorders, take two Pepto-Bismol tablets (or another anti-nausea medication) with meals, plus two at bedtime (you can safely take this dosage for up to three weeks).

Use a sunscreen. While you may think you look better with a little color, it's easy to overdo sun exposure in tropical climates, even if you're just out shop-ping. Use a sunscreen with a Sun Pro-tection Factor (SPF) of 15 or more, and a pair of UV-protective sunglasses in any warm-weather spot. Try to stay out of the sun during the time of day when rays are strongest (between 11 A.M. and 3 P.M.). Schedule museum visits and naps dur-ing those hours.

Soothe "honeymoon cystitis," otherwise known as a urinary-tract infection. Since this infection is more common during periods of increased sexual activ-ity, such as a honeymoon, ask your gyne-cologist to prescribe medication, and pack it, just in case. (Common symptoms are burning during urination and increased frequency of urination; in bad cases, blood in the urine.) Make sure you keep the pills in the original container to avoid hassles at customs.

Prepare ahead for motion sickness. Island hopping or cruising? Pack anti-nausea pills, such as Dramamine, Bonine, or Travel Garde acupressure cloth wristbands to help prevent motion sickness from ruining your trip.

Guard against bugs. If you'll be outside a lot, particularly in a humid climate, bring along insect repellent to ward off mosquitoes. Consult guidebooks to determine the level of protection you'll need for the time of your trip.

Guard against allergies. Pack any allergy medications you normally take in their original bottles.

If you become ill while traveling abroad, ask your hotel or the U.S. embassy or consulate for a referral to an English-speaking doctor. Before you leave, write to the International Association for Medical Assistance to Travelers for a list of doctors overseas (see Appendix, under Chapter 19, "Going Away").

Travel Dilemmas

I want to go to the beach; he wants to ski. What should we do? The secret is compromise. Will he settle for water-skiing? If not, try to work in some of your favorite things, too. Agree that you'll ski mornings, then spend the afternoon together shopping, sightseeing, hot-tubbing, and getting to know your fireplace. Or, do a "sea and ski" honeymoon—one week in a warm climate, the next week at a ski resort.

My fiancé wants to plan a surprise honeymoon for me, but I'm worried I won't pack the right things. Any ideas? Make sure the surprise doesn't go sour; ask him to tell you what type of destination you're heading for (tropical island, big city, mountain resort), what temperatures to pack for, and how formal or casual it is. Or have him confide in your maid of honor, who can steer you in the right direction.

We're honeymooning at my parents' Florida condo, which fits our budget. How can we make the trip special? Why not travel by train—a romantic journey? Once you arrive, indulge in an elaborate beach picnic. Fill the place with a rainbow of flowers and eat out at special places a few times. Rent a convertible. Put a "Do Not Disturb" sign on the door.

What if we lose our plane/train/cruise tickets? Tickets are the equivalent of cash, so act quickly. Call your travel agent—he or she may be able to get new tickets delivered, even to your hotel. If you're already at the airport, airlines will ask you to file a lost-ticket claim. You'll have to buy new tickets, but the airline will refund your money within ninety days if no one finds and uses the originals. It's wise to keep a copy of your plane tickets. Then you can call the airline and report the specific ticket number lost; airline officials may be able to intercept the ticket if someone tries to use or change it. If you have proof of purchase (a credit-card receipt), an airline ticket-agent or his or her manager may re-issue the tickets for you (each airline's policy varies).

On Amtrak, and all trains, tickets are viewed like cash; if you lose them, they're gone. (You'll have to repurchase them at full cost.)

For cruise tickets, find the company representative at the pier. Since a room has been reserved in your name, if you provide identification, he or she should be able to issue a new ticket with little trouble.

What if we miss the plane/train/boat? Phone ahead, if possible. Airlines will rebook you on the next available flight, even on another airline, and accept the tickets you hold. (If you had nonrefundable tickets, there might be a nominal additional fee.)

Amtrak and most railroad companies will book you on the next available train.

An agent of a cruise line or the local port authority will tell you whether it's possible to charter a launch if the ship is still in sight or how to fly to meet it. If, when booking a cruise, you also book your airfare through the cruise line, it's the responsibility of the cruise line to get you to the ship if the flight is delayed.

What if our luggage doesn't show up after our flight or in our room on a cruise? Some luggage mishaps can be prevented by attaching indestructible identification tags on the outside of bags; enclosing identification cards inside luggage, as well; and making sure luggage is tagged for the correct destination by the airline when you check in. Also get to the baggage-claim area promptly to minimize the likelihood that bags might be stolen off the carousel. (Tie ribbon to the handles to ensure that they're easy to spot.)

If your luggage doesn't show up on the carousel, tell the representative in the baggage office at the airport and present your luggage-check tags. You'll be asked to fill out a form describing the pieces to help airline personnel conduct a search. In nearly all cases, the bags will arrive on the next flight or within twenty-four hours; the airlines will transport them to your hotel. If they still don't turn up, you'll need to describe the bags' appearance clearly; the airlines then tap into a computerized network that matches stray bags with their owners. If the bags still don't surface, you'll need to describe the contents in detail; the airlines will reimburse you. (Reimbursements top out at $2,500 for domestic flights; $9.07 per pound of baggage on international flights. You must provide sales slips for any big-ticket items lost.) The airlines will also provide varying amounts of money to cover any expenses you incur while buying the necessities you need.

While it's rare that cruise companies lose luggage, report any missing bags to the ship's purser. Slip-ups can occur with air-to-sea transfers. If you have purchased your airline ticket through the cruise line, personnel from the ship can search the airport for passengers' luggage as soon as it's reported missing. Use the color-coded luggage tags provided by your cruise company. If there's a delay in getting luggage to you, the cruise company should provide funds to enable you to buy essentials; if bags are never located, they will reimburse you in the range of $300 per person. If you have booked your flight separately, see if the cruise line can assist you, or call the airline directly.

What if we arrive at a hotel and they don't have a room for us? Here's where it helps to have a paper confirmation of your reservation. When you present a confirmation number, the hotel is obligated to find a way to accommodate you—either by upgrading you to a better room or by finding you a room at an equivalent hotel nearby and providing transportation to it.

What if the room is not what we wanted? (There are twin beds, no view, it's too dark, or too cold.) Call the manager, tell him or her the problem, and ask politely but firmly to be moved. In many cases, you can be moved or the problem fixed. It can't hurt to add that you are honeymooners.

What if the resort is not the way it was described in the brochure? Brochures alone may not tell the true story. Rely on personal referrals from friends, a travel agent, or a reputable magazine. For example, *on the water* might mean a waterway separates the hotel and beach. *Traditional* may translate to dated, not quaint. *Deluxe* may be the smallest room, while *junior suite* and *grand-luxe* are more spacious. Ask for specifics on your room size and view; on-site facilities; the location of the beach; restaurants; nightlife.

Also be aware that new resorts and hotels may need up to a year to perfect operations. Research the site carefully before you book. Are rooms fully furnished? Are electricity and hot water connected? Are sports facilities operating smoothly? Are restaurants open? The date of project completion may often be behind schedule; expect up to a six-month delay. Do check if the hotel is offering any special low rates during construction; you should not have to pay full price for diminished services.

What if one of us gets seriously ill? Many hotels have doctors on call (English-speaking in foreign countries) who can come to your room. Some credit-card companies can also put card holders in touch with local physicians. If you have a pre-existing health problem, such as diabetes or asthma, you may want to research doctors and health facilities and consult your own doctor before you leave.

What if we lose our passports? Look around very carefully, then report the loss to the nearest U.S. embassy, and they will instruct you. It will help to have your passport number, date, and place of issue in a safe place, separate from your passport. It also helps to bring along a photocopy of the passport, packed separately from the passport.

What if we run out of money? When traveling, it's always wise to budget several hundred dollars extra to allow for emergencies—the dress that needs dry-cleaning, the muffler that needs repair, the illness that necessitates a doctor's visit. For this reason, too, it's wise to leave home with all of your credit-card bills paid, so that you have the maximum credit limit available to you. Billing your honeymoon accommodations to your credit card will also give you recourse if there is a problem during your stay.

A hotel may agree to send all or part of your bill home. Hotels can often cash checks for small to moderate amounts.

carry-on items

Don't check essential items! Pack them in a carry-on and take them with you on the plane—just in case other luggage is lost or delayed. (Check with your airline for carry-on restrictions.) Include:

- tickets (plus copies, in a separate bag)
- passports, visas, and other proof of citizenship (plus photocopies of each)
- driver's licenses (and photocopies)
- address book
- itinerary with phone numbers
- hotel and car-rental confirmations
- cash for taxis, tipping, and small purchases
- traveler's checks, and major credit cards (write numbers down and pack separately)
- birth control and prescription drugs in original containers
- good jewelry (pack the minimum)
- camera and film
- house and car keys
- change of clothes, underwear, and socks
- swimsuit, coverup, and sunscreen
- glasses, sunglasses, contact-lens case, and solution
- copies of all documents, numbers of traveler's checks, and credit cards, separately.

If you're in a foreign country and funds are getting low, call your hometown bank and arrange for an international draft in the local currency. These days, you'll generally be able to find ATMs in even the smallest cities throughout the world. Check with your bank to see if your card and/or PIN number will work in machines abroad.

How to Pack

Less is more when packing for a honeymoon. You won't want to be burdened with too much luggage. (Remember, you *can* do laundry while traveling.) To get the most into the least space, follow these tips:

Do your research. Read guidebooks, surf the Internet, and/or call the tourist board office of the place you'll be visiting to check on average temperatures and local dress codes.

Make a list. You don't want to forget essentials like underwear, or a bathing suit, or your birth control.

Divide things up. Put half your things in his luggage, half of his in yours. That way if your bags get lost—or vice versa—you'll both be able to function.

Pack heavy things first. Place shoes, hair dryer, travel iron, next to the hinge of the suitcase.

Make a layer of no-wrinkle items. Pack jeans, sweaters, underwear. Fill empty spaces with socks or underpants. Stuff belts and costume jewelry into shoes.

Pack everything that requires careful folding next. Layer in dresses, slacks, skirts, and blouses. Make as few folds as possible. Put plastic bags or tissue paper between layers to cushion against wrinkles; the bags can be used on your trip home for damp swimsuits and dirty laundry.

Pack a collapsible suitcase. This will be useful for carrying souvenirs home.

Pack the items you'll need first, last. If you're planning on hitting the beach right after you check in, pack your swimsuit and sunscreen on top.

Travel Protocol

There used to be a strict code of etiquette for behavior aboard ships, trains, and airplanes. Today, however, common courtesy is the only thing you really need observe (see Appendix, under Chapter 19, "Going Away"). And, pay attention to the following:

Honeymoon Tipping

WHOM TO TIP	HOW MUCH TO TIP	WHEN TO TIP
AIRPORT		
Sky cap	$1.00 per bag	Delivery of luggage to check-in or curb
SHIP		
Cabin Stewards	$5.00 to $6.00 each day, per couple	End of voyage
Waiter	$5.00 to $6.00 each day, per couple	End of voyage
Busboy	$3.00 each day, per couple	End of voyage
Bar & Wine Stewards	15–20% of bill added automatically	With each bill
TRAIN		
Redcap	$1.00 per bag	After service is performed
Cabin Steward	$6.00–10.00 per couple, per night	Each night
Dining Car Waiters	15–20% of bill	Each meal
HOTEL		
Bellhop	$5.00 for bringing bags to your room	When service is delivered
Chambermaid	$2.00–$5.00 per day	Before you leave the room each day (maids usually rotate)
Doorman	$1.00 per bag; $1.00 for hailing taxi	When service is delivered
Maitre 'd/Headwaiter	$5.00 per week for special service	Upon seating
Waiter	15–20% of bill when no service charge	Each meal
Room-Service Waiter	15–20% of the cost of the meal (excluding the room-service charge)	Each meal
TAXI		
Driver	15–20% for good service	Completion of ride
INSTRUCTORS		
Water Skiing, Horseback Riding, etc.	15–20% of bill (unless they own the business)	End of lesson
GOLF		
Caddie	30% over the caddie fee with good service	End of the round
BUS		
Tour Guide	$5.00 per couple, per half day	End of ride

Air travel. Allow plenty of time for travel to the airport, checking luggage, and rechecking seat assignments (you'd hate to be seated three rows apart on your honeymoon). Also make any requests early for vegetarian, diabetic, salt-free, or kosher meals. (To get your honeymoon off to a sparkling start, you might also request on-board champagne.) Tip sky-caps, curbside attendants, and taxi drivers for each bag they handle (see "Honeymoon Tipping" chart).

If your flight is delayed or canceled, which in turn affects your connections, or if your luggage is lost, ask to see a special-service representative and ask him or her to arrange for lodging, a new flight, and money for replacement clothes.

Train travel. On overnight train trips, tip the porter each night for making up your berth and for wake-up calls.

Cruise lines. It's customary to find out where you are seated for dinner as soon as possible and to request any table changes within two days after arrival; tip the steward for this service. On board a cruise ship, except for captains and doctors with professional titles, all personnel are addressed as "Mr." (or "Miss," "Mrs.," or "Ms.").

Hotels. Don't be afraid to remind the staff at check-in you are newlyweds; you may get special treatment (complimentary champagne or cocktails, fruit, candy, or flowers).

Tip the bellman for carrying suitcases to your room. Any problems with the room should be directed to the general manager.

Often, the housekeeping department can handle requests for smaller items, such as extra pillows, towels, blankets, and hair-dryers. Leave a tip at the end of your stay.

To save time when checking out, you can call the front desk in advance to have them prepare your bill or use automated check-out; call the bell desk when your luggage is ready and a bellman will appear shortly to help. Double-check the room—drawers, closets, the bathroom, and any balconies or terraces—to make sure you have all your belongings.

Foreign countries. Master the native words for "please" and "thank-you"; it may improve the service received. Always tip in the local currency. Ask if restaurants include gratuities in the bill.

Honeymoon tipping. Think ahead. Decisions about tipping can be embarrassing and confusing; factors such as quality of service and the economy of the country you visit should always be taken into consideration. (See "Honeymoon Tipping" chart.)

Coming Home

Once again, you may want to repeat the wedding custom of the bride being carried over the threshold of her new home by her husband (see Chapter 2, "Wedding Customs"). This ritual dates from a time when it was thought that carrying the bride would prevent the evil spirits that lurked around doorways from entering through the soles of her feet. Carrying the bride over the threshold ensured future good luck.

The threshold gift. Jewish parents or close friends of the married couple may observe the tradition of the *threshold gift.* Candles, bread, and salt are brought to the new home to express the wish that there may always be light, joy, and plenty to eat in the home.

Visiting around. In the Amish community, newlywed couples spend the first several months of married life visiting family and friends. Even some non-Amish couples tack a few extra days on their honeymoon to visit relatives or friends who couldn't attend the wedding.

Newlywed Checklist

Once you're home from your honeymoon and ready to start married life, you'll find that there are still some postwedding plans and tasks to take care of. Some of these things can be delegated to friends and relatives. Others can be accomplished during the first few months. Settle in and follow this checklist:

Say thanks for wedding help. Call or write to attendants, clergymembers, and others who made your wedding special.

Write thank-you notes. Every gift should receive a prompt handwritten thank-you note, even if you thanked the giver at the wedding (see Chapter 17, "Wedding Gifts" and Appendix, under Chapter 17).

Preserve your wedding dress. Have your gown, veil, and headpiece professionally dry-cleaned (see Chapter 7, "Wedding Clothes"). Inquire about various storage methods with those who specialize in wedding-dress care (see Appendix, under Chapter 7, "Wedding Clothes," for source).

If you changed your name when you were married, change it on all documents, if you haven't already done so. (See Chapter 4, "Planning Your Wedding," "The Name Decision" section.)

Update financial records. Deposit wedding-gift checks, bonds, and stock certificates (if it wasn't already done by attendants). Pay outstanding wedding bills. If you haven't already done so, this is also the time to start discussing a household budget and savings plan.

Evaluate insurance needs. Health, car, and life insurance may have to be adjusted to reflect your married status. Have wedding gifts appraised and insured. Consult your insurance agent if necessary. (See Chapter 17, "Wedding-Gift Protection.")

Unpack, exchange, and store wedding gifts. Consider the giver's feelings before exchanging gifts.

Select photographs and review video. Have any film taken at the wedding and on your honeymoon developed. Look at the photographer's wedding proofs; review the wedding video. Choose photos for your wedding album and order wedding prints for yourselves, relatives, and friends. Put other photos in albums.

Invite family and friends to your home. Plan some time shortly after your honeymoon to get together with attendants, friends, and family members to show them your honeymoon photos and video, as well as your home with their wedding gifts in use. Don't delay these gatherings; even if there are still a few unpacked boxes, everyone will want to see you and share in your happiness.

REAFFIRMATION

Reaffirming your wedding vows is a popular way to pledge your love and commitment to one another all over again. The reaffirmation, while solemn, is not a legal act, so this time you won't need a license, certificate, or blood test. If you want the reaffirmation ceremony to be in a church or synagogue, however, you will need a clergymember to sanction your vows. While the reaffirmation may include many elements of your first wedding, the emphasis now is on the two of you and the personal things that have made your marriage special.

Why a Reaffirmation?

There are many reasons couples decide to reaffirm their marriage vows, and each will influence the style of the reaffirmation service and celebration.

The first ceremony was a civil ceremony, or the couple eloped. Perhaps this was due to religious differences, pregnancy, or a difficult divorce. If you want your religion's blessing of your marriage, you may approach church officials about creating a private church service where you can reaffirm your vows. Many will be more than eager to oblige. You might even include the reaffirmation in a Sunday church or Friday evening synagogue service, with friends and family in attendance.

The couple wish to mark a milestone in their relationship. On their fifteenth—or fiftieth—anniversary, they are proud to announce that they're happy to be married to the same person they fell in love with years before. Or maybe they want to mark the birth of a long-awaited child or a long-strived-for graduation. This cou-

reaffirmation newspaper announcements

Today, it is not uncommon to read announcements of reaffirmations in newspapers. Tips for reaffirming couples:

- Call the lifestyle editors of local newspapers to ask if reaffirmation news should be submitted according to standard wedding announcement guidelines.

- If not, write the news up in the style of a press release, explaining why the decision was made to have a reaffirmation and how it was planned. If reaffirmations are uncommon in that area, it may be reported as a feature story.

- Include the same details found in a wedding announcement (see Chapter 16, "Photography, Videography, & Publicity").

- Be sure to add the number of years married, names of children, and that it is a reaffirmation of marriage vows. Include the text of the reaffirmation vows used.

ple can repeat the same vows they spoke long ago or write new ones that express how their feelings have deepened. The ceremony might resemble a wedding before a congregation in a church or synagogue, with their children included. Or the clergy can visit the couple's home for a private ceremony, followed by a gala celebration. Another option: A reaffirmation at the site where you met (a ski lodge, for example); invite close family and friends.

The couple are finally able to afford the "wedding of their dreams." Perhaps when they first married, money was tight. Invitations might be extended to those who attended the original ceremony and to any new friends or family members with whom the couple would like to celebrate.

The couple recently overcame hardship. Perhaps an ill child has recovered, or one spouse has returned home from serving overseas—and they would like to reaffirm their commitment to one another and to their family. Or maybe a

couple separated for a time and considered divorce but have now decided to reconcile. These couples might invite those who helped them through their difficult period, encouraging them to now join in toasting happy times. Or a couple might feel that their reaffirmation is a ceremony they'd like to share only with one another, stressing the strength of their love in their vows. Following the ceremony, they can plan a romantic dinner for two at a favorite restaurant.

The couple's children wish to host a reaffirmation for their parents. Often, in honor of a milestone anniversary, the couple's children and grandchildren plan and host a reaffirmation ceremony and reception for their parents. The celebration may be a formal ceremony and seated reception, similar to their original wedding, or it may be the big wedding they never had. It may also take place at home, as a cocktail party or backyard barbecue. Some families plan their reaffirmation ceremonies during family-reunion weekends.

Reaffirmation Questions

How soon after our first ceremony can we renew our vows? A reaffirmation, or "Service of Blessing," as it is sometimes known, can take place anytime after a wedding—two days or twenty-five years later.

Can music be part of a reaffirmation ceremony? Yes, as can poetry, Scripture readings, and a blessing of the original wedding rings or new reaffirmation rings. You will want to select music for the processional and recessional—perhaps a few popular songs that are meaningful to you. Include special touches such as the lighting of a Unity Candle (see Chapter 10, "Special Weddings & New Ways to Wed") or the sharing of a cup of wine. Distribute a flower to each member of the congregation. Ask married couples in the pews to rise and renew their vows with you, or, later, to witness the planting of a tree to symbolize the ongoing life of your love and marriage.

Must a reaffirmation ceremony be presided over by a clergymember? Any authority figure may officiate at a reaffirmation, since unlike the actual wedding, this is not a legal function. For those who see renewal of their vows as a religious commitment, a clergymember is the right officiant. A judge might appeal to those who want someone who represents the community to give sanction to their vows. At the family reunion, the patriarch of the clan might preside. A military commander might fill the role for a couple in the service; for a faculty pair, the college president.

How far in advance should planning for a reaffirmation begin? Allow up to twelve months to plan a gala reaffirmation (the same amount of time needed to plan a large, formal wedding); less time for a simpler celebration.

How much money should be budgeted for a reaffirmation? Expect to spend money on the details you didn't have at your first wedding—or on those you want to repeat— such as bouquets, centerpieces, a photographer (and also a videographer to record the event), a seated dinner, and band for dancing after the ceremony. As when planning a budget for a wedding, the celebration can be as simple or elaborate as you choose.

Is it necessary to have a wedding party? Attendants are unnecessary at a reaffirmation ceremony, but some couples choose to invite their original bridesmaids and ushers back to reprise their roles. Many couples also have their children and grandchildren escort them down the aisle, stand at the altar, perform a reading during the ceremony, or make toasts at the reception.

Reaffirmation Preparation

If the couple want a religious reaffirmation, they should visit with their clergymember. Their feelings about the service, vows, music, and readings will be discussed. They'll see existing services and receive guidelines for writing their own.

In some churches and synagogues, reaffirmations may be an annual event. Couples come together at an annual reaffirmation ceremony, often during a weekly worship service, to rededicate themselves to their marriages. All couples in the congregation celebrating an anniversary are invited to participate.

The couple might consider attending an enrichment program for couples. A program such as this may help strengthen and renew their relationship. Worldwide Marriage

---

reaffirmation sites

- a church or synagogue
- a home
- a scenic location (the beach at sunset, or a mountaintop)
- a park or garden
- a sentimental place (the art gallery where you met, the chapel you visited on your honeymoon)
- a historic building or an elegant mansion
- a vacation spot

Encounter, Inc., is a Christian-based organization dedicated to keeping married love alive. During two-day weekend retreats (held away from home), husbands and wives learn to share feelings they may find hard to talk about back home—everything from how much money to invest in savings to how often they make love. At the end of every weekend, all couples are invited to renew their marriage vows. There are many interfaith and nondenominational organizations that provide marriage-enrichment programs. (See the Appendix, under Chapter 20, "Reaffirmation," for marriage-enrichment programs.)

Reaffirmation Invitations

Compiling the guest list. The reaffirming couple should review their wedding guest book, holiday card list, and address book to be sure they are not forgetting any guests. The couple should be sure to include guests who missed their first wedding (a baby was born or someone was overseas in the service). If children wish to invite a few friends to this family celebration, the reaffirming couple should consider it; it shows their children are proud, too!

Selecting the invitation style. Personal handwritten notes are appropriate if the guest list is small; cheery, colorful invitations are suitable if the celebration style is festive (such as a summer barbecue). If the reaffirmation will include a formal ceremony and seated meal, printed or engraved cards are preferred. Couples might personalize their invitations with a reproduced original wedding photo or their own thoughts, in verse, on renewing their vows.

Reaffirmation invitation:

The honour of your presence
is requested at the reaffirmation
of the wedding vows of
Mr. and Mrs. John David Smith
Saturday, the eighth of March
two thousand and three
at three o'clock
All Saints Church
New York, New York

Simplified reception card:

Reception
immediately following
the ceremony
The Plaza Hotel

Kindly respond
860 Park Avenue
New York, New York 10021

Invitation issued by children:

The children of
Daniel and Sarah Patterson
request the honour of your presence
at the reaffirmation ceremony of their
parents
Saturday, the twentieth of June
two thousand and three
at six o'clock in the evening
Bethany Memorial Church
201 Main Street
Bethany, West Virginia

R.s.v.p.
Jan Patterson
21 Highland Avenue
Wheeling, West Virginia 26003

Reaffirmation Attire

As is true for any wedding, what the remarrying bride and groom wear depends on the style and formality of the ceremony and celebration.

THE BRIDE

A new dress. The reaffirming bride may choose a stylish cocktail dress or suit, or a formal evening dress. Depending on the style of the ceremony, the dress may be floor-length (without a train), ballet-length, or skim the knee. As for color, it should be in a soft shade from the traditional bridal palette: white, ivory, pale peach, ecru, or platinum.

The headpiece. If you choose to wear one, it should be something simple and understated, such as jeweled hair sticks or combs, or perhaps some floral accents. A wedding veil, long a traditional symbol of youth and innnocence, is not worn for a reaffirmation ceremony.

The flowers. Fresh blossoms are a beautiful addition to a reaffirming bride's ceremony attire. For an island locale, she might choose to wear a lei; for a garden ceremony, she might carry an armful of bright field flowers or a colorful handtied bouquet.

The accessories. A remarrying bride can complement her dress with the pearls she received from her groom on their wedding day; the diamond eternity ring received on a milestone anniversary; a locket with photos of her children; a three-stone diamond necklace, representing past, present and future; and, of course, her wedding ring, which will be blessed again if the reaffirmation is a religious service.

THE GROOM

New formalwear. If the reaffirmation ceremony is before 5 P.M., for a semi-formal or informal ceremony, the reaffirming groom may wear a dark suit and tie or blazer; for a formal ceremony, a gray cutaway, waistcoat, striped trousers, shirt, and striped tie. If the celebration begins after 5 P.M., for a semiformal ceremony, he may wear a tuxedo or dinner jacket; for a formal ceremony, a tuxedo; for a very formal ceremony, white tie—or a full-dress tailcoat, matching trousers, white waistcoat, wing-collared shirt, and white bow tie.

The accessories. The reaffirming groom can complement his outfit with gifts of jewelry his wife has given him over the years—cuff links, his engagement watch, a new bow tie and cummerbund.

The flowers. The reaffirming groom should always wear a simple fresh floral boutonniere on his left lapel.

THE ATTENDANTS

Attendants' dresses. Female attendants might wear any short or long elegant dress, or dinner suit that matches the bride's formality. The reaffirming bride should ask them to wear dresses of similar length, style, and perhaps color.

reaffirmation gifts

Gifts should not be expected for a reaffirmation, although many guests will probably want to give the couple a memento to mark the happy occasion. The reaffirming couple may:

- Register for items not received the first time around (a completer set to their china pattern or a soup tureen) at a local department store's wedding gift registry (see Chapter 17, "Wedding Gifts").

- Register at specialty stores for leisure-time gifts (golf equipment, picnic accessories).

- Stress that this is a celebration of love by suggesting (by word of mouth, not in writing) that in place of gifts, friends might make a donation to a favorite charity in the couple's names.

Ushers' formalwear. The men's attire should complement the reaffirming groom's (See "The Groom" section.)

Children's attire. Children should wear their best outfits, or perhaps a new outfit specially purchased for the occasion (for a young child, this can be similar to what a flower girl or ring bearer might wear).

Children's flowers. Fresh, colorful nosegays and boutonnieres will add to the spirit of the day and make children feel even more special.

Reaffirmation Vows

Meaningful vows are the focal point of the recommitment that a couple make.

Write original vows. This will ensure that you say what you feel. It will also help to make your relationship healthier by forcing the two of you to address any long-buried issues. You might mention the qualities you most love about each other, describe the things you've created and shared together, mention any hardships overcome, make pledges relating to patience and a sense of humor.

Thank family and friends. Being acknowledged for what they've contributed to the couple's relationship will make guests feel as if they are a vital part of the ceremony.

Alter the traditional marriage vows for a reaffirmation ceremony. Ask the clergymember to use the words *"renewing their promise in the presence of God"* in the service. Or look into the revised marriage services many faiths now offer. Almost every faith celebrates reaffirmation. Some churches have created standard services. Look in *The Book of Common Prayer*, from the Episcopal faith, for "The Blessing of a Civil Marriage;" this ceremony is for couples previously married in a civil ceremony who want to reaffirm their vows in a religious ceremony. The Methodist church uses several services from *A Service of a Christian Marriage*, including "Renewal of Vows," "The Blessing of a Civil Marriage," and "Anniversaries of Marriages." In a reaffirmation ceremony, couples may repeat their original vows, use their church's or synagogue's traditional wedding-ceremony vows, or alter the vows to reflect that the ceremony is a reaffirmation. For example, when the clergymember asks, *"Do you take this woman/man?"* you might answer, *"I did and I do,"* or *"I still take . . ."* Or the clergymember might say, *"William, you have taken Joan to be your wife. Do you promise to love her, comfort her, honor and keep her, in sickness and in health; and, forsaking all others, to be faithful to her as long as you both shall live?"* Guests might be asked *"to uphold these two people in their marriage."*

Reaffirmation Rings

Similar to a wedding ceremony, the reaffirmation ceremony is a time when the clergymember will ask for the couple's original wedding rings, or the new ones they may wear in the future. These rings will be blessed before the reaffirming bride and groom present them to each other with a pledge of love (*"We have lived and loved as we promised long ago in the presence of God, and our past and future are a circle unbroken . . . like this ring, with which I renew my pledge to you of never-ending devotion."*) The couple might ask the clergymember to also bless the gifts that may be given to their children to commemorate the day—a gold charm, locket, or birthstone ring.

The Reaffirmation Reception

The party can be any style— a candlelit dinner for family or a large cocktail party.

Food can be creative. A reaffirmation reception can feature finger foods and drinks; a hearty buffet of favorite family recipes; or a seated dinner with traditional ethnic dishes (see Chapter 4, "Planning Your Wedding"). Some classic touches, such as champagne for toasts and a festive reaffirmation cake, should be included. Use your original wedding-cake topper again.

Delegate planning tasks. This time, the two of you may be the hosts and may be making the arrangements yourselves. It might be a more carefree celebration, though, if you rely on wedding professionals, such as a wedding consultant (see Chapter 4, "Planning Your Wedding"). As hosts, you'll want to spend time with each guest and oversee hospitality details. Don't hesitate to delegate some responsibilities (e.g., writing out place cards or making a list of must-take photos) to children, relatives, and friends.

Include wedding traditions. A receiving line should be included at a large reaffirmation to ensure that the couple have a chance to greet every guest. The reception can include some— or all—of the traditional wedding customs: the first dance, toasts, the cake cutting. Throwing the bouquet may not seem as appropriate; you might choose another way to pass on your "good fortune" to guests. You might present them with symbolic favors—rooted sprigs of forget-me-nots (signifying true love) or ivy or veronica (meaning fidelity) to take home and plant.

Don't forget decorations. The reaffirmation site might be trimmed with fresh, colorful floral arrangements and nostalgic items (enlarged pictures of your original wedding— with space around the borders of one special photo for all guests to sign; place cards printed with your engagement photo).

reaffirmation-ring ideas

- reaffirmation wedding bands of diamonds or gemstones that stack, or are worn on either side of your original wedding band

- an anniversary ring (usually a band of diamonds, meant to be worn alone or as a complement to the original wedding band)

- a gemstone ring (precious stones set with the birthstones of the husband and wife, as well as each child)

- an eternity ring (with a diamond or other precious stone for each year together)

reaffirmation favors

Guests will appreciate a token to remember the reaffirmation. The reaffirming couple might consider:

• a picture of their family

• a CD with "their song"

• a scroll or small book that contains an inspirational passage that has shaped their marriage

Plan to have keepsakes and mementos. Since you will want to cherish the memories of this special day, hire a professional photographer and/or videographer to record all the happy moments. Everyone will have fun leafing through the original guest book; don't forget to provide another for guests to write new messages, good wishes, and humorous recollections.

A Second Honeymoon

You may want to take a celebratory trip, either directly after the reaffirmation or in the near future. All of the preparations and the excitement of the occasion will rekindle romance, and romance is good for marriage! It might be just the right time for you to take the trip you've always dreamed of, or it may be a chance to splurge for a weekend at an elegant resort. Give yourselves a little private time and space to reflect on all the joy you've rediscovered.

APPENDIX

The following publications, organizations and services can help provide further information and support for every step of your wedding-planning experience.

1. YOUR ENGAGEMENT

American Gem Society (for a free consumer kit on diamonds and fine jewelry)
8881 W. Sahara Avenue
Las Vegas, NV 89117
(800) 346-8485
Fax: (702) 255-7420
www.ags.org

Cultured Pearl Information Center
c/o Tele-press Associates
321 E. 53rd Street
New York, NY 10022
(212) 688-5580
Fax: (212) 688-5857
www.pearlinfo.com

Diamond Information Center
466 Lexington Avenue
New York, NY 10017
(212) 210-7920
www.diamondinformationcenter.com

Diamond Ring Buying Guide: How to Evaluate, Identify and Select Diamonds and Diamond Jewelry, 6th Ed., by Renee Newman. International Jewelry Publications, 2002.

Engagement and Wedding Rings, 2nd Ed.: The Definitive Buying Guide for People in Love, by Antoinette Matlins, Antonio C. Bonanno. GemStone Press, 1999.

Gemological Institute of America (G.I.A.) Trade Laboratory (appraisals)
(800) 421-7250
gia.org/gemtradelab/index.cfm

International Colored Gemstone Association (for colored gemstone information)
19 West 21st Street, #705
New York, NY 10010-6805
www.gemstone.org

Jewelers of America
52 Vanderbilt Avenue, 19th floor
New York, NY 10017
(800) 223-0673
(646) 658-0246
Fax: (646) 658-0256
jewelers.org

The Jewelers' Vigilance Committee (if you think a jeweler has been deceptive about a stone you purchased)
25 West 45th Street, Suite 400
New York, NY 10036
(212) 997-2002
Fax: (212) 997-9148
jvclegal.org

New York City Department of Consumer Affairs Their pamphlet, *Avoiding the Wedding Bell Blues*, is now available free, online at:
www.nyc.gov/html/dca/html/wedding.html

Popping the Question: Real-Life Stories of Marriage Proposals from the Romantic to the Bizarre, by Sheree Bykofsky, Laurie Viera. Walker & Co., 1997.

World Gold Council (brochures)
(212) 317-3800
Fax: (212) 688-0410
www.gold.org

2. WEDDING CUSTOMS

American Folklife Center
Folklife Reading Room
Library of Congress
101 Independence Ave. SE
Washington, DC 20540-4610
(202) 707-5510
Fax: (202) 707-2076
http://lcweb.loc.gov/folklife/

askginka.com (for information on a wide variety of ethnic, religious and theme wedding traditions and celebrations)

BRIDE'S Little Book of Customs and Keepsakes, by the Editors of BRIDE'S. Clarkson Potter, 1994.

Irish Wedding Traditions: Using Your Irish Heritage to Create the Perfect Wedding, by Shannon McMahon-Lichte. Hyperion, 2001.

Jumping the Broom: The African-American Wedding Planner, by Harriette Cole. Henry Holt & Co., 1995.

Marriage Customs in Many Lands, by Henry Neville Hutchinson. Gale Research, 1975.

The Nubian Wedding Book: Words and Rituals to Celebrate and Plan an African-American Wedding, by Ingrid Sturgis. Crown, 1997.

Quaker Information Center
1501 Cherry Street
Philadelphia, PA 19102
(215) 241-7024
Fax: (215) 567-2096
http://www.afsc.org/qic.htm

Wild Geese and Tea; An Asian-American Wedding Planner, by Shu Shu Costa. Riverhead Books, 1997.

3. PREWEDDING PARTIES

Bridal Showers, 2nd Ed.: Special Touches and Unique Ideas for Throwing a Fabulous Shower, by Beverly Clark. Wilshire Publications, 1999.

The Complete Idiot's Guide to Bridal Showers, by Jennifer Barr. MacMillan, 1999.

The Wedding Shower Book, by Janet Anastasio. Adams Media, 1994.

4. PLANNING YOUR WEDDING

American Association for Marriage and Family Therapy
112 S. Alfred Street
Alexandria, VA 22314
(703) 838-9809
Fax: (703) 838-9805
www.aamft.org

American Ethical Union (for referrals to local affiliates and listings of officiants who perform interfaith and nondenominational ceremonies)
2 West 64th Street
New York, NY 10023
(212) 873-6500
Fax: (212) 362-0850
www.aeu.org

American Rental Association (owners of party-rental and referrals for party-stores nationwide)
1900 19th Street
Moline, IL 61265
(800) 334-2177
Fax: (309) 764-1533
www.ararental.org

The Amy Vanderbilt Complete Book of Etiquette, by Nancy Tuckerman and Nancy Dunnan. Doubleday, 1995.

Association for Couples in Marriage Enrichment (A.C.M.E.)
P.O. Box 10596
Winston-Salem, NC 27108
(800) 634-8325
Fax: (336) 721-4746
www.bettermarriages.org

Association of Bridal Consultants
200 Chestnutland Road
New Milford, CT 06776-2521
(860) 355-0464
Fax: (860) 354-1404
www.bridalassn.com

Bentley Meeker Lighting & Staging, Inc.
432 East 91st Street, 3rd floor
New York, NY 10128
(212) 722-3349
Fax: (212) 722-8803
bentleymeeker.com

BRIDE'S Wedding Planner, by the Editors of BRIDE'S. Fawcett Books, 1997.

The Complete Idiot's Guide to the Perfect Wedding, by Teddy Lenderman. MacMillan, 1997.

Emily Post on Weddings, by Elizabeth L. Post. HarperCollins, 1994.

Emily Post's Wedding Etiquette: Cherished Traditions and Contemporary Ideas for a Joyous Celebration (4th Ed.), by Peggy Post. Harper Resource, 2001.

Emily Post's Weddings [Abridged], by Emily Post, Peggy Post (Audiocassette). Harper Audio, 1999.

The Everything Wedding Book: Everything You Need to Know to Survive Your Wedding Day and Actually Even Enjoy It, by Janet Anastasio, Michelle Bevilacqua. Adams Media, 2000.

How to Have the Wedding You Want, by Danielle Claro. Berkley Books, 1995.

Insurance Information Institute
110 William Street
New York, NY 10038
(212) 346-5500
www.iii.org

Interfaith Wedding Ceremonies: Samples and Sources, **edited by Joan Hawxhurst.** Dovetail Publishing, 1997.

International Special Events Society (ISES) (organization of party-planning professionals)
401 N. Michigan Avenue
Chicago, IL 60611-4267
(800) 688-4737
Fax: (312) 673-6953
www.ises.com

Jumping the Broom: The African-American Wedding Planner, by Harriette Cole. Henry Holt & Co., 1995.

June Wedding, Inc. (for referrals to bridal consultants in your area)
4041 Raphael Drive
Plano, TX 75093-6912
(702) 474-9558
www.junewedding.com

Legendary Brides: From the Most Romantic Weddings Ever, Inspired Ideas for Today's Brides, by Letitia Baldridge. Harper Collins, 2000.

Marry Like a Man: The Essential Guide for Grooms, by Peter N. Nelson. Plume, 1992.

Miss Manners on Weddings, by Judith Martin. Crown Publishers, 1999.

National Easter Seal Society (for information on making your wedding site accessible to disabled guests)
230 West Monroe Street
Suite 1800
Chicago, IL 60606
(800) 221 6827
Fax: (312) 726-1494
www.easter-seals.org

National Limousine Association (for member referrals in your area)
49 S. Maple Avenue
Marlton, NJ 08053
(800) NLA-7007 [652-7007]
Fax: (856) 596-2145
www.limo.org/consumer.jsp

The Nubian Wedding Book: Words and Rituals to Celebrate and Plan an African-American Wedding, by Ingrid Sturgis. Crown, 1997.

PAIRS (Practical Application of Intimate Relationship Skills) (for premarital counseling)
PAIRS Foundation, Ltd.
1056 Creekford Drive
Weston, FL 33326
(888) 724-7748
www.pairs.org

The Perfect Wedding, by Maria McBride-Mellinger, Harper-Collins, 1997.

Places: A Directory of Public Places for Private Events & Private Places for Public Functions, by Hannelore Hahn and Tatiana Stoumen. Tenth House Enterprises, Inc. 1998.

Planned Parenthood Federation of America, Inc. (for birth control brochures and information)
810 Seventh Avenue
New York, NY 10019
(212) 541-7800
Fax: (212) 245-1845
www.ppfa.org/ppfa

PREPARE (for a list of trained clergy and counselors in your area, send a self-addressed, stamped envelope to:)
PREPARE
P.O. Box 190
Minneapolis, MN 55440-0190
(800) 331-1661
Fax: (651) 636-1668
www.lifeinnovation.com

Proflowers.com (sells flowers at near-wholesale prices)
5005 Waterbridge Vista Drive, Suite 200
San Diego, CA 92121
(888) FRESHEST [373-7437]
www.proflowers.com

Rabbinic Center for Research and Counseling (for a fee, this group will send related articles, plus a list of rabbis who will perform interfaith marriages)
128 East Dudley Avenue
Westfield, NJ 07090
(908) 233-0419
Fax: (908) 233-6459
www.rcronline.org

Real Weddings: A Celebration of Personal Style, by Sally Kilbridge, Mallory Samson. Clarkson Potter, 1999.

Registry of Interpreters for the Deaf
333 Commerce Street
Alexandria, VA 22314
(703) 838-0030
Fax: (703) 838-0454
www.rid.org

SIECUS (Sexuality Information and Education Council of the U.S.)
130 W. 42nd Street
Suite 350
New York, NY 10036-7802
(212) 819-9770
Fax: (212) 819-9776
www.siecus.org

There Must Be Something for the Groom to Do, by Paula Begoun and Stephanie Bell. Beginning Press, 1996.

Wedding Details, by Mary Norden, Polly Wreford. Harper Resource, 2000.

The Wedding Library
50 East 81st Street
New York, NY 10028
(212) 327-0100
weddinglibrary.net

Weddings, by Colin Cowie, Jean T. Barrett. Little Brown & Company, 1998.

Weddings: A Celebration, by Beverly Clark. Wilshire Publications, 1996.

Weddings for Dummies, by Marcy Blum, Laura Fisher Kaiser. Wiley Publishing, Inc., 1997.

Weddingsurance (insurance coverage for wedding gifts, photography, wedding clothing, cancellation, illness, liability, and other items)
Fireman's Fund
R. V. Nunncio & Associates
P.O. Box 307
Fawnskin, CA 92333
(800) ENGAGED [364-2433]
Fax: (909) 866-4659
www.firemansfund.com/products/personal/event/wedding.html

Wild Geese and Tea; An Asian-American Wedding Planner, by Shu Shu Costa. Riverhead Books, 1997.

5. INVITATIONS & ANNOUNCEMENTS

The Air Force Wife Handbook: A Complete Social Guide, by Ann Crossley and Carol E. Keller. ABI Press, 1992.

C. R. Gibson Company
501 Nelson Place
Nashville, TN 37214
(615) 889-9000
Fax: (615) 391-3166

Rae Michaels Ltd.
521 Madison Avenue
New York, NY 10022
(212) 688-2256
Fax: (212) 688-2004

Rexcraft
Rexburg, ID 83441
(800) 635-4653
Fax: (800) 826-2712

Service Etiquette, by Oretha D. Swartz. Naval Institute Press, 1988. For information on ordering and fee contact:
U.S. Naval Institute
2062 Generals Highway
Annapolis, MD 21401
(800) 233-8764

The Social Secretary (a computerized calligraphy and printing service in 500 stationery, party, and card stores, nationwide)

(212) 956-2707
Fax: (212) 956-2904

Society for Calligraphy
P.O. Box 64174
Los Angeles, CA 90064-0174
(323) 931-6146
www.societyforcalligraphy.com

6. THE WEDDING PARTY

Weddings: A Celebration, by Beverly Clark. Wilshire Publications, 1996.

7. WEDDING CLOTHES

12251 Tech Road
Silver Spring, MD 20904
(800) 638-2627
(301) 622-1900
www.ifi.org

International Formalwear Association
401 North Michigan Avenue, Suite 2200
Chicago, IL 60611
(312) 644-6610, ext. 338
Fax: (312) 321-4098
www.formalwear.org

Legendary Brides: From the Most Romantic Weddings Ever, Inspired Ideas for Today's Brides, by Letitia

Baldridge. Harper Collins, 2000.

StyleNoir: The First How-To Guide to Fashion Written with Black Women in Mind, by Constance C. R. White. Perigee, 1998.

Vera Wang on Weddings, by Vera Wang. Harper Resource, 2001.

Wedding Gowns and Other Bridal Apparel, by Jo Packham. Sterling Publishing Co., 1994.

International Fabricare Institute (contact this organization for wedding-gown dry cleaning questions, or problems, or for help in restoring an antique wedding gown.)

8. YOUR WEDDING CEREMONY

American Bible Society (suppliers for Today's English Version of the Bible)
1865 Broadway
New York, NY 10023
(212) 408-1200
www.americanbible.org

Bride's Little Book of Vows and Rings, by the Editors of BRIDE'S. Clarkson Potter, 1994.

The Everything Wedding Vows Book, by Janet Anastasio and Michelle Bevilacqua. Adams Media, 2001.

I Do: A Guide to Creating Your Own Unique Wedding Ceremony, by Sydney Barbara Metrick. Celestial Arts Publishing, 2001.

Into the Garden: A Wedding Anthology, by Robert Hass and Stephen Mitchell. HarperPerennial, 1994.

Marriage in Christ (a participation booklet for the Nuptial Mass)
The Liturgical Press
Saint John's Abbey
P.O. Box 7500
Collegeville, MN 56321-7500
(800) 858-5450

Fax: (800) 455-5899
www.litpress.org

Wedding Readings, by Eleanor Munro. Viking Penguin, 1996.

Weddings from the Heart, by Daphne Rose Kingma. Conari Press, 1995.

With These Words I Thee Wed: Contemporary Wedding Vows for Today's Couples, by Barbara Royster Eklof. Adams Media, 1989.

9. RELIGIOUS RITUALS AND REQUIREMENTS

Beth Din of America (Jewish/Orthodox)
305 Seventh Avenue

New York, NY 10001-6008
(212) 807-9042
Fax: (212) 807-9183
www.bethdin.org

Church of Jesus Christ of Latter-Day Saints (Mormon)
Public Affairs Department
50 E. North Temple Street
Salt Lake City, UT 84150
(801) 240-1000
http://www.lds.org

Evangelical Lutheran Church in America
8765 West Higgins Road
Chicago, IL 60631
(800) 638-3522
Fax: (773) 380-1465
http://www.elca.org

General Council Assemblies of God
1445 Boonville Avenue
Springfield, MO 65802-1894
(417) 862-2781
www.ag.org

Greek Orthodox Archdiocese of America
10 East 79th Street
New York, NY 10021
(212) 570-3500
Fax: (212) 570-3569
www.goarch.org

Presbyterian Center, News Services Office
100 Witherspoon Street
Louisville, KY 40202-1396
(800) 872-3283
Fax: (502) 569-5018
www.pcusa.org

Quaker Information Center
(For information on Quaker marriage procedures)
1501 Cherry Street
Philadelphia, PA 19102
(215) 241-7024
Fax: (215) 567-2096
www.afsc.org/qic.htm

The New Jewish Wedding, by Anita Diamant. Fireside, 2001.

Union of American Hebrew Congregations (Jewish/Reform)
633 Third Avenue
New York, NY 10017-6778
(888) 634-8242
(212) 650-4190
www.uahc.org

Unitarian Universalist Association
(for information on interfaith and nondenominational ceremonies)
25 Beacon Street
Boston, MA 02108
(617) 742-2100
www.uua.org

10. SPECIAL WEDDINGS & NEW WAYS TO WED

askginka.com (for information on a wide variety of ethnic, religious and theme wedding traditions and celebrations)

The Creative Wedding Idea Book: Bold Suggestions to Make Every Aspect of Your Wedding Special, by Jacqueline Smith. Adams Media, 1994.

151 Ways to Make Your Wedding Special, by Don Altman. Moon Lake Media, 1994.

Service Etiquette, by Oretha D. Swartz. Naval Institute Press, 1989. For information on ordering and fee contact:

U.S. Naval Institute
2062 Generals Highway
Annapolis, MD 21401
(800) 233-8764

Wedded Bliss: A Victorian Bride's Handbook, by Molly Dolan Blayney. Abbeville Press, 1992.

www.getawayweddings.com (for information on destination and faraway weddings, including hiring consultants)

11. REMARRIAGE

Making Your Second Marriage a First-Class Success, by Douglas Moseley, Naomi Moseley. Prima Publishing Group, 1998.

The Stepfamily Foundation
333 West End Avenue
New York, NY 10023
(212) 877-3244

Fax: (212) 362-7030
www.stepfamily.org

Weddings for Complicated Families: The New Etiquette for Couples with Divorced Parents and Those Planning a Remarriage, by Margorie Engel. Mount Ivey Press, 1993.

12. STICKY SITUATIONS, UNEXPECTED SITUATIONS

Better Business Bureau of Metropolitan New York (send for wedding advisory material; contact for ordering information and fee)
257 Park Avenue South
New York, NY 10010-7384
(212) 533-6200
www.newyork.bbb.org

or

Council of Better Business Bureaus (locate a Better Business Bureau by state or zip code)
4200 Wilson Boulevard
Arlington, VA 22203
(703) 276-0100
Fax: (703) 525-8277
www.bbbonline.org

The Bride Did What? Etiquette for the Wedding-Impaired, by Martha Woodham. Longstreet Press, 1995.

Consumer Information Center
Pueblo, Colorado 81009
(888) 8-PUEBLO [878-3256]
www.pueblo.gsa.gov

Weddings for Complicated Families: The New Etiquette for Couples with Divorced Parents and Those Planning a Remarriage, by Margorie Engel. Mount Ivey Press, 1993.

13. YOUR RECEPTION

A Passion for Parties, by David Tutera, Laura Morton. Simon & Schuster, 2001.

The Bride & Groom's Menu Cookbook, by Abigail Kirsch with Susan M. Greenberg. Broadway Books, 2002.

Bride's Little Book of Cakes and Toasts, by the Editors of BRIDE'S. Clarkson Potter, 1993.

Cakewalk: Adventures with Sugar, by Margaret Braun, Quentin Bacon. Rizzoli, 2001.

Cater Your Own Wedding, by Michael Flowers and Donna Bankhead. New Page Books, 2000.

Colette's Wedding Cakes, by Colette Peters. Little, Brown and Co., 1997.

The Complete Book of Wedding Toasts, by John William McCluskey, Lois E. Frevert. Arden Book Co., 2000.

Fireworks by Grucci
1 Grucci Lane
Brookhaven, NY 11719
(631) 286-0088
Fax: (631) 286-9036
www.grucci.com

mycoolgift.com/cdw100.html (for custom-created CD wedding favors, stamped with your names and wedding date)

National Limousine Association (for member referrals in your area)
49 S. Maple Avenue
Marlton, NJ 08053
(800) NLA-7007 [652-7007]
Fax: (856) 596-2145
www.limo.org/consumer.jsp

New York Cake & Baking Center (store selling wedding-cake baking supplies)
56 West 22nd Street
New York, NY 10010
(212) 675-2253

The Perfect Wedding Cake, by Kate Manchester, Sylvia Weinstock, Zeva Oelbaum. Stewart Tabori & Chang, 2001.

The Perfect Wedding Reception: Stylish Ideas for Every Season, by Maria McBride-Mellinger, Siobhan McGowan, Ross Whitaker. Harper Resource, 2000.

Romantic Wedding Cakes, by Kerry Vincent. Merehurst, Ltd., 2001.

Toastmasters International (Contact for local referrals to toastmasters and masters of ceremony.)
23182 Arroyo Vista
Rancho Santa Margarita, CA 92688
(949) 858-8255
Fax: (949) 858-1207
www.toastmasters.org

www.wilton.com (online cake-decorating resource)
Wilton Industries
(800) 794-5866
Fax: (888) 824-9520

14. WEDDING MUSIC

American Federation of Musicians
1501 Broadway
Suite 600
New York, NY 10036
(212) 869-1330
Fax: (212) 764-6134
www.afm.org

American Society of Composers, Authors and Publishers (ASCAP) (information about songs and reprinting)
One Lincoln Plaza
New York, NY 10023
(212) 621-6000
Fax: (212) 724-9064
www.ascap.com

BRIDE'S Guide to Wedding Music (CD or cassette)
Angel Classics [#64899], 1993.
(800) 426-9922, Dept. 525154

Cantor's Assembly (Conservative)
Jewish Theological Seminary
3080 Broadway
Suite 613
New York, NY 10027
(212) 678-8834
Fax: (212) 662-8989

New Traditions (for a free brochure on original, contemporary wedding music selections)
P.O. Box 827
East Longmeadow, MA 01028
(800) 447-6647
www.new-wedding-traditions.com/

The New Complete Book of Wedding Music
Hansen House
1820 West Avenue
Miami Beach, FL 33139
(305) 532-5461
Fax: (305) 672-8729

Transcontinental Music Publications (the music-publishing division of the Jewish Reform Movement)
633 Third Avenue
New York, NY 10017
(800) 455-5223
(212) 650-4101
Fax: (212) 650-4109
www.uahc.org/transmp/

Wedding Album for the Classical Pianist, Warner Brothers Publications, 2000.

15. WEDDING FLOWERS

Bouquets: A Year of Flowers for the Bride, by Marsha Heckman, Richard Jung. Stewart Tabori & Chang, 2000.

Bridal Flowers: Arrangements for a Perfect Wedding, by Maria McBride-Mellinger, William Stites. Bulfinch Press, 1992.

BRIDE'S Little Book of Bouquets and Flowers, by the Editors of BRIDE'S. Clarkson Potter, 1993.

Jane Packer's Flowers, by Jane Packer, Simon Brown. Conran Octopus, 2001.

Shane Connolly's Wedding Flowers, by Shane Connolly, Jan Baldwin. Trafalgar Square, 1998.

Teleflora (free brochures available at Teleflora florists)
11444 West Olympic Boulevard, 4th floor
Los Angeles, CA 90064-1544
(800) 898-7484
www.teleflora.com

16. PHOTOGRAPHY, VIDEOGRAPHY, & PUBLICITY

Professional Photographers of America, Inc. (for referrals in your area)
229 Peachtree Street, NE
Suite 2000
Atlanta, GA 30303
(800) 786-6277
www.ppa.com

Wedding and Event Videographers Association, International (for referrals in your area)
8499 S. Tamiami Trail, PMB 208
Sarasota, FL 34238

(941) 923-5334
Fax: (941) 921-3836
www.weva.com

Wedding and Portrait Photographers International (for referrals to photographers in your area)
1312 Lincoln Boulevard
P.O. Box 2003
Santa Monica, CA 90406-2003
(310) 451-0090
Fax: (310) 395-9058
www.wppi-online.com

17. WEDDING GIFTS

Consumer's Resource Handbook (for a sample complaint letter and information about consumer protection)
Consumer Information Center
Dept. 6203D
Pueblo, CO 81009
(888) 8-PUEBLO (878-3256)
www.pueblo.gsa.gov

Crate & Barrel (registry and store information)
(800) 967-6696
www.crateandbarrel.com

Fortunoff (registry and store information)
(800) 367-8866
www.fortunoff.com

Gifts That Make a Difference: How to Buy Hundreds of Great Gifts Sold Through Nonprofits, by Ellen Berry.
Foxglove Publishing, 1992.

Honeymoon Registry Websites
www.honeyluna.com
www.thehoneymoon.com

L. L. Bean (registry information)
(800) 443-8552/(800) 441-5713
www.llbean.com

National Bridal Service (over 1,000 members: bridal salons, small gift shops, fashion, tabletop, and jewelry stores nationwide)
5001 W. Broad Street, Suite 214
Richmond, VA 23230
(804) 288-1220
Fax: (804) 288-1242
www.nationalbridal.com

International Housewares Association
6400 Schafer Court
Suite 650
Rosemont, IL 60018
(847) 292-4200
Fax: (847) 292-4211
www.housewares.org

Target (registry and store information)
(800) 800-8800/(888)-304-4000
www.target.com

The Gift Registry Alliance (registry and store information)
Bloomingdale's (888) 269-3187
The Bon Marché (800) 638-9656
Burdines (800) 878-9783
Goldsmith's (800) 777-BRIDES
Lazarus (800) 777-BRIDES
Macy's (East Coast) (800) 44-WEDDING
Macy's (West Coast) (888) 92-BRIDES
Rich's (800) 777-BRIDES

Tiffany & Co. (registry and store information)
(800) 843-3269
www.tiffany.com

The WeddingChannel.com (internet-based registry service)
www.weddingchannel.com

Williams-Sonoma (registry and store information)
(800) 541-0015/(877) 812-6235
www.williams-sonoma.com

18. WEDDING GUESTS

Miss Manners' Guide to Excruciatingly Correct Behavior, by Judith Martin. Budget Book Service, 1997.

The Amy Vanderbilt Complete Book of Etiquette, by Nancy Tuckerman and Nancy Dunnan. Doubleday, 1995.

19. GOING AWAY

American Citizens' Services/U.S. Department of State
(Contact for up-to-date information on foreign travel, passports, and visa requirements)
United States Department of State
Bureau of Consular Affairs
Room 4811
2201 C Street NW

Washington, DC 20520-4818
(888) 407-4747
(202) 647-5225 (for travel info)
(202) 663-1225 (passport/visa services)
Fax: (202) 647-3000
www.travel.state.gov

Overseas Citizens Services 24-hour Hotline (for emergency help from the state department)
(202) 647-5225

American Society for the Prevention of Cruelty to Animals (A.S.P.C.A.) (for information on traveling with pets)
Public Information Department
424 East 92nd Street
New York, NY 10128-6804
(212) 876-7700
www.aspca.org

American Society of Travel Agents (for a list of members)
(800) 965-2782
(703) 739-2782
Fax: (703) 684-8319
www.astanet.com

Amtrak
60 Massachusetts Avenue NE
Washington, DC 20002-4225
(202) 484-7540
(800) 872-7245
http://www.amtrak.com

Better Business Bureau of Metropolitan New York (Travel packet available for a fee.)
257 Park Avenue South
New York, NY 10010-7384
(212) 533-6200
www.newyork.bbb.org

The Consumer Reports Travel Letter (Contact for details on subscribing, or sign up for their email newsletter.)
P.O. Box 53629
Boulder, CO 80322
(800) 365-0396
www.consumerreports.org/Services/travel.html

Cruise Lines International Association (Send self-addressed, 55-cent stamped envelope for free booklet, "Answers to the Most-Asked Questions About Cruising.")
500 Fifth Avenue
Suite 1407
New York, NY 10110
(212) 921-0066
Fax: (212) 921-0549
www.cruising.org

European Travel Commission (go online for information on "Planning Your Trip to Europe," or to order a booklet of current European travel deals and events)

One Rockefeller Plaza, Suite 214
New York, NY 10020
www.visiteurope.com

Frommer's Caribbean Hideaways, by Ian Keown. Frommer, 2001.

Hawaii for Dummies, by Cheryl Farr Leas. Hungry Minds, Inc., 2000.

International Association for Medical Assistance to Travelers (travel packet available; contact for information)
417 Center Street
Lewiston, NY 14092
(716) 754-4883
www.sentex.net/~iamat

International Travelers Hotline (information on disease control by region)
Department of Health and Human Services
United States Public Health Service
Centers for Disease Control and Prevention
Quarantine Division/Travelers Health Section
Atlanta, GA 30333
(877) FYI-TRIP [394-8747]
(800) 331-3435
Fax: (888) 232-3299
www.cdc.gov

100 Best Romantic Resorts of the World, 3rd Ed., by Katharine D. Dyson, Paula Brisco. Globe Pequot Press, 2000.

Travel Health Services (for information on disease control, by country)
50 East 69th Street
New York, NY 10021
(212) 734-3000
travelhealth.net

United States Government Printing Office (for information and brochures on various foreign regions, search under "Tips for Travelers".)
www.access.gpo.gov/su_docs

Wendy Perrin's Secrets Every Smart Traveler Should Know, by Wendy Perrin. Fodor's Travel Publications, 1997.

www.honeymoons.about.com (for general information and links to hundreds of related websites)

20. REAFFIRMATION

ENRICH (Ask your clergymember, see the website, or send a self-addressed, stamped envelope for information on this marriage-enrichment program for married couples.)
ENRICH
P.O. Box 190
Minneapolis, MN 55440-0190
(800) 331-1661
Fax: (651) 636-1668
www.lifeinnovation.com

Jewish Marriage Encounter (for married or engaged couples; call for a referral to a group in your area)
Jewish Marriage Enhancement
P.O. Box 4494
Woodland Hills, CA 91308-4494
(818) 225-0099
http://home.earthlink.net/~rvw/index.htm

United Marriage Encounter (for married couples)
P.O. Box 209
Muscatine, IA 52761-0209
(800) 334-8920
(563) 264-8889
Fax: (563) 264-3363
www.ume1975.org

Worldwide Marriage Encounter (for married couples; weekends presented in 12 faith expressions and several languages; contact for a group in your area)
2210 East Highland Avenue
Suite 106
San Bernardino, CA 92404-4666
(909) 863-9963
(800) 795-LOVE (795-5683)
Fax: (909) 863-9986
www.wwme.org

Marriage Laws

STATE	AGE WITH PARENTAL CONSENT		AGE WITHOUT CONSENT		MEDICAL EXAM REQUIRED	WAITING PERIOD BEFORE LICENSE IS ISSUED	MAXIMUM TIME BETWEEN EXAM AND LICENSE	LICENSE VALID
	Male	Female	Male	Female				
Alabama*	14a	14a	18	18	none	none	none	30 days
Alaska	16b	16b	18	18	none	3 days, i	none	90 days
Arizona	16b	16b	18	18	none	none	none	1 year
Arkansas	17c	16c	18	18	none	none	none	60 days
California	no age limits		18	18	none	none, i	30 days	90 days
Colorado*	16b	16b	18	18	none	none	none	30 days
Connecticut	16b	16b	18	18	V.D., l	4 days, i	none	25-35 days
Delaware	18c	16c	18	18	none	1 day	none	30 days
Dist. of Columbia*	16a	16a	18	18	V.D.	3 days, i	30 days	indefinitely
Florida	16a, c	16a, c	18	18	none	3 days	none	60 days
Georgia*	16c	16c	18	18	V.D.	none	none	30 days
Hawaii	16b	16b	18	18	V.D.	none	none	30 days
Idaho*	16b	16b	18	18	none	none	none	indefinitely
Illinois	16b	16b	18	18	none	none	none	30 days, q
Indiana*	17b	17b	18	18	none	none	none	60 days
Iowa*	16b	16b	18	18	none	3 days, n	none	none
Kansas*✦	14b	12b	18	18	none	3 days, i	none	6 months
Kentucky	18e	18e	18	18	none	none	none	29 days
Louisiana	18	18	18	18	none	3 days, i	10 days	30 days
Maine	16b	16b	18	18	none	3 days, i, n	none	90 days
Maryland	16c, f	16c, f	18	18	none	2 days, i	none	180 days
Massachusetts	14e	12e	18	18	V.D., l	3 days, n	60 days	60 days
Michigan	16b	16b	18	18	V.D.	3 days, i	30 days	33 days
Minnesota	16b	16b	18	18	none	5 days, i	none	6 months
Mississippi	17	15	21	21	V.D.	3 days, i	30 days	90 days
Missouri	15d, 18b	15d, 18b	18	18	none	none	none	30 days
Montana*✦	16e, h	16e, h	18	18	V.D.	none	none	180 days
Nebraska✦	17	17	19	19	V.D.	none	none	1 year
Nevada	16b	16b	18	18	none	none	none	1 year
New Hampshire	14e	13e	18	18	none	3 days, n	none	90 days
New Jersey	16b, c	16b, c	18	18	none	3 days, i	30 days	30 days
New Mexico✦	16d	16d	18	18	V.D.	none	30 days	indefinitely
New York	16e	16e	18	18	k	none	none	60 days, q
North Carolina	16c	16c	18	18	none	none	none	60 days
North Dakota	16	16	18	18	none	none	none	60 days
Ohio*	18b, c	16b, c	18	18	none	5 days, i	30 days	60 days
Oklahoma*	16c	16c	18	18	V.D.	3 days, p	30 days	30 days
Oregon	17	17	18	18	none	3 days, i	none	60 days
Pennsylvania*	16d	16d	18	18	V.D.	3 days, i	30 days	60 days
Puerto Rico✦	18b, c, d	16b, c, d	21	21c	none	none	none	indefinitely
Rhode Island*	18d	16d	18	18	j	none	none	90 days
South Carolina*	16c	14c	18	18	none	1 day	none	indefinitely
South Dakota	16c	16c	18	18	none	none	none	20 days
Tennessee	16d	16d	18	18	none	3 days, p	none	30 days
Texas*✦	14e, g	14e, g	18	18	none	3 days	none	30 days
Utah*✦	14e, g	14e, g	18h	18h	none	none	30 days	30 days
Vermont	16b	16b	18	18	V.D.	1 day, i	30 days	60 days
Virginia	16a, c	16a, c	18	18	r	none	none	60 days
Washington	17d	17d	18	18	m	3 days	none	60 days
West Virginia	16e	16e	18	18	V.D.	3 days, i	none	indefinitely
Wisconsin	16d	16d	18	18	s	5 days, i	none	30 days
Wyoming	16d	16d	18	18	V.D.	none	none	indefinitely

* Indicates 1987 common-law marriage is recognized; many states only recognize such marriages if entered into many years before.

✦ Proxy marriages are valid under certain conditions.

a Parental consent not required if minor was previously married.

b Younger parties may marry with parental consent and/or permission of a judge. In Connecticut, judicial approval.

c Younger parties may obtain license in case of pregnancy or birth of a child.

d Younger parties may obtain a license in special circumstances.

e Parental consent and/or permission of a judge required.

f If parties are 16, proof of age and consent of parents in person is required.

g Younger parties need parental consent and permission of a judge.

h Authorizes counties to provide for premarital counseling as a requisite to issuance of license to persons under 19 and persons previously divorced.

i Waiting period may be avoided.

j Mental incompetence, infectious tuberculosis, venereal disease, and rubella (certain counties only).

k Tests for sickle-cell anemia may be required for certain applicants. If positive, marriage prohibited unless it is established that procreation is not possible.

l Rubella (for female).

m No medical exam required; however, applicants must file affidavit showing non-affliction of contagious venereal disease.

n Parties must file notice of intention to marry with local clerk.

o Waived if parties are 18 or over, or female is pregnant, or applicants are the parents of a living child born out of wedlock.

p Unless parties are over 18.

q License effective one day after issuance, unless court orders otherwise.

r Required offer of HIV test, and/or must be provided with information on AIDS and tests available.

s Applicants must receive information on AIDS and certify having read it.

INDEX